WHAT EVERY
VISUAL C++ 2™
PROGRAMMER
SHOULD KNOW

WHAT EVERY
VISUAL
C++ 2™
PROGRAMMER
SHOULD KNOW

PETER D. HIPSON

SAMS
PUBLISHING

201 West 103rd Street, Indianapolis, Indiana 46290 USA

This book is dedicated to Manneeya Tonyai, a very special granddaughter!

Copyright © 1994 by Sams Publishing

FIRST EDITION

International Standard Book Number: 0-672-30493-7

Library of Congress Catalog Card Number: 93-87653

97 96 95 94   4   3   2   1

Interpretation of the printing code: the rightmost double-digit number is the year of the book's printing; the rightmost single-digit, the number of the book's printing. For example, a printing code of 94-1 shows that the first printing of the book occurred in 1994.

Composed in Goudy, Helvetica, and MCPdigital by Macmillan Computer Publishing

Printed in the United States of America

Trademarks

OVERVIEW

CONTENTS

About the Author

Peter D. Hipson and his wife live, work, and play in New Hampshire. He has worked with computers since 1972, both in hardware design and software development. He has developed a number of applications for PCs under both DOS and Windows. Hipson holds patents in the field of CPU design and has been involved with microcomputers since their inception. He is the developer of the STARmanager Windows application. When not writing books or software, Hipson often can be found bicycling around the New England countryside.

Acknowledgments

The author would like to thank Greg Croy, Brad Jones, Greg Guntle, Gayle Johnson, and Ryan Rader at Sams. Thanks also go to Brad Silverberg, John Brown, and Dave Brown at Microsoft. A very special thanks to my wife, who missed her summer vacation so that I could get the book done on time!

INTRODUCTION

This book is written for two different groups of people. The first group is made up of people who have purchased Visual C++ 2.0 and are looking for ways to get the most out of it. The second group is made up of people who are seriously considering either upgrading to or purchasing Visual C++ 2.0 and who want to review the new features of the product prior to making their decision.

When it introduced Visual C++ 1.0 in 1993, Microsoft took the lead in C/C++ compilers for the Windows environment for the first time. Now, with the introduction of Visual C++ 2.0, Microsoft continues to lead the industry in Windows-based compilers. Visual C++ 2.0 is a powerful 32-bit development environment that enables developers to create 32-bit applications for Windows. Visual C++ 2.0 also enables the Windows programmer to port Windows applications to the Apple Macintosh 68xxx platform.

Visual C++ 2.0 gives programmers many new features that the Visual C++ 1.x 16-bit and 32-bit editions didn't include, such as Microsoft Foundation Classes (MFC) 3.0, Object Linking and Embedding (OLE) version 2, OLC Custom Controls, and Open Database Connectivity (ODBC) 32-bit support. Visual C++ 2.0 is the first major revision of the Visual C++ product line, and it's being released about 18 months after Visual C++ 1.0.

In addition to these new features, a number of improvements to the various development tools are part of Visual C++. Generally, with Visual C++ you have a product that packs a lot of bang for the buck.

Visual C++ 2.0 is available only on CD-ROM, because Microsoft estimated that to distribute it on disks would require about 100 3 1/2-inch disks, which is more than most people are willing to deal with. As a benefit, if you really want to, you can run the product directly from the CD, so that you'll need to dedicate only a small portion of your hard disk to the product. You'll find that the product runs more slowly when run from the CD unless you have a really fast (triple or quad speed) CD drive.

A full installation on the hard disk typically takes between 75 and 100 MB of hard disk space. Most of the documentation for the product, as well as many samples, is installed on the hard disk when you use the full installation. However, the space required doesn't include Books OnLine or additional MFC or OLE samples, totaling about 30 MB of executable files; they remain on the CD.

If you don't plan to compile the sample applications that are included with Visual C++ 2.0, you can elect to keep the sample code on the CD as well, which reduces the amount of required hard disk space. All of the documentation is available using the Books OnLine help system. Gone are the 14 or so different help files. It annoyed me to no end to have a help file open, only to find that the topic I wanted was in one of the other files! This is no longer a problem because Books OnLine offers everything in one place, in addition to a better search that searches text as well as topic titles.

WHY MORE?

I think we've all asked the question "Why do applications—including compilers and development tools—keep getting bigger and bigger?" In the late 1970s, I managed a large computer center at a graduate school. I had a dream that someday I would have a computer sitting on my desk that was as powerful as the IBM mainframe at the university. At that time, the term "personal computer" connoted a finicky toy put together by electronics nuts. With the level of technology available at the time, there was no such thing as a graphical user interface (just 80x25 monochrome screens), and the average wait between pressing Enter and getting a response to your command could easily be several minutes.

However, things aren't as bad today. My main platform for Visual C++ 2.0 consists of a 386/33 with 8 MB of RAM and a 200 MB hard disk. This system is networked to a server with several gigabytes of disk, but I have no doubt that with a bit of careful planning I could be productive with just a single computer. The 386/33 is really at the bottom of the performance ladder. I would recommend a 486 with 16 MB of RAM and perhaps 500 MB of hard disk space. In today's world, such a system really is neither excessive nor expensive.

The ultimate system to run Visual C++ 2.0 (as of fall 1994) is a 100 MHz Pentium system with 32 MB of RAM and a 2 gigabyte hard disk. There are several systems meeting this specification that cost between $3,000 and $4,000. For a professional developing a product that will be sold retail, the investment will be returned many times over in improved productivity. A compile that takes two or three minutes on the 386/33 will be completed in only a few seconds on the 100 MHz Pentium.

The computers I use today (I have three networked computers sitting in my work area) are substantially more powerful than that state-of-the-art IBM mainframe of 15 years ago. The user interface available today is much better. In my word processor, I can see between 50 and 70 lines of text and up to 130 characters per line. I can see pictures, maps, drawings, charts, spreadsheets, and a whole slew of other things using my computer. "Things?" There has to be a better word, and there is—*objects*. We've gone object-crazy, no question about it!

Of course, Visual C++ 2.0 isn't the end of the bigger and better applications trend. As we demand more and more from computers, the applications that do the work for the user must become more and more complex.

Throughout this book, I refer to things as *objects* (now there's a case of a word defining itself!). Objects come in many varieties: the user's objects, such as those pesky pictures, maps, spreadsheets, and so on; the system's objects, such as programs; and the programmer's objects, including C++ classes, OLE Custom Controls, and data objects. Like it or not, the world of microcomputers is becoming object-oriented.

Handling an object, such as an OLE object, generally is much easier for the programmer. That person doesn't have to worry about the object's internal format, but simply relies on the object to take care of the details, such as drawing, itself.

OLE, from Where?

Object Linking and Embedding, generally referred to as OLE, was developed from Dynamic Data Exchange (DDE). DDE was incorporated into earlier versions of Windows to allow programs to exchange data directly. This exchange of data was complex, and very few programs supported DDE. Microsoft moved to correct DDE's shortcomings by implementing the next generation of the transfer of objects using OLE. The first versions of OLE were a major improvement over DDE, but they still left much to be desired. With OLE 1, much programming effort was still required.

OLE went through several stages of development on the way to the current standard of OLE 2. With OLE 2, an application can be a client, a server, or a container. Full OLE functionality includes such support as Drag and Drop, Visual Editing, and OLE Automation.

ODBC

You know the questions: Is your application ODBC-compatible? Does your application support OLE 2? Most of us have a general knowledge of what these terms mean, even if our Windows applications don't yet support them.

Some important features included with Visual C++ 2.0 are the ODBC SDK, the OLE 2 SDK, and the OLE Custom Control developer's kit. These developer's kits contribute to a major part of the appeal of Visual C++ 2.0.

Of course, the addition of MFC 3.0 is also important, because it adds some functionality that isn't available with Visual C++ 1.x.

HOW THIS BOOK IS ORGANIZED

This book is divided into four parts. The first part is a review of what is included with Visual C++ 2.0. The second part covers programming for Windows. The third part covers OLE Custom Controls. The fourth and final part, which covers 32-bit ODBC, places special emphasis on including ODBC in existing applications.

Part I introduces Visual C++ 2.0.

Chapter 1 introduces Visual C++ 2.0. It covers in general terms what has been changed and added.

Chapter 2 discusses the programmer's interface with Visual C++ 2.0. This interface, commonly called the IDE, has been greatly enhanced with the addition of customizable floating toolbars, dockable windows, and enhancements in the integration of resource editing. Visual C++ 2.0's project management facilities have been greatly enhanced with the addition of a better build facility that now enables the developer to retain both debug and release versions of applications being developed.

Chapter 3 presents the new features of Visual C++ 2.0's C/C++ compiler, version 9.0. This compiler may be run from a command-line prompt using the familiar CL command syntax.

Chapter 4 looks at what's new and improved in MFC 3.0, the C++ class interface for Windows programmers.

Chapter 5 describes the new debugging techniques that are available with Visual C++ 2.0. Included is information about Just-In-Time debugging, a new feature of Visual C++ 2.0.

Chapter 6 focuses on the external utilities that are supplied with Visual C++ 2.0. These utilities—such as Spy++, PView, and PortTool—greatly enhance the Visual C++ 2.0 programmer's efficiency.

Part II introduces the new features found in Visual C++ 2.0 that support Unicode, multithreaded programming, and tabbed dialogs (often called *property boxes*).

Chapter 7 presents Unicode, the new character system used in Windows NT 3.5. Unicode overcomes the limitations of the current character-based display systems, allowing for a character set of about 60,000 characters. Unicode is only partially supported under Chicago, which has some Unicode support in the OLE system.

Chapter 8 outlines multithreaded programming, with which the programmer can create separate tasks to perform operations that might otherwise seriously affect the user's perception of performance.

Chapter 9 focuses on tabbed dialog boxes (referred to as property page dialogs), which allow for much more efficient management of complex dialog boxes. A typical example of a tabbed dialog box is Visual C++ 2.0's ClassWizard.

Part III introduces the OLE Custom Control development kit, as well as the concepts of properties, methods, and events.

Chapter 10 introduces OLE Controls and their concepts.

Chapter 11 describes the tools available for developing OLE Controls, including ControlWizard, Test Container, WPS, and the register/unregister control utilities.

Chapter 12 covers the creation of an OLE Control. We start with a shell developed with ControlWizard, and then we develop a digital clock and include it in an Access form.

Chapter 13 discusses the inclusion of OLE Controls in applications. Special attention is given to Access's use of OLE Controls, because Access was the first Windows application to support OLE Controls.

Part IV introduces Open Database Connectivity (ODBC). Visual C++ 1.5 offered ODBC in 16-bit environments. Now, with Visual C++ 2.0, ODBC is supported in 32-bit environments.

Chapter 14 provides an introduction to ODBC, which can be accessed using one of two methods: MFC classes or calls to the C database functions (these functions are prefaced with **SQL**).

Chapter 15 describes ODBC servers, which act as the "glue" between an ODBC-compliant application and a specific DataSource. Each ODBC driver offers both standard functionality and some optional enhanced functionality.

Chapter 16 introduces SQL, the standardized database language that ODBC uses. An ODBC programmer can create SQL statements both at development time and at runtime. The MFC ODBC classes have a number of basic SQL capabilities built in.

Chapter 17 describes the process of creating an ODBC shell application. AppWizard can create the necessary code to manage record navigation. For a minimum application, the programmer only needs to display the DataSource's records using standard dialog controls.

Chapter 18 focuses on the steps needed to add ODBC to an existing application. For many applications that need to import data, ODBC is an excellent way to get data from a number of different DataSources.

Chapter 19 presents the process of connecting an application to a DataSource.

Chapter 20 discusses the process of getting information back from the ODBC drivers.

At the end of the book are five appendixes. Appendix A is a glossary of common terms. Appendix B lists the command-line compiler's options. Appendix C lists the command-line linker's options. Appendix D lists the command-line resource compiler's options. Appendix E lists some applications and utilities available from other sources that might enhance your usage of Visual C++ 2.0.

CONVENTIONS

This book uses the following conventions:

All code appears in `monospace`. If the listing title shows a filename, that file is available on the sample code disk. (See the following sidebar for information on ordering the sample code disk.) If no filename is mentioned, that code isn't available on the disk and probably was extracted from one of the other listings. For any chapter that describes creating a program (such as Chapter 12), that program's source is on the sample code disk.

When it's significant to the discussion, the code in listings and elsewhere that has been modified by the Visual C++ wizards (ClassWizard, AppWizard, and so on) appears in **`bold monospace italic`**.

In listings and elsewhere, code that I've modified or added (such as additions to an AppWizard- or ClassWizard-supplied code section) appears in **bold monospace**.

Something that must be substituted (such as a variable, filename, or value) appears in *monospace italic*.

Keywords in a chapter's text are **bold**.

Command Syntax

Throughout this book, the descriptions of commands with arguments are shown in square brackets ([...]) or angle brackets (<...>). The arguments enclosed in square brackets are optional, and the arguments in angle brackets are required.

```
CL [options] <filename>
```

In this example, [*options*] is allowed but not required, and <*filename*> is a required parameter.

Menu options are separated by a vertical bar. For example, File | Open means to select the Open option from the File menu.

AND IN THE END...

Thank you for purchasing *What Every Visual C++ 2 Programmer Should Know*. I hope that this book provides you with a good introduction to Visual C++ 2.0.

Please feel free to contact me, either at the address given for the WEVCPSK Disk Offer, or by sending CompuServe mail to 70444,52. When writing, enclosing an SASE will greatly enhance the chances that I will reply! Please don't telephone, even if you find my number. If you have a question, write and be as detailed as you can. Most of the time, I will reply to CompuServe mail within a few hours of receipt.

Source code for *What Every Visual C++ 2 Programmer Should Know* is available from the author on a 3 1/2-inch high-density disk. Send a check or money order for $14.95 ($19.95 outside the U.S.), payable in U.S. currency, drawn on a U.S. bank, to:

WEVCPSK Disk Offer
Peter D. Hipson
P.O. Box 88
West Peterborough, NH 03468-0088

Make checks payable to **Peter D. Hipson**. Be sure to include your name and address. Orders will be shipped within 15 days of receipt. Sending a money order will expedite your order. I promise!

Good luck with Visual C++ 2.0, and remember Peter's golden rule:

Always back up your disk frequently!

The programming information in this book is based on information for developing applications for Windows 95 made public by Microsoft as of 9/9/94. Since this information was made public before the final release of the product, there may have been changes to some of the programming interfaces by the time the product is finally released. We encourage you to check the updated development information that should be part of your development system for resolving issues that might arise.

The end-user information in this book is based on information on Windows 95 made public by Microsoft as of 9/9/94. Since this information was made public before the release of the product, we encourage you to visit your local bookstore at that time for updated books on Windows 95.

If you have a modem or access to the Internet, you can always get up-to-the-minute information on Windows 95 direct from Microsoft on WinNews:

On CompuServe: `GO WINNEWS`

On the Internet: `ftp://ftp.microsoft.com/PerOpSys/Win_New /Chicagohttp://www.microsoft.com`

On AOL: keyword WINNEWS

On Prodigy: jumpword WINNEWS

On GEnie: WINNEWS file area on Windows RTC

You can also subscribe to Microsoft's WinNews electronic newsletter by sending Internet e-mail to news@microsoft.nwnet.com and putting the words SUBSCRIBE WINNEWS in the text of the e-mail.

PART

I

AN INTRODUCTION TO VISUAL C++

THE VISUAL C++ ENVIRONMENT

Using the Visual C++ environment to create a Windows application has resulted in a Windows application development cycle that is considerably quicker than was possible using earlier versions of the Microsoft C compiler. With Visual C++ 2.0, programmers can quickly and easily develop applications that support 32-bit Windows, MFC 3.0, OLE 2, and ODBC through the use of the Visual Workbench.

Visual C++ 2.0 isn't meant to completely replace Visual C++ 1.5. Instead, until the usage of Windows 3.x has declined to a point where it's no longer feasible to develop or maintain 16-bit Windows applications, Visual C++ 1.5 will continue to be the platform of choice for 16-bit Windows development for most Windows programmers. Figure 1.1 shows the relationships among the various versions of Visual C++ and their key components.

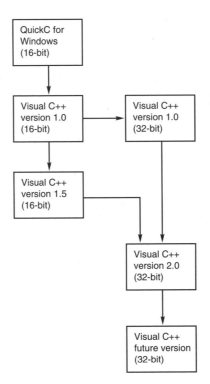

Figure 1.1. The progression of Visual C++.

Figure 1.1 shows that the first member in the Visual C++ family is a product called QuickC for Windows. I included QuickC for Windows in this figure because many of Visual C++'s features (including the Windows development environment and the ability to create a shell Windows application) were first introduced in QuickC for Windows. QuickC for Windows didn't offer support for C++.

As a product, QuickC for Windows didn't have a long life span. It was quickly replaced with the personal version of Visual C++ 1.0. The creation of two editions of the Visual C++ products (a personal and a professional edition) was dropped when the next version was released. At that time, Microsoft was pricing the Visual C++ product so aggressively that there was little need or demand for a low-cost, stripped version of Visual C++.

DIFFERENCES BETWEEN VERSIONS OF VISUAL C++

Visual C++ has always come in two versions: a 16-bit version and a 32-bit version. The development interface of these two products hasn't been identical. In particular, the 32-bit version of Visual C++ has always offered better programmer support than the 16-bit versions did.

Each version of Visual C++ has offered support for the MFC library. MFC has evolved through three major versions (1.0, 2.0, and 2.5). Support for OLE also has gone through a number of versions (OLE 1 and then OLE 2, which will be followed by OLE version 3.0). Microsoft has decided to drop the number portion of the name of OLE and call the product just *OLE*. This means that there will not be an OLE 3, for example.

Programmers who are using MFC will enjoy a relatively painless method of upgrading. Microsoft has been careful not to significantly affect MFC users by changing or removing features from the MFC library. The only changes are those necessary to correct bugs or deficiencies that have been discovered in prior versions of MFC.

Visual C++ 2.0 provides a tighter integration between resource editing and the source code editor. With earlier versions of Visual C++, resources were edited using AppStudio, a stand-alone utility that was called from Visual C++. In Visual C++ 2.0, resources are edited directly in Visual C++'s development environment. This means that there is no switching between (and having to remember to save) Visual C++ and AppStudio. Figure 1.2 shows Visual C++ 2.0 with the Clock project loaded and a dialog box open.

You can develop applications for any platform that is supported by Windows NT, including the RISC (Reduced Instruction Set Computer) platforms, by using the add-on RISC compilers that are available from Microsoft.

For developers who are creating applications that will have to be ported to different, non-Windows platforms, Visual C++ 2.0 supports cross-platform development for the Macintosh line of computers from Apple. Windows applications may be easily ported to the 68xxx platform using Visual C++ 2.0.

In the past, when a programmer developed a new Windows application, it could take months to complete the shell. What required months of time and expertise can now be done with a few keystrokes in just a few minutes. No, I haven't timed how long it takes to develop a Windows program using AppWizard, but it's not long. I did time how long it took me to create the basic shell of the first Windows program—it was well over four months. To develop this first application, I used some rather crude tools: a simple dialog editor (you could use it to locate and size controls but not much else), a simple icon editor, and a DOS command-line-based editor. Until Windows 3.x was released, it wasn't really possible to develop Windows programs while running Windows—there wasn't enough memory for the compiler or linker to run. The best development systems were networks of Windows and OS/2 machines in which the editing and program building was done on the OS/2 machine while the actual testing was done on the other system that ran Windows.

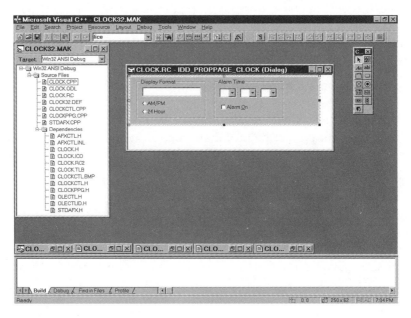

Figure 1.2. Visual C++ 2.0 with a dialog resource open.

Today, things are much better. Using Windows NT and Windows 95's protected modes, development tools can access much more memory than was possible with versions of Windows prior to 3.0. In addition, since Windows applications (including Visual C++'s tools) are run in protected mode, they have access to more memory than the earlier, real-mode development tools.

A classic example of a development tool that has benefited from being able to utilize more memory is the Visual Workbench program. The original program for creating dialog boxes, DLGEDIT, had only basic functionality: it could create only dialog boxes. To create other resources, such as cursors and icons, you had to use other applications. With Visual C++'s Visual Workbench, you have access to a rich set of features that allow you to create virtually all the resources you need in Windows applications, to edit source files, to manage projects, and to actually create the final program by invoking the compiler and linker.

Today, with Visual C++, you can develop a Windows program's shell in a few minutes. You can create dialog boxes, attach the necessary C++ classes, draw icons, define menus, and build and test your applications in a small fraction of the time that it took just a few years ago.

SUMMARY

This chapter introduced Visual C++ 2.0, which offers many powerful features for the Windows programmer. This chapter covered the overall differences between Visual C++ 2.0 and earlier versions of Visual C++. The following topics were covered:

- The origins of the Visual C++ products
- The progression of the Microsoft Foundation Class library
- The progression of OLE

New Features of Visual C++ 2.0

Once upon a time, it took months for a programmer to complete the shell of a Windows program. What used to take months of time and a great deal of expertise can now be done in just a few minutes with a few keystrokes using Visual C++.

Improvements in the developer's tools continue to increase productivity and make the task of writing Windows applications easier. This chapter reviews the new features of Visual C++ 2.0 and describes how to use them.

THE VISUAL WORKBENCH

The Visual Workbench is the programmer's interface with Visual C++. With the Visual Workbench, a programmer can access the Visual C++ source code editor; use the built-in debugger; and create, load, and build projects. In addition, you can create all the resources that a Windows application will use. The Visual Workbench is often referred to as an *IDE* (Integrated Development Environment or Editor). However, because IDE is a commonly used acronym for Integrated Drive Electronics (an interface standard for hard disk drives), I won't use the term IDE again in this book.

With Visual C++ 2.0, Visual Workbench's basic user interface has changed from the user interface found in Visual C++ 1.0 and 1.5. There have been some major changes, such as the integration of AppWizard into the Visual Workbench. However, even with these changes, the overall user interface is very similar to that of the earlier version. Experienced Visual C++ programmers will quickly adapt to, and welcome, the new features that Visual C++ 2.0 offers.

This chapter covers the Visual Workbench's user interface and reviews the Visual Workbench editor. Also in this chapter is information about each of the tools that form part of the Visual Workbench: the editor, AppWizard, AppStudio, Class Wizard, and Browser integrated utilities.

THE VISUAL WORKBENCH USER INTERFACE

The Visual Workbench offers a well-planned user interface. It has evolved over the past few years as Microsoft has listened to the users of Visual C++ to determine what they want when programming for Windows.

The programmer can access a rich set of features through Visual Workbench's menu structure and toolbars. Five toolbars are available, and users can create new toolbars to suit their needs. Figure 2.1 shows the Visual Workbench with the project HELLO loaded (from the samples supplied with Visual C++ 2.0) following a rebuild of the project. Behind the Output window, you can see a source file loaded into one editor window, while another window shows the source file's header (include) file.

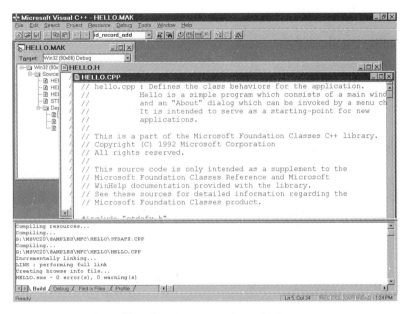

Figure 2.1. The Visual Workbench with a project being built.

The following sections look at the features available on Visual Workbench's menus.

The File Menu

The File menu enables you to create a new file or an entire project, select a file to edit, save the current file (either to the original name or a new name), and save all the currently open files.

The File | New option also enables you to create a new Visual Workbench project. This menu option brings up a dialog box that prompts you for the project's name and the type of program (the program's platform) that this project will create (see Figure 2.2). This process was derived from earlier versions of Visual C++ that called AppWizard from the Project menu.

The valid platform types for Visual C++ are listed in Table 2.1. To use a platform other than Win32, you must have the appropriate cross-development compiler installed. Also, in the New Project Name and Type dialog, you can choose whether to include support for Microsoft Foundation Classes.

Figure 2.2. Visual Workbench's New Project Name and Type dialog.

TABLE 2.1. VISUAL C++ PLATFORM TYPES.	
Program Type	*Hardware Type*
Win32 application (.EXE)	IBM-compatible PCs
Apple Macintosh application	Apple Macintosh 68xxx systems
Win32 application	Alpha systems running Windows NT
Win32 application	MIPS systems running Windows NT

As you can see from Table 2.1, Visual C++ can create programs that can be executed under a number of different platforms. Microsoft is committed to creating new cross-development platforms for Visual C++ 2.0. The standard version of Visual C++ 2.0 will create IBM-compatible (80x86) applications. Other versions of Visual C++ 2.0 will be available for the MIPS, Alpha, and Macintosh systems.

After you specify the project's name and the type of project, you are presented with a second dialog in which you select the project's type. You set the new application's attributes in this dialog using the Next and Back buttons. Each of the six panes in this dialog represents a different aspect of the project creation process:

1. You can create MDI, SDI, and dialog-based applications.
2. You can include ODBC support on the following levels:
   - No ODBC support
   - Header files only, so that ODBC can be added later
   - Database view only, with no support for database files
   - Full database support for both views and files

3. You can include OLE support on the following levels:
   - No OLE support
   - Container support only
   - Miniserver support only
   - Full-server support
   - Both container and server support
4. You can include support for the following:
   - Dockable toolbars
   - Initial status bars
   - Print and print preview
   - Context-sensitive help
   - Use of 3D controls (CTRL3D.DLL)
   - The number of files in the MRU list
   - Advanced options, including the document template settings, and the MainFrame's options, including the use of a splitter window and MDI Child Frame
5. Source comments, makefile type, and MFC library usage.
6. The names used for the application's classes and the filenames of the files that will contain these classes.

If you want to create an application that will support database files without having view support, select the Header Files Only option and use ClassWizard to create the **CRecordSet** class after you've created the application's project.

The final step in the project creation process is to verify that the project's options are the ones you want it to have. Figure 2.3 shows the Visual Workbench Project Files dialog.

The file types that a typical project would include are listed in Table 2.2. Using the File | New menu option, you can create any of these types of files.

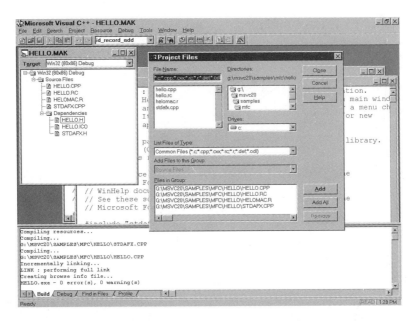

Figure 2.3. Visual Workbench's Project Files dialog.

TABLE 2.2. FILES TYPICALLY INCLUDED IN A PROJECT.	
File Type	**Extension**
Code/text file	.C, .CPP, .CXX, .H
Project file	.MAK
Resource script file	.RC
Bitmap file	.BMP, .DIB
Icon file	.ICO
Cursor file	.CUR

Not all projects will have all of these types of files. Generally, a Windows project must have source files, a definition file (which Visual C++ creates automatically), and resource files. A Windows project might have static link libraries and/or object files as well.

Page Setup

Printing support also includes Page Setup, which you can use to define the format of the listing printout. Page format consists of setting margins and (optionally) defining a header and/or a footer. In either the header or footer, you can choose to include substituted information by specifying a substitution code in the header or footer's text string. Table 2.3 shows the valid page header and footer formatting codes.

TABLE 2.3. PAGE LAYOUT HEADER AND FOOTER FORMATTING CODES.	
Code	Description
&f	Substitutes the filename of the file being printed.
&p	Substitutes the current page number.
&t	Inserts the current system time.
&d	Inserts the current system date.
&l	Causes the header or footer to be left-aligned.
&c	Causes the header or footer to be centered.
&r	Causes the header or footer to be right-aligned.

Print

Also provided on the File menu is printing support. You can print part (the current selection) or all of the current file.

MRU File Lists

The next-to-last option on the File menu is the list of most recently used (MRU) files, which allows you to quickly open one of the four most recently opened files. These lists are subdivided into two parts: The first lists the most recently used source files, and the second lists the most recently opened projects.

Exit

You use the Exit menu option to end the current Visual C++ session. This option is the same as pressing Alt-F4, selecting Close from the System Menu, or clicking on the title bar's exit button.

The Edit Menu

The next Visual Workbench menu is Edit. The Edit menu controls Visual C++'s interface with the clipboard, Undo and Redo, and the Properties dialog.

Undo and Redo

The first part of the Edit menu is the Undo and Redo support. With Undo, you can take back any changes you've made to the files being edited. The number of edits that may be undone is limited by the size of the undo buffer, which is set by selecting Tools | Options | Editor... (described later). The Redo option is the converse of the Undo option: Redo enables you to "undo" an undo, restoring the edits that were removed by the undo command. Redo is very handy when you have undone a large number of edits before realizing that the edits were, in fact, acceptable.

Cut, Copy, Paste, and Delete

The Edit menu also includes the clipboard interface. You will find that the clipboard interface features of the Edit menu closely follow Windows standards, offering the following capabilities:

Edit offers the capability to cut and discard the currently selected text in the active edit window. Copy enables the user to copy the currently selected text in the active edit window to the clipboard, where it then may be copied to other windows or applications. With Paste, you can copy the current clipboard's contents to the cursor position (if the clipboard offers an object that can be converted to text). Edit's Del menu selection works like the Delete key—it deletes the current selection without copying it to the clipboard.

Select All

The Edit menu includes an option that enables you to select the current file's contents without altering the current text cursor's position.

Properties

You can set properties for a window (editable windows, but not the standard output windows). This menu option calls up the appropriate File Properties menu, based on the currently active edit window. The exact properties that can be set depend on the type of file that is in the currently active window.

Following are the properties that are available for text windows. For windows showing resources, such as dialog boxes, the properties offered will vary.

Properties Dialog: Read-Only

You can set the read-only mode for any file. The advantage of read-only is that you can prevent inadvertent modification of the file while it's loaded in the editor. All of the Visual Workbench's standard debugging windows (Output, Watch, Locals, Registers, Memory, Call Stack, and Disassembly) are read-only.

Properties Dialog: Language

This option, in the Properties dialog, allows various parts of the syntax of a C (or C++) program to be displayed in different colors. The different syntax items that may be colored include comments, constants (both numeric and character), and keywords.

The editor's default is to enable syntax coloring based on the file's extension (the extensions of .C and .CPP use the C or C++ syntax coloring). This dialog selection enables you to override the default (to specify C++ syntax coloring for a .C file, or to specify C syntax coloring for a .CPP file) or to simply turn off the syntax coloring.

Personally, I find syntax coloring to be quite valuable. It can help the programmer spot errors in variable types, such as using a double where you intended an integer, or having a long integer where you really wanted a short integer. Of course, turning on syntax coloring for files that aren't C or C++ source code doesn't make much sense.

The Search Menu

The next menu in the Visual Workbench is Search. In earlier versions of Visual C++, the searching functionality was part of the Edit menu.

Find and Replace

The Visual Workbench editor uses Find to support searching for text in a file that is being edited. In addition, you can replace text using the Replace functionality. Text being searched for can be either regular text or text formed using regular expressions (which are described in the next section).

Find in Files...

With the Find in Files menu option, you can search for a text string in the files that you select. The text string searched for can be regular text, or it can contain regular expressions. There is no subdirectory option, which makes searching a subdirectory tree a bit awkward. Figure 2.4 shows the Find in Files dialog.

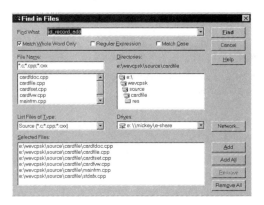

Figure 2.4. The Find in Files dialog box.

Match Brace...

The next selection on the Search menu is Match Brace, which enables you to jump to the line containing the brace that matches the brace you have selected.

Go To...

Go To... lets you jump to a line by specifying its line number. To use this option, you must know the number of the line that you want to jump to. You might find that, for many purposes, the bookmark function (described later) provides a better way of moving to specific lines in a file. The Go To... function is most commonly used to move to a line in an error message.

Next Error and Previous Error

The next two selections on the Search menu usually are used together. Next Error and the Previous Error enable you to locate the line where an error or warning occurred, following a build that produced compile error or warning messages. While you're using the Next Error and Previous Error functions, the text of the error or warning message is placed in the output area of the Visual Workbench's status bar. This makes it easy to see both the offending line and the description of the problem that the compiler encountered. Unfortunately, for errors other than compiler errors, the Next Error and Previous Error message feature isn't useful, because only compiler errors contain line number information.

Bookmarks

The next four options under Search support bookmarks. You use bookmarks to return to a specific line in a source file. When you set a bookmark at a line, that line is highlighted with a small rectangle in the left margin (the default color is cyan on most systems). You may have as many bookmarked lines in a source file as you want. However, if you mark too many lines, it might become tedious to find the bookmarked line you want to jump to. Typically, I have three or four lines marked when using bookmarks; however, I've had as many as 10 marked at a time.

Toggle Bookmark

The first menu option that supports bookmarks is Toggle Bookmark. When this item is selected, the current line's marking status is toggled. Therefore, if the current line was marked, the bookmark is turned off; if the current line was not bookmarked, it becomes marked.

Next Bookmark

The next Search menu option is Next Bookmark, which lets you jump forward (toward the end of the file) to the next line that has a bookmark defined. If there are no defined bookmarks, the Next Bookmark option has no effect. When the end of the file is reached, Visual Workbench returns to the beginning of the file and restarts the search for bookmarks.

Previous Bookmark

Following the Next Bookmark option is Previous Bookmark, which enables you to jump backward (toward the beginning of the file) to the next line that has a bookmark defined. If there are no defined bookmarks, the Previous Bookmark option has no effect. When the beginning of the file is reached, Visual Workbench starts searching again at the end of the file.

Clear All Bookmarks

The final bookmark selection is Clear All Bookmarks. With this option you can clear all of the bookmarks that have been set in the current file. This is useful when you find that you have created too many bookmarks to be really effective.

Go to Definition

The Go to Definition option on the Search menu enables you to jump to the first place where the selected symbol has been defined. You may select the symbol either in a source window or in the Browse window.

Go to Reference

The Go to Reference option allows you to jump to the first place where the selected symbol is referenced. You may select the symbol either in a source window or in the Browse window.

Next Definition

The Next Definition option enables you to jump to the next definition or reference. Next is always used after Go to Definition or Go to Reference.

Previous Definition

Previous Definition is used following Go to Definition or Go to Reference to jump to the previous definition or reference.

Pop Context

When used after Go to Definition or Go to Reference, this option returns to the symbol that was last used.

Browse

The Browse option allows you to move to various parts of the source so that you can quickly find the definitions and references for symbols. Symbols being browsed can be selected in either the source window or the Browse window. The final part of the Browse menu option calls the Browse functions. You create a Browse window by selecting Project | Open....

The Project Menu

The Project menu comes after the Search menu in the Visual Workbench. You use Project to create, modify, and save your programming projects.

OK, you say, what is a project? A project is the mechanism that combines all the source components of an application (which could be a Windows program, a DLL, or perhaps a .LIB file). A project is actually contained in a file that has an extension of .MAK. It's important to note that not all .MAK files are Visual C++ project files. Some .MAK files have been created simply to provide input to the NMake utility. (Those that are intended to be used only with NMake are referred to as *external make* or *external project* files.) However, all project files can also be used with NMake if you wish. If you use NMake directly with a project file, you won't get the benefits that Visual Workbench offers, such as the capability to jump to errors. AppWizard is one way to create a project file. It creates projects that are compatible with Visual Workbench, or external projects that can be used only with NMake.

Why create external makefiles? With Visual Workbench project files, you must use the Visual Workbench to modify the project file. This limits some of the things that can be done in the project file. With an external makefile, you can edit and change the makefile to your heart's content. You can convert a Visual

Workbench project file to an external project file simply by editing it. You'll find the project files created by either AppWizard or Visual Workbench to be concise and well organized, but a bit difficult to read if you're not experienced with their syntax. For further information about makefiles, you should refer to the documentation for the NMake utility.

Each Project menu option is covered in the following paragraphs.

Files

The Project menu's first option is Files, which enables you to add or delete files from the current project. This functionality was part of the Edit menu selection in Visual C++ 1.5 and earlier versions.

New Group

New Group enables you to manage the Visual C++ project hierarchy.

Settings

The Settings option displays the Settings dialog box. You use Settings to alter the project's modifiable options, which include the following:

- General: Foundation class usage, and directories
- Debug: Settings for the debug environment are made here
- C/C++: Settings that affect the compiler, such as warning level and defines, are set with this option
- Link: Used to set the linker's options and libraries
- Resources: Used to set the project's resource options
- OLE Types: Used to set OLE type options
- Browse: Used to set the browse options

You also can specify the application's target type. Choices include the following:

- Win32 Release
- Win32 Debug
- Macintosh Release
- Macintosh Debug

In addition, you can use these target types:

- Win32 Application
- Win32 Dynamic Link Library (.DLL)

- Win32 Static Link Library (.LIB)
- Win32 Console Application (runs in a DOS window)

The Macintosh versions are available only if you have the add-on Macintosh compiler option installed.

Targets

The Project | Targets menu option allows you to change the project's target type. See the section titled "Settings" for more information.

Compile <file>...

You can tell Visual Workbench to compile the current file by selecting Project | Compile <file>.... This menu item compiles only the current file. It won't invoke the linker or any other build tools. If the current file is the project's resource script, the Resource Compiler will be called rather than the Visual C++ compiler.

Build <file>...

The Build <file>... menu option enables you to compile whatever source files have been changed. (Source files that have not changed, and for which there is an existing object file, are not compiled.) If no errors are generated during the compile process, the other project build tools will be called to create the final project file.

Rebuild All...

Rebuild All... allows you to compile all source files, regardless of whether they have been changed or not. If there are no errors from the compile process, the other project build tools will be called to create the final project file.

Batch Build...

Batch Build... opens the Batch Build dialog box, which enables you to rebuild more than one project in a single step. This menu option is very useful if your project contains .DLL or .LIB files in addition to the main application and you wish to rebuild all the parts of a project.

Stop Build

Let's say that you select Build or Rebuild All. The compiler starts and you see a problem, perhaps with one of your header files. You decide it would be pointless to continue the build process because all the compiles would fail. Or perhaps the compile only generated warning messages (that won't stop the build process), but you want to fix the problems that generated the messages before completing the build. You can stop the build process at almost any point by selecting Project | Stop Build. At some points in the build process, you have to select Stop Build twice. Sometimes, during the link process, you'll find that the first time Stop Build is selected, the linker will be stopped, but then the next build step will start. If this happens, simply select Stop Build a second time.

Microsoft has added Ctrl-Break as the hot key to access Stop Build. This makes sense, because many programmers instinctively press Ctrl-Break to stop a process.

Execute <file>

The next option on the Project menu is Execute <file>. With Execute <file>, you can run the project's program (assuming that the project is for an executable program and not for a link library, DLL, or VBX control). Execute starts the program but doesn't run it under the Visual Workbench debugger. Generally, you'll use Execute for programs that have been built using the Release option (see the section titled "Options"). Any program that has been built without the debugging options can be run, but you won't be able to access any of the Visual Workbench's debugging options.

To run a program under the debugger, you must use the toolbar's go button or select Debug | Go.

Update Dependencies

With Project | Update Dependencies you can scan the current source file— if it's a resource script, C, or C++ source file—to determine which include (header) files this source file is dependent on. These dependencies are then added to the project's list of include files. If you've added a header file to the current source file, you then use Update Dependencies to update the project. Generally, you don't need to update dependencies when adding standard C and C++ header files that are part of Visual C++, because these files won't be changed.

> Never change the standard C and C++ include files found in the \MSVC\INCLUDE directory.

If you have a header file that you never want to include in the dependencies list, you can add it to the file SYSINCL.DAT, which is found in the \MSVC\BIN directory. Any file found here will never be added to the dependencies. If you peruse this file, you'll find that it lists all of Visual C++'s include files. Listing 2.1 shows a small part of SYSINCL.DAT.

LISTING 2.1. A PARTIAL LISTING OF SYSINCL.DAT.

```
AFX.H
AFX.INL
AFXCOLL.H
AFXCOLL.INL
AFXDB.H
AFXDB.INL
AFXDB.RC
AFXDD_.H
AFXDISP.H
AFXDLGS.H
AFXDLGS.INL
AFXDLL_.H
AFXDLLX.H
AFXEXT.H
AFXEXT.INL
AFXMSG_.H
AFXODLGS.H
AFXOLE.H
AFXOLE.INL
AFXOLECL.RC
AFXOLESV.RC
AFXPEN.H
AFXPEN.INL
AFXPRINT.RC
AFXPRIV.H
AFXRES.H
AFXRES.RC
AFXV_DLL.H
AFXV_DOS.H
AFXVER_.H
...
```

Update All Dependencies

With Project | Update All Dependencies, you can scan all of the source files (.RC, .C, .CPP, and .CXX) to determine which include (header) files are part of the project. The dependencies are then added to the project. This option is useful if you've updated the include files for a number of source files. You probably would use this option if you had doubts as to whether all the header files had been properly included in the project. Generally, Update All Dependencies is fast. I try to run it from time to time just to be sure that I've correctly included all the header files in the project. Especially with C++ code, you can create some serious problems if the project doesn't include all the dependencies.

ClassWizard

ClassWizard is a utility that enables you to create new classes and map Windows messages to member functions. You can use ClassWizard to work with classes that manage dialog box controls.

The ClassWizard utility contains a single tabbed dialog box. The main tabs offer support for these areas (for most applications):

- Message Maps: The management of classes that interact with Windows messages
- Member Variables: The management of variables that are part of a given class
- OLE Automation: The management of OLE automation
- OLE Events: The management of OLE events
- Class Info: The overall management of classes

You can add classes, member variables, and member functions and perform a host of other functions on MFC classes that are part of your application.

Close Browse Info File

The Close Browse Info File menu option enables you to close the currently open Browser information file.

Build Browse Info File

The Build Browse Info File menu option allows you to create, on demand, a Browser information file. This menu selection is useful if you've turned on the Update Browse Info File on Demand option under Project | Settings | Browse Info.

The Resource Menu

The Resource menu lets you manage your project's resources. Because Visual C++ 2.0 has built into the Visual Workbench all of the functionality that was part of AppStudio, it's now much easier to work with a Windows program's resources.

New

Resource | New enables you to create a new resource. The types of resources that Visual C++ can create include the following:

- Accelerator tables
- Bitmaps
- Cursors
- Dialog boxes
- Icons
- Menus
- String table entries
- Version tables

One nice feature is the capability to create version tables using a standardized input format.

Open Binary Data
The Open Binary Data menu option enables you to open a binary edit window for resources that can be edited in binary format.

Import
Using Import, you can import an icon, cursor, or bitmap into the current resource file.

Export
Using Export, you can export an icon, cursor, or bitmap from the current resource file to an external file.

Symbols
The Symbols menu option opens the Symbol Browser dialog, which lists each resource symbol, the symbol's value, and whether the symbol is currently being used. You can create new symbols, change existing symbols, and delete unused symbols using this dialog.

Set Includes
The Set Includes menu option opens the Set Includes dialog, which lists each of the files that are included with the application's resources. The default is usually to include AFXRES.H, while non-MFC applications usually include WINDOWS.H. You can add new include files and compile-time (resource compile) directives in this dialog.

The Debug Menu

The Debug menu is used when debugging applications that you've developed using Visual C++. The Visual Workbench integrated debugger allows source-level debugging. Also, by using the mixed assembly/source listing option, you often can quickly spot those subtle programming blunders that are difficult to see in C/C++.

The following descriptions of the Debug menu items will serve as your introduction to the Visual Workbench debugger. Like most things in life, learning the debugger is best done by practice. Use the debugger, and try each of its options and features. I promise you, it will be a lot more frustrating to learn the debugger when you have a program that won't run and you must have the program completed and running in a few hours.

Go

If the current project is for a program and not a library, the Go option tells Visual Workbench's debugger to begin the execution program if it isn't already running. If the program is currently running and is stopped at a breakpoint, the Go menu option starts the program's execution from the breakpoint. Execution continues until the program ends (normally or otherwise) or a breakpoint is reached. If the current project isn't for a program but is actually a library, the Go menu option has no effect. If the program has been modified and hasn't been rebuilt, Visual Workbench asks you whether you want to rebuild the program.

Restart

The Restart menu option restarts the program being debugged. Restart is active when the program being debugged has been stopped either by an error that signals the debugger to break or by reaching a breakpoint. The Restart command is equivalent to selecting Debug | Stop Debugging and then selecting Debug | Go.

Stop Debugging

Once a program has been started and has stopped due to an error or a breakpoint, you can terminate its execution by selecting Debug | Stop Debugging. Stop Debugging returns you to Visual Workbench's normal development state.

Break

The Break menu option stops at its current location the program that is being debugged. This menu item is useful if you're unsure of where you are in the program's execution.

Remote Debugger

The Remote Debugger menu option executes Visual C++ 2.0's remote debugging facility. See Chapter 5, "Debugging With Visual C++," for more information about remote debugging.

Step Into

The Debug menu's Step commands enable you to control the single-step mode of the Visual Workbench debugger. Step Into, which follows calls to functions, enables you to execute the program one statement at a time.

Step Over

Unlike Step Into, the Step Over menu option allows you to not follow function calls. When a call to a function is reached, the debugger executes the function without stepping into the function. Using Step Over can significantly shorten the debugging process when you know that the function being called is error-free.

Step Out

With the Step Out menu option, you can suspend line-by-line stepping until the end of the current function has been reached. The next stop is at the line after the call to the function where Step Out was used.

Run to Cursor

When you place the editor's insert cursor (the I-beam) where you want the debugger to stop, and then select Debug | Run to Cursor, the debugger executes the program and stops at the line where the cursor is. It's very important that the cursor be on a line that contains an executable statement. A good test for an executable statement is to find a line that ends in a semicolon and isn't a variable allocation.

Exceptions

This menu option opens the Exceptions dialog box, which is used to determine the action taken by the debugger for individual exceptions. This menu item is active only when debugging. The exceptions you can manage are listed in Table 2.4.

TABLE 2.4. EXCEPTION CONDITIONS HANDLED BY THE DEBUGGER.

Exception	Default Action
Control C	Stop always.
Control Break	Stop always.
Datatype misalignment	Stop if not handled.
Access Violation	Stop if not handled.
In Page Error	Stop if not handled.
No Memory	Stop if not handled.
Illegal Instruction	Stop if not handled.
Non-configurable Exception	Stop if not handled.
Invalid Disposition	Stop if not handled.
Array Bounds Exceeded	Stop if not handled.
Floating Point Denormal Operand	Stop if not handled.
Floating Point Divide by Zero	Stop if not handled.
Floating Point Inexact Result	Stop if not handled.
Floating Point Overflow	Stop if not handled.
Floating Point Stack Check	Stop if not handled.
Floating Point Underflow	Stop if not handled.
Floating Point Invalid Operation	Stop if not handled.
Integer Divide by Zero	Stop if not handled.
Integer Overflow	Stop if not handled.
Privileged Instruction	Stop if not handled.
Stack Overflow	Stop if not handled.
DLL Initialization Failed	Stop if not handled.
Microsoft C++ Exception	Stop if not handled.

Threads

The Threads menu option opens the Threads dialog box, which you can use to suspend a thread, resume a thread, terminate a thread, or set a thread's focus. The Threads dialog box shows the status of all active threads, including state, priority, and current location (either by function name or address).

Breakpoints

The Breakpoints menu option enables you to set and clear breakpoints. This menu option displays the Breakpoints dialog box, shown in Figure 2.5, in which you can add, disable, delete, and clear all breakpoints. The easiest method to set and clear a breakpoint is to use the breakpoint tool from the main toolbar.

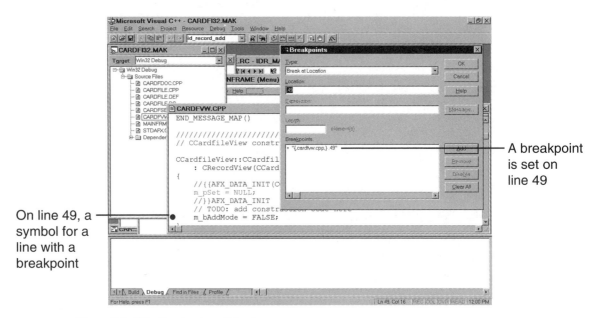

On line 49, a symbol for a line with a breakpoint

A breakpoint is set on line 49

Figure 2.5. The Breakpoints dialog box.

QuickWatch

You can use Debug | QuickWatch to look at the variable that is currently selected in a source window. If the variable is a structure, union, or class, you can examine all its members. If the variable selected is a scalar variable, its current contents will be provided. When you select a variable using QuickWatch, you have the option of adding it to the watch window. The QuickWatch dialog is shown in Figure 2.6.

Watch

Watch opens the Visual Workbench Watch window, which is used to view the contents of variables while debugging. If the Watch window is already open, this menu option brings the window to the top.

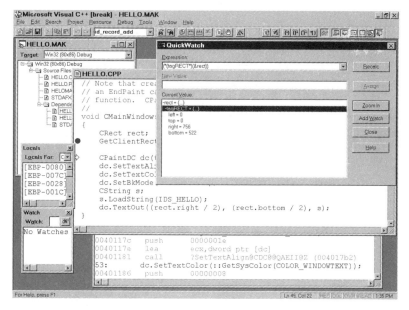

Figure 2.6. The QuickWatch dialog.

Locals

The Locals menu option opens the Visual Workbench Local window, which is used to view the contents of local variables while debugging. If the Local window is already open, this menu option brings the window to the top.

Registers

The Registers menu option opens the Visual Workbench registers window that is used to view the contents of the CPU's registers while debugging. If the Registers window is already open, this menu option brings the window to the top.

Memory

The Memory menu option opens the Visual Workbench Memory window, which is used to view the contents of the system memory (RAM) while debugging. If the Memory window is already open, this menu option brings the window to the top.

Call Stack

When a program stops due to an error condition at some point in the Windows operating system, it's important to find out which function called the Windows

API that failed. Because many APIs might have been called from many places in your program, you can use the Call Stack option to display a window that shows the current state of the call stack. By using the window's contents, you can review each of the calls and jump to the calling code in a source window. An example of the Call Stack window is shown in Figure 2.7.

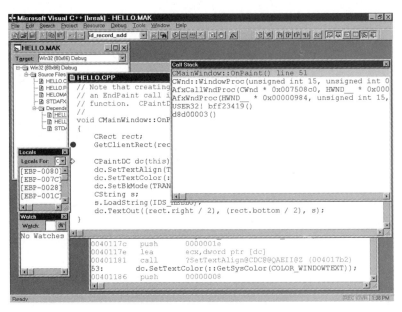

Figure 2.7. The Visual Workbench's Call Stack window.

Disassembly

The Disassembly option opens a Visual Workbench Disassembly window, which is used to view a source module's source in mixed C/C++ and assembly.

When debugging, it's useful to be able to look at the assembly language that the compiler has produced for a source file. By selecting Debug | Disassembly, you can view a mixed assembly and C/C++ source listing. To use this option, your application must be running in debug mode. Once it's running, you can select the Disassembly option. When you terminate the application you're debugging, Visual Workbench deletes the Disassembly window.

The Tools Menu

Visual Workbench's Tools menu allows you to access various development tools quickly and easily. As a switch from Visual C++ 1.5, in which the Tools menu was a utility launcher, Visual C++ 2.0 offers a fixed set of menu selections that enable you to configure Visual C++'s toolbars, customize the environment, set options, record (simple) keystroke macros, set up the Visual C++ profiler, and update the remote target. The capability to create menu items to launch other applications is still available under the Tools menu (see the section titled "Customize").

Toolbars

The toolbars menu option enables you to configure Visual C++'s toolbars. Unlike earlier versions of Visual C++, Visual C++ 2.0 comes with five standard toolbars and with a methodology to enable the programmer to add new toolbars as desired. The five standard toolbars are as follows:

- Standard: Allows working with files, searching, building projects, and so on.
- Edit: Allows the setting of bookmarks, searching, indenting and unindenting, and window management.
- Resource: Allows the creation of resources (dialogs, menus, and so on) and edit symbols.
- Debug: Allows the use of most of the debugging commands (see the section titled "The Debug Menu").
- Browse: Allows interaction with Visual C++ 2.0's Browser.

All toolbars can be customized by dragging applicable icons from the toolbar customization dialog (see the next section). In addition to these stock toolbars, you can create your own customized toolbars.

Customize

The Customize menu option enables you to add new items to the Tools menu. Each item added is linked to an executable file. You can customize the Tools menu text for the new command and provide default arguments as necessary.

The Customize menu option also lets you customize toolbars and create keyboard shortcut keys. For example, I've assigned F12 to the Window | Cascade option, which puts Visual C++'s edit windows in a cascade arrangement.

With the Customize dialog, you can create custom tools that are available under the Tools menu (see the section titled "The Tools Menu"). The Customize dialog displays the current contents of the customizable portion of the Tools menu in the Tools tab. You may add, edit, delete, move up, or move down the menu items in the Tools menu. When defining tools, you can set the following:

- Command line
- Menu text
- Arguments
- Initial directory

In some circumstances, you'll want to elect to have Visual Workbench prompt for arguments for the tool. To do so, you can select the Prompt for Arguments check box. The argument's parameter can be a constant value, or you can select one of the predefined identifiers listed in Table 2.5.

TABLE 2.5. TOOLS PREDEFINED IDENTIFIERS.	
Macro	*Description*
$CmdLine	The command-line arguments to be passed to the application. These are set using Project | Settings | General Properties.
$col	The current column number.
$CurText	The word that the insertion cursor is on, or the current single-line selection.
$dir	The current directory.
$File	The current filename, fully qualified but without an extension.
$Filedir	The current file's directory. Ends in a backslash (\ ).
$Filename	The current filename, fully qualified but with an extension.
$line	The current line number.
$Proj	The current project's name.
$Projdir	The current project's directory.
$RC	The name of the project's resource file.
$Target	The current target. For example, a Windows application would be $Target.exe.

Options

The Options menu item enables the programmer to customize a number of Visual C++ Visual Workbench functions. The areas that can be customized are arranged as tabs in a tabbed dialog. The tabs are as follows:

- Editor: You can set tabs, the format of the edit windows (scroll bars, editing modes, window recycling, and so on), and the save options.

- Colors: You can set the colors for items in the editor that are colored by context (such as comments, keywords, and strings). The Colors tab enables you to set the colors of various windows and the syntax coloring if syntax coloring is active. Table 2.6 shows the items that may have their color set.

- Fonts: You can set the font used in the edit windows. I recommend that you use a fixed-space font when programming so that columns will be aligned.

- Debug: You can configure the windows for Disassembly, Registers, Call Stack, and Memory. You also can enable the Just-in-Time debugging mode and remote debugging.

- Directories: You set the default directories using this option. You set directories for each platform in three categories: Executable, Include, and Library files.

- Workspace: You configure the workspace in this option. You can choose which of the debugging and output windows (Output, Watch, Locals, Registers, Memory, Call Stack, and Disassembly) are dockable. You can also turn off the status bar.

- Help: You specify in this option the help files that are searched when F1 is pressed to do a keyword search.

TABLE 2.6. ITEMS IN THE COLOR DIALOG.	
Item	*What Gets Colored*
Watch window	The entire window.
Locals window	The entire window.
Registers window	The entire window.
Memory window	The entire window.

continues

Table 2.6. continued

Item	What Gets Colored
Calls window	The entire window.
Disassembly window	The entire window.
Output window	The entire window.
Registers highlight	Highlighted items.
Memory highlight	Highlighted items.
Calls highlight	Highlighted items.
Breakpoint line	The breakpoint line in the editor window.
Current statement	The current line in the editor.
Current error/tag	The line where the error has been located using the View menu's Next Error or Previous Error options.
Bookmark	The lines that have been defined as bookmark lines.
Text selection	Any text selected in a window.
Source text	Default color for all text that isn't colored for some other reason.
C keyword	All C keywords.
C++ keyword	All C++ keywords.
Identifier	The names of functions, symbols, `#define` symbols, and so on.
Comment	All C and C++ comments.
Number	All short and long integers.
Real	All float and double numbers.
String	All character strings (always delimited with double quotes).
Wizard-modified code	Code that is modified by a Wizard.
User-defined type	User-defined types.

Record Keystrokes

This option allows the creation of a single unnamed keystroke macro. This macro can't be saved, nor can more than one macro exist at a time.

Playback Recording

This option allows the unnamed keystroke macro to be played back.

Profile

The Profile option enables you to invoke the Visual C++ 2.0 profiler on the current application. To use the profiler, you must create your application with profiling enabled. For more information about profiling, see Chapter 5, "Debugging with Visual C++."

Spy++

This option executes the Spy++ program.

MFC Tracer

This option displays the MFC Trace Options dialog so that you can configure the amount of runtime debugging information that is displayed in the output window.

The Window Menu

The Window menu enables you to configure the display of Visual Workbench's MDI windows. Window menu items enable you to select specific windows, display the debugging and output windows (Watch, Locals, Registers, Call Stack, Memory, Locals, and Output), and manage windows currently being displayed. An open window is any window that isn't iconized.

New Window

The New Window option enables you to create a new window for the object that is currently being displayed in the active window. The active window must be a project file and not a debugging window.

You use the New Window option to create a second view of an open file. This allows you to view two or more different places in a single file.

Split

Edit windows can be split to allow concurrent viewing of two places in a single file. This is an alternative to creating a new window for the object being displayed in the edit window.

Hide

A debug window (Locals, Watch, and so on) may be hidden if desired.

Cascade

Window | Cascade enables you to arrange all the currently open windows. The open windows are arranged starting at the upper-left and moving to the lower-right in an overlapped fashion.

Tile Horizontally

Tile Horizontally tiles all nondocked windows in a horizontal manner. The tiling of windows allows you to see some part of each window. If there are many open windows, the view of the windows will be rather small.

Tile Vertically

Tile Vertically tiles all nondocked windows in a vertical manner. The tiling of windows allows you to see some part of each window. If there are many open windows, the view of the windows will be rather small.

Close All

The Close All option enables you to close all open files and their windows.

Output

The Output option opens the Visual Workbench output window. If the output window is already open, this menu option brings the window to the top. The output window is used both to receive debugging messages from your application (such as output from the **TRACE()** macros and the **OutputDebugString()** function) and to receive output from the various project-building tools (such as the compiler, resource compiler, and linker).

Open Windows List

The Open Windows list enables you to select a window from a list. All open edit windows are listed.

The Help Menu

The Help menu enables the programmer to interface with the Visual C++ help files.

Quick Reference

This option opens the Visual C++ help facility contents Browser window.

Books OnLine

This option opens the Books OnLine help file. Books OnLine is the collection of all the major help files. With Books OnLine, you can search all the various help files for items of interest.

Foundation Classes

This option opens the help file that documents the MFC 3.0 classes.

Windows API

This option opens the documentation for the Win32 API.

C/C++ Language

This option opens the language documentation file.

Run-Time Routines

This option opens the documentation for the runtime libraries.

Keyword Search

This option opens a dialog in which you can enter a keyword to search for. This is similar to placing the insertion cursor on a keyword and pressing F1.

Technical Support

This option opens a help file that describes how to obtain technical support from Microsoft.

About Microsoft Visual C++...

The About dialog contains the version number, the registered owner, and the product ID number.

CREATING A NEW PROJECT

This part of the chapter looks at the process used to create a new application. This process involves creating a new project file, then customizing the project's source to meet your needs.

There was a time, not too long ago, when the Windows programmer spent about two to five months developing a Windows application's user interface and shell. This initial development programming amounted to building a user interface, developing the basic necessary resources (such as icons, cursors, and bitmaps), adding calls to the help system, and so on. The user interface in a Windows application is expected to meet certain universal standards that exist to make it easy for a user to learn Windows applications. These standards consist of defining the basic menu structure, the application's appearance, the appearance of certain dialog boxes, and so on.

For our example, we will create a program called WevCalc. This program is a simple, four-function calculator. Later in this chapter, we will modify and improve this program to improve its user interface.

The AppWizard User Interface

AppWizard's user interface is a series of dialog boxes. You start AppWizard by selecting File | New, then selecting Project from the New Filetype dialog. When AppWizard is started, it presents the dialog box shown in Figure 2.8.

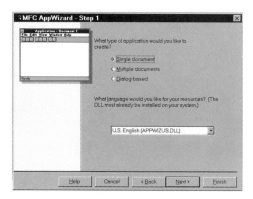

Figure 2.8. Visual Workbench's new project Step 1 dialog.

AppWizard presents a series of *chained* dialogs. You can move forward using the Next button and backward using the Back button through the chain of dialogs. The following is a list of the four AppWizard application creation dialogs that are presented when you create a dialog-based application:

1. With AppWizard's Step 1 dialog, the programmer needs to specify the application's type as Single document (SDI), Multiple document (MDI), or Dialog-based (an application that uses a dialog box as its user interface). For our program, WevCalc, we will select Dialog-based. There is also a provision to select the application's language. For people in the United States, selecting U.S. English is the most logical choice. If you're programming for a non-U.S. market, select the language that meets your target market's needs.

2. AppWizard's Step 2 of 4 dialog allows you to select support for the following items:

- About Box: The application can have a standard About box created by AppWizard that can be modified by the programmer. The default is to include an About box.
- Context Sensitive Help: You can include support for context-sensitive help in your new application. The default is not to have context-sensitive help.
- Use 3D Controls: The controls used in the application can be managed by the CTL3D.DLL 3D dialog control library. The default is to include the usage of 3D controls.

Additionally, step 2 allows you to select the title for the dialog. The default title is the same as the application's name.

3. AppWizard's Step 3 of 4 dialog allows you to select support for the following items:

- The inclusion of Source File Comments. The default is to include comments.
- You can select the type of makefile that this project will have, choosing either a Visual C++ makefile or an External (using NMake) makefile. The default is a Visual C++ makefile.
- The linkage to MFC's library, for applications that are created with MFC, is the final option in this step. The choices are to use MFC in a static (nonshared) library or to use MFC in a shared DLL environment (the default). The shared DLL environment is useful when you have a number of MFC applications that could share a single copy of the MFC library.

Step 3's defaults generally are acceptable for the majority of projects created. Usually, the only option that might be changed is the usage of the MFC .DLL file.

4. AppWizard's Step 4 of 4 dialog allows you to select the classes that will be created for this application. The classes are listed, along with the class they were derived from and the filenames that the classes will be placed in. For the application class (based on **CWinApp**) you can't make any changes, but for other classes you can change the filenames to suit your naming standards.

The four steps are specifically for an application that is dialog-based.

When you've finished with AppWizard's creation dialogs, you're presented with a final "sanity check" dialog, which enables you to review your new project's specifications. If you notice an error at this stage, you can click on Cancel and return to the project definition stage.

For an MDI or SDI application, you'll have a different number of steps to follow. You'll find, however, that AppWizard's dialogs are well documented and easy to use, even the first time.

The options described in Tables 2.7 and 2.8 can be used with all Windows applications except dialog-based programs. With SDI and MDI applications, you can select OLE (Object Linking and Embedding) options and ODBC (Open Database Connectivity) options. First are the OLE options, described in Table 2.7. A further discussion of the OLE options is found in Chapter 10, "An Introduction to OLE Custom Controls."

Table 2.7. OLE options.	
Option	*Description*
No OLE support	Tells AppWizard that the application being generated will have no OLE support. This option is the default. Many simpler applications will be created with this option. While there is no requirement that an application support OLE, there will be a time when virtually all Windows applications will support OLE as a container, a server, or both.
Container support only	A container application is a program that can have objects created by other applications embedded or linked in the container application's document. A document that has embedded or linked objects is called a compound document.

Option	Description
Miniserver support only	A miniserver is a program that supports embedded objects. A miniserver won't support linked objects or run as a stand-alone application. Because a miniserver isn't a stand-alone application, it won't have support such as open, save, or create for files.
Full server support	A full server is a functional application whose documents can be used even if they're not embedded in a container application's document. An example of a full server is a graphing program in which a graph may be printed directly in the graphing program or embedded in a word processing document to form a complete report.
Container-server support	A container-server application combines the container application (just described) with a full server. It isn't possible to have a container-server in which the server is a miniserver, because a container application must provide file and document support.
Automation support	Automation enables a server application to provide additional services to the container application. With these additional services, you can do the following: You can create applications to expose objects to programming tools that will be able to manipulate these objects, and expose objects to macro languages such as VBA. Your applications can create and manipulate OLE objects to be exposed in one application from another of your applications. You also can create tools that can access and manipulate OLE objects. The tools that you can create include functions such as an embedded macro language or a programming tool. This option is not selected by default.

Another part of AppWizard's options is the Database options, which enable you to create an application that has ODBC support already built in. In setting the Database options, you are presented with a number of choices. These choices are outlined in Table 2.8.

Table 2.8. Database options.	
Option	Description
No ODBC Support	This option tells AppWizard not to include support for ODBC. If you later decide to add database support, you will have to manually add the necessary classes to your application. Information about the ODBC classes can be found in Part IV of this book. This is the default option.
Include Header File	This option installs the ODBC support header files. It doesn't create any specific source code. It simply modifies STDAFX.H (to which an #include AFXDB.H is included) and the .RC file that has an #include AFXDB.RC added.
Database Support, No File Support	This option installs support for ODBC views (**CRecordView**) but doesn't add file support (**CRecordSet**). You must specify both the database file and (if applicable for the specified datafile) a table. If you don't yet have a database file, you can't create the application.
Database and File Support	This option installs support for ODBC (**CRecordSet**), including support for file open and save. You will have to specify both the database file and (if applicable for the specified datafile) a table. If you don't yet have a database file, you won't be able to create the application.

After you set the application's main options and any OLE or ODBC options, you can modify the classes that AppWizard will create. The possible modifications vary depending on which class is being modified, but common changes made include the class's name and the name of the file that will hold the class's code.

When you're done defining the application, you can click on the OK button to create the application. Doing so displays a dialog box that describes the application being created (see Figure 2.9). If the application's creation options are acceptable, you can click on OK to create the application. However, if you see that the application's options don't meet the specifications, click on Cancel and return to AppWizard to modify the specification or option you want.

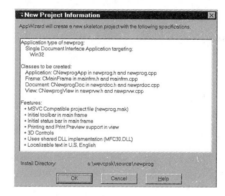

Figure 2.9. AppWizard's New Project Information dialog.

AppWizard provides a quick and easy way to create a Windows application. Once the shell is created, it is necessary to fill in the missing pieces—the parts of the application that AppWizard is unable to create. For this purpose, you use Visual Workbench's editor, which is described in more detail later.

To show how easy it is to create a Windows application using AppWizard, let's create a program together. Frankly, I'm getting rather tired of "hello" programs that don't really offer the programmer any challenge. Even though a fine calculator program is included with Windows, a calculator program is an excellent example of how to create a form view-type application.

WevCalc Calculator

First, we must create a design specification. If we don't plan, we won't get the results we expect! How can you get desired results without knowing, in advance, what results you want? For WevCalc, we'll set some simple specifications. The calculator will support the standard four functions (add, subtract, multiply, and divide) and provide an eight-digit display. We'll also need clear entry (CE) and clear all (C) keys. Face it, we're creating a classic "four-banger." Later, you can add to your version of the calculator and include new functions (such as the standard scientific functions) if you choose.

Visual Workbench's AppWizard used MFC's **CDialog** classes to create a form view type of Windows application. This type of application allows the programmer to create a program that simply presents a main window that looks like a standard dialog box and includes whatever dialog controls you need. With this interface we can create an edit control for user output and buttons for input.

To begin this project, start AppWizard by selecting File | New | Project. When AppWizard starts, a predefined set of project defaults is selected, some of which must be changed. The first thing required is the project's name. You also need to select the directory in which to place the program's files. Select the correct directory, then enter the program's name (WevCalc).

After providing the program name, click on the Create button. This button causes the AppWizard - Step 1 dialog to be displayed (see Figure 2.10). In this dialog, select the Dialog-based check box (WevCalc will be a dialog box-based program). Make sure that the correct language is selected, then click on the Next button. In the next dialog (Step 2), select About Box and Use 3D Controls. Make sure that Context Sensitive Help isn't selected. Name the dialog to be used "WevCalc," then click on the Next button. In the Step 3 dialog, use the default options—Yes, please; Visual C++ makefile; and Use MFC in a static library—then click on the Next button. In the Step 4 dialog, simply accept the defaults for the class names and class filenames. When you're done, click on the Finish button. At that point, you're presented with the project review dialog.

Figures 2.10 through 2.14 show each of AppWizard's project creation dialog boxes.

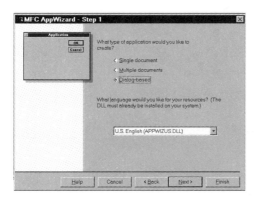

Figure 2.10. AppWizard's Step 1 dialog.

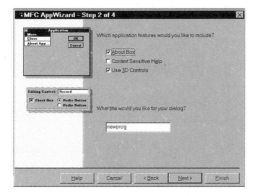

Figure 2.11. AppWizard's Step 2 of 4 dialog.

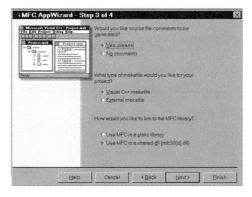

Figure 2.12. AppWizard's Step 3 of 4 dialog.

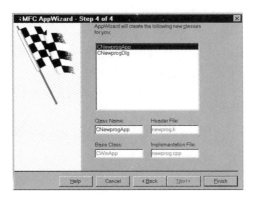

Figure 2.13. AppWizard's Step 4 of 4 dialog.

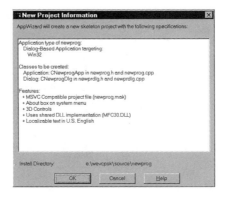

Figure 2.14. AppWizard's New Project Information dialog.

As the final step of the project creation process, AppWizard displays a status dialog that describes the application that is being created. Review the information contained in this dialog, and if everything meets your expectations, click on OK. If you notice any problems, click on Cancel to return to App Wizard's main dialog box (the final Step dialog), where you can make the necessary changes to your project.

When the project is complete, a number of files are saved in the specified directory. I have listed these files in Listing 2.2. This list of files was created after the first compile of the WevCalc program. (Your dates and sizes may differ.) This first compile, which created the debugging version of WevCalc, placed files in the subdirectory WINDEBUG. The files created by the project build process appear in bold. When the final release version of WevCalc is created, the results of the build are placed in a subdirectory called WINREL. This allows you to maintain both a release and a debugging version of your program at the same time, something that earlier versions of Visual C++ wouldn't let you do.

LISTING 2.2. FILES CREATED BY VISUAL C++ 2.0'S APPWIZARD.

```
Volume in drive E is E-SHARE

Directory of E:\WEVCPSK\SOURCE\WevCalc

.                <DIR>        06-14-94   2:57p
..               <DIR>        06-14-94   2:57p
RES              <DIR>        06-14-94   2:57p
WINDEBUG         <DIR>        06-14-94   2:59p
FILES    DIR           0      06-14-94   3:25p
README   TXT       3,224      06-14-94   2:56p
RESOURCE H           556      06-14-94   2:56p
STDAFX   CPP         205      06-14-94   2:56p
STDAFX   H           284      06-14-94   2:56p
WEVCADLG CPP       4,103      06-14-94   2:56p
WEVCADLG H           912      06-14-94   2:56p
WevCalc  APS      13,753      06-14-94   2:57p
WevCalc  CLW       1,054      06-14-94   2:56p
WevCalc  CPP       1,960      06-14-94   2:56p
WevCalc  H           905      06-14-94   2:56p
WevCalc  MAK       7,580      06-14-94   2:56p
WevCalc  RC        3,979      06-14-94   2:56p
        17 file(s)      38,515 bytes

Directory of E:\WEVCPSK\SOURCE\WevCalc\RES

.                <DIR>        06-14-94   2:57p
..               <DIR>        06-14-94   2:57p
WevCalc  ICO       1,078      06-14-94   2:56p
WevCalc  RC2         379      06-14-94   2:56p
         4 file(s)       1,457 bytes

Directory of E:\WEVCPSK\SOURCE\WevCalc\WINDEBUG

.                <DIR>        06-14-94   2:59p
..               <DIR>        06-14-94   2:59p
STDAFX   OBJ      41,518      06-14-94   2:59p
STDAFX   SBR     523,592      06-14-94   2:59p
WEVCADLG OBJ      15,810      06-14-94   3:00p
WEVCADLG SBR           0      06-14-94   3:04p
WevCalc  BSC     708,802      06-14-94   3:03p
WevCalc  EXE     561,664      06-14-94   3:02p
WevCalc  ILK     999,020      06-14-94   3:02p
WevCalc  OBJ       9,797      06-14-94   2:59p
WevCalc  PCH   2,152,288      06-14-94   2:59p
WevCalc  PDB   1,937,408      06-14-94   3:02p
WevCalc  RES      15,324      06-14-94   3:00p
WevCalc  SBR           0      06-14-94   3:04p
        14 file(s)   6,965,223 bytes
```

continues

LISTING 2.2. CONTINUED

```
Total files listed:
      35 file(s)      7,005,195 bytes
                     73,547,776 bytes free
```

In the list of files, RES is a subdirectory used to hold files that are specific to the project's resources.

The next step in creating our program is to form the calculator's layout. Later in this chapter, Figure 2.15 shows my layout. You don't have to follow this layout, but you should have the same keys. The figure has been annotated with the dialog control IDs so that you can use the same identifiers I used. The exact process of laying out WevCalc's dialog is covered later in this chapter.

The next section of this chapter covers the ways in which Visual Workbench's editor works with resources. For example, we can use the Visual Workbench editor to create dialog boxes; specifically, we'll modify the main dialog for WevCalc. In WevCalc, an application based on a dialog box, the main window's controls are laid out using a dialog box template.

Why a Dialog-Based Program?

Why create a dialog-based program as the first example in this book? Wouldn't a standard WYSIWYG program be more useful? Well, I have several reasons for creating a dialog-based application first. Before the existence of Visual C++ and MFC, creating a dialog-based application was a difficult and complex process. AppWizard has made creating a dialog-based application as easy as possible, actually easier than creating a WYSIWYG application.

Next, consider how a formview application can be used. One application is used as a calculator. Another classic application is to allow access to database records. Or, you might write a Rolodex-type program to create a simple personal information manager for names, addresses, and telephone numbers.

The Visual Workbench Editor

A major part of the Visual Workbench is its editor. The editor is part of Visual Workbench's MDI support. It enables you to open multiple source and resource files, each in its own window.

Editing Source C/C++ Files

You can set your editor preferences with the Editor tab in the Options dialog (select Tools | Options). The editor configuration tabs (Editor, Colors, and Fonts) affect how the edit windows look and work. Many programmers set their tab stops every four columns. Some programmers, however, set their tabs at three or five columns. The first option in the Editor configuration dialog allows you to set tab stops. You also have the option of either keeping the tabs or converting them to spaces when the file is saved.

Found in the Editor tab of the Options dialog are the scroll bars' Enable check boxes. You can elect to turn on or off the vertical, horizontal, or both scroll bars. With a scroll bar turned off, you can still scroll using the cursor: simply move the cursor to the edge of the screen and the window will scroll automatically. I prefer to have scroll bars in my edit windows.

The Editor tab of the Options dialog enables you to define the action performed on source code in certain situations. To automatically save your source files before running tools, select the Save Before Running Tools check box. You also can have the Visual Workbench prompt you before you saving any file. To activate a prompt prior to saving, check the Prompt Before Saving Files check box.

Unlike earlier versions of Visual C++, Visual C++ 2.0 doesn't allow direct configuration of the undo buffer. The number of undos allowed is determined by a value set in the registry. Using RegEdit or another registry editor, you need to add (or modify, if it already exists) HKEY_CURRENT_USER\Software\Microsoft\Visual C++ 2.0\General data item UndoLevels. This item, of datatype **REG_DWORD**, contains an integer count of the number of undo levels allowed. If the UndoLevels data item doesn't exist, a default of 10 undo levels is assumed.

Also in the Options dialog is a tab called Fonts. With Fonts you can select the font for a window and set the default font for all windows. With more and more programmers using high-resolution monitors (1024 x 768 and better), the selection of a font and point size that are easy to read becomes increasingly important. Because programming is basically columnar, it's generally accepted that a monospace font should be used, such as Courier, Courier New, or Courier New OEM. However, several other monospace fonts that you might prefer are becoming available. Typical font sizes range from 10 points to about 16 points, but other sizes might be useful, depending on your screen size and resolution. On my 1024 x 768, 20-inch monitor, I use a 10- or 11-point font.

Some of the features supported by the Visual Workbench editor are listed in Table 2.9.

TABLE 2.9. THE VISUAL WORKBENCH'S EDITOR FEATURES.

Feature	Description
Syntax coloring	This option allows various parts of the syntax of a C or C++ program to be colored differently. Examples of the different syntax items that may be colored include comments, constants (both numeric and character), and keywords.
Clipboard	The Visual Workbench's clipboard support is much like most other Windows applications. You can copy text to and from the clipboard, both within the Visual Workbench and with external applications. The editor also supports drag-and-drop editing.
Find/replace	The Visual Workbench editor supports searching for text in a file that is being edited. Also, you can replace text using the replace functionality. Text being searched for can be regular text or text formed using regular expressions (which are described later).
Read-only files	Any file edited can be made read-only. The advantage of read-only is that it prevents inadvertent modification of the file while the file is loaded in the editor. All of the Visual Workbench's standard debugging windows (Watch, Locals, Registers, and Output) are read-only.

Feature	Description
Undo buffer	The Visual Workbench editor has an undo function that enables you to trace back and undo changes made to a source file. Many times programmers start to make a change, only to realize that the change won't work. The undo function allows changes to be undone one at a time. Also, whenever editing is being undone, you can restore the edits that have been undone by using the redo function.
View modes	Generally, you will view files as C/C++ source files. However, while debugging, you can view a source file in the mixed assembly/source format.
Jump to line	You can jump to any line in the currently active window by specifying its number.
Move to compiler error	Following a compile that generates either warning or error messages, pressing F4 forces the editor to jump to the line that contains the error. If the file that contains the error isn't loaded, the Visual Workbench will automatically load the file. The error-message text, found in the Output window, will be displayed in Visual Workbench's status bar.
Bookmarks	While editing a file, you can mark lines using the bookmark function (Ctrl-F2). After you have marked a line or lines, you can press the F2 key to jump to the marked line. If you have more than one line marked, Visual Workbench jumps to each in turn. Bookmarks can be toggled on and off using Ctrl-F2.

Using the Visual Workbench editor is simple. Generally, programmers have enough experience with editors to make using the Visual Workbench editor intuitive. Because this editor is rather simple, we'll devote the remainder of this chapter to tips for using it.

Tabs or spaces? You can configure the editor to either keep tabs in the files that are being edited or to replace the tabs with spaces. When you keep tabs in your text (that is, when you don't convert tabs to spaces), it's much easier to indent and unindent sections of code. When tabs are replaced with spaces, it can be easier to print the file or to import the file into some other utility. Generally, I keep tabs in the source files, since I always seem to be changing the indent level—it's easier to delete one tab than to delete four spaces.

Syntax coloring is one of the better features that any programming editor can offer. With syntax coloring you can see at a glance variable types, comments, strings, and so on. Incorrect variable types and improper usage of keywords quickly jump out at you (usually, you see these errors as you are typing).

Bookmarks are useful because they enable you to jump between two or more places in a given file. A bookmark is deleted when the line that has the bookmark is deleted, so lines copied to the clipboard don't include a bookmark. There is one limitation: Bookmarks don't survive the closing of a file, whether you use the Close command or exit Visual C++. It would be nice if bookmarks were saved in the workspace, but for now they're not.

Have you ever written code that had no errors? It does happen, but not often. Generally, each time you modify and add to a program's code, you generate compile-time error and warning messages. Use Jump to Next Error (F4) and Jump to Previous Error (Shift-F4) to find the code that generated each error. With these functions, the editor takes into consideration that you might add or delete lines when it computes the line that the error is on.

Use the Project (.MAK) window to open files whenever possible. This window shows the files that are part of the project and their relationships. For files that aren't listed in the Project window, use the tollbar's open file button (the second one on the left), which will show only files that are part of the currently loaded project. With the open file button, you can quickly open a file without having to navigate Visual Workbench's open file dialogs.

Editing Resource Objects

With earlier versions of Visual C++, resource objects (dialog boxes, menus, string tables, and so on) had to be edited with the Visual Workbench editor. Visual C++ 2.0 has integrated the functionality of AppStudio with the Visual

Workbench editor. Now, when you open a project's resource (.RC) file, you're presented with a hierarchical view of the project's resources. You can then select any resource (see Table 2.10) and open it in its own edit window.

Most of the resource editing functionality is similar to that of AppStudio. Some changes have been made to the way things work, mostly extending the functionality of the resource editor. In addition, Visual C++ can now edit version resource objects in a user-friendly manner. (AppWizard will actually create a shell version resource for new projects.)

Table 2.10. Visual Workbench-supported resources.

Resource	Description
Accelerator	Used to map keys to a specific functionality.
Bitmap	Used for many purposes, including toolbar button images.
Cursor	Used to create custom cursors.
Dialog	Dialog boxes are a major part of a Windows application's user interface.
Icon	The application's icon is used to show the application both when it's minimized and when it's displayed in Program Manager's group boxes.
Menu	A program's menu structure is the main user interface.
String	String constants should be used whenever possible. String resources reduce usage of the default data segment (when you're creating a 16-bit application). String resources enable you to easily modify strings, typically when you're converting the application to a foreign language.
Version	Information that describes the application. Windows uses this information to help manage the program after it's been installed. The version resource has information such as the program's copyright, operating system, and filetype.

Modifying Dialog Boxes

In this chapter we'll use the Visual Workbench to modify the default resources that AppWizard created for our WevCalc program. Our first change is to add new controls to the default dialog that is used to create WevCalc's main window. AppWizard initially creates this dialog (**IDD_WEVCALC_FORM**) with two buttons, OK and Cancel, and a single text control telling you to locate the application's controls in this dialog.

First, you need to delete the default text control created by AppWizard by selecting this control and pressing the Delete key. After deleting the AppWizard default text control, you should also delete the OK and Cancel buttons. Create 18 buttons: the numbers 0 through 9, a decimal point, C for clear, CE for clear entry, the four operations (add, subtract, multiply, and divide), and an equals sign.

Refer to Figure 2.15 to see my layout for the calculator. Although you don't have to follow this layout, you should make sure that you've included all the necessary buttons. After creating the buttons, you need to create the edit control that will be used to display WevCalc's output. As with all simple calculators, the number being entered is displayed in the output window. Whenever a math operation is performed, the operation's results are displayed in the output window as well.

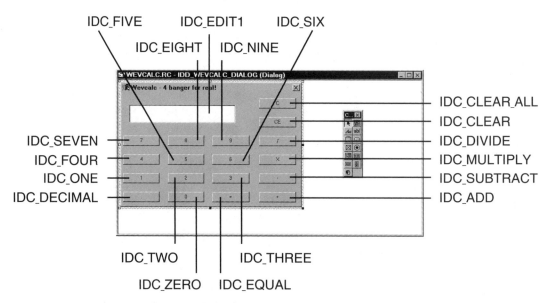

Figure 2.15. WevCalc's main dialog layout.

Laying out the dialog box is relatively easy. You can choose to align the dialog box's controls, make groups of controls the same size, and even define the font that will be used with the dialog box. For WevCalc, I created a single button and used Ctrl-click to copy the control, creating each of the 18 controls that WevCalc requires. After copying the control, I then renamed and labeled it.

After making the changes to the dialog box, it's a good idea to save all the files in the project.

Adding Code for a Dialog Box

After you've created a dialog box using Visual Workbench's resource editor, you need to add code to the dialog box handler to manage the new controls. Generating the shells for the new functions (one function for each new button) is an easy task using ClassWizard. After saving the dialog box, simply activate ClassWizard using the accelerator key Ctrl-W. Next, select the dialog box's class (**CWevcalcDlg**) and the Message Maps tab in ClassWizard. In the Object IDs: list box you'll see the identifiers for each of the new controls that you've added to the dialog box. In the Messages: list box are two messages for a pushbutton, **BN_CLICKED** and **BN_DOUBLECLICKED**.

WevCalc uses only single clicks, so we won't assign a handler for double-clicks. The process for creating handlers for the new controls in WevCalc looks like this:

1. Select a button's identifier (**ID_ADD**, for example) in the Object IDs: list box.
2. Select **BN_CLICKED** in the Messages: list box.
3. Click on Add Function.
4. Click on OK to accept the default name (or enter a new name of your choosing and click on OK).
5. Repeat steps 1 through 4 for each button.

Once you've created handlers for WevCalc's 18 buttons, you must create a variable for the edit control that serves as the user's output area. To create a variable for an edit control, select the Member Variables tab in the ClassWizard dialog. This displays the member variables part of ClassWizard's dialog. In the Control IDs: list box, select the edit control's identifier (**IDC_EDIT1**). Then click on the Add Variable button. You'll be presented with the Add Member Variable dialog box. You must supply a name for the new member variable (ClassWizard provides a default *m_* prefix). For WevCalc, I used the variable name *m_Accumulator*. You must also change the variable's type from **CString** to

double, because WevCalc will put floating-point numbers in the edit control. One nice thing about MFC is that it takes care of formatting and displaying the contents of the edit controls automatically.

When you've named the edit control's variable and changed its type to **double**, click on OK. You'll see that the Control IDs: list box has been updated with the new variable, which is listed after **ID_EDIT1**. When **ID_EDIT1** is selected, you see at the bottom of ClassWizard's dialog two new edit controls, Minimum Value: and Maximum Value:, which allow you to specify a minimum and maximum value that can be placed in the variable *m_Accumulator*.

Finally, after you've created the variable for **IDC_EDIT1** and the handlers for the buttons, you can select the Message Maps tab, select the first button you created, and click on the Edit Code button in ClassWizard. This closes ClassWizard and takes you to the function that was created for the first button. You can use the Edit Code button at any time, not just after creating a new handler.

After you create the handlers for the buttons, your WEVCADLG.CPP file will look like the one shown in Listing 2.3. Notice that, although there are functions for each control, these functions do nothing. Also notice that ClassWizard has updated the message map (**BEGIN_MESSAGE_MAP**) to tell Windows which control handler is for which button.

Listing 2.3. WevCalc's WEVCADLG.CPP file with button handlers.

```
// WEVCADLG.CPP: Implementation file
//

#include "stdafx.h"
#include "wevcalc.h"
#include "wevcadlg.h"

#ifdef _DEBUG
#undef THIS_FILE
static char BASED_CODE THIS_FILE[] = __FILE__;
#endif

/////////////////////////////////////////////////////////////////////////////
// CAboutDlg dialog used for App About

class CAboutDlg : public CDialog
{
public:
    CAboutDlg();
```

```
// Dialog data
    //{{AFX_DATA(CAboutDlg)
    enum { IDD = IDD_ABOUTBOX };
    //}}AFX_DATA

// Implementation
protected:
    virtual void DoDataExchange(CDataExchange* pDX);    // DDX/DDV support
    //{{AFX_MSG(CAboutDlg)
    virtual BOOL OnInitDialog();
    //}}AFX_MSG
    DECLARE_MESSAGE_MAP()
};

CAboutDlg::CAboutDlg() : CDialog(CAboutDlg::IDD)
{
    //{{AFX_DATA_INIT(CAboutDlg)
    //}}AFX_DATA_INIT
}

void CAboutDlg::DoDataExchange(CDataExchange* pDX)
{
    CDialog::DoDataExchange(pDX);
    //{{AFX_DATA_MAP(CAboutDlg)
    //}}AFX_DATA_MAP
}

BEGIN_MESSAGE_MAP(CAboutDlg, CDialog)
    //{{AFX_MSG_MAP(CAboutDlg)
        // No message handlers
    //}}AFX_MSG_MAP
END_MESSAGE_MAP()

////////////////////////////////////////////////////////////////////////
// CAboutDlg message handlers

BOOL CAboutDlg::OnInitDialog()
{
    CDialog::OnInitDialog();
    CenterWindow();

    // TODO: Add extra about dialog initialization here

    return TRUE;  // Return TRUE  unless you set the focus to a control
}

////////////////////////////////////////////////////////////////////////
// CWevcalcDlg dialog

CWevcalcDlg::CWevcalcDlg(CWnd* pParent /*=NULL*/)
    : CDialog(CWevcalcDlg::IDD, pParent)
{
    //{{AFX_DATA_INIT(CWevcalcDlg)
    m_Accumulator = 0;
    //}}AFX_DATA_INIT
    // Note that LoadIcon does not require a subsequent DestroyIcon in Win32
    m_hIcon = AfxGetApp()->LoadIcon(IDR_MAINFRAME);
```

continues

LISTING 2.3. CONTINUED

```cpp
}

void CWevcalcDlg::DoDataExchange(CDataExchange* pDX)
{
    CDialog::DoDataExchange(pDX);
    //{{AFX_DATA_MAP(CWevcalcDlg)
    DDX_Text(pDX, IDC_EDIT1, m_Accumulator);
    //}}AFX_DATA_MAP
}

BEGIN_MESSAGE_MAP(CWevcalcDlg, CDialog)
    //{{AFX_MSG_MAP(CWevcalcDlg)
    ON_WM_SYSCOMMAND()
    ON_WM_PAINT()
    ON_WM_QUERYDRAGICON()
    ON_BN_CLICKED(IDC_ADD, OnAdd)
    ON_BN_CLICKED(IDC_CLEAR_ALL, OnClearAll)
    ON_BN_CLICKED(IDC_CLEAR_ENTRY, OnClearEntry)
    ON_BN_CLICKED(IDC_DECIMAL, OnDecimal)
    ON_BN_CLICKED(IDC_DIVIDE, OnDivide)
    ON_BN_CLICKED(IDC_EIGHT, OnEight)
    ON_BN_CLICKED(IDC_EQUAL, OnEqual)
    ON_BN_CLICKED(IDC_FIVE, OnFive)
    ON_BN_CLICKED(IDC_FOUR, OnFour)
    ON_BN_CLICKED(IDC_MULTIPLY, OnMultiply)
    ON_BN_CLICKED(IDC_NINE, OnNine)
    ON_BN_CLICKED(IDC_ONE, OnOne)
    ON_BN_CLICKED(IDC_SEVEN, OnSeven)
    ON_BN_CLICKED(IDC_SIX, OnSix)
    ON_BN_CLICKED(IDC_SUBTRACT, OnSubtract)
    ON_BN_CLICKED(IDC_THREE, OnThree)
    ON_BN_CLICKED(IDC_TWO, OnTwo)
    ON_BN_CLICKED(IDC_ZERO, OnZero)
    //}}AFX_MSG_MAP
END_MESSAGE_MAP()

/////////////////////////////////////////////////////////////////////////////
// CWevcalcDlg message handlers

BOOL CWevcalcDlg::OnInitDialog()
{
    CDialog::OnInitDialog();
    CenterWindow();

    // Add "About..." menu item to system menu

    // IDM_ABOUTBOX must be in the system command range
    ASSERT((IDM_ABOUTBOX & 0xFFF0) == IDM_ABOUTBOX);
    ASSERT(IDM_ABOUTBOX < 0xF000);

    CMenu* pSysMenu = GetSystemMenu(FALSE);
    CString strAboutMenu;
    strAboutMenu.LoadString(IDS_ABOUTBOX);
    if (!strAboutMenu.IsEmpty())
    {
        pSysMenu->AppendMenu(MF_SEPARATOR);
```

```
            pSysMenu->AppendMenu(MF_STRING, IDM_ABOUTBOX, strAboutMenu);
    }

    // TODO: Add extra initialization here

    return TRUE;  // Return TRUE unless you set the focus to a control
}

void CWevcalcDlg::OnSysCommand(UINT nID, LPARAM lParam)
{
    if ((nID & 0xFFF0) == IDM_ABOUTBOX)
    {
        CAboutDlg dlgAbout;
        dlgAbout.DoModal();
    }
    else
    {
        CDialog::OnSysCommand(nID, lParam);
    }
}

// If you add a minimize button to your dialog, you will need the code below
// to draw the icon. For MFC applications using the document/view model,
// this is automatically done for you by the framework.

void CWevcalcDlg::OnPaint()
{
    if (IsIconic())
    {
        CPaintDC dc(this);  // Device context for painting

        SendMessage(WM_ICONERASEBKGND, (WPARAM) dc.GetSafeHdc(), 0);

        // Center icon in client rectangle
        int cxIcon = GetSystemMetrics(SM_CXICON);
        int cyIcon = GetSystemMetrics(SM_CYICON);
        CRect rect;
        GetClientRect(&rect);
        int x = (rect.Width() - cxIcon + 1) / 2;
        int y = (rect.Height() - cyIcon + 1) / 2;

        // Draw the icon
        dc.DrawIcon(x, y, m_hIcon);
    }
    else
    {
        CDialog::OnPaint();
    }
}

// The system calls this to obtain the cursor to display while the user drags
// the minimized window
HCURSOR CWevcalcDlg::OnQueryDragIcon()
{
    return (HCURSOR) m_hIcon;
}
```

continues

Listing 2.3. continued

```
void CWevcalcDlg::OnClearAll()
{
    // TODO: Add your control notification handler code here
}

void CWevcalcDlg::OnClearEntry()
{
    // TODO: Add your control notification handler code here
}

void CWevcalcDlg::OnDecimal()
{
    // TODO: Add your control notification handler code here
}

void CWevcalcDlg::OnAdd()
{
    // TODO: Add your control notification handler code here
}

void CWevcalcDlg::OnMultiply()
{
    // TODO: Add your control notification handler code here
}

void CWevcalcDlg::OnSubtract()
{
    // TODO: Add your control notification handler code here
}

void CWevcalcDlg::OnDivide()
{
    // TODO: Add your control notification handler code here
}

void CWevcalcDlg::OnEqual()
{
    // TODO: Add your control notification handler code here
}

void CWevcalcDlg::OnZero()
{
    // TODO: Add your control notification handler code here
}

void CWevcalcDlg::OnOne()
{
    // TODO: Add your control notification handler code here
}

void CWevcalcDlg::OnTwo()
{
    // TODO: Add your control notification handler code here
}
```

```
void CWevcalcDlg::OnThree()
{
    // TODO: Add your control notification handler code here
}

void CWevcalcDlg::OnFour()
{
    // TODO: Add your control notification handler code here
}

void CWevcalcDlg::OnFive()
{
    // TODO: Add your control notification handler code here
}

void CWevcalcDlg::OnSix()
{
    // TODO: Add your control notification handler code here
}

void CWevcalcDlg::OnSeven()
{
    // TODO: Add your control notification handler code here
}

void CWevcalcDlg::OnEight()
{
    // TODO: Add your control notification handler code here
}

void CWevcalcDlg::OnNine()
{
    // TODO: Add your control notification handler code here
}
```

Next, we must add code to make our calculator work. For instance, if the user presses a number button, we must make that number appear in the edit window. We must take care to manage the entered number's magnitude.

For the operations buttons, we must move the current accumulator's contents to a new location (we'll call the new, temporary accumulator *m_Accumulator1*), save the current operation, and set a flag to tell WevCalc to clear the current accumulator when the next nonfunction button is pressed. When the execute button (the equals button) is pressed, we then take the contents of *m_Accumulator* and *m_Accumulator1* and perform the operation that was saved when the last operation key was pressed.

Finally, we must code the two clear buttons to clear the main accumulator when clear entry (CE) is selected, or both accumulators when clear all (C) is selected.

This code fragment shows the new variables we've added to WevCalc:

```
m_dAccumulator1 = 0.0;          // Save accumulator
m_nDecimal = 0;                 // Current digit's magnitude
m_nPreviousOperation = FALSE;   // Last operation key pressed
m_bClear = FALSE;   // If !FALSE, clear accumulator on next digit entered
```

I also added one new helper function to WevCalc, **ClearEntry()**, which clears the current accumulator and resets the other related variables to their default values:

```
void CWevcalcDlg::ClearEntry()
{// Clear the current accumulator (only)
    m_Accumulator = 0.0;
    m_nDecimal = 0;
    m_bClear = FALSE;
}
```

Listing 2.4 shows WEVCADLG.H, the header file for WevCalc. I've included this file to show (in bold) the addition of the function prototype for `ClearEntry()` and the four new variables that must be added.

LISTING 2.4. WEVCADLG.H, THE HEADER FILE FOR WevCalc.

```
// WEVCADLG.H: Header file
//

///////////////////////////////////////////////////////////////////////////
// CWevcalcDlg dialog

class CWevcalcDlg : public CDialog
{
// Construction
public:
    CWevcalcDlg(CWnd* pParent = NULL);   // Standard constructor

// Dialog data
    //{{AFX_DATA(CWevcalcDlg)
    enum { IDD = IDD_WEVCALC_DIALOG };
    double      m_Accumulator;
    //}}AFX_DATA

    double      m_dAccumulator1;
    int         m_nDecimal;
    int         m_nPreviousOperation;
    BOOL    m_bClear;

    // ClassWizard-generated virtual function overrides
    //{{AFX_VIRTUAL(CWevcalcDlg)
    protected:
    virtual void DoDataExchange(CDataExchange* pDX);   // DDX/DDV support
    //}}AFX_VIRTUAL
```

```
// Implementation
protected:
    HICON m_hIcon;
    void    ClearEntry();
    // Generated message map functions
    //{{AFX_MSG(CWevcalcDlg)
    virtual BOOL OnInitDialog();
    afx_msg void OnSysCommand(UINT nID, LPARAM lParam);
    afx_msg void OnPaint();
    afx_msg HCURSOR OnQueryDragIcon();
    afx_msg void OnAdd();
    afx_msg void OnClearAll();
    afx_msg void OnClearEntry();
    afx_msg void OnDecimal();
    afx_msg void OnDivide();
    afx_msg void OnEight();
    afx_msg void OnEqual();
    afx_msg void OnFive();
    afx_msg void OnFour();
    afx_msg void OnMultiply();
    afx_msg void OnNine();
    afx_msg void OnOne();
    afx_msg void OnSeven();
    afx_msg void OnSix();
    afx_msg void OnSubtract();
    afx_msg void OnThree();
    afx_msg void OnTwo();
    afx_msg void OnZero();
    //}}AFX_MSG
    DECLARE_MESSAGE_MAP()
};
```

Listing 2.5 shows the final code for WEVCADLG.CPP. The lines I added to the ClassWizard code appear in bold.

LISTING 2.5. WevCalc's dialog box manager (WEVCADLG.CPP) completed.

```
// WEVCADLG.CPP: Implementation file
//

#include "stdafx.h"
#include "wevcalc.h"
#include "wevcadlg.h"

#ifdef _DEBUG
#undef THIS_FILE
static char BASED_CODE THIS_FILE[] = __FILE__;
#endif

/////////////////////////////////////////////////////////////////////////////
// CAboutDlg dialog used for App About
```

continues

Listing 2.5. continued

```
class CAboutDlg : public CDialog
{
public:
    CAboutDlg();

// Dialog data
    //{{AFX_DATA(CAboutDlg)
    enum { IDD = IDD_ABOUTBOX };
    //}}AFX_DATA

// Implementation
protected:
    virtual void DoDataExchange(CDataExchange* pDX);   // DDX/DDV support
    //{{AFX_MSG(CAboutDlg)
    virtual BOOL OnInitDialog();
    //}}AFX_MSG
    DECLARE_MESSAGE_MAP()
};

CAboutDlg::CAboutDlg() : CDialog(CAboutDlg::IDD)
{
    //{{AFX_DATA_INIT(CAboutDlg)
    //}}AFX_DATA_INIT
}

void CAboutDlg::DoDataExchange(CDataExchange* pDX)
{
    CDialog::DoDataExchange(pDX);
    //{{AFX_DATA_MAP(CAboutDlg)
    //}}AFX_DATA_MAP
}

BEGIN_MESSAGE_MAP(CAboutDlg, CDialog)
    //{{AFX_MSG_MAP(CAboutDlg)
        // No message handlers
    //}}AFX_MSG_MAP
END_MESSAGE_MAP()

/////////////////////////////////////////////////////////////////////////////
// CAboutDlg message handlers

BOOL CAboutDlg::OnInitDialog()
{
    CDialog::OnInitDialog();
    CenterWindow();

    // TODO: Add extra about dialog initialization here

    return TRUE;  // Return TRUE  unless you set the focus to a control
}

/////////////////////////////////////////////////////////////////////////////
// CWevcalcDlg dialog

CWevcalcDlg::CWevcalcDlg(CWnd* pParent /*=NULL*/)
    : CDialog(CWevcalcDlg::IDD, pParent)
```

```
{
    //{{AFX_DATA_INIT(CWevcalcDlg)
    m_Accumulator = 0;
    //}}AFX_DATA_INIT
    // Note that LoadIcon does not require a subsequent DestroyIcon in Win32
    m_hIcon = AfxGetApp()->LoadIcon(IDR_MAINFRAME);

    m_dAccumulator1 = 0.0;
    m_nDecimal = 0;
    m_nPreviousOperation = FALSE;
    m_bClear = FALSE;

}

void CWevcalcDlg::DoDataExchange(CDataExchange* pDX)
{
    CDialog::DoDataExchange(pDX);
    //{{AFX_DATA_MAP(CWevcalcDlg)
    DDX_Text(pDX, IDC_EDIT1, m_Accumulator);
    //}}AFX_DATA_MAP
}

BEGIN_MESSAGE_MAP(CWevcalcDlg, CDialog)
    //{{AFX_MSG_MAP(CWevcalcDlg)
    ON_WM_SYSCOMMAND()
    ON_WM_PAINT()
    ON_WM_QUERYDRAGICON()
    ON_BN_CLICKED(IDC_ADD, OnAdd)
    ON_BN_CLICKED(IDC_CLEAR_ALL, OnClearAll)
    ON_BN_CLICKED(IDC_CLEAR_ENTRY, OnClearEntry)
    ON_BN_CLICKED(IDC_DECIMAL, OnDecimal)
    ON_BN_CLICKED(IDC_DIVIDE, OnDivide)
    ON_BN_CLICKED(IDC_EIGHT, OnEight)
    ON_BN_CLICKED(IDC_EQUAL, OnEqual)
    ON_BN_CLICKED(IDC_FIVE, OnFive)
    ON_BN_CLICKED(IDC_FOUR, OnFour)
    ON_BN_CLICKED(IDC_MULTIPLY, OnMultiply)
    ON_BN_CLICKED(IDC_NINE, OnNine)
    ON_BN_CLICKED(IDC_ONE, OnOne)
    ON_BN_CLICKED(IDC_SEVEN, OnSeven)
    ON_BN_CLICKED(IDC_SIX, OnSix)
    ON_BN_CLICKED(IDC_SUBTRACT, OnSubtract)
    ON_BN_CLICKED(IDC_THREE, OnThree)
    ON_BN_CLICKED(IDC_TWO, OnTwo)
    ON_BN_CLICKED(IDC_ZERO, OnZero)
    //}}AFX_MSG_MAP
END_MESSAGE_MAP()

/////////////////////////////////////////////////////////////////////////////
// CWevcalcDlg message handlers

BOOL CWevcalcDlg::OnInitDialog()
{
    CDialog::OnInitDialog();
    CenterWindow();

    // Add "About..." menu item to system menu
```

continues

Listing 2.5. continued

```
    // IDM_ABOUTBOX must be in the system command range
    ASSERT((IDM_ABOUTBOX & 0xFFF0) == IDM_ABOUTBOX);
    ASSERT(IDM_ABOUTBOX < 0xF000);

    CMenu* pSysMenu = GetSystemMenu(FALSE);
    CString strAboutMenu;
    strAboutMenu.LoadString(IDS_ABOUTBOX);
    if (!strAboutMenu.IsEmpty())
    {
        pSysMenu->AppendMenu(MF_SEPARATOR);
        pSysMenu->AppendMenu(MF_STRING, IDM_ABOUTBOX, strAboutMenu);
    }

    // TODO: Add extra initialization here

    return TRUE;   // Return TRUE  unless you set the focus to a control
}

void CWevcalcDlg::OnSysCommand(UINT nID, LPARAM lParam)
{
    if ((nID & 0xFFF0) == IDM_ABOUTBOX)
    {
        CAboutDlg dlgAbout;
        dlgAbout.DoModal();
    }
    else
    {
        CDialog::OnSysCommand(nID, lParam);
    }
}

// If you add a minimize button to your dialog, you will need the code below
// to draw the icon. For MFC applications using the document/view model,
// this is automatically done for you by the framework.

void CWevcalcDlg::OnPaint()
{
    if (IsIconic())
    {
        CPaintDC dc(this);  // Device context for painting

        SendMessage(WM_ICONERASEBKGND, (WPARAM) dc.GetSafeHdc(), 0);

        // Center icon in client rectangle
        int cxIcon = GetSystemMetrics(SM_CXICON);
        int cyIcon = GetSystemMetrics(SM_CYICON);
        CRect rect;
        GetClientRect(&rect);
        int x = (rect.Width() - cxIcon + 1) / 2;
        int y = (rect.Height() - cyIcon + 1) / 2;

        // Draw the icon
        dc.DrawIcon(x, y, m_hIcon);
    }
    else
    {
```

```
        CDialog::OnPaint();
    }
}

// The system calls this to obtain the cursor to display while the user drags
// the minimized window
HCURSOR CWevcalcDlg::OnQueryDragIcon()
{
    return (HCURSOR) m_hIcon;
}

void CWevcalcDlg::ClearEntry()
{// Clear the current accumulator (only)
    m_Accumulator = 0.0;
    m_nDecimal = 0;
    m_bClear = FALSE;
}

void CWevcalcDlg::OnClearAll()
{
    // TODO: Add your control notification handler code here
    ClearEntry();
    m_dAccumulator1 = 0.0;
    UpdateData(FALSE);
}

void CWevcalcDlg::OnClearEntry()
{
    // TODO: Add your control notification handler code here
    ClearEntry();
    UpdateData(FALSE);
}

void CWevcalcDlg::OnDecimal()
{
    // TODO: Add your control notification handler code here
    if (m_bClear)
        ClearEntry();

    if (m_nDecimal == 0)
    {// Set decimal point only if not already set; otherwise, ignore it
        m_nDecimal = 10;
    }
}

void CWevcalcDlg::OnAdd()
{
    // TODO: Add your control notification handler code here
// Next operation is:
//        Add m_Accumulator and m_dAccumulator1.
//        Perform the previous operation, place result in m_dAccumulator1,
//        and display the result in m_Accumulator (and the edit window).
//        The next button pressed will clear m_Accumulator
//        and reset the edit window...

// First, perform previous operation (if any), then set up for next number...
```

continues

Listing 2.5. continued

```
    switch (m_nPreviousOperation)
    {
        case IDC_ADD:          // Add
            m_dAccumulator1 +=    m_Accumulator;
            break;
        case IDC_MULTIPLY:     // Multiply
            m_dAccumulator1 *=    m_Accumulator;
            break;
        case IDC_SUBTRACT:     // Subtract
            m_dAccumulator1 -=    m_Accumulator;
            break;
        case IDC_DIVIDE:       // Divide (check for divide by zero!)
            if (m_Accumulator != 0.0)
            {
                m_dAccumulator1 /=    m_Accumulator;
            }
            break;
        default:                  // Move, no previous operation...
            m_dAccumulator1 = m_Accumulator;
            break;
    }
    m_nPreviousOperation = IDC_ADD;
    m_Accumulator    =    m_dAccumulator1;
    m_bClear         =    TRUE;
    UpdateData(FALSE);
}

void CWevcalcDlg::OnMultiply()
{
    // TODO: Add your control notification handler code here
// Next operation is:
//        Multiply m_Accumulator and m_dAccumulator1.
//        Perform the previous operation, place result in m_dAccumulator1,
//        and display the result in m_Accumulator (and the edit window).
//        The next button pressed will clear m_Accumulator
//        and reset the edit window...

// First, perform previous operation (if any), then set up for next number...

    switch (m_nPreviousOperation)
    {
        case IDC_ADD:          // Add
            m_dAccumulator1 +=    m_Accumulator;
            break;
        case IDC_MULTIPLY:     // Multiply
            m_dAccumulator1 *=    m_Accumulator;
            break;
        case IDC_SUBTRACT:     // Subtract
            m_dAccumulator1 -=    m_Accumulator;
            break;
        case IDC_DIVIDE:       // Divide (check for divide by zero!)
            if (m_Accumulator != 0.0)
            {
                m_dAccumulator1 /=    m_Accumulator;
            }
            break;
```

```
        default:                  // Move, no previous operation...
            m_dAccumulator1 = m_Accumulator;
            break;
    }
    m_nPreviousOperation = IDC_MULTIPLY;
    m_Accumulator    =    m_dAccumulator1;
    m_bClear         =    TRUE;
    UpdateData(FALSE);
}

void CWevcalcDlg::OnSubtract()
{
    // TODO: Add your control notification handler code here
// Next operation is:
//        Subtract m_Accumulator and m_dAccumulator1.
//        Perform the previous operation, place result in m_dAccumulator1,
//        and display the result in m_Accumulator (and the edit window).
//        The next button pressed will clear m_Accumulator
//        and reset the edit window...

// First, perform previous operation (if any), then set up for next number...

    switch (m_nPreviousOperation)
    {
        case IDC_ADD:            // Add
            m_dAccumulator1 +=    m_Accumulator;
            break;
        case IDC_MULTIPLY:    // Multiply
            m_dAccumulator1 *=    m_Accumulator;
            break;
        case IDC_SUBTRACT:    // Subtract
            m_dAccumulator1 -=    m_Accumulator;
            break;
        case IDC_DIVIDE:        // Divide (check for divide by zero!)
            if (m_Accumulator != 0.0)
            {
                m_dAccumulator1 /=    m_Accumulator;
            }
            break;
        default:                  // Move, no previous operation...
            m_dAccumulator1 = m_Accumulator;
            break;
    }
    m_nPreviousOperation = IDC_SUBTRACT;
    m_Accumulator    =    m_dAccumulator1;
    m_bClear         =    TRUE;
    UpdateData(FALSE);
}

void CWevcalcDlg::OnDivide()
{
    // TODO: Add your control notification handler code here
// Next operation is:
//        Divide m_Accumulator and m_dAccumulator1.
//        Perform the previous operation, place result in m_dAccumulator1,
//        and display the result in m_Accumulator (and the edit window).
//        The next button pressed will clear m_Accumulator
```

continues

Listing 2.5. continued

```
//         and reset the edit window...

// First, perform previous operation (if any), then set up for next number...

    switch (m_nPreviousOperation)
    {
        case IDC_ADD:          // Add
            m_dAccumulator1 +=    m_Accumulator;
            break;
        case IDC_MULTIPLY:     // Multiply
            m_dAccumulator1 *=    m_Accumulator;
            break;
        case IDC_SUBTRACT:     // Subtract
            m_dAccumulator1 -=    m_Accumulator;
            break;
        case IDC_DIVIDE:       // Divide (check for divide by zero!)
            if (m_Accumulator != 0.0)
            {
                m_dAccumulator1 /=    m_Accumulator;
            }
            break;
        default:               // Move, no previous operation...
            m_dAccumulator1 = m_Accumulator;
            break;
    }
    m_nPreviousOperation = IDC_DIVIDE;
    m_Accumulator     =    m_dAccumulator1;
    m_bClear          =    TRUE;
    UpdateData(FALSE);
}

void CWevcalcDlg::OnEqual()
{
    // TODO: Add your control notification handler code here
    switch (m_nPreviousOperation)
    {
        case IDC_ADD:          // Add
            m_dAccumulator1 +=    m_Accumulator;
            break;
        case IDC_MULTIPLY:     // Multiply
            m_dAccumulator1 *=    m_Accumulator;
            break;
        case IDC_SUBTRACT:     // Subtract
            m_dAccumulator1 -=    m_Accumulator;
            break;
        case IDC_DIVIDE:       // Divide (check for divide by zero!)
            if (m_Accumulator != 0.0)
            {
                m_dAccumulator1 /=    m_Accumulator;
            }
            break;
        default:               // Move, no previous operation...
            m_dAccumulator1 = m_Accumulator;
            break;
    }
    m_nPreviousOperation = FALSE;
```

```
    m_Accumulator    =    m_dAccumulator1;
    m_bClear         =    TRUE;
    UpdateData(FALSE);
}

void CWevcalcDlg::OnZero()
{
    // TODO: Add your control notification handler code here
    if (m_bClear)
        ClearEntry();

    if (m_nDecimal > 0)
    {// Entering digits to right of decimal point. Shift digit m_nDecimal
    //   to the right and add it to accumulator.
        m_nDecimal *= 10;
    }
    else
    {// Entering to the left of decimal point. Shift left; add the digit.
        m_Accumulator *= 10.0;
    }
    UpdateData(FALSE);
}

void CWevcalcDlg::OnOne()
{
    // TODO: Add your control notification handler code here
    if (m_bClear)
        ClearEntry();

    if (m_nDecimal > 0)
    {// Entering digits to right of decimal point. Shift digit m_nDecimal
     // to the right and add it to accumulator.
        m_Accumulator += (1.0 / (double)m_nDecimal);
        m_nDecimal *= 10;
    }
    else
    {// Entering to the left of decimal point. Shift left; add the digit.
        m_Accumulator *= 10.0;
        m_Accumulator += 1.0;
    }
    UpdateData(FALSE);
}

void CWevcalcDlg::OnTwo()
{
    // TODO: Add your control notification handler code here
    if (m_bClear)
        ClearEntry();

    if (m_nDecimal > 0)
    {// Entering digits to right of decimal point. Shift digit m_nDecimal
     // to the right and add it to accumulator.
        m_Accumulator += (2.0 / (double)m_nDecimal);
        m_nDecimal *= 10;
    }
    else
    {// Entering to the left of decimal point. Shift left; add the digit.
```

continues

Listing 2.5. continued

```
        m_Accumulator *= 10.0;
        m_Accumulator += 2.0;
    }
    UpdateData(FALSE);
}

void CWevcalcDlg::OnThree()
{
    // TODO: Add your control notification handler code here
    if (m_bClear)
        ClearEntry();

    if (m_nDecimal > 0)
    {// Entering digits to right of decimal point. Shift digit m_nDecimal
     // to the right and add it to accumulator.
        m_Accumulator += (3.0 / (double)m_nDecimal);
        m_nDecimal *= 10;
    }
    else
    {// Entering to the left of decimal point. Shift left; add the digit.
        m_Accumulator *= 10.0;
        m_Accumulator += 3.0;
    }
    UpdateData(FALSE);
}

void CWevcalcDlg::OnFour()
{
    // TODO: Add your control notification handler code here
    if (m_bClear)
        ClearEntry();

    if (m_nDecimal > 0)
    {// Entering digits to right of decimal point. Shift digit m_nDecimal
     // to the right and add it to accumulator.
        m_Accumulator += (4.0 / (double)m_nDecimal);
        m_nDecimal *= 10;
    }
    else
    {// Entering to the left of decimal point. Shift left; add the digit.
        m_Accumulator *= 10.0;
        m_Accumulator += 4.0;
    }
    UpdateData(FALSE);
}

void CWevcalcDlg::OnFive()
{
    // TODO: Add your control notification handler code here
    if (m_bClear)
        ClearEntry();

    if (m_nDecimal > 0)
    {// Entering digits to right of decimal point. Shift digit m_nDecimal
     // to the right and add it to accumulator.
        m_Accumulator += (5.0 / (double)m_nDecimal);
```

```
        m_nDecimal *= 10;
    }
    else
    {// Entering to the left of decimal point. Shift left; add the digit.
        m_Accumulator *= 10.0;
        m_Accumulator += 5.0;
    }
    UpdateData(FALSE);
}

void CWevcalcDlg::OnSix()
{
    // TODO: Add your control notification handler code here
    if (m_bClear)
        ClearEntry();

    if (m_nDecimal > 0)
    {// Entering digits to right of decimal point. Shift digit m_nDecimal
     // to the right and add it to accumulator.
        m_Accumulator += (6.0 / (double)m_nDecimal);
        m_nDecimal *= 10;
    }
    else
    {// Entering to the left of decimal point. Shift left; add the digit.
        m_Accumulator *= 10.0;
        m_Accumulator += 6.0;
    }
    UpdateData(FALSE);
}

void CWevcalcDlg::OnSeven()
{
    // TODO: Add your control notification handler code here
    if (m_bClear)
        ClearEntry();

    if (m_nDecimal > 0)
    {// Entering digits to right of decimal point. Shift digit m_nDecimal
     // to the right and add it to accumulator.
        m_Accumulator += (7.0 / (double)m_nDecimal);
        m_nDecimal *= 10;
    }
    else
    {// Entering to the left of decimal point. Shift left; add the digit.
        m_Accumulator *= 10.0;
        m_Accumulator += 7.0;
    }
    UpdateData(FALSE);
}

void CWevcalcDlg::OnEight()
{
    // TODO: Add your control notification handler code here
    if (m_bClear)
        ClearEntry();

    if (m_nDecimal > 0)
```

continues

LISTING 2.5. CONTINUED

```
    {// Entering digits to right of decimal point. Shift digit m_nDecimal
     // to the right and add it to accumulator.
        m_Accumulator += (8.0 / (double)m_nDecimal);
        m_nDecimal *= 10;
    }
    else
    {// Entering to the left of decimal point. Shift left; add the digit.
        m_Accumulator *= 10.0;
        m_Accumulator += 8.0;
    }
    UpdateData(FALSE);
}

void CWevcalcDlg::OnNine()
{
    // TODO: Add your control notification handler code here
    if (m_bClear)
        ClearEntry();

    if (m_nDecimal > 0)
    {// Entering digits to right of decimal point. Shift digit m_nDecimal
     // to the right and add it to accumulator.
        m_Accumulator += (9.0 / (double)m_nDecimal);
        m_nDecimal *= 10;
    }
    else
    {// Entering to the left of decimal point. Shift left; add the digit.
        m_Accumulator *= 10.0;
        m_Accumulator += 9.0;
    }
    UpdateData(FALSE);
}
```

Notice that the handler for each button calls the UpdateData() function. This function manages the transfer of data to and from the dialog's edit controls and the variables assigned to them. If UpdateData() is called with a FALSE parameter, the contents of the variable are displayed in the control. If UpdateData() is called with a parameter of TRUE, the variable is updated with the contents of the control.

After you've modified WEVCADLG.CPP and WEVCADLG.H, you should have a working calculator program. Try it and see what you think. Of course, if your calculator doesn't work, you've just been presented with an excellent opportunity to practice your debugging skills!

Our program exhibits a weakness: you must use the mouse to interact with WevCalc. It would be nice if WevCalc could use the keyboard's numeric keypad for data entry. By now you should know that you interact with the keyboard by using accelerators, which are part of a resource called an accelerator table.

WevCalc presents a unique problem because it doesn't use a standard Windows message loop. Because WevCalc is based on a dialog box, it uses the Windows dialog message handler that isn't aware of accelerator keys. This could have been a problem. However, there is a simple solution we can implement.

Adding Accelerators to WevCalc

I have added to the accelerator table to allow the user to enter data into WevCalc with the numeric keypad. Because all the necessary keys (except for an equals key) are present on the numeric keypad, user input is easy to perform with the numeric keypad. WevCalc doesn't use the numeric keypad's Enter key, so I defined it as the equals key.

If you look at Listing 2.6, you can see the accelerators I've defined. Each of the buttons used by WevCalc has one accelerator. There is no reason why a function couldn't be served by two different keys (such as a keypad number and a number from the number row on the main keyboard). How you define your accelerators is up to you. Simply keep in mind the basic standards that Microsoft has established, as well as how the user will be using your application.

LISTING 2.6. WEVCALC'S ACCELERATOR TABLE (FROM WEVCALC.RC).

```
///////////////////////////////////////////////////////////////////////////////
//
// Accelerator
//

IDR_ACCELERATOR1 ACCELERATORS DISCARDABLE
BEGIN
    VK_ADD,         IDC_ADD,            VIRTKEY, NOINVERT
    VK_BACK,        IDC_CLEAR_ALL,      VIRTKEY, NOINVERT
    VK_DECIMAL,     IDC_DECIMAL,        VIRTKEY, NOINVERT
    VK_DELETE,      IDC_CLEAR_ENTRY,    VIRTKEY, NOINVERT
    VK_DIVIDE,      IDC_DIVIDE,         VIRTKEY, NOINVERT
    VK_MULTIPLY,    IDC_MULTIPLY,       VIRTKEY, NOINVERT
    VK_NUMPAD0,     IDC_ZERO,           VIRTKEY, NOINVERT
    VK_NUMPAD1,     IDC_ONE,            VIRTKEY, NOINVERT
    VK_NUMPAD2,     IDC_TWO,            VIRTKEY, NOINVERT
    VK_NUMPAD3,     IDC_THREE,          VIRTKEY, NOINVERT
    VK_NUMPAD4,     IDC_FOUR,           VIRTKEY, NOINVERT
    VK_NUMPAD5,     IDC_FIVE,           VIRTKEY, NOINVERT
    VK_NUMPAD6,     IDC_SIX,            VIRTKEY, NOINVERT
    VK_NUMPAD7,     IDC_SEVEN,          VIRTKEY, NOINVERT
    VK_NUMPAD8,     IDC_EIGHT,          VIRTKEY, NOINVERT
    VK_NUMPAD9,     IDC_NINE,           VIRTKEY, NOINVERT
    VK_RETURN,      IDC_EQUAL,          VIRTKEY, NOINVERT
    VK_SUBTRACT,    IDC_SUBTRACT,       VIRTKEY, NOINVERT
END
```

Next, it's necessary to make some changes in WevCalc's main .CPP file. This file contains the program initialization code, which we need to modify slightly. First, in Listing 2.7, is WEVCALC.H, the header file for WevCalc. In this file we must add a variable of **HACCEL** type and a function prototype for a new function that we will create, **ProcessMessageFilter()**. This function overrides the **ProcessMessageFilter()** that is part of the **CWinApp** class, the class upon which WevCalc is based. Note that the lines that I added appear in bold.

LISTING 2.7. WEVCALC.H, WevCalc's header file.

```
// WEVCALC.H: Main header file for the WEVCALC application
//

#ifndef __AFXWIN_H__
    #error include 'stdafx.h' before including this file for PCH
#endif

#include "resource.h"        // Main symbols

/////////////////////////////////////////////////////////////////////////////
// CWevcalcApp:
// See WEVCALC.CPP for the implementation of this class
//

class CWevcalcApp : public CWinApp
{
public:

    HACCEL     hAccelTable;

    CWevcalcApp();

// Overrides
    // ClassWizard-generated virtual function overrides
    //{{AFX_VIRTUAL(CWevcalcApp)
    public:
    virtual BOOL InitInstance();
    //}}AFX_VIRTUAL

    BOOL ProcessMessageFilter(int code, LPMSG lpMsg);
// Implementation

    //{{AFX_MSG(CWevcalcApp)
        // NOTE: ClassWizard adds and removes member functions here.
        // DO NOT EDIT what you see in these blocks of generated code!
    //}}AFX_MSG
    DECLARE_MESSAGE_MAP()
};


/////////////////////////////////////////////////////////////////////////////
```

In WEVCALC.CPP, shown in Listing 2.8, I show the implementation of the code to process accelerators in a dialog-based program. This code appears in bold.

LISTING 2.8. WEVCALC.CPP WITH THE ACCELERATOR HANDLER ADDED.

```
// WEVCALC.CPP: Defines the class behaviors for the application
//

#include "stdafx.h"
#include "wevcalc.h"
#include "wevcadlg.h"

#ifdef _DEBUG
#undef THIS_FILE
static char BASED_CODE THIS_FILE[] = __FILE__;
#endif

/////////////////////////////////////////////////////////////////////////////
// CWevcalcApp

BEGIN_MESSAGE_MAP(CWevcalcApp, CWinApp)
    //{{AFX_MSG_MAP(CWevcalcApp)
        // NOTE: ClassWizard adds and removes mapping macros here.
        // DO NOT EDIT what you see in these blocks of generated code!
    //}}AFX_MSG
    ON_COMMAND(ID_HELP, CWinApp::OnHelp)
END_MESSAGE_MAP()

/////////////////////////////////////////////////////////////////////////////
// CWevcalcApp construction

CWevcalcApp::CWevcalcApp()
{
    // TODO: Add construction code here
    // Place all significant initialization in InitInstance
}

/////////////////////////////////////////////////////////////////////////////
// The one and only CWevcalcApp object

CWevcalcApp theApp;

/////////////////////////////////////////////////////////////////////////////
// CWevcalcApp initialization

BOOL CWevcalcApp::InitInstance()
{
    // Standard initialization
    // If you are not using these features and wish to reduce the size
    // of your final executable, you should remove from the following
    // the specific initialization routines you do not need.
```

continues

Listing 2.8. continued

```
    Enable3dControls();
    LoadStdProfileSettings();   // Load standard .INI file options
                                // (including MRU)

    // Load accelerator table. See ProcessMessageFilter() below for more info.
    hAccelTable = LoadAccelerators(AfxGetInstanceHandle(),
        MAKEINTRESOURCE(IDR_ACCELERATOR1));

    CWevcalcDlg dlg;
    m_pMainWnd = &dlg;
    int nResponse = dlg.DoModal();
    if (nResponse == IDOK)
    {
        // TODO: Place code here to handle when the dialog is
        // dismissed with OK
    }
    else if (nResponse == IDCANCEL)
    {
        // TODO: Place code here to handle when the dialog is
        // dismissed with Cancel
    }

    // Since the dialog has been closed, return FALSE so that we exit the
    // application rather than start the application's message pump
    return FALSE;
}

BOOL CWevcalcApp::ProcessMessageFilter(int code, LPMSG lpMsg)
{
    if (code < 0)
        CWinApp::ProcessMessageFilter(code, lpMsg);

    if (m_pMainWnd && hAccelTable)
    {
        if (::TranslateAccelerator(m_pMainWnd->m_hWnd, hAccelTable, lpMsg))
            return(TRUE);
    }

    return (CWinApp::ProcessMessageFilter(code, lpMsg));
}
```

The ProcessMessageFilter() function processes the messages and calls **TranslateAccelerator()** to translate them. When a message is translated, **TranslateAccelerator()** returns a non-FALSE value and ProcessMessageFilter() returns TRUE. If **TranslateAccelerator()** returns a FALSE value, ProcessMessageFilter() calls **CWinApp::ProcessMessageFilter()** to process the message.

Presenting: WevCalc

Creating WevCalc required major modifications to both of the source files that AppWizard created. These files, WEVCADLG.CPP and WEVCALC.CPP, provide the interface between the application and the user. Several other files were also modified (the header files and the resource files), but the changes were minimal. For example, I modified the dialog box to add the controls for the user interface.

WevCalc shows how a simple Windows application (that doesn't have a document to save) can be developed with a minimum of effort.

Summary

This chapter reviewed the Visual Workbench and the editor. The Visual Workbench is the programmer's main interface with Visual C++. The editor is a major part of the Visual Workbench, in that it's used to create and modify source input files. We also used the Visual C++ AppWizard program to create a simple application. In the final part of this chapter, we looked at creating WevCalc, a simple four-function calculator.

The following topics were covered in this chapter:

- The Visual Workbench menu structure
- The Visual Workbench source editor
- The Visual Workbench resource editor
- Visual C++'s AppWizard, a utility to create Windows application shells

New Compiler Features

The Visual C++ 2.0 compiler offers several new features for the Windows programmer. I have grouped these features into two categories:

- Templates
- Exception handling

With templates, you can create C++ template objects. Templates offer the programmer a great deal of flexibility and enable easy programming of non-type–specific objects. This chapter covers the usage of templates and gives a few simple examples of how templates are used.

Exception handling enables the programmer to plan ahead for certain runtime problems. In Visual C++ 2.0, exception handling is divided into two distinct (and exclusive) parts:

- Structured exception handling, in which exceptions are generally system level. Structured exception handling is supported by Win32 and is system-specific (in other words, what causes an exception under Windows in an Intel environment might not cause the same exception in a MIPS environment).

- C++ exception handling, in which exceptions usually are generated (triggered) at the software level. Many MFC functions throw (cause) an exception when an error occurs.

One problem with having two methods of exception handling is that they're somewhat mutually exclusive. A module can support either structured exception handling or C++ exception handling, but not both. Each method of exception handling offers both advantages and disadvantages. Later sections of this chapter look at each type of exception handling, the advantages and disadvantages, and how to use them. First, however, let's take a look at Visual C++ 2.0's support for templates.

TEMPLATES

Templates are a part of C++ that previous versions of Visual C++ haven't supported. Many programmers have wanted template support, and Microsoft responded: Visual C++ 2.0 offers full template support.

Visual C++ 2.0 supports templates as described in ISO WG21/ANSI X3J16, which outlines the work that is being done to create a standardized C++ language.

What Are Templates?

Not all programmers know just what templates are. Let's try to dispel some of the mystery that surrounds them. First I'll define some terms that I'll use when I discuss templates.

- Typeless parameter: Any parameter or return value that didn't have a specific type when the code was written. The compiler will substitute a type when the template is actually used. When a template is used with a given type, the compiler will create a function that handles the specified type.

- Instantiation: A specific, compiler-created implementation of a class or function for a specified data type.

In a template, an object (either a class or function) is defined using the following format:

```
template <class sub_class_1[, class sub_class_2]> object
```

The keyword **template** is a required keyword that identifies this object as a template. The < and > are required in order to delimit the keyword **class** and its operand. You will have one (or more) **class** keywords in a template definition. In the preceding example, *sub_class_1* and *sub_class_2* are placeholders for which the compiler will later substitute the desired types (when the template is used). These placeholders often are referred to as *abstracted types*.

Template Functions

To understand what a template function is, assume that your program must swap two adjacent items in an array. Typically, you would place the first variable's contents in a temporary storage object, place the second variable's contents in the first variable, and then place the temporary storage object's contents in the second variable.

For integers, a function to perform this might look like the following:

```
// SwapInt(): swaps two integers

void  SwapInt(int& First, int& Second)
{
int TemporaryStorage;

    TemporaryStorage = First;
    First = Second;
    Second = TemporaryStorage;
}
```

If you wanted to expand the SwapInt function to include the ability to swap other data types (such as double), you would have to write an overloaded function. If you wanted to include more data types, you would have to write an overloaded function for each type. Because a number of different data types are available to use with C/C++, the process of creating a separate, overloaded function for each data type could become rather tedious.

A simpler solution would be to create a single template function and let the compiler take care of creating the necessary overloaded functions. For example, our swap function could be modified like this:

```
// SwapIt(): swaps two objects of any type

template <class Thing> void  SwapIt(Thing& First, Thing& Second)
{
Thing   TemporaryStorage;

    TemporaryStorage = First;
    First = Second;
    Second = TemporaryStorage;
}
```

In the preceding example, the SwapIt() function could be called with **int**, **WORD**, **char**, or any valid C/C++ data type. This function would even work for objects such as **CStrings**, as the following example shows:

```
CString Bozo;
CString Clown;
CString GoofOff;

    Bozo = "What a goofoff";
    Clown = "A Bozo for sure";
    GoofOff = "Smile, it's a clown";

// Swap 'em to make the sayings correct

    SwapIt(Bozo, Clown);
    SwapIt(Clown, GoofOff);

//   Now each CString is correct
```

However, because we've defined a single template type of *Thing*, we can't pass more than one type to SwapIt(). For example:

```
CString Bozo;
int     nHowMany;

    Bozo = "There are many Bozos";
    nHowMany = 10000;

//   Wrong: Compiler will generate an error!
    SwapIt(Bozo, nHowMany);
```

The program in Listing 3.1 shows my program TEPLDEMO, which implements the code fragments just shown into an actual program. TEPLDEMO is a simple 32-bit console application that you can create by using AppWizard to create a console application, then adding TEPLDEMO.CPP to the project (as its only source file). The TEPLDEMO program will run from the command line in both Windows 95 and Windows NT.

LISTING 3.1. TEPLDEMO.CPP, A PROGRAM TO SHOW TEMPLATES.

```c
#include <stdio.h>


template <class Thing> void SwapIt(Thing& First, Thing& Second)
{
Thing     TemporaryStorage;

    TemporaryStorage = First;
    First = Second;
    Second = TemporaryStorage;
}


void main()
{
int        i;
int        j;
double  dI;
double  dJ;

    i = 5;
    j = 500;

    dI = 5.5;
    dJ = 500.5;

    SwapIt(i, j);

    printf("(int) SwapIt(5, 500) returned (%d, %d)\n", i, j);

    SwapIt(dI, dJ);

    printf("(double) SwapIt(5.5, 500.5) returned (%f, %f)\n", dI, dJ);

    return;
}
```

Here are the results of running TEPLDEMO:

```
Win-32 15:57:29 E:\WEVCPSK\SOURCE\TEPLDEMO\WINDEBUG

tepldemo
(int) SwapIt(5, 500) returned (500, 5)
(double) SwapIt(5.5, 500.5) returned (500.500000, 5.500000)

Win-32 15:57:29 E:\WEVCPSK\SOURCE\TEPLDEMO\WINDEBUG
```

Two very useful template-derived functions are the Min() and Max() functions. These two functions typically are implemented as macros. However, by using a template function, you can avoid one of the most serious problems that plagues macros: multiple evaluations of the macro's arguments. An example of Min() and Max() as a set of template functions is shown in Listing 3.2.

```
// Min() and Max() as templates

template <class Thing> Thing Min(Thing First, Thing Second)
{
    return((First < Second) ? First : Second);
}

template <class Thing> Thing Max(Thing First, Thing Second)
{
    return((First > Second) ? First : Second);
}
```

In Listing 3.2, the parameters passed can be used with the prefix (or postfix) operators, such as the following:

```
int    i = 10;
int    j = 100;

printf("The minimum of (%d and %d) is %d\n", i, j, Min(i++, j++));
```

This code fragment would print

```
The minimum of (10 and 100) is 10
```

After the line containing the `printf()` call is executed, the variables **i** and **j** will be 11 and 101, respectively. If the macro version were used, the resultant message would look like this:

```
The minimum of (10 and 100) is 11
```

After the line containing the `printf()` call (with the macro) is executed, the variable **i** will be 12 (**i** was incremented twice: once when tested and once when used) and **j** will be 101, which probably is not what you would have expected.

The final version of TEPLDEMO is shown in Listing 3.3. I appended the results of the program's execution to the end of the listing.

Listing 3.3. TEPLDEMO.CPP (final version).

```
#include <stdio.h>

template <class Thing> void SwapIt(Thing& First, Thing& Second)
{
Thing    TemporaryStorage;
```

```
        TemporaryStorage = First;
        First = Second;
        Second = TemporaryStorage;
}

// Don't use the macro versions. It gives bad results if
// not used carefully!

#define MIN(First, Second) ((First < Second) ? First : Second)
#define MAX(First, Second) ((First > Second) ? First : Second)

template <class Thing> Thing Min(Thing First, Thing Second)
{
    return((First < Second) ? First : Second);
}

template <class Thing> Thing Max(Thing First, Thing Second)
{
    return((First > Second) ? First : Second);
}

void main()
{
int        i;
int        j;
double  dI;
double  dJ;

    i = 5;
    j = 500;

    dI = 5.5;
    dJ = 500.5;

    SwapIt(i, j);

    printf("(int) SwapIt(5, 500) returned (%d, %d)\n", i, j);

    SwapIt(dI, dJ);

    printf("(double) SwapIt(5.5, 500.5) returned (%f, %f)\n", dI, dJ);

    i = 10;
    j = 100;

    printf("Min (10, 100) is %d\n", Min(i++, j++));
    printf("i = %d j = %d\n", i, j);

    i = 10;
    j = 100;

    printf("MIN (10, 100) is %d\n", MIN(i++, j++));
    printf("i = %d j = %d\n", i, j);

    return;
}
/* Execution results:
```

continues

Listing 3.3. continued

```
Win-32 15:57:29 E:\WEVCPSK\SOURCE\TEPLDEMO\WINDEBUG

tepldemo
(int) SwapIt(5, 500) returned (500, 5)
(double) SwapIt(5.5, 500.5) returned (500.500000, 5.500000)
Min (10, 100) is 10
i = 11 j = 101
MIN (10, 100) is 11
i = 12 j = 101

Win-32 15:57:29 E:\WEVCPSK\SOURCE\TEPLDEMO\WINDEBUG

*/
```

Template Classes

Templates aren't limited to simple functions. You can create an entire class of objects that are based on templates. MFC uses templates to implement some of the new classes that MFC 3.0 provides—CArray, CList, CMap, CTypedPtrArray, CTypedPtrList, and CTypedPtrMap. Using templates with classes enables the programmer to develop powerful classes in which the object of the class is a basic C/C++ data type or class.

A typical example of using templates in a class is found when you create a linked list class. The list may be of any type, such as int, double, or perhaps CString. Each object in the list is linked to the object that follows it in the list and to the object that precedes it in the list. It's up to the class's member functions to manage the addition, deletion, and query of objects contained in the list.

The code to create a class based on templates is very similar to that used to create a template function. For example, let's create a class that creates a list of objects and manages them. In this example, I won't try to create all the functionality needed (you probably would need code to expand and contract the list, search for a member object, and so on).

First, in Listing 3.4, is the file TEPLCLAS.H, which is the header file needed to create a template base class. When creating a definition of a template class, you must be sure that the function prototypes are correctly formatted. Note the usage of the < and > operators. As in a template-derived function, you can have more than one abstracted type.

LISTING 3.4. TEPLCLAS'S HEADER FILE, TEPLCLAS.H.

```
// Class templates

template <class Thing>
    class TemplateClass
{
public:
    TemplateClass(void);
    ~TemplateClass(void);
    int         AddMember(Thing aThing);
    Thing       GetMember(int    nItem);
private:
    Thing       ThingArray[300];
    int         nPointerBack[300];
    int         nPointerForward[300];
    int         nFreeItem;
};

template <class Thing>
    TemplateClass<Thing>::TemplateClass(void)
{// Constructor
    int         i;
//  First free item in list
    nFreeItem = 0;

    for (i = 0; i < 300; i++)
    {
        nPointerBack[i] = 0;
        nPointerForward[i] = 0;
    }
}

template <class Thing>
    TemplateClass<Thing>::~TemplateClass(void)
{// Destructor

}

template <class Thing>
    int TemplateClass<Thing>::AddMember(Thing aThing)
{// Add a new member to the list
    ThingArray[nFreeItem] = aThing;
    return(nFreeItem++);
}

template <class Thing>
    Thing TemplateClass<Thing>::GetMember(int nItem)
{// Get member value
    return(ThingArray[nItem]);
}
```

Let's take a closer look at the template-based class. First, in the definition of the class, we use the `template` keyword and define the abstracted type (*Thing*). Many of the member functions refer to the abstracted type, and an array of type *Thing* is created in the class. In a properly created class, you would create the arrays dynamically (at runtime) so that you wouldn't be limited to the hardcoded sizes (300) that this example uses.

```
template <class Thing>
    class TemplateClass
{
public:
    TemplateClass(void);
    ~TemplateClass(void);
    int        AddMember(Thing aThing);
    Thing      GetMember(int    nItem);
private:
    Thing      ThingArray[300];
    int        nPointerBack[300];
    int        nPointerForward[300];
    int        nFreeItem;
};
```

The constructor and destructor for the `TemplateClass` are rather standard. The constructor will initialize the variables. Notice that I didn't attempt to initialize the member variable *ThingArray*. However, I could have used a **memcopy()** call to zero out *ThingArray*'s memory, if necessary.

The two member functions `AddMember()` and `GetMember()` simply add a new member to the list and retrieve the value contained in a specified member. In a more functional class, these members would also have updated the pointers to create a linked list.

Notice how the `GetMember()` function returns the value for a *Thing* object. This function doesn't know (or care, for that matter) what type *ThingArray* is. When the compiler instantiates a copy of `TemplateClass`, it will "plug in" the correct types.

```
template <class Thing>
    int TemplateClass<Thing>::AddMember(Thing aThing)
{// Add a new member to the list
    ThingArray[nFreeItem] = aThing;
    return(nFreeItem++);
}
template <class Thing>
    Thing TemplateClass<Thing>::GetMember(int nItem)
{// Get member value
    return(ThingArray[nItem]);
}
```

After instantiation with a type of int, the AddMember() function would become

```
int TemplateClass::AddMember(int aThing)
{// Add a new member to the list
    ThingArray[nFreeItem] = aThing;
    return(nFreeItem++);
}
```

After instantiation with a type of int, the GetMember() function would become

```
int TemplateClass::GetMember(int nItem)
{// Get member value
    return(ThingArray[nItem]);
}
```

Using the class defined in Listing 3.4, we could then write a calling program such as the one shown in Listing 3.5. In TEPLCLAS.CPP, we create two objects of the TemplateClass type. The first object is int-based, and the second one is based on a floating-point double. In both cases, the compiler makes sure that the necessary functions are present to allow for the different types for the abstracted type variable *Thing*.

LISTING 3.5. TEPLCLAS's **main()** FUNCTION.

```
#include "stdio.h"
#include "teplclas.h"

void main()
{
    int         nIndex = 0;

    TemplateClass <int> OurIntClass;

    nIndex = OurIntClass.AddMember(123);
    printf("number %d is %d\n", nIndex, OurIntClass.GetMember(nIndex));

    nIndex = OurIntClass.AddMember(456);
    printf("number %d is %d\n", nIndex, OurIntClass.GetMember(nIndex));

    nIndex = OurIntClass.AddMember(789);
    printf("number %d is %d\n", nIndex, OurIntClass.GetMember(nIndex));

    TemplateClass <double> OurDoubleClass;

    nIndex = OurDoubleClass.AddMember(123.321);
    printf("number %d is %f\n", nIndex, OurDoubleClass.GetMember(nIndex));

    nIndex = OurDoubleClass.AddMember(456.654);
    printf("number %d is %f\n", nIndex, OurDoubleClass.GetMember(nIndex));

    nIndex = OurDoubleClass.AddMember(789.987);
    printf("number %d is %f\n", nIndex, OurDoubleClass.GetMember(nIndex));

}
```

The output from TEPLCLAS is as follows:

```
/* TEPLCLAS program output

Win-32 21:19:40 E:\WEVCPSK\SOURCE\TEPLCLAS\WINDEBUG
teplclas
number 0 is 123
number 1 is 456
number 2 is 789
number 0 is 123.321000
number 1 is 456.654000
number 2 is 789.987000

Win-32 21:19:40 E:\WEVCPSK\SOURCE\TEPLCLAS\WINDEBUG

*/
```

As TEPLCLAS shows, creating a template-based class isn't that difficult. You should try the sample programs, perhaps modifying them to suit your needs. You also can gain some insight into how Microsoft has implemented some template-based classes by looking at the file AFXTEMPL.H, which can be found in the directory \MSVC20\MFC\INCLUDE.

Exception Handling

Sometimes I think that simply writing an error-free program is an exception. In reality, however, error-free programs are exceptional. You might wonder: Just what is exception handling? Why do we need two methods of exception handling, when with 16-bit Windows programming we were able to make do with no real exception handling at all? And, to really clear things up, just what are exceptions? Why do we need them? Finally, you might wonder: What is a stack? Why does exception handling have to unwind the stack? Who wound the stack up, anyway? Never fear, my friends. Once you've finished this chapter, your programming will be exceptional, and you will be able to implement exception handling!

Let's answer some of those tough questions we've raised. First, what are exceptions, and why do we need them?

Exceptions are errors that occur at runtime. Generally they're not triggered by programming errors, but by factors that are external to the application. Typical exception errors include invalid data, a hardware failure, or the lack of a required resource.

Secondly, what is exception handling? Exception handling is a methodology to handle these error conditions at runtime. With exception handling, the programmer isn't required to actually test at every possible point for errors. He or she simply places program lines that might cause problems in an exception block (or body) and provides an exception handler for exceptions that might be raised during the execution of the code in the exception block.

Why do we need two methods for exception handling? First, let's list and define the two methods of exception handling—structured exception handling and C++ exception handling:

- Structured exception handling is a methodology provided by Windows and generally is language-independent. For instance, structured exception handling works with C code, while C++ exception handling doesn't. This methodology is portable in that applications written for one platform (such as Intel) can be ported to another platform (such as MIPS) without the need for rewriting the exception handling. Structured exception handling can be used with both kernel and user mode software. It also can treat both hardware and software exceptions in an identical fashion. Finally, structured exception handling is supported by the Visual C++ 2.0 debugger.

  With structured exception handling, you deal with only one exception type, which is always `unsigned int`.

  A downside of structured exception handling is that it doesn't work well with C++ objects. Particularly, when some C++ objects are created as part of a function call, the structured exception handling routines don't always properly call the object's destructors.

- C++ exception handling is available to applications modules written in C++. For C code you must use structured exception handling. With C++ exception handling, you deal with more than one exception type.

When structured exception handling is used, the exception is identified using an `unsigned int` value (called the *exception context*). Each of the handlers (called *filters*) examines the exception context and determines whether the handler can handle the exception. If the exception handler can process the exception, it does so. If the handler is unable to process the exception, it either ignores the exception or passes it on to the next handler.

With C++ exception handling, your handlers can catch exceptions of any of the following types:

- Exceptions of the same type as the exception object
- References of the same type as the exception object
- The same base type as the exception object
- A pointer to the exception object
- Exceptions of any type (specified using `catch(...)` syntax)

Finally, what is a stack, why does exception handling have to unwind the stack, and who wound the stack up, anyway? Well, Grasshopper, you *would* have to ask that one....

The stack is a block of memory that stores information that your program uses when it runs. Think of the stack as a pile of paper on top of which you can add new pieces of paper (one on top of another) or remove pieces of paper (one at a time, always from the top). Each piece of paper is numbered starting from the bottom of the stack, and on each piece of paper is a single object. The objects on the stack can be examined randomly by simply "peeking" at a certain piece of paper.

What's on the stack? Well, lots of stuff: return addresses, which are used to tell a function where to return to; local (dynamic) variables that, before they are initialized, house the junk left over from the last thing that occupied a location on the stack; and other information that the compiler has placed on the stack. The stack is really just an area where things of a temporary nature can be stored.

When a function returns to its caller, the function's local variables, saved registers, and the like are removed from the stack. Actually, nothing is changed. An internal (to the CPU) variable tells the system where the top of the stack is. This variable is simply decremented to indicate a lower point in the stack.

Parts two and three of this question can be answered more easily if we reverse them. Who wound up the stack? (Maybe I'm pushing it here. We don't really refer to using the stack as "winding it up.") Each time a function is called, it uses parts of the stack for the function's local variables, its internal storage, and the function's return address.

Assume that you have three functions: A(), B(), and C(). In function A() there is an exception handler. In function C() there is a condition that causes an exception. If function A() calls function B() and function B() calls function C(), there will be information on the stack for function A(), followed by function B(), and then function C(). To get back from function C() (where the error is) to function A() (where the exception handler is), the system needs to work its way back through the stack to find function A()'s place. This process of tracing back through the stack is called "unwinding the stack."

In the process of unwinding the stack, it's important that C++ objects that are being destroyed have their destructors called. This allows these objects to properly clean up after themselves. Without this cleanup, your application might later experience unpredictable problems.

Structured Exception Handling

Structured exception handling is a source-language–independent method for handling errors (it works equally well with C or C++). It's implemented by the system, not the language. Structured exception handling isn't part of the proposed C++ standard.

In Visual C++ 2.0, the interface to structured exception handling is a series of keywords:

- **__try**
- **__finally**
- **__leave**
- **__except** (*filter*)

Note that each of these keywords is prefixed with two underscores.

Let's take a closer look at each of these keywords.

__try

The **__try** keyword is used to mark the beginning of a block of statements where your program will want to handle any exceptions that occur. A typical **__try** block might look like this:

```
int    i = 0;
int    j = 0;

    __try
    {
        j = 100 / i;   // Divide-by-zero error!
    }
```

__finally

The **__finally** keyword is used to mark a block of code that will always be executed after the **__try** block has completed. The execution of the **__finally** block is automatic: you can't jump into a **__finally** block (using a goto). You can jump out of a **__finally** block by using either a return or a goto statement, but I *don't* recommend it. The **__finally** block is used to ensure that your code cleans up after itself.

__leave

The __**leave** keyword is used to jump from a __**try** block. You can visualize the __**leave** statement as a way to (prematurely) stop executing the statements in a __**try** block. The following code fragment shows an implementation of the __**leave** keyword:

```
int    i = 0;
int    j = 0;

    __try
    {// Something that might fail
        if (j == 0)  // Something's wrong. End this madness.
            __leave;

        j = 100 / i;  // Divide-by-zero error!
    }
    __finally
    {// Cleanup

    }
```

__except (filter)

The __**except** keyword is used to mark the beginning of the exception handler. An exception handler consists of a compound block of statements that are executed if the filter returns a value of **EXCEPTION_EXECUTE_HANDLER**. The filter must evaluate to one of the following values:

- **EXCEPTION_EXECUTE_HANDLER**
- **EXCEPTION_CONTINUE_EXECUTION**
- **EXCEPTION_CONTINUE_SEARCH**

After the filter evaluates to **EXCEPTION_EXECUTE_HANDLER**, the code in the exception handler is executed. After the code in the __**except** block is executed, execution continues with the **NEXT** statement after the __**except** block. Control isn't returned to the __**try** block where the error occurred.

The filter, if it is a function, can attempt to correct the error. If the filter function can correct the error condition, it should return **EXCEPTION_CONTINUE_EXECUTION**. When **EXCEPTION_CONTINUE_EXECUTION** is returned, the instruction that caused the error is retried. Because the statement where the error occurred is re-executed, the filter must be sure that it has corrected the error, or that it can properly handle a possible subsequent error.

Finally, the filter can return **EXCEPTION_CONTINUE_SEARCH**. When **EXCEPTION_CONTINUE_SEARCH** is returned, the system traces up the stack (it "unwinds" the stack), searching for another __**except** block. If another

__except block is found, its filter is evaluated and action appropriate to the filter's return value is taken. If there are no more **__except** blocks, a system error message is displayed and the task is terminated.

What Is This Exception?

The filter (and the exception handler) need to know which exception occurred. Visual C++ provides the function **DWORD GetExceptionCode(void)**, which returns an identifier telling what the exception is. This function returns one of the values listed in Table 3.1.

TABLE 3.1. `GetExceptionCode()` RETURN VALUES.	
Exception	*Description*
EXCEPTION_ACCESS_VIOLATION	An attempt was made to read from or write to a memory address for which the thread does not have the appropriate access privileges.
EXCEPTION_BREAKPOINT	A breakpoint has been reached.
EXCEPTION_DATATYPE_MISALIGNMENT	On systems where data objects must be aligned, the thread has attempted to access data that was misaligned. For example, aligned simple objects usually must start on an address that is a multiple of their size.
EXCEPTION_SINGLE_STEP	The system's single-step mechanism has reported to the system that a single instruction has been executed.
EXCEPTION_ARRAY_BOUNDS_EXCEEDED	On systems that support array bounds checking, an attempt has been made to access an array element that was not within the bounds of the array.

continues

Table 3.1. continued	
Exception	*Description*
EXCEPTION_FLT_DENORMAL_OPERAND	An operand in a floating-point operation is too small to be represented as a standard floating-point value.
EXCEPTION_FLT_DIVIDE_BY_ZERO	A floating-point divide-by-zero error occurred.
EXCEPTION_FLT_INEXACT_RESULT	A result in a floating-point operation can't be represented exactly as a decimal fraction.
EXCEPTION_FLT_INVALID_OPERATION	Any floating-point error that is not otherwise included in this list.
EXCEPTION_FLT_OVERFLOW	The resultant exponent is too large to be stored in the specified floating-point type.
EXCEPTION_FLT_STACK_CHECK	There was a floating-point stack overflow or underflow. The floating-point stack is different from the program's stack.
EXCEPTION_FLT_UNDERFLOW	The resultant exponent is too small to be stored in the specified floating-point type.
EXCEPTION_INT_DIVIDE_BY_ZERO	There was an integer divide-by-zero error.
EXCEPTION_INT_OVERFLOW	The size of the result of an integer operation was too large. One or more bits of precision were lost.
EXCEPTION_PRIV_INSTRUCTION	An attempt was made to execute an instruction by a thread that doesn't have sufficient privilege.
STATUS_NONCONTINUABLE_EXCEPTION	A noncontinuable exception occurred, and the thread attempted to continue.

C++ Exception Handling

The C++ exception handling process is very similar to the structured exception-handling process described earlier. C++ exception handling incorporates three keywords:

- **try**
- **catch**(*exception_declaration*)
- **throw**

The C++ exception-handling **try** keyword works like **__try** in structured exception handling. You have a block of code within the **try** block; when an exception occurs, the code contained in the **catch** block is evaluated.

The **try**, **catch**, and **throw** statements work much like the structured exception-handling keywords. You wrap the code that could produce an exception in a **try** block, then use **catch** blocks to handle whatever exceptions have occurred. The **throw** statement allows you to throw (create) an exception of your own.

Listing 3.6 shows a simple console application that implements a **try/catch** block. This program throws an exception when the assignment line attempts to divide the variable **i** by zero.

LISTING 3.6. CEH.CPP, A PROGRAM TO SHOW try/catch BLOCKS.

```
#include <stdio.h>
#include <eh.h>
#include <process.h>
#include <iostream.h>

void main()
{// Program to show C++ exception handling
int        i;
int        j;
int        k;

    i = 1;
    j = 0;
    k = 0;

    try
    {
        printf("Start of 'try' block, i = %d j = %d k = %d \n", i, j, k);

        k = i / j;

        printf("After bad math, i = %d j = %d k = %d \n", i, j, k);
```

continues

LISTING 3.6. CONTINUED

```
    }
    catch(int me)
    {
        printf("in catch(int me = %d), i = %d j = %d k = %d \n", me, i, j, k);
    }
    catch(...)
    {
        printf("in catch(...), i = %d j = %d k = %d \n", i, j, k);
    }

    printf("end of try/catch blocks, i = %d j = %d k = %d \n", i, j, k);
}
```

Proper implementation of exception handling can do much to make your application seem more robust. If your application can catch the errors before the operating system does and provide a logical handler for these errors, the program's user often will never realize that anything went wrong. Should an unhandled exception occur, however, your program's user will find out about the problem in a rather abrupt manner: Windows will simply end the program with a message box explaining that the program did something wrong.

SUMMARY

This chapter covers some of the new features that Visual C++ 2.0 offers. The two most important features that C++ programmers have wanted are exception handling and templates, both of which Visual C++ 2.0 offers.

Topics covered in this chapter include the following:

- Templates, which can be used to create typeless functions and classes
- Structured exception handling, in which exceptions can be handled in C and C++ code
- C++ exception handling, in which exceptions can be handled in C++ code only

CHAPTER 4

WHAT'S NEW IN MFC

The MFC library offers a number of new features for the Visual C++ 2.0 programmer. While almost all of the functionality of MFC 2.0 (included with Visual C++ 1.0) and MFC 2.5 (included with Visual C++ 1.5) has been retained, the exception macros (**TRY**, **CATCH**, **AND_CATCH**, and **THROW**) have been redefined to the new C++ exception handling statements. You shouldn't use the **TRY**, **CATCH**, **AND_CATCH**, and **THROW** exception handlers in your Visual C++ 2.0 code.

This chapter outlines the improvements that have been made to MFC 3.0. It is beyond the scope of this chapter to cover each of these new features in depth. However, the major features (such as exception handling, Unicode support, and so on) are covered in more detail in other chapters.

Support for 32-Bit Programs

With MFC 3.0, you now have support for writing 32-bit programs for the Intel systems (Windows NT and Windows 95) and the MIPS Windows NT environment. You have to create only one version of your application, and that version will be able to run on either platform.

New GDI Functions

MFC 3.0 offers improved support for the new GDI functions, such as the Bézier and path functions. The Bézier functions are used to draw complex curves. With Bézier functions, you can define a complex curve using two end points and two modifying points. With the path functions, you can create logical polygons that may then be filled or otherwise manipulated under program control. Charles Petzold has written several articles for *PC Magazine* showing how to use both Bézier curves and path functions.

New USER Functions

MFC 3.0 offers improved support for the new **USER** functions. Improvements in MFC classes that support dialog applications (applications that present only a dialog box as the user interface) typify the changes to the **USER** functions. Because the Windows **USER** functionality hasn't changed in Visual C++ 2.0, there are no additional **USER** functions as such.

Support for Exception Handling

Versions of MFC prior to 3.0 used macros to implement exception handling. With the inclusion of C++ exception handling in Visual C++ 2.0, MFC 3.0 now supports true exception handling. The original macros that were defined to process exceptions have been redefined to implement C++ exception handling. New code should always implement either structured exception handling or C++ exception handling.

C++ TEMPLATE CLASSES FOR COLLECTIONS

MFC 3.0 has defined a number of new classes for collections of objects. These classes include the following:

- **CArray**: A template class that implements an array of the type specified, with member functions to add, insert, remove, expand, and shrink the array. The type of the object in the array is specified when the **CArray** object is created.

- **CMap**: A template class that is used to map a set of unique keys to specific values. The process used is called using a *hash table*. There are member functions to look up, set, and remove items in the table.

- **CList**: A template class used to maintain lists of nonunique objects. The scheme used to manage the **CList** objects is similar to a doubly linked list. There are functions to get the first, last, or any specified object from the list.

- **CTypedPtrArray**: A template class that implements an array of pointers class, with member functions to add, insert, remove, expand, and shrink the array. The type of the object in the array is specified when the **CTypedPtrArray** object is created.

- **CTypedPtrList**: A template class used to maintain lists of nonunique pointers objects. The scheme used to manage the **CTypedPtrList** objects is similar to a doubly linked list. There are functions to get the first, last, or any specified object from the list.

- **CTypedPtrMap**: A template class that is used to map a set of unique keys to specific pointers. The process used is called using a hash table. There are member functions to look up, set, and remove items in the table.

Using the template classes, you can create your own type-safe classes.

TABBED DIALOG BOXES (PROPERTY SHEETS)

With tabbed dialog boxes, also called property sheets, you can create complex yet easy-to-use dialog boxes. For an example of a tabbed dialog box, simply look at Visual C++ 2.0's Class Wizard. Support for tabbed dialog boxes is provided with the **CPropertyPage** and **CPropertySheet** classes. I cover tabbed dialog boxes in more detail in Chapter 9, "Tabbed Dialog Boxes."

Improved Toolbar Support

Toolbar support has been improved in two major areas.

MFC 3.0 now supports *dockable* toolbars, in which the user can dock the toolbar to any side of the parent window. When the toolbar isn't docked (when it's floating), it can be placed in a mini-frame window.

In addition, toolbars now support *tool tips*, small help windows that pop up whenever the mouse moves over a toolbar button. Tool tips give a one- or two-word explanation of the toolbar button's function.

Visual C++ 2.0 is an example of an application that uses dockable toolbars and tool tips.

Unicode and Double-Byte Character Set (DBCS) Support

MFC 3.0 supports both Unicode and DBCS character sets. Generally, if you're writing applications for Windows NT, you'll want to include support for Unicode. Because Windows 95 doesn't support Unicode, you don't need to include support for Unicode in Windows 95-only applications. You must be careful when creating Unicode-aware applications under Windows NT not to make your applications incompatible with Windows 95. Your applications can be more easily internationalized using Unicode or DBCS strings.

For more information on Unicode, see Chapter 7, "Using Unicode."

> Windows 95 programmers should remember that, although the OLE support in MFC is available only in Unicode, Visual C++ 2.0 takes care of making the necessary conversions to and from Unicode when working under Windows 95.

New 3D Controls

When you add a call to `CWinApp::Enable3DControls()` in your application's `InitInstance()` function, the application will be able to use the new 3D controls in dialog boxes. You don't need to use CTRL3D.DLL with Visual C++ 2.0 applications.

Thin Caption Bar Windows

You can use an object created from `CMiniFrameWnd` to create a window that has the thin caption bar attribute. A window with the thin caption bar style looks much like a Visual C++ property window.

Assigning a Single Handler for a Range of Command or Control IDs in MFC

You may now map a number of consecutive command IDs to a single handler. A single mouse button handler can be implemented with only one function rather than the three (for up, down, and double click) that were required.

MFC 3.0 Has Added New Functionality to *CString*

The `CString` class has new added functionality. The functions added include member functions to support formatted strings (similar to the C library function **sprintf()**). The new functions include the following:

- **Format(LPCTSTR szFormat, ...)**: The **Format()** member function works like the **sprintf()** function found in the C library. **Format()** accepts a format string, which specifies both constant data as well as substitution variable type and formatting.

- **FreeExtra()**: You can use the **FreeExtra()** function to free any excess memory that has been allocated to this **CString** object. Normally, **CString** objects will grow as needed. However, they won't shrink unless **FreeExtra()** is called. The new size of the memory for the **CString** object will be equal to the value returned by the **CString::GetLength()** function.

OLE Class Support When Moving from MFC 2.0

MFC 2.5 and MFC 3.0 offer a set of OLE class objects that make it easier for you to create both OLE server and OLE container applications. The OLE classes enable you to create applications that support OLE Automation.

Part III of this book covers the OLE Custom Controls that have been added to MFC.

Support for Database Interaction When Moving from MFC 2.0

MFC 2.5 and MFC 3.0 offer a set of database class objects that make it easier for you to create applications that interact with DataSources. The process of database support (called ODBC or Open Database Connectivity) allows an application to work with data from a number of different sources, including SQL servers, Access, dBASE, text, and FoxPro.

Part IV of this book covers using the ODBC support provided by MFC 3.0.

Summary

This chapter covered some of the new features that MFC 3.0 offers. MFC 3.0 also has many minor improvements (such as performance enhancements) that you'll notice when MFC 3.0 is incorporated into your application. Topics covered in this chapter include the following:

- Support for 32-bit programming
- New GDI and **USER** support, including paths and Bézier functions
- Support for Unicode, tabbed dialog boxes, and exception handling
- Support for thin caption bar dialog boxes
- Additions to the **CString** class that allow easy formatting of output
- Improvements in and changes to OLE support
- ODBC support using MFC 3.0

DEBUGGING WITH VISUAL C++

Many of the debugging features found in Visual C++ 2.0 are similar to those found in earlier versions of Visual C++. For example, there are separate Watch, Locals, and Registers windows. In addition to these debugging windows, Visual C++ 2.0 also offers the Memory, Call Stack, and Disassembly debugging windows. Earlier versions of Visual C++ implemented Call Stack as a modal dialog box under the Debug pull-down menu. Now Call Stack is a window that is accessible to the programmer whenever Visual C++ 2.0 is in debugging mode.

In this chapter, I frequently use the phrase "your program fails." This means that the program has crashed (perhaps because of a GPF or an invalid page fault), not that there is a logic flaw. No debugger will find logic flaws if there is not an accompanying crash.

Standard Debugging with Visual C++ 2.0

Standard debugging with Visual C++ 2.0 is very similar to debugging using Visual C++ 1.0 or 1.5. You start the Visual Workbench, load the debugging version of your program, and run it. When the program fails, you are placed at the offending line in your code.

Actually, if the program failed in your code, you would be placed at the offending line. However, if the failure occurred in a part of the MFC code, you would see the MFC source. You could then use the Call Stack window to trace the execution of your program back to the point in your code where the failure was triggered.

If there is a failure in one of the Windows API or C library functions, you get a message that "no source code exists" for this location (the location of the error). This is not a major problem because you can always look at the Call Stack window to see where the failure really is. To trace back using the Call Stack window, look for names that are part of your program, such as MainFame or the view or document class names.

Let's look at what happens when a program is executed under the Visual Workbench's debugger. First, you run your program using either F5, the start button, or the Debug | Go menu selection. Generally, the following steps take place:

1. The Debug toolbar is displayed. This toolbar may be fixed, attached to another menu, or floating. Buttons on the Debug toolbar include the following:

    • Restart: Restarts the program from the current instruction pointer.

    • Stop Debugging: Stops the program's execution, exits debug mode, and returns you to development mode. The debugging windows will be closed, so be sure to save any information you might need for development prior to stopping the debugging session.

    • Step Into: Works like Visual C++ 1.x's Step Into command, which continues execution line-by-line into called functions.

    • Step Over: Works like Visual C++ 1.x's Step Over command, which continues execution line-by-line but doesn't trace calls into other functions.

    • Step Out: Works like Visual C++ 1.x's Step Out command, which continues execution line-by-line, with the next statement following the line that called the current function.

- Run to Cursor: Works like Visual C++ 1.x's Run to Cursor (F7) command, which continues execution until the line that contains the cursor is encountered. The cursor must be on a line containing an executable statement.
- Quick Watch: Activates the Quick Watch window. The variable under the cursor will be displayed in the Quick Watch window if the variable is in a block of code that is currently active and if the variable can be evaluated. Any variable in the Quick Watch window can be added to the Watch window. In Visual C++ 2.0, the Quick Watch window supports expressions.
- Watch: Displays or hides the Watch window.
- Locals: Displays or hides the Locals window.
- Registers: Displays or hides the Registers window.
- Memory: Displays or hides the Memory window.
- Call Stack: Displays or hides the Call Stack window.
- Disassembly: Displays or hides the Disassembly window.

Of course, you can choose to customize the Debug toolbar, adding and removing tools as you see fit. I recommend keeping the Debug toolbar as supplied until you're experienced with its use, then adding tools as you see a need.

2. Any debugging windows flagged as active are opened. If these debugging windows are docked (usually at the bottom of the main Visual Workbench window), the contents of the Visual Workbench are shifted up (during the debugging session only) to make space for the docked debugging windows. If the debugging windows aren't docked, they're placed on top of the current Visual Workbench edit windows.

3. The application and the application's symbols are loaded, and the application is started. The application runs until any one of the following events occurs:
   - A breakpoint is reached.
   - A break condition occurs, such as setting a break when a variable or memory location is modified or accessed.
   - An application error, such as a GPF or an Invalid Page Fault, occurs.

- An error is signaled, perhaps by an assertion-type error, usually in an MFC module.

- The application ends normally.

  After an application has started, you can still return to Visual C++ 2.0's Visual Workbench and set a breakpoint. Breakpoints are updated whenever they're set or cleared. It doesn't matter if the program is running or not.

As soon as the application being debugged has been started, it runs as it would under Windows. This application becomes the current task. Figure 5.1 shows the WevCalc application running under Visual C++ 2.0 in debugging mode. To switch back to Visual C++ 2.0, press Alt-Tab or select the Visual Workbench (if it's visible) using the mouse.

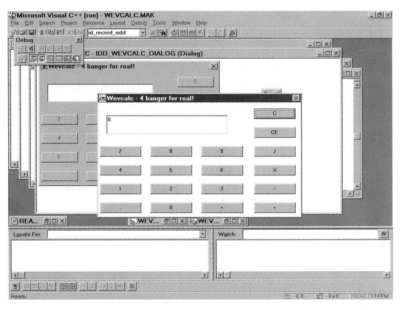

Figure 5.1. WevCalc being debugged.

When a program has been halted in the debugger, you can do an enormous amount of damage! First, you can change the contents of virtually all variables in the program. There will be no special error checking, other than that performed by your application, to see if the new value is either correct or logical. Obviously, modifying a variable must be done with a great deal of caution, because plugging an inappropriate value into a variable often results in the crash of the application.

The Disassembly Window

The Disassembly window is used to show a mixed source/assembly listing of the current location. For example, setting a breakpoint at a given line shows a disassembly listing for the line at the breakpoint. In Listing 5.1, I have copied part of the display from the Disassembly window. The actual line that the cursor was displayed at is in bold italic. I have also added some comments, which are in bold. Figure 5.2 shows the Disassembly window displayed in Visual C++ 2.0.

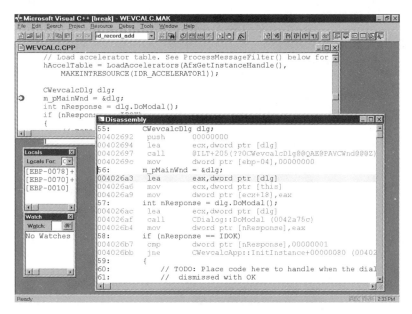

Figure 5.2. A program stopped in the debugger with the Disassembly window.

Suppose that you were debugging a Windows program. If you knew that the **m_pMainWnd** member variable wasn't being set correctly, and you needed to see how the compiler was making the assignment, you could look at the disassembly. If you understood the CPU's assembly/machine language, you would be able to see the actual machine instructions that made the assignment. In this example, assigning a pointer to a pointer variable requires three machine instructions.

Listing 5.1. WEVCALC.CPP in the Disassembly window.

```
55:        CWevcalcDlg dlg;
00402692   push       00000000
00402694   lea        ecx,dword ptr [dlg]
00402697   call       @ILT+205(??0CWevcalcDlg@@QAE@PAVCWnd@@@Z) (004010cd)
0040269c   mov        dword ptr [ebp-04],00000000
56:        m_pMainWnd = &dlg;
004026a3   lea        eax,dword ptr [dlg]         ;Load eax with pointer to dlg
004026a6   mov        ecx,dword ptr [this]        ;load ecx with pointer to 'this'
004026a9   mov        dword ptr [ecx+18],eax      ;m_pMainWnd is +18 from 'this'
57:        int nResponse = dlg.DoModal();
004026ac   lea        ecx,dword ptr [dlg]
004026af   call       CDialog::DoModal (0042a75c)
004026b4   mov        dword ptr [nResponse],eax
58:        if (nResponse == IDOK)
004026b7   cmp        dword ptr [nResponse],00000001
004026bb   jne        CWevcalcApp::InitInstance+00000080 (004026c6)
59:        {
60:            // TODO: Place code here to handle when the dialog is
61:            // dismissed with OK
62:        }
63:        else if (nResponse == IDCANCEL)
004026c1   jmp        CWevcalcApp::InitInstance+0000008a (004026d0)
004026c6   cmp        dword ptr [nResponse],00000002
004026ca   jne        CWevcalcApp::InitInstance+0000008a (004026d0)
64:        {
65:            // TODO: Place code here to handle when the dialog is
66:            // dismissed with Cancel
67:        }
68:
69:    // Since the dialog has been closed, return FALSE so that we exit the
70:    // application, rather than start the application's message pump.
71:        return FALSE;
004026d0   mov        dword ptr [ebp-74],00000000
004026d7   mov        dword ptr [ebp-04],ffffffff
004026de   call       $L21510 (004026eb)
004026e3   mov        eax,dword ptr [ebp-74]
004026e6   jmp        $L21509+0000000a (004026fe)
72:    }
004026eb   lea        ecx,dword ptr [dlg]
004026ee   call       @ILT+120(??1CWevcalcDlg@@UAE@XZ) (00401078)
004026f3   ret
$L21509:
004026f4   mov        eax,004730b8
004026f9   jmp        ___CxxFrameHandler (004031d5)
004026fe   mov        ecx,dword ptr [ebp-0c]
00402701   mov        dword ptr fs:[00000000],ecx
00402708   pop        edi
00402709   pop        esi
0040270a   pop        ebx
0040270b   leave
0040270c   ret
```

Listing 5.2 shows WEVCALC.CPP. The line where the breakpoint was set appears in bold.

LISTING 5.2. WEVCALC.CPP WITH THE BREAKPOINT LINE IN BOLD.

```
// wevcalc.cpp: Defines the class behaviors for the application.
//

#include "stdafx.h"
#include "wevcalc.h"
#include "wevcadlg.h"

#ifdef _DEBUG
#undef THIS_FILE
static char BASED_CODE THIS_FILE[] = __FILE__;
#endif

/////////////////////////////////////////////////////////////////////////////
// CWevcalcApp

BEGIN_MESSAGE_MAP(CWevcalcApp, CWinApp)
    //{{AFX_MSG_MAP(CWevcalcApp)
        // NOTE - the ClassWizard will add and remove mapping macros here.
        //    DO NOT EDIT what you see in these blocks of generated code!
    //}}AFX_MSG
    ON_COMMAND(ID_HELP, CWinApp::OnHelp)
END_MESSAGE_MAP()

/////////////////////////////////////////////////////////////////////////////
// CWevcalcApp construction

CWevcalcApp::CWevcalcApp()
{
    // TODO: Add construction code here
    // Place all significant initialization in InitInstance
}

/////////////////////////////////////////////////////////////////////////////
// The one and only CWevcalcApp object

CWevcalcApp theApp;

/////////////////////////////////////////////////////////////////////////////
// CWevcalcApp initialization

BOOL CWevcalcApp::InitInstance()
{
    // Standard initialization
    // If you are not using these features and wish to reduce the size
    //   of your final executable, you should remove from the following
    //   the specific initialization routines you do not need.

    Enable3dControls();
    LoadStdProfileSettings();  // Load standard INI file
                               // options (including MRU)
```

continues

LISTING 5.2. CONTINUED

```
    // Load accelerator table. See ProcessMessageFilter()
    // below for more info.
    hAccelTable = LoadAccelerators(AfxGetInstanceHandle(),
        MAKEINTRESOURCE(IDR_ACCELERATOR1));

    CWevcalcDlg dlg;
    m_pMainWnd = &dlg;   // BREAKPOINT IS THIS LINE!
    int nResponse = dlg.DoModal();
    if (nResponse == IDOK)
    {
        // TODO: Place code here to handle when
        // the dialog is dismissed with OK
    }
    else if (nResponse == IDCANCEL)
    {
        // TODO: Place code here to handle when
        // the dialog is dismissed with Cancel
    }

    // Since the dialog has been closed, return FALSE so that we exit the
    //  application, rather than start the application's message pump.
    return FALSE;
}

BOOL CWevcalcApp::ProcessMessageFilter(int code, LPMSG lpMsg)
{
    if (code < 0)
        CWinApp::ProcessMessageFilter(code, lpMsg);

    if (m_pMainWnd && hAccelTable)
    {
        if (::TranslateAccelerator(m_pMainWnd->m_hWnd, hAccelTable, lpMsg))
            return(TRUE);
    }

    return (CWinApp::ProcessMessageFilter(code, lpMsg));
}
```

Earlier versions of Visual C++ simply replaced the current source window's contents with a mixed source/assembly listing. This method allowed the programmer to see the assembly instructions but was somewhat awkward to use. You had to select each source file for which you wanted a disassembly listing produced, and the actual process of creating a disassembly listing was lengthy.

The Memory Window

The Memory window is a feature new to Visual C++ 2.0. With the Memory window, the programmer can examine specific areas of memory. In the preceding example, I noted that the **m_pMainWnd** memory variable was +18 (18 bytes) from the this pointer. Looking at the Locals Window, you see that the address for the this pointer is 0x00470000. You also can see the contents of the applicable class object using the Locals For window (see Listing 5.3).

It's then possible to start a Memory window and set the Address control or scroll back using the scroll bar to address 0x00470000. At this address you can see the one-to-one correspondence between the actual contents of memory (in the Memory window—see Listing 5.4) and the MFC objects that are located there.

LISTING 5.3. THE CONTENTS OF THE LOCALS FOR WINDOW.

```
[EBP-0078]-CWevcalcApp * const this = 0x00470000
 -CWinApp CWinApp = {...}
   -CWinThread CWinThread = {...}
     +CCmdTarget CCmdTarget = {...}
     +CRuntimeClass classCWinThread = {...}
     +CWnd * m_pMainWnd = 0x00000000
      int m_bAutoDelete = 1
     +void * m_hThread = 0xfffffffe
      unsigned long m_nThreadID = 2165713148
      int m_nDisablePumpCount = 0
     +tagMSG m_msgCur = {...}
     +void * m_pThreadParams = 0x00000000
      unsigned int (void *)* m_pfnThreadProc = 0x00000000
     +CPoint m_ptCursorLast = {...} protected
      unsigned int m_nMsgLast = 0 protected
   +CRuntimeClass classCWinApp = {...}
```

LISTING 5.4. THE MEMORY WINDOW'S CONTENTS WITH m_pMainWnd IN BOLD.

```
address   0  1  2  3  4  5  6  7  8  9  A  B  C  D  E  F
0046FFF0  00 00 00 00 00 00 00 00 00 00 00 00 00 00 00 00   ..............
00470000  00 31 47 00 01 00 00 00 00 00 00 00 00 00 00 00   .1G...........
00470010  00 00 00 00 01 00 00 00 00 00 00 00 01 00 00 00   ..............
00470020  FE FF FF FF FC 28 16 81 00 00 00 00 00 00 00 00   .....(........
00470030  00 00 00 00 00 00 00 00 00 00 00 00 00 00 00 00   ..............
00470040  00 00 00 00 00 00 00 00 00 00 00 00 00 00 00 00   ..............
00470050  44 01 00 00 30 00 00 00 00 00 00 00 00 00 40 00   D...0........@.
00470060  00 00 00 00 2A 28 16 81 01 00 00 00 00 00 00 00   ....*(........
```

Looking at the Memory window in Listing 5.4, you see that I've marked in bold the 4 bytes starting at 0x00470018. A **CWnd*** variable is a pointer that is 4 bytes long. The next variable in the object is the **m_bAutoDelete** variable, a 32-bit integer whose value currently is 1 (the identifier **TRUE** probably was used to initialize this variable). It's important to note that the Intel processor has the bytes swapped when a value is stored in memory—that is, the lowest bits in the range are the least significant. This is a logical choice, but it means that you must reverse the order of the bytes when looking at a dump of memory. For example, if you see the bytes 12 34 56 78 in a memory dump, the actual variables' contents are 0x78563412 (or 2018915346 in decimal).

Just-In-Time Debugging

Just-In-Time debugging? Isn't that an oxymoron? If your application has a bug, you weren't just in time—you were a little too late!

OK, to be a bit more serious, let's look at this thing called Just-In-Time debugging. Just-In-Time debugging enables you to run your application from outside the Visual C++ Visual Workbench and its integrated debugger without having to worry about the issues of running the Visual Workbench. All's fine until your program fails (let's say there's a GPF). With earlier versions of Visual C++ and Windows, you had to run DrWatson, have a symbol file for your application (created with MapSym from the .MAP file), dig through the DrWatson.LOG file, and try to find the line in the program that failed.

Granted, most of the time you could find the offending line of code and fix the problem. The down side was that locating the problem could take a lot of time.

With Just-In-Time debugging, you don't have to worry about DrWatson, symbol files, map files, log files, and the like. What you do is enable Just-In-Time debugging so that when your program fails, Windows will launch the debugger for your application.

Once the debugger is started, you can do anything you might have done if you had started with Visual C++ 2.0's Visual Workbench. The main advantage is that you don't need to have Visual C++ 2.0 running each time you start your application. Without Visual C++ 2.0 running, you'll probably have better response time from the system, because Visual C++ 2.0 is a large program that demands resources. Also, using Just-In-Time debugging can make your testing simpler because you don't have to start a debugger as a separate step.

Whom is Just-In-Time debugging for? First, it's not for end-users. You need to have a compatible debugger (Visual C++ 2.0), and you'll need the application's source code and debugging information (in a format that the debugger understands). However, for in-house (alpha) testing, Just-In-Time debugging can be very useful, because you don't need to have a number of testers running

Visual C++ 2.0 to enable debugging of the application. Instead, when the application fails, Visual C++ 2.0 starts, and a developer can use the machine to find the problem.

You must follow a few steps to enable Just-In-Time debugging on a Windows system. First, if you're using Windows NT, you can choose the Tools | Options menu selection. Next, select the Debug tab from the Options dialog box that is displayed and check the Just In Time Debugging check box at the bottom-right of the dialog box.

The information about Just-In-Time debugging is contained in the registry in both Windows 95 and Windows NT. The section is

```
\Software\Microsoft\Windows NT\CurrentVersion\AeDebug
```

Figure 5.3 shows a system fault dialog box that includes the button to launch the debugger. Prior to starting the debugger, you should request the details portion of the dialog so that you can see where the instruction pointer was and what was in the registers. This information could be valuable if, after the debugger has started, a further problem prevents the debugger from functioning correctly.

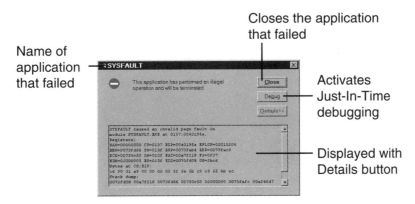

Figure 5.3. The System Error dialog box with the Debug button.

After you've found and corrected the problem in your program, you'll need to rebuild it. Because Visual C++ 2.0 is already running, this is an easy task.

PROFILING

Your application isn't complete until you profile it. But what is a profile, you ask?

This is a common question for many Windows programmers. No, profiling isn't looking at your product from the side! *Profiling* is determining, during both typical and atypical usage, where the computer occupies most of its time when your program is executing. For example, you might profile a program to determine which functions are called most frequently, which functions use the most time on the system, and which functions are never called. Let's look at each of these situations and why they are important to you as the application developer.

Which Functions Are Used Most Frequently?

The need to determine which functions are called most frequently might give you justification to make frequently-called functions in-line. A function that isn't too large and that is called frequently from a few locations can be made in-line, thereby saving the overhead of the function call. It's not uncommon for a call to a simple function to consume more overhead than the actual code in the function itself.

Which Functions Utilize the Most Time?

Determining which functions are utilizing the most time enables you to find functions that are poorly written. When a single function utilizes a substantial amount of a program's execution, that function might benefit from a rewrite. Sometimes, if the offending function is large, you'll want to profile it by line also. That way, you can see which lines in the function are using the majority of the time.

Which Functions Are Never Called?

A function that is never called is often a relatively minor problem. An uncalled function could make your executable larger, but usually only slightly. There is a problem when a function that you know should be called is not. How often have you had a function that wasn't executing properly, and no matter what you changed, you couldn't fix it? Don't laugh; it's happened to many of us! The most common error is to have a name in mixed case (which the compiler will treat as a unique name), which is the same as a name in a library that is being included from some other source, such as the standard libraries or an aftermarket product. The problem is that the linker normally will ignore the case and link in the first name found. Because the linker doesn't do any error checking for parameters and so on, the results can be very difficult to find if you aren't careful. Pity the poor programmer who has his own function named *SprintF()* and thinks that the library function `sprintf()` will be ignored. Not likely!

> When your program has been built with the profiling options set, you're not getting the best from either Visual C++ 2.0 or the other debugging and program-building facilities. When you've completed your profiling, turn off the profiling options and rebuild your project.

PREPARING A PROGRAM FOR PROFILING

To prepare a program for profiling, you need to perform a few steps. You must set the profiling option in the linker configuration. To enable profiling, you must set to on the Enable Profiling option, under Project Settings in the Link tab, General Category. This option tells the linker to create a map file (Visual C++ 2.0 normally doesn't use map files) and to store debugging information in the executable file rather than in Visual C++ 2.0's PDB file.

> ### PERFORMANCE HIT
>
> Turning on the profiling option disables incremental linking, so your project build link process will take longer to complete. Turn off profiling when you're not using it and rebuild your project.

Profiling is a multistep process. Select Tools | Profile. This option displays a dialog box that lists the profiling options (see Figure 5.4).

Figure 5.4. Profiler options under Windows 95.

Let's look at the profiler options and what they can do for you. In the Profile dialog box you see a group box, called Profile Type, with a set of options. The options for profile type include the following:

- Function Timing: Profiling by function timing lets you determine which functions utilize the majority of the system's resources (the CPU in this case). The breakdown is by function, so for lengthy functions you'll have to determine which part of the function is inefficient.

- Function Coverage: Looking at function coverage enables you to see which functions are being called and which are not. A function that is not called might be a piece of "dead" (unused) code or simply a piece of code that is used infrequently, such as an error handler.

- Line Coverage: Like function coverage, line coverage enables you to determine which lines in your program are being executed and which are not. Because many lines in conditional blocks (`if... else...`) aren't always executed, you must look carefully at the code to determine why a line of code wasn't executed.

- Merge: The profiler is built as a series of steps that are executed in order. It's not necessary to run the `PREP` stage (discussed later) prior to each profiling run. Once `PREP` has created the PBI and PBT files, they can be reused with the profiler to create a number of PBO files. The resultant PBO files can then be automatically merged using the Merge option.

- Custom Settings: The Custom Settings option enables you to create customized profiling based on your own set of options. You can customize the profiling to your needs (for example, limiting the profiling to a given set of source files).

- Advanced Settings: The Advanced Settings option enables you to set options for phase one of the PREP process.

Profiling is performed in the following steps:

1. When you begin a profiling session, the profiler system is initialized. The Output window is set to the Profile tab and the PREP stage is started.

2. The PREP command is executed, creating the PBI and PBT files that are used in the next stages of profiling.

3. The PROFILE command is executed, executing your program and gathering the information that the profiler needs.

4. When the program being profiled ends, the PROFILE command writes the PBO file and then ends.

5. The PREP command is again executed, processing the output from the PROFILE command.

6. The results of the profile are loaded into the Output window (under the Profile tab).

Considering what we've had to do with previous versions of Visual C++, the profiling facilities included with Visual C++ 2.0 are fairly good. You still must create custom batch files to customize your profile sessions, but now you can profile while using the Visual Workbench.

SUMMARY

This chapter covered debugging under Visual C++ 2.0. Topics discussed include the following:

- Using the Visual Workbench built-in debugger
- New features found in the Visual Workbench debugger, such as the Memory window, the Call Stack window, and the Disassembly window
- Using Just-In-Time debugging to make locating and correcting bugs in a running application easier
- Using the Profiler to create an execution profile of the application

EXTERNAL VISUAL C++ UTILITIES

The Visual C++ package includes a number of utilities. You will use these utilities to create and debug programs, monitor the system, and do other miscellaneous things. Many of these utilities haven't changed appreciably since the introduction of Visual C++, but some have been extensively rewritten. An example of a utility that hasn't really changed is ZoomIn, which is essentially the same as it was with Visual C++ 1.0. The Spy++ program is a complete rewrite of the old Spy program that was included with earlier versions of Visual C++. The new Spy++ offers much more functionality, and it actually replaces several other utilities that are no longer included with Visual C++ 2.0.

The usefulness of any of these utilities depends on the skills of the programmer. You can get much use from most of them, but you must be able to interpret the utilities' output correctly.

Some of these tools run from the Visual C++ 2.0 program group. The remainder are 32-bit console applications that look and feel like DOS command-line utilities. You can run them by selecting their icon in the file list or by entering their name at a command-line prompt. With Windows 4.0, entering a Windows program's name at a DOS command prompt launches the Windows application. Most of these utilities return information; for example, Spy++ returns information about a selected window, thread, or process. This chapter looks at how to use each of the Visual C++ 2.0 external utilities.

PortTool

The utility PortTool enables you to convert applications that were written for 16-bit versions of Windows to run under 32-bit versions of Windows (such as Windows NT). PortTool was introduced in the 32-bit version of Visual C++.

PortTool also enables programmers who write Windows NT applications to port their applications to Windows 95. PortTool can flag the differences between the version of Windows that the application was written for and the target version of Windows. The programmer can customize the control file that controls PortTool's actions.

This utility examines the code of your program, source module by source module, and reports any lines that might not function correctly under the different versions of 32-bit Windows.

Microsoft has decided to include the source for PortTool with Visual C++ 2.0. This source can be found in the directory \MSVC20\SAMPLES \SDKTOOLS\PORTTOOL. If you have the Windows NT version of Visual C++, you also can look there for the source for these tools.

Spy++

Visual C++ 2.0 offers a new, enhanced version of the Spy utility, Spy++. It replaces the Spy utility that was supplied with earlier versions of Visual C++ and the Windows SDKs.

I've found Spy++ to be one of the most valuable tools available for Windows. Spy++ wasn't designed to be educational, but you'll find that not only can you monitor messages, processes, threads, and windows, but you also can see the relationships among these elements. For example, when monitoring a message, you can see the message's effect on the window.

To use Spy++, start it by double-clicking on its icon. This will bring up Spy++'s

main menu. To select a new window to spy on, select Spy | Find Window....
Doing so displays the Find Window dialog box (as shown in Figure 6.1).

Figure 6.1. Spy++'s Find Window dialog box.

Spy++ has six menus. The first, Spy, lets you select which part of Windows
you'll spy on. Tree allows you to manage trees, expanding and collapsing them.
View allows you to set fonts, display the toolbar and/or status bar, and set
properties for the current window. Messages allows you to start and stop the
logging of message activity, configure the Message window's attributes, and
clear the Message window. The Window menu is a standard MDI menu that
lets you manage Spy++'s MDI windows. The final menu, Help, provides an
interface with Spy++'s help file and the obligatory About box.

The Spy Menu

The Spy menu has six options. The first four control what you'll be spying on,
and the fifth activates the Window Finder dialog box. The final item on the Spy
menu is Exit, which ends Spy++. Let's take a quick look at the first five menu
options under Spy:

- Messages...: The Messages menu option activates the Message Options
  dialog and allows you to select a window to spy on. To select a window, click and drag the finder tool (shaped like a target sight) over the
  window that you want to spy on and release the button.

After selecting the window to spy on, you can set options for spying. The window spy options are subdivided into three categories: Windows, Messages, and Output.

- Windows: The Windows menu option opens another MDI client window with a listing of the windows currently available (open) on the system. Generally, each application that is running has one window (or sometimes more). Each window in the listing is accompanied by its handle, title (if there is one), and class.

- Processes: The Processes menu option opens another MDI client window with a listing of the processes currently running on the system. Each application is a separate process, and a number of system processes will be running as well. Each process listed can be expanded to show the threads and windows that are part of the process.

- Threads: The Threads menu option opens another MDI client window with a listing of the threads currently running on the system. Each thread has an owner (see Processes), and one or more windows may be associated with a thread.

- Find Window...: The Find Window menu option opens a dialog box that allows you to select a window and obtain information about that window. You can view the window's message stream (see Windows), but you can't set the options for messages from this dialog.

The Tree Menu

The Tree menu allows you to expand and collapse the trees that are shown in the Windows, Processes, and Threads MDI windows. You can choose from these options:

- Expand One Level: Expands the current branch one level.
- Expand Branch: Expands the current branch fully.
- Expand All: Expands all branches fully.
- Collapse: Collapses the current branch. There is no Collapse All option.

The View Menu

The View menu allows you to set the font used, display the toolbar and status bar, and view properties for the current Windows, Processes, and Threads MDI windows:

- Font: The Font menu selection displays the standard Fonts dialog box. This dialog allows you to select a font and its attributes (such as bold and italic) and size. You can make the selected font the default font.

- Toolbar: The Toolbar menu option allows you to turn the display of the toolbar on and off.

- Status bar: The Status bar menu option allows you to turn the display of the Status bar on and off.

- Properties: The Properties menu option displays a Properties dialog box for the current window. The information displayed in the Properties window varies depending on what the current MDI window's type is (Window, Processes, or Threads).

The Messages Menu

The Messages menu allows you to start or stop the logging of messages, set options (such as the filters used), and clear the current Messages window. All options on the Messages menu are active only when the current MDI window is a Messages window.

- Start (or Stop) Logging: This option allows you to start (if currently stopped) or stop (if currently started) the logging of messages.

- Options: The Options menu selection allows you to configure the current Message window. Options that can be set include the following:

  Scope (Parent, Children, Windows of Same Thread, Windows of Same Process, or All Windows in System).

  Messages that aren't logged.

  Output format (Message Nesting Level, Raw Message Parameters, Decoded Message Parameters, Raw Return Values, and Decoded Return Values).

You also can specify the size of the buffer that the messages are stored in. The default buffer size is 750 lines, which should be adequate for most applications.

- Clear: The Clear menu selection enables you to clear the current Messages window.

The Window Menu

The Window menu enables you to arrange the MDI child windows, refresh the current window's contents, or select a specific window from the list. This menu is typical of all MDI applications.

The Help Menu

The Help menu allows you to access the help file for Spy++ and to view the About box.

DDE Spy

DDE Spy allows you to look at DDE processes. DDE Spy is a very powerful utility that is invaluable in determining what's happening with data transfers between two applications.

Command-Line Compiler

Visual C++ 2.0 makes available a command-line-driven compiler (CL) that follows the syntax of previous versions of Microsoft C/C++ compilers. The Visual C++ 2.0 command-line compiler supports the 32-bit environment of Windows NT, Windows 95, and Win32s.

The options that CL supports are listed in Table 6.1. These options are divided into seven broad categories: Optimization, Code Generation, Output Files, Preprocessor, Language, Miscellaneous, and Linking.

	TABLE 6.1. THE VISUAL C++ 2.0 CL COMPILER OPTIONS.	

Option	New or Changed	Description
Optimization		
/O1		Optimizes to create the smallest output.
/O2		Optimizes to create the fastest code.
/Oa		Turns off aliasing.
/Ob<n>		Enables (= 1 or = 2) or disables (= 0) inline expansion.
/Od		Disables all optimizations.
/Og		Enables optimization at the global level.
/Oi		Turns on intrinsic (inline rather than calls to library) functions.
/Op[-]		Optimizes to create floating-point consistency.
/Os		Optimizes to minimize code size.
/Ot		Optimizes to improve code speed.
/Ow		Establishes that aliasing may occur between functions.
/Ox		Maximum optimization. Equivalent to /Ogityb1/Gs.
/Oy[-]	•	Tells compiler not to create stack frames on the call stack.
Code Generation		
/G3		Optimizes for the 80386 CPU.
/G4	•	Optimizes for the 80486 CPU.
/G5	•	Optimizes for the Pentium CPU.

continues

	Table 6.1. continued	
Option	New or Changed	Description
Code Generation		
/GB	•	Optimizes to favor the Pentium, but not to seriously affect performance when run on 80386/80486 systems.
/Gd		Uses the __cdecl calling convention.
/Ge		Turns on stack calls when functions are entered.
/Gf		Turns on string pooling. String constants are reused if possible.
/Gh	•	Generates a call to __penter for each function or method called.
/Gr		Uses the __fastcall calling convention.
/Gs[num]		Customizes the stack probes. Setting a nondefault value for [num] can cause problems.
/GX	•	Enables the calling of destructors when the stack is unwound during exception handling.
/GX-	•	Disables the calling of destructors when the stack is unwound during exception handling.
/Gy		Creates separate functions for the linker.
/Gz	•	Uses the __stdcall calling convention.
Output Files		
/Fa[file]		Creates and optionally names the assembly listing file.

Option	New or Changed	Description
/FA[*sc*]	•	Customizes the /**Fa** assembly listing. **s** = assembly with source, **c** = assembly with machine code, and **sc** = assembly with machine code and source.
/Fd[*file*]		Creates and optionally names the .PDB file.
/Fe<*file*>		Specifies the name of the executable file.
/Fm[*file*]		Creates and optionally names the map file.
/Fo<*file*>		Specifies the name of the object file.
/Fp<*file*>		Specifies the name of the precompiled header file.
/Fr[*file*]		Creates and optionally names the source Browser file.
/FR[*file*]		Creates and optionally names the extended .SBR file.
Preprocessor		
/C		Leaves comments in the preprocessor output.
/D<*name*>{=¦#}<*text*>		Creates a macro.
/E		Writes the preprocessor output to stdout.
/EP		Writes the preprocessor output to stdout, suppressing the line numbers.
/FI<*file*>	•	Forces the named file to be included.
/I<*dir*>		Adds an additional path to the include search path.

continues

	TABLE 6.1. CONTINUED	
Option	New or Changed	Description
Preprocessor		
/P		Writes the preprocessor output to a file.
/u		Removes all existing macros.
/U<name>		Removes an existing macro.
/X		Ignores the standard search order.
Language		
/vd{0¦1}		Enables or disables the addition of the hidden **vtordisp** constructor displacement member. Useful only if virtual bases are used.
/vm<x>		Member pointer type. **s** = single inheritance, **m** = multiple inheritance, and **v** = any class.
/Z7		Creates CodeView debugging information in C7 style.
/Za		Disables Microsoft extensions to the C/C++ language (implies /Op).
/Zd		Writes line number information to the object file.
/Ze		Enables Microsoft extensions to the C/C++ language (implies /Op).
/Zg		Generates function prototypes.
/Zi		Creates CodeView-compatible output.
/Zl		Doesn't write library names in the object files.
/Zp[n]		Packs (aligns) structures to be on n byte boundaries.
/Zs		Performs a syntax check only; doesn't write an object file.

Option	New or Changed	Description
	*Miscellaneous*	
/? and /help		Display a quick list of options.
/c		Performs a compile only. Doesn't link.
/H<num>		Sets the maximum external name length. Used for some aftermarket linkers.
/J		Makes the default **char** type unsigned.
/nologo		Doesn't display the sign-on banner and copyright message.
/Tc<source file>		Compiles as if the input file had an extension of .C.
/Tp<source file>		Compiles as if the input file had an extension of .CPP.
/V<string>		Adds a string to the object file. Useful for copyright branding.
/w		Turns off all warnings.
/W<n>		Sets the warning level. The default is $n = 1$.
/WX		Treats all warnings as errors.
/Yc[file]		Creates a .PCH (precompiled header) file.
/Yd	•	Adds debugging information to each object file created. This option has been changed slightly from earlier versions of Visual C++.
/Yu[file]		Uses the user-specified .PCH file.
/YX[file]		Uses a precompiled header file and creates the .PCH if it doesn't exist.
/Zn		Disables source Browser packing for .SBR files.

continues

TABLE 6.1. CONTINUED		

Option	New or Changed	Description
		Linker
/F<*num*>		Defines the stack size.
/LD	•	Creates a DLL (Dynamic Link Library) rather than an executable program. The case of this option has changed from /Ld to /LD.
/link		Allows the passing of options and libraries to the linker.
/MD	•	Creates a multithreaded application using MSVCRT.LIB.
/ML	•	Creates a single-threaded application using LIBC.LIB.
/MT	•	Creates a multithreaded application using LIBCMT.LIB.

Most programmers won't want to use the command-line compiler. It really doesn't make sense not to use Visual Workbench's interface with the compiler. However, some projects (generally ones that are older and that were created for compilers other than Visual C++) still require the command-line compiler.

Most programmers who are going to use the command-line compiler will be calling it using NMake or some other make-type utility.

LINK

The linker supplied with Visual C++ 2.0 is a powerful, 32-bit, incremental linker. The current version is 2.5. The inputs to the linker are standard object modules (in COFF, or Common Object File Format) and static libraries. The output from the linker is either an executable program (.EXE) or a dynamic link library.

Incremental linking allows the linker to shorten the time taken to relink an existing project's output file. There are some circumstances in which the linker is unable to use an incremental link, such as when incremental linking is turned off; the .ILK file is missing, read-only, or corrupted; there have been added library calls; and so on. When an incremental link can't be performed, the linker performs a standard full link.

The linker uses a number of options, which are listed in Table 6.2. Note that the linker's options have changed substantially because the linker was totally rewritten.

	TABLE 6.2. LINKER OPTIONS.	
Option	New or Changed	Description
/ALIGN:_n_		A command-line option used to specify the alignment of each section within the linear address space. The default for _n_ is 4096, and it must be a power of 2.
/BASE:{_address_ ¦ _@filename, key_**}**	•	An output-type option used to set the base address of the program. For Windows NT programs, the default address is 0x400000. When loading the program, Windows can alter the base if necessary. However, altering the program's base will significantly affect the program's loading performance. Note: Windows NT and

continues

	TABLE 6.2. CONTINUED	

Option	New or Changed	Description
		Windows 95 have different program-loading addresses. If you're targeting a specific version of Windows, be sure that the correct base address is specified.
/COMMENT:*comment*	•	A command-line option used to insert a comment string into the header of the output file. The comment can be used for copyright information or version identification.
/DEBUG	•	A debugging option that tells the linker to include debugging information with the output file.
/DEBUGTYPE:{CV ¦ COFF ¦ BOTH}	•	A debugging option used to specify which type of debugging information is included with the output file. You can choose to have the debugging information stored in CodeView, COFF, or both formats.

Option	New or Changed	Description
/DEF:*filename*	•	A command-line option used to specify the module definition file. A module definition file isn't required with this version of the linker.
/DEFAULTLIB:*library*[, *library*]	•	A command-line option used to add libraries in addition to the ones already defined.
/DLL	•	A command-line option used to tell the linker to build a dynamic link library instead of an executable file.
/ENTRY:*symbol*	•	An output option that sets the entry point for an executable program or a dynamic link library.
/EXETYPE:{DEV386 ¦ DYNAMIC}	•	A command-line option used when creating a virtual device driver (a **VXD**). You specify **DEV386** to create a **VXD** that is loaded when the calling program is loaded. If **DYNAMIC** is specified, the **VXD** is dynamically loaded.
/EXPORT:*symbol*	•	A command-line option that allows you to specify which functions are exported and accessible to other programs.

continues

Option	New or Changed	Description
Table 6.2. continued		
/FIXED	•	A command-line option that tells Windows that the program can be loaded only at its specified base address (see **/BASE**).
/FORCE[:{MULTIPLE ¦ UNRESOLVED}]	•	An option that tells the linker to create a valid executable file even if there are unresolved or multiply-defined symbols.
/HEAP:*reserve*[,*commit*]	•	A command-line option that sets the heap size. The default size is 1,048,576 (1 MB).
/IMPLIB:*filename*	•	A command-line option used to override the default name for the import library created by link. An import library is created whenever an output file contains exported functions.
/INCLUDE:*symbol*	•	An input option that tells the linker to include a symbol in the symbol table.
/INCREMENTAL:{YES¦NO}	•	An option used to change the default behavior of the incremental linker.

Option	New or Changed	Description
/MAC:creator:*name*	•	An option that specifies the name of the creator of the Macintosh application.
/MAC:*type*:	•	An option that specifies the type of Macintosh application. The default is **APPL**.
/MAC:{BUNDLE ¦ NOBUNDLE}	•	An option that specifies whether the application has a bundle resource. The bundled resource has information about the application's icons for both the application and the the application's documents.
/MACDATA:*path*	•	An option that specifies the path of the Macintosh Data Fork File Name box.
/MACHINE:{IX86 ¦ M68K}	•	A command-line option used to specify the target machine as either Intel 80x86/Pentium (IBM PC-compatible) or Motorola 68xxx (Macintosh-compatible).
/MACRES:*filename*	•	An option that specifies the name of the Macintosh resource file.

continues

	TABLE 6.2. CONTINUED	

Option	New or Changed	Description
/MAP[:filename]		An option used to specify the creation of a map file (which lists the symbols and their locations in a program) and optionally the name of the map file.
/NODEFAULTLIB[:library [, library...]]	•	An option that tells the linker to ignore all the default libraries that may be specified in an object module. This option has changed from other versions of the Linker.
/NOENTRY	•	A command-line option used to create a dynamic link library that has only resources and no callable functions.
/NOLOGO		An option that tells the linker not to display a startup logo or copyright notice.
/OPT:{REF ¦ NOREF}	•	A command-line option used to tell the linker how to optimize the output file.
/ORDER:@filename	•	An option that allows you to specify the order of certain packaged functions in the final output file.

Option	New or Changed	Description
/OUT:*filename*	•	An option used to specify an output filename that is different from the default.
/PDB:{*filename* ¦ NONE}	•	An option that tells the linker whether or not to create a program database, a file used for debugging.
/PROFILE	•	An option that enables the inclusion, in the output file, of information that the profiler requires.
/RELEASE	•	An option used to set the output file's checksum. Device drivers are required to have a valid checksum, and it's recommended that all files include checksum information.
/SECTION:*section*,[E][R][W][S] [D][K][L][P][X]	•	An option used to change the attributes of the specified *section*. Options include E (execute), R (read), W (write), S (shared), P (paged virtual memory), D (discardable), and K (cached virtual memory).

continues

	Table 6.2. continued		
Option	New or Changed	Description
/STACK:*reserve*[, *commit*]	•	An option that allows the stack size to be specified. The default size is 1,048,576 (1 MB). The *reserve* and *commit* options are new to Visual C++ 2.0.
/STUB:*filename*		An option that enables you to specify the name of the stub program. A stub program is run when a Windows program is executed under DOS without Windows running.
/SUBSYSTEM:{NATIVE ¦ WINDOWS ¦ CONSOLE ¦ POSIX}[,#[.##]]	•	A command-line option that enables you to specify the type of application you will generate. A **NATIVE** subsystem is a Windows NT device driver. A **WINDOWS** subsystem is an application that creates its own windows. A **CONSOLE** application runs in Windows NT and Windows 95 console mode (Windows 95's DOS windows mode). A **POSIX** application runs under POSIX in Windows NT.

Option	New or Changed	Description
/VERBOSE	•	An option that tells the linker to provide a detailed report of the progress of the link.
/VERSION:#[.#]	•	An option that allows you to specify the version information (a major version and optionally a minor version) in the output file's header.
/VXD	•	A command-line option that tells the linker to create a VXD (virtual device driver) file.
/WARN[:*warninglevel*]	•	A command-line option that specifies what level of warnings you want to see. Setting *warninglevel* to 0 suppresses all warnings. Setting *warninglevel* to 1 displays most warnings. Setting *warninglevel* to 2 displays all warnings.

Like the compiler, most Visual C++ users allow the Visual Workbench to manage the link process. However, for some projects the linker will be needed outside the Visual Workbench. It is uncommon not to use a makefile to control the linker.

LIB

The library utility Lib is used to create libraries, import libraries, and export files that the linker can use. The Lib command can be used to do the following:

- Create or modify a COFF (Common Object File Format) library.
- Extract a member from a COFF format library.
- Create an export file and an import library.

The Lib utility supports the options listed in Table 6.3. It's been rewritten for Visual C++ 2.0, so all its options are new.

TABLE 6.3. LIB OPTIONS.	
Option	*Description*
/DEBUGTYPE:{COFF ¦ CV ¦ BOTH}	A debugging option used to specify which type of debugging information is included with the output file. You can choose to have the debugging information stored in CodeView, COFF, or both formats.
/DEF:[*filename*]	A command-line option used to specify the module definition file. A module definition file isn't required with this version of the linker.
/EXPORT:*symbol*	A command-line option that allows you to specify which functions are exported (and accessible to other programs).
/EXTRACT:*membername*	Tells Lib to extract the specified membername from the library and place it in an .OBJ file.
/INCLUDE:*symbol*	This input option tells the linker to include a symbol in the symbol table.

Option	Description
/LIST[:*filename*]	Tells Lib to list the contents (the members) of a library and optionally to place this listing into the file ***filename***.
/MACHINE:{IX86 ¦ M68K}	A command-line option used to specify the target machine as either Intel 80x86/Pentium (IBM PC-compatible) or Motorola 68xxx (Macintosh-compatible).
/NAME:*filename*	Allows you to specify the name of the output file created.
/NOLOGO	Tells Lib not to display a startup logo or copyright notice.
/OUT:*filename*	Specifies the name for the member extracted using /EXTRACT:*membername*.
/REMOVE:*membername*	Allows you to remove a member from the library.
/SUBSYSTEM:{NATIVE ¦ WINDOWS ¦ CONSOLE ¦ POSIX}[,#[.#]]	A command-line option that allows you to specify the type of application you will generate. A **NATIVE** subsystem is a Windows NT device driver. A **WINDOWS** subsystem is an application that creates its own windows. A **CONSOLE** application runs in Windows NT and Windows 95 console mode (Windows 95's DOS windows). A **POSIX** application runs under POSIX in Windows NT.
/VERBOSE	Tells Lib to provide a detailed report of progress.

The Lib utility makes it possible to create and manage static link libraries from the command-line environment.

PROFILER

The Profiler can be run from the Visual Workbench. For applications that require it, you can run the DOS command-line–based Profiler. The Profiler is a collection of programs that allow you to determine which parts of your program occupy the majority of the CPU's resources.

You might be surprised at which parts of your program are the most inefficient. One program that I wrote had an infrequently called function that was using about 20 percent of the CPU's resources. I figured, incorrectly, that since this function wasn't called often, it didn't have to be efficient.

The Profiler is divided into three major parts:

- Prep: The Prep program is run both before and after you execute your program. The first time it's executed, it creates the .PBI and .PBT files. The second time, it updates the .PBT file that will be used by Plist.
- Profile: The Profile program is run after the first run of Prep. Profile is given the name of the program to be profiled, and then it starts the program.
- Plist: The Plist program converts the results of the second run of Prep into a report file.

Six batch files are provided to enable the programmer to use the Profiler facility. They are found in the \MSVC20\BIN directory:

- FCOUNT.BAT
- FCOVER.BAT
- FSAMPLE.BAT
- FTIME.BAT
- LCOUNT.BAT
- LCOVER.BAT

These batch files can be used as they are, or you can modify them to suit your needs.

Most projects created with Visual C++ 2.0 are profiled with the Visual Workbench Profiler, not the command-line versions.

BSCMAKE

The BSCMAKE utility is used to build browse information files. If you are creating a project from the command-line tools, you might want to create a browse information file. BSCMAKE uses the options listed in Table 6.4.

TABLE 6.4. BSCMAKE OPTIONS.	
Option	Description
@<file>	Reads BSCMAKE options and arguments from file.
/Esi <file> i(<files>) r<symbol> r(<symbols>) l m...	Excludes from the Browser file these system files:
	i Named include file.
	i Named include file list in files.
	r Named symbol symbol.
	r Named symbol list symbols.
	l Local variables.
	m Macro expanded symbols.
/Iu	Include:
	u Unreferenced symbols.
/S <file>	The file file is simple. Process it once, then exclude it.
/S (<files>)	The files files are simple. Process them once, then exclude them.
/o <file>	Specifies the output name.
/n	The no incremental mode, with full builds. All source Browser files (.SBR) will be preserved.
/v	Tells BSCMAKE to provide a detailed report of progress.
/nologo	Tells BSCMAKE not to display a startup logo or copyright notice.
/? or /help	Displays a quick list of options.

Generally, BSCMAKE won't be run from the command line. The output that BSCMAKE produces can be used only by Visual Workbench's Browse system.

DumpBin

The DumpBin utility runs from the DOS command line. To execute this command from the Visual Workbench, you must add it as a menu item under the Tools menu. The DumpBin utility enables you to obtain information about a binary (COFF, executable, or DLL) file. DumpBin supports the options listed in Table 6.5. Because DumpBin is a new utility to Visual C++ 2.0, all its options are new as well.

TABLE 6.5. DumpBin options.	
Option	Description
/ALL	Displays all information available (with the exception of disassembly).
/ARCHIVEMEMBERS	Displays information about member objects in a library.
/DISASM	Provides a disassembly listing (address, raw bytes, disassembly) of the code sections.
/EXPORTS	Displays all exported objects.
/FPO	Displays all the frame pointer optimization records.
/HEADERS	Displays the file and section header records.
/IMPORTS	Displays all imported objects.
/LINENUMBERS	Displays the line numbers contained in a COFF format file. The file must have been compiled with the line numbers option.

Option	Description
/LINKERMEMBER[:{1 ¦ 2}]	Displays the public symbols. If the option is 1, they are displayed in object order with offsets. If the option is 2, they are displayed in alphabetical order. Specify no option to get both listing types.
/OUT:*filename*	Specifies the output filename.
/RAWDATA[:{NONE ¦ BYTES ¦ SHORTS ¦ LONGS}[,*n*]]	Specifies the formatting of the raw data for each section. The format includes the following:

NONE	Displays no raw data.
BYTES	Displays as bytes with ASCII-translated characters.
SHORTS	Displays as hex WORDs.
LONGS	Displays as hex DWORDs.
n	Specifies the width of the lines.

Option	Description
/RELOCATIONS	Displays information about relocations.
/SECTION:*name*	Reports only on the specified section.
/SUMMARY	Displays summary information about the sections.
/SYMBOLS	Displays the COFF symbol table.

DumpBin provides one of the first disassemblers that will work on protected-mode executable programs. It also provides the information that EXEHDR provided, and more.

EditBin

The EditBin utility runs from the DOS command line. To execute this command from the Visual Workbench, you must add it as a menu item under the Tools menu. The EditBin utility allows you to modify binary (COFF, executable, or DLL) files and to convert a file in the OMF (object module format) to COFF format. EditBin supports the options listed in Table 6.6. Because EditBin is a new utility to Visual C++ 2.0, all its options are new as well.

TABLE 6.6. EditBin options.	
Option	*Description*
`/BIND[:PATH=path]`	Sets the executable file's or DLL's entry point into the import address table.
`/HEAP:reserve[,commit]`	A command-line option that sets the heap size. The default size is 1,048,576 (1 MB).
`/NOLOGO`	Tells EditBin not to display a startup logo or copyright notice.
`/REBASE[:[BASE=address][,BASEFILE]` `[, DOWN]]`	Modifies the base address for a DLL or executable file. The default base is 0x400000. The **BASEFILE** option creates a text file (COFFBASE.TXT) that has the correct format for Link's **/BASE** option. The **DOWN** option sets the addresses down from the **BASE** address specified.
`/RELEASE`	Used to set the output file's checksum. Device drivers are required to have a valid checksum, and it's recommended that all files include checksum information.

Option	Description
`/SECTION:name[=newname][,[[!]` `{cdeikomprsuw}][a{1248ptsx}]]`	Sets the attribute specified in the **name** section (which can be renamed to **newname**). To unset an attribute, prefix the attribute with an exclamation point (!). Attributes include the following: **c** Code. **d** Discardable. **e** Executable. **i** Initialized data. **k** Cached virtual memory. **m** Link remove. **o** Link info. **p** Paged virtual memory. **r** Read. **s** Shared. **u** Uninitialized data. **w** Write. Alignment can be specified as **an** where **n** is: **1** On byte boundaries. **2** On even 16-bit boundaries. **4** On even 32-bit boundaries. **8** On even 64-bit boundaries. **p** On even 128-bit boundaries. **t** On even 256-bit boundaries. **b** On even 512-bit boundaries. **x** Alignment isn't specified.
`/STACK:reserve[,commit]`	A command-line option that sets the stack size. The default size is 1,048,576 (1 MB).

The EditBin utility allows the skilled programmer to make modifications to an existing binary file. If you're unsure of the effects of changing an attribute for an existing binary file (better yet, even if you're sure of the effects), make a backup of the file first. Save the backup until you're sure that your change hasn't introduced an undesirable side effect.

NMAKE

The NMake utility is a make-type utility that can be used to build projects directly. Even project files that have been created for Visual Workbench can be used with NMake. To build (recompile only the changed modules), issue this command:

```
NMAKE /F name.mak
```

To rebuild (recompile all modules), issue this command:

```
NMAKE /A name.mak
```

In both of these examples, *name.mak* is a placeholder for the name of your Visual C++ project file.

NMake supports the options listed in Table 6.7. NMake hasn't changed substantially since the introduction of Visual C++ 2.0.

TABLE 6.7. NMAKE OPTIONS.

Option	Description
/A	Tells NMake to build all objects in the project.
/B	Tells NMake to build the objects if the time stamps are equal.
/C	Tells NMake not to display output messages.
/D	Tells NMake to display build information, such as timestamps, from each object.
/E	Tells NMake to ignore the environment variables.
/? or /HELP	Displays a quick list of options.
/I	Normally, NMake exits when a command returns an error return code. This option tells NMake to continue, ignoring error exit codes from commands.

Option	Description
/K	Like /I, tells NMake to ignore error return codes. However, rebuilding continues with the next unrelated section.
/N	Tells NMake to process the makefile, but not to actually execute the commands. Instead of being executed, each command is displayed on the **stdout** (terminal) device. Useful for debugging custom makefiles.
/NOLOGO	Doesn't display the sign-on banner and copyright message.
/P	Tells NMake to display information about macros, inference rules, targets, and .SUFFIXES lists.
/Q	Tells NMake to check whether the project is up-to-date. If the project's target is up-to-date, NMake returns a zero return code. If the project's target is out-of-date, NMake returns a nonzero return code.
/R	Tells NMake to ignore predefined rules and macros.
/S	Tells NMake not to display the commands that are being executed.
/T	Updates the time stamps of each of the objects referenced in the makefile but doesn't rebuild them.
/X *filename*	Tells NMake to send output to the file specified by filename.

NMake provides an acceptable alternative to using Visual Workbench for project building. There's no reason to create an access to NMake in the Tools menu, because clicking on the Build or Re-Build All buttons will call NMake.

RESOURCE COMPILER

The Resource Compiler (RC) is a program that builds a program's resources into a format that the linker can use. As part of the link process, the linker includes the resources with the output module.

The resource compiler is usually called either automatically by the Visual Workbench or by a makefile. Most programmers have no need to directly interact with the resource compiler.

RC supports the options listed in Table 6.8.

TABLE 6.8. RC OPTIONS.	
Option	Description
-r	Tells RC to create a .RES compiled resource file.
-v	Tells RC to display progress messages.
-d	Defines a symbol for the resource file being compiled.
-fo	Renames an existing .RES file. (Don't use DOS's RENAME command.)
-l	Sets the default language ID. Specifies the value in hex.
-i	Sets an additional path for include file searches.
-x	Tells RC to ignore the INCLUDE environment variable.
-c	Sets the CodePage used by NLS (national language support) conversion. This option is new to Visual C++ 2.0's version of the resource compiler.

PVIEW

The PView utility is a Windows program that provides information about processes running under Windows NT.

With PView, you can examine and modify attributes of processes and threads. Spy++ can monitor these attributes but can't modify them.

PView can make changes to the system and its components that can halt Windows. Make sure you've saved all your files before you run PView and make changes.

A really long time ago, when I was running a mainframe computer at a university, we had a utility like PView. I killed the computer and everybody was really upset.

> If you kill a computer that others are using, immediately jump up and yell, "Who did that?"

PView has no command-line options or menu. Its user interface is a dialog box that has several buttons. These are described in Table 6.9.

TABLE 6.9. PVIEW'S BUTTONS.

Button	Function
Exit	Ends the PView session. The same functionality as Alt-F4.
Memory Details	Displays the Memory Details dialog box (the replacement for HeapWalk).
Kill Process	Ends the selected process. This option is dangerous because the application isn't notified that it's being killed.
Refresh	Tells PView to update the dialog boxes.
Connect	Displays information about the network computer in the Computer text box.

PView provides an interesting insight into Windows internals. By using PView with Spy++, you can access valuable information about processes and threads.

HELP COMPILER

The help compiler (HC30 and HC31) is a tool that developers use to create .HLP files. The input to the help compiler is a file created in RTF (rich text format) by a word processor that supports that format. The WordPad editor edits RTF files, and it could be used to create simple help files. However, more-complex help files may necessitate the use of a word processor such as Word for Windows.

WinDiff

WinDiff is a Windows-based utility that enables the programmer to view the differences between two files or two directories. This utility is similar to FC, but with a Windows interface.

Using WinDiff from the DOS prompt is easy, because it accepts its input from this command line:

```
WINDIFF path1 [path2] [-s [options] savefile]
```

In this example, *path1* is the path of the directory to compare files with, and *path2* is the directory to compare *path1* with. If *path2* isn't specified, the current directory is used. The *options* can be any of those in Table 6.10.

TABLE 6.10. WinDiff options.	
Option	Description
s	Compares files that exist in both paths.
l	Compares only files in the first path.
r	Compares only files in the second path.
d	Compares different files in both paths.

The *savefile* parameter specifies the name of a text file to which the results of the comparison are written.

One of the nice things that WinDiff does is comparing multiple files in a single pass. This means that you don't have to enter the compare command multiple times.

ZoomIn

The ZoomIn program is a utility that you can use to magnify part of the screen. This allows you to easily see individual pixels on-screen without digging in the drawer for a magnifying glass. This makes it easy to look at the details of things such as small toolbar buttons and other highly detailed objects on-screen.

Start ZoomIn and enlarge its window to about 20 percent of the screen's size. Then zoom into ZoomIn, making sure that the scroll bar is captured. Scroll, and you'll see that ZoomIn doesn't capture a static image; in fact, the image in ZoomIn's window is rather dynamic. Zooming into the clock utility is another interesting effect. Each time the scroll bar is updated (try simply holding the up button while it's at the top), watch the clock's image get updated in the ZoomIn window.

ZoomIn has three main menus: Edit, Options, and Help.

- Edit: The Edit menu allows you to copy the contents of ZoomIn's window to the clipboard and to force a refresh of the ZoomIn window's contents.
- Options: The Options menu displays one item, Refresh Rate. This menu selection allows you to select the rate of automatic refresh and to enable or disable automatic refresh.
- Help: The Help menu allows you to display the About box for ZoomIn.

This utility is useful when looking at icons and toolbar bitmaps to see detail in them.

THE DEBUGGING VERSION OF WINDOWS

The debugging version of Windows doesn't come with Visual C++ 2.0. However, it's a valuable tool that can be purchased separately from Windows. With most versions of Windows, you get the debugging version with the SDK that can be purchased separately from Windows. Windows comes in two flavors: the retail version, which all users get, and the debugging version, which applications developers get. To be able to fully test your applications, you need to install and use the debugging version of Windows. Part of the installation of the debugging version of Windows is to configure it after it's installed.

Because there are a number of different versions of Windows, it is beyond the scope of this book to describe the debugging versions of each. Please refer to the documentation that was provided with the SDK for information about installing the debugging version of windows.

> If you're testing on a machine other than the one you're debugging on, you'll need to install the debugging version of Windows on the machine that you're testing on.

MFC Trace Options

The MFC Trace Options program (TRACER.EXE) enables you to customize the MFC trace facility. These options are active from within the Visual Workbench and don't require that you install the debugging version of Windows.

The MFC Trace Options program's window is shown in Figure 6.2. This figure and Table 6.11 show the options available to the program. Except for Enable Tracing, all of the options shown in the figure modify the TraceFlags flag in AFX.INI, which is shown in Listing 6.1.

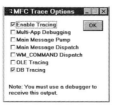

Figure 6.2. MFC trace options.

Table 6.11. MFC trace options.	
Option	*Description*
Enable Tracing	When checked, this option turns on the tracing process and allows tracing by setting the AFX.INI flag **TraceEnabled** = 1.
Multi-App Debugging	With this option, each trace message is prefaced with the name of the application. This option affects both TRACE macros used within your program and tracing resulting from the selection of the other options listed in this table.
Main Message Pump	Generates a trace message for each Windows message that is received in **CWinApp**'s message handling functions. The output includes the window handle, the message name or number, and the message's parameters. This report is

Option	Description
	made after the `GetMessage()` call but before any translation or dispatching is performed. Additionally, any DDE messages also display additional data that is relevant to debugging. This flag reports on messages posted but not dispatched.
Main Message Dispatch	Works like Main Message Pump but causes the reporting of messages that have been posted and messages that have been sent and are about to be dispatched.
WM_COMMAND Dispatch	This option is used for extended WM_COMMAND (OnCommand) message handling. Reports the progress of the message, which class receives the command (based on the message map table), and the location of classes that won't receive the message (those in which the message map table doesn't specify this message). Microsoft recommends this option as being "especially useful to track the flow of command messages in multiple document interface (MDI) applications."
OLE Tracing	Traces significant OLE notifications or requests. Use this option to trace an OLE client or server's communications between the OLE DLLs and the OLE application.
DB Tracing	Reports significant ODBC events. Turn this option on for an ODBC application when you need to monitor ODBC events. Visual C++ documentation for this option isn't thorough. If you're debugging an ODBC application, enable this option and examine the output. This option is separate from the tracing that the ODBC driver performs.

All of these options are saved in the file AFX.INI, found in the WINDOWS directory. This file is shown in Listing 6.1. AFX.INI currently consists of three lines of code and a few comment lines, but more items might be added to the file in later releases of Visual C++.

Listing 6.1. AFX.INI (from Visual C++).

```
; Copy this file to your Windows directory in order to modify
; the default behavior of diagnostic messages.

; By default, messages are ignored. You can use CodeView to set
; the variable afxTraceEnabled to TRUE to observe TRACE output
; or you can change TraceEnabled in the [Diagnostics] section of
; this file to 1. You must have a dumb debug terminal or run
; CodeView to see TRACE output. If you do not have one of
; those and you set TraceEnabled to 1, you will see the Windows
; MessageBox "Cannot Write to AUX."

; See the Technical Note TN007 for more information on the TraceFlags.

; This is a part of the Microsoft Foundation Classes C++ library.
; Copyright (c) 1992 Microsoft Corporation
; All rights reserved.
;
; This source code is intended only as a supplement to the
; Microsoft Foundation Classes Reference and Microsoft
; QuickHelp and/or WinHelp documentation provided with the library.
; See these sources for detailed information regarding the
; Microsoft Foundation Classes product.


[Diagnostics]
TraceEnabled = 1
TraceFlags = 0
```

If you don't have AFX.INI in your WINDOWS directory, you can copy the file from your \MSVC20\MFC\SRC directory to your WINDOWS directory.

Shed: The Segmented Hypergraphics Hotspot Editor

The Hotspot editor is used to create hypergraphics in any Windows metafile or bitmap image. You load the bitmap into the Hotspot editor, mark your hotspots, and save the bitmap in the hypergraphic format. This format saves both the image and the hotspots that you've defined.

Examples of when to use hotspots include defining hotspots that link parts of a graphic image to other help topics and graphics, executing a help macro, or linking to multimedia objects (assuming that you can provide support for these multimedia events with an external DLL file).

To add a graphic that has hotspots defined, you must include it by reference, using the bmc, bml, or bmr formats. These formats are described in Chapter 10, "Adding Graphics," in the *Windows Help Authoring Guide*.

Figure 6.3 shows the main window of Hotspot in action. I've loaded a simple bitmap and created a hotspot (called "Hotspot 1"). This hotspot is the box with "Quick C for Windows (16-bit)" in it. When this file is saved, it's saved with the extension of .SHG.

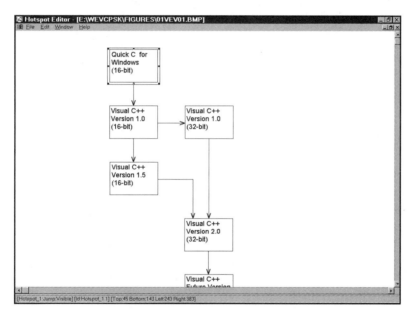

Figure 6.3. Hotspot editor in action.

If you're still writing Windows 3.0 applications, the Hotspot editor won't work. Windows 3.0 programmers must create hypergraphic links without using Hotspot. This procedure is detailed in the *Windows Help Authoring Guide*. The basic procedure is to create a number of smaller bitmaps, one for each hotspot. You then tile these bitmaps to form the overall image. This process isn't efficient, because the WinHelp program must load and position a number of different bitmaps (requiring numerous disk accesses) rather than one single, large bitmap.

Help Files

Visual C++ 2.0 has a number of useful help files. One of the most important is Books OnLine. Books OnLine is a very large help file that remains on the CD, so to use it you must have the Visual C++ 2.0 CD in the drive. The user can elect to have the other help files copied to the hard drive during the installation procedure. If you find that a help file hasn't been copied to the \MSVC20\HELP directory, and you can't have the MSVC20 CD in the CD-ROM drive, you can copy the help file to the \MSVC20\HELP directory yourself. One of the benefits of copying the help files to the \MSVC20\HELP directory is that, generally speaking, your hard drive has a much faster access time than the CD-ROM drive.

Books OnLine has a Contents window that allows you to navigate through the various sections covered. Generally, pressing F1 for help inside the Visual Workbench brings up the Visual C++ Help system. You can then switch to Books OnLine either by pressing the Books OnLine button or by selecting the Books OnLine icon in the Visual C++ 2.0 group. All topics covered in Visual C++ 2.0 Help are also covered in Books OnLine. Often, a Visual C++ 2.0 Help file is a subset of the Books OnLine documentation.

For your convenience, in some instances help files are loaded automatically by the Visual Workbench when you press the F1 (help) key. An example of automatic loading is when an error message is displayed in the Output window. All error messages are a single line long, and often the error message's text doesn't really explain what's wrong. Placing the cursor on the error message and pressing F1 brings up the help on errors. WinHelp displays additional information about the particular error, possible conditions that cause the error to occur, and suggested corrective actions.

Books OnLine covers the following topics:

- User's Guide

    Introducing Visual C++: Describes how to install Visual C++, introduces the product to the customer, and provides tutorials on using Visual C++ and the MFC library.

    Visual C++ User's Guide: Describes the features of Visual C++ and all its tools.

    Help Compiler User's Guide: Describes how to create application help files.

- MFC

  Programming with MFC: Provides procedural and conceptual information about the MFC Library.

  Class Library Reference: Provides a complete description of the MFC library.

  MFC Samples: Provides source code samples for the Microsoft Foundation Class Library.

  MFC Technotes: Supplies technical notes that reflect requests for information from users, as well as specialized information that the MFC developers anticipate advanced users will want.

- C/C++

  Programming Techniques: Introduces programming techniques for new features and discusses migrating from other platforms and compilers.

  C Language Reference: Describes the Microsoft implementation of C.

  C++ Language Reference: Describes the Microsoft implementation of C++.

  Run-Time Library Reference: Describes the Visual C++ runtime library.

  iostream Reference: Describes the iostream class library.

  Preprocessor Reference: Describes the C/C++ preprocessor.

  C/C++ Samples: Provides programming samples.

- Win32 SDK

  API 32 Functions: Describes the 32-bit Windows API functions.

  Open GL Functions: Describes the Open GL functions, which are used to render two- and three-dimensional objects.

  Win32s Programmer's Reference: Describes the Win32s API.

  Windows Sockets: Describes sockets as supported by Microsoft Windows.

- OLE 2 SDK

  OLE 2 Programmer's Reference, Volume 1.

  OLE 2 Automation Programmer's Reference, Volume 2.

- ODBC SDK

  Part 1 Introduction to ODBC: Describes ODBC.

  Part 2 Developing Guidelines: Describes the guidelines for developing ODBC applications.

  Part 3 Developing Drivers: Describes the process of developing ODBC drivers.

  Part 4 Installing and Configuring ODBC Software: Describes the process of installing and configuring ODBC.

  Part 5 API Reference: Describes the ODBC API.

  Part 6 Appendixes: Describes error codes, state tables, SQL grammar, data types, embedded SQL and ODBC differences, scalar functions, and the ODBC Cursor Library.

- Extensions: 68K Porting

  68K Porting Getting Started: Covers setup and installation of Visual C++ Cross-Development Edition for Macintosh.

  68K Porting Programmer's Guide: Includes overview, porting procedures, and reference information for the tools for the Cross-Development Edition.

  68K Porting Reference: Describes functions and portability issues.

- Extensions: Articles

  Technical Articles: Contains a nubmer of useful articles about topics of interest to the Visual C++ 2.0 programmer.

  CompuServe Corner: Contains articles about using CompuServe to get technical assistance.

Table 6.12 describes the topics that the Visual C++ 2.0 Help system covers.

TABLE 6.12. THE VISUAL C++ 2.0 HELP SYSTEM.	
Topic	*Section*
Visual C++ tools	Visual C++
Module-definition file statements	Miscellaneous Tools
Resource-file statements	Miscellaneous Tools
Build errors	Build Errors

Topic	Section
C/C++ language	Language
Microsoft foundation classes	Foundation Classes
C/C++ runtime library	Run-Time Routines
iostream class library	iostream Classes
OLE 2.0 classes	Foundation Classes
Database classes	Foundation Classes
Win32 API	Windows API
OLE 2.0 API	OLE API
ODBC API	ODBC API
68K porting issues	68K Porting Reference

If you experience difficulty finding information about a topic when using Visual C++ 2.0 help, you should try the Books OnLine files.

Visual C++ 2.0 also includes a number of other help files that cover a variety of topics. Table 6.13 lists the other help files.

TABLE 6.13. OTHER HELP FILES IN VISUAL C++ 2.0.

File	Description
SPYXX.HLP	Provides help on the Spy++ utility.
WIN32KB.HLP	Presents a selection of Windows NT Knowledge Base articles.
PSS.HLP	Provides information on how to obtain support for Microsoft products.
WINSOCK.HLP	Provides information about Windows Sockets.
UNIPAD.HLP	Provides information about the Windows NT Unipad editor. Windows 95 users should use the WinPad help supplied with Windows 95.
SHED.HLP	Provides information about the WinHelp Hotspot editor.

Generally, although the number of help files shipped with Visual C++ has decreased, the coverage has actually been enhanced. The rearrangement of the help files, along with the provision of a single access method for these files, has improved Visual C++ 2.0's help facilities substantially.

Summary

This chapter covered the various utilities and tools that are supplied with Visual C++. Most of these tools can be called from icons in the Microsoft Visual C program group found in Program Manager.

Many of the help files can be accessed from the icons in Program Manager's Microsoft Visual C program group. Help files that are directly related to programming can be accessed from Visual C++'s Visual Workbench.

Topics covered in this chapter include the following:

- Spy++, a utility to spy on processes, threads, and windows.
- CL, the command-line compiler.
- Link, the 32-bit incremental linker.
- Profiler, a utility to profile an application.
- Lib, the static object library management tool.
- BSCMAKE, a utility to create and maintain Browser files.
- DumpBin, a utility to dump binary (COFF, executable, and DLL) files.
- EditBin, a utility to modify the attributes of a binary file.
- NMake, a makefile utility.
- RC, the resource compiler.
- DDESpy, a utility to spy on DDE transactions.
- PView, a utility to view (and modify) attributes for a process or thread.
- ZoomIn, a utility to enlarge a portion of the screen.
- WinDiff, a utility to determine the differences between two directories or files.
- HC, the help compiler utility.
- AFX Trace Options, a utility to set the options for the AFX trace facility.
- Shed, a utility to set hypergraphic hot spots.

- The Windows debugging version. (Comes with the SDK and not with Visual C++ 2.0.)
- The Visual C++ 2.0 help system, which consists of two major parts, the Visual C++ 2.0 Help system and the Books OnLine system. A number of smaller, specialized help files also are available.

P A R T

II

PROGRAMMING
FOR WINDOWS

USING UNICODE

One major problem with creating applications that are offered to a broad-based international market has been the issue of supporting the language of the target country. For countries that use characters based on the Romantic languages, the character sets that people who speak English have been using are adequate. English, the most common Romantic language, uses a simple character set of 26 letters. Five or six are vowels, and the remainder are consonants. Additional characters (numbers, punctuation marks, and other symbols) bring the total number of characters to about 200. Because the Romantic languages have few letters, it has been possible to represent these letters and other characters using an 8-bit-wide value, giving a total of 256 possible characters. The standardization of these character sets is set out in what is usually referred to as the ANSI (American National Standards Institute) character set. The first 128 characters are basic characters used by all Romantic languages. The second 128 characters usually include special characters that aren't necessarily used in all the languages, along with a number of special characters that are used for special purposes.

A Romantic language: Sounds something like a quiet table in a restaurant, soft music, and someone you care about. But the truth is that a Romantic language is based on Latin, the original language of Rome. Romantic languages are centered around Europe and areas that were conquered or settled by Europeans (such as North and South America). Some examples of Romantic languages are English, French, Spanish, Dutch, German, and Italian. All of these languages use very similar character sets. The major difference is that some of the languages have few additional characters.

Although most people understand at least one Romantic language, the real hitch comes when you consider the rest of the world. Believe it or not, English is the most commonly used language in India. The many different dialects necessitate the use of English for business transactions. You could get along quite easily in Malaysia, where the people speak excellent English. On the other hand, just to the North of Malaysia in Thailand, it would be difficult to find anyone outside the city who can (or will) speak English. Further complicating matters, the Thai language is based on a character set that people who know only English find very difficult to read.

Traveling throughout East Asia, you find many different and unusual languages. The Chinese, Japanese, and Korean languages use Chinese ideographs, which include about 20,000 characters—quite literally a character for each word! There is no way to fit those 20,000 characters into the standard 256 spaces found in the 8-bit character format of the ANSI character set.

The SBCS Character Set

The term *SBCS* (Single-Byte Character Set) refers to the ANSI character set, which is used by Windows 3.x and earlier. Windows 95 also uses the ANSI character set (and not Unicode). If you're creating applications that are only for Windows 95, then much of the material in this chapter will be of little value to you. Only Windows NT, and versions of Windows that are derived from Windows NT, support Unicode.

Figure 7.1 shows the first 128 characters of the ANSI character set, and Figure 7.2 shows the final 128 characters. The characters in these figures are shown in the Arial font that is supplied with Windows 3.1 and later. In Figure 7.1, I've annotated the first 32 characters with their *control-code* equivalents. These have no characters assigned to them in either the ANSI or Unicode character sets.

	0	1	2	3	4	5	6	7	8	9	A	B	C	D	E	F
0	nul	soh	stx	etx	edt	enq	ack	bel	bs	ht	lf	vt	ff	cr	so	si
1	dle	dc1	dc2	dc3	dc4	nak	syn	etb	can	em	sub	esc	fs	gs	rs	us
2		!	"	#	$	%	&	'	(	)	*	+	,	-	.	/
3	0	1	2	3	4	5	6	7	8	9	:	;	<	=	>	?
4	@	A	B	C	D	E	F	G	H	I	J	K	L	M	N	P
5	P	Q	R	S	T	U	V	W	X	Y	Z	[	\	]	^	_
6	`	a	b	c	d	e	f	g	h	I	j	k	l	m	n	o
7	p	q	r	s	t	u	v	w	x	y	z	{	|	}	~	del

Figure 7.1. The first 128 characters in the ANSI character set.

	0	1	2	3	4	5	6	7	8	9	A	B	C	D	E	F
8	□	□	‚	ƒ	„	…	†	‡	^	‰	Š	‹	Œ	□	□	□
9	□	‘	’	"	"	•	–	—	~	™	š	›	œ	□	□	Ÿ
A		¡	¢	£	¤	¥	¦	§	¨	©	ª	«	¬	-	®	¯
B	°	±	²	³	´	µ	¶	·	¸	¹	º	»	¼	½	¾	¿
C	À	Á	Â	Ã	Ä	Å	Æ	Ç	È	É	Ê	Ë	Ì	Í	Î	Ï
D	Ð	Ñ	Ò	Ó	Ô	Õ	Ö	×	Ø	Ù	Ú	Û	Ü	Ý	Þ	ß
E	à	á	â	ã	ä	å	æ	ç	è	é	ê	ë	ì	í	î	ï
F	ð	ñ	ò	ó	ô	õ	ö	÷	ø	ù	ú	û	ü	ý	þ	ÿ

Figure 7.2. The last 128 characters in the ANSI character set.

In Figure 7.1, the characters shown with a two- or three-character code (such as NUL) are control codes. Officially, no characters are assigned to these 32 positions, but the IBM PC character set actually defines characters for them. Using the first 32 characters is difficult, and therefore most programmers don't take advantage of them.

The ANSI character set is derived from the ASCII (American Standard Code for Information Interchange) standard.

THE DBCS CHARACTER SET

The *DBCS* (Double-Byte Character Set) is an attempt to solve the problem of having too many characters without a large-enough address space for those characters. Unlike Unicode, DBCS doesn't replace the conventional character set, but extends it. The extension is done by examining a given character's value. If it's one of the DBCS extension values, the function **IsDBCSLeadByte()** returns **TRUE**.

Unlike Unicode, DBCS isn't easy to implement. Generally, to implement DBCS, you must modify your application. These changes might be extensive. When you do finally convert the application to run solely under Unicode, many of the changes made for DBCS must be removed or modified.

DBCS has been used in the Japanese versions of Windows. Applications that will support Windows 3.x (or Windows 95) with Japanese character sets should consider the use of DBCS, because Unicode is available only under Windows NT.

Because DBCS isn't a new feature of Visual C++ 2.0, it isn't covered in this book.

THE UNICODE CHARACTER SET

The Unicode character set is an extension to Windows that was added to Windows NT. It's truly unfortunate that Windows 95 doesn't offer support for Unicode; however, at this time Unicode is available only to Windows NT users.

First, let's take a look at how Unicode came to be. The first standardization of character sets was a code called ASCII. ASCII offered standardization for 128 characters (ASCII is a 7-bit code). ASCII was (and still is) widely used for many minicomputers and virtually all microcomputers. Very few microcomputers used EBCDIC (developed by IBM for its mini and mainframe computers) or other specialized character sets. The IBM PC used the ASCII character set, but then extended it, adding a second block of 128 characters that included line drawing and a number of common characters used in other Romantic languages. These common characters are often referred to as the international characters.

Derived from the ASCII character set was the ANSI character set, a set of 256 characters. The first 128 characters are the ASCII characters, and the second

128 are mostly international characters, including a few special symbols (such as the copyright symbol).

In the international market, a number of other standards were developed. These include the following:

- ISO-8859-1: A character set often called the Latin character set. The Unicode character set uses the ISO-8859-1 character set for the first 256 characters.
- ISCII: The Indian Standard Code for Information Interchange. The Indian equivalent of ASCII.
- GB-2312: The Chinese standard for characters.
- JIS-X-0208 and JIS-X-0212: The Japanese Industrial Standard character sets.
- CNS 11643: The character set standard for Taiwan.

A number of other standards were used in the development of Unicode.

Unicode is made up of a large block of more than 65,000 characters. The first 256 typically are those found in the ANSI character set for Windows, but there are some minor differences. Figure 7.3 shows the first 256 characters under Unicode.

Notice that the first 128 characters in Figure 7.3 (except for the control codes— the first 32 characters) are identical to the characters shown in Figure 7.1. Of the final 128 characters in Figure 7.3, the first 32 aren't defined and therefore aren't identical to those shown in Figure 7.2.

Figure 7.4 shows the layout of the Unicode character set. It shows all the major parts, and some of the major sizes and starting locations are noted. Notice that the Unicode character set is divided into four separate blocks called *zones*. The zones are as follows:

- A-Zone: Alphabets, syllabaries, and symbols
- I-Zone: Ideographs (Chinese, Japanese, and Korean)
- O-Zone: Reserved for future assignments
- R-Zone: Restricted-use zone

The A-Zone is divided into three major parts:

- General character sets
- Symbol character sets
- Chinese, Japanese, and Korean auxiliary

	0	1	2	3	4	5	6	7	8	9	A	B	C	D	E	F
0	☐	☐	☐	☐	☐	☐	☐	☐	☐	☐	☐	☐	☐	☐	☐	☐
1	☐	☐	☐	☐	☐	☐	☐	☐	☐	☐	☐	☐	☐	☐	☐	☐
2		!	"	#	$	%	&	'	(	)	*	+	,	-	.	/
3	0	1	2	3	4	5	6	7	8	9	:	;	<	=	>	?
4	@	A	B	C	D	E	F	G	H	I	J	K	L	M	N	P
5	P	Q	R	S	T	U	V	W	X	Y	Z	[	\	]	^	_
6	`	a	b	c	d	e	f	g	h	I	j	k	l	m	n	o
7	p	q	r	s	t	u	v	w	x	y	z	{	|	}	~	☐
8	☐	☐	☐	☐	☐	☐	☐	☐	☐	☐	☐	☐	☐	☐	☐	☐
9	☐	☐	☐	☐	☐	☐	☐	☐	☐	☐	☐	☐	☐	☐	☐	☐
A		¡	¢	£	¤	¥	¦	§	¨	©	ª	«	¬	-	®	¯
B	°	±	²	³	´	µ	¶	·	¸	¹	º	»	¼	½	¾	¿
C	À	Á	Â	Ã	Ä	Å	Æ	Ç	È	É	Ê	Ë	Ì	Í	Î	Ï
D	Ð	Ñ	Ò	Ó	Ô	Õ	Ö	×	Ø	Ù	Ú	Û	Ü	Ý	Þ	ß
E	à	á	â	ã	ä	å	æ	ç	è	é	ê	ë	ì	í	î	ï
F	ð	ñ	ò	ó	ô	õ	ö	÷	ø	ù	ú	û	ü	ý	þ	ÿ

Figure 7.3. The first 256 characters in the Unicode character set.

The I-Zone holds the CJK ideographs. These are the actual characters that make up the languages. Note that these characters aren't subdivided into separate parts, but are simply treated as a single block.

The O-Zone is a block of 16,384 bytes that are reserved for future use.

The R-Zone is a block that holds three major parts:

- Private Usage: The use of these characters isn't defined by the standard, except that the corporate area is defined as starting at 0xF8FF and grows down, and the end-user area begins at 0xE000 and grows upward.

- Compatibility: The compatibility section includes presentation formats.

- Special Purpose: A set of 14 characters. The positions 0xFFFE and 0xFFFF aren't defined.

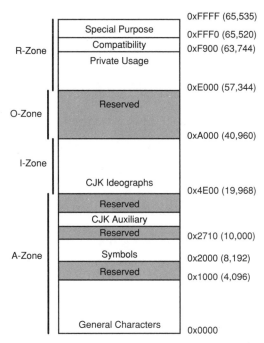

Figure 7.4. The Unicode map.

Figure 7.4 shows the allocation of characters in Unicode. This allocation is covered in the Unicode Standard version 1.1, available from the Unicode Consortium.

Table 7.1 shows a detailed breakdown of the zones and languages that are currently part of the Unicode Standard 1.1. (Where there are several listings for a specific language, a - A or - B sometimes follows the name. The - A and - B are used to distinguish between the different sections.)

	TABLE 7.1. LANGUAGES AND ZONES IN UNICODE STANDARD 1.1.			
From	*To*	*Length*	*Zone*	*Description*
0x0000	0x001F	0x001F	A	Special use (control character mapping)
0x0020	0x007E	0x005E	A	Basic Latin
0x007E	0x007F	0x0001	A	Delete character mapping

continues

From	To	Length	Zone	Description
0x0080	0x009F	0x001F	A	Special use (control character mapping)
0x00a0	0x00FF	0x005F	A	Latin-1 supplement
0x0100	0x017F	0x007F	A	Latin extended - A
0x0180	0x024F	0x00CF	A	Latin extended - B
0x0250	0x02AF	0x005F	A	IPA extensions
0x02B0	0x02B1	0x0002	A	Unknown use
0x02B2	0x02FF	0x004D	A	Spacing modifier letters
0x0300	0x036F	0x006F	A	Combining diacritical marks
0x0370	0x03CF	0x005F	A	Basic Greek
0x03D0	0x03FF	0x002F	A	Greek symbols and Coptic
0x0400	0x04FF	0x00FF	A	Cyrillic
0x0500	0x052F	0x002F	A	Unknown use
0x0530	0x058F	0x005F	A	Armenian
0x0590	0x05CF	0x003F	A	Hebrew extended - A
0x05D0	0x05EA	0x001A	A	Basic Hebrew
0x05EB	0x05FF	0x0014	A	Hebrew extended - B
0x0600	0x0652	0x0052	A	Basic Arabic
0x0653	0x06FF	0x00AC	A	Arabic extended
0x0900	0x097F	0x007F	A	Devanagari
0x0980	0x09FF	0x007F	A	Bengali
0x0A00	0x0A7F	0x007F	A	Gurmukhi
0x0A80	0x0AFF	0x007F	A	Gujarati
0x0B00	0x0B7F	0x007F	A	Oriya
0x0B80	0x0BFF	0x007F	A	Tamil
0x0C00	0x0C7F	0x007F	A	Telugu
0x0C80	0x0CFF	0x007F	A	Kannada
0x0D00	0x0D7F	0x007F	A	Malayalam
0x0D80	0x0DFF	0x007F	A	Unused area

Table 7.1. continued

From	To	Length	Zone	Description
0x0E00	0x0E7F	0x007F	A	Thai
0x0E80	0x0EFF	0x007F	A	Lao
0x0F00	0x1000	0x0100	A	Unused area
0x1000	0x109F	0x00CF ·	A	Reserved area
0x10A0	0x10CF	0x002F	A	Georgian extended
0x10D0	0x10FF	0x002F	A	Basic Georgian
0x1100	0x11FF	0x00FF	A	Hanguljamo
0x1E00	0x1EFF	0x00FF	A	Latin extended additional
0x1F00	0x1FFF	0x00FF	A	Greek extended
0x2000	0x206F	0x006F	A	Genera punctuation
0x2070	0x209F	0x002F	A	Superscripts and subscripts
0x20A0	0x20CF	0x002F	A	Currency symbols
0x20D0	0x20FF	0x002F	A	Combining diacritical marks for symbols
0x2100	0x214F	0x004F	A	Letter-like symbols
0x2150	0x218F	0x003F	A	Number forms
0x2190	0x21FF	0x006F	A	Arrows
0x2200	0x22FF	0x00FF	A	Mathematical operators
0x2300	0x23FF	0x00FF	A	Miscellaneous technical
0x2400	0x243F	0x003F	A	Control pictures
0x2440	0x245F	0x001F	A	Optical character recognition
0x2460	0x24FF	0x009F	A	Enclosed alphanumerics
0x2500	0x257F	0x007F	A	Box drawing
0x2580	0x259F	0x001F	A	Block elements
0x25A0	0x25FF	0x005F	A	Geometric shapes
0x2600	0x26FF	0x00FF	A	Miscellaneous symbols
0x2700	0x27BF	0x00BF	A	Dingbats
0x27C0	0x27FF	0x003F	A	Unused area
0x3000	0x303F	0x003F	A	CJK symbols and punctuation
0x3040	0x309F	0x005F	A	Hiragana
0x30A0	0x30FF	0x005F	A	Katakana

continues

		TABLE 7.1. CONTINUED		
From	*To*	*Length*	*Zone*	*Description*
0x3100	0x312F	0x002F	A	Bopomofo
0x3130	0x318F	0x005F	A	Hangul compatibility Jamo
0x3190	0x319F	0x000F	A	CJK miscellaneous
0x319A0	0x31FF	0x005F	A	CJK miscellaneous
0x3200	0x32FF	0x00FF	A	Enclosed CJK letters and months
0x3300	0x33FF	0x00FF	A	CJK compatibility
0x3400	0x3D2D	0x092D	A	Hangul
0x3D2E	0x44B7	0x0789	A	Hangul supplementary - A
0x44B8	0x4DFF	0x0947	A	Hangul supplementary - B
0x4E00	0x9FFF	0x51FF	I	CJK unified ideographs
0xA000	0xDFFF	0x3FFF	O	Reserved area
0xE000	0xF8FF	0x18FF	R	Private use area
0xF900	0xFAFF	0x01FF	R	CJK compatibility ideographs
0xFB00	0xFB4F	0x004F	R	Alphabetic presentation forms
0xFB50	0xFDFF	0x02AF	R	Arabic presentation forms - A
0xFE00	0xFE1F	0x001F	R	Unused area
0xFE20	0xFE2F	0x000F	R	Combining half marks
0xFE30	0xFE4F	0x001F	R	CJK compatibility forms
0xFE50	0xFE6F	0x001F	R	Small form variants
0xFE70	0xFEFE	0x008E	R	Arabic presentation forms - B
0xFF00	0xFFEF	0x00EF	R	Half-width and full-width forms
0xFFF0	0xFFFD	0x000D	R	Specials (Note: 0xFFFE and 0xFFFF are undefined)

As Table 7.1 shows, the Unicode standard has a large number of areas (both languages and zones). These areas are from the Unicode Standard 1.1 and other sources. Areas for which I was unable to determine the usage are described as "unused." Note that this table differs somewhat from the information shown in Figure 7.4. This figure's information (also from the Unicode standard) was derived from the text of the standard, while the information contained in Table 7.1 is from a table found in the standard.

Including Unicode Support in Your Applications

You must make some minor (thank goodness) changes to your applications so that they will support Unicode. First, remember that all good Windows programmers make sure that their character strings are part of their resources, and never code strings as constants in their applications. You might have wondered whether the practice of including all character strings in the program's resources was worth the effort. Well, now you know. When implementing multi-language support, having your strings in a single place definitely makes your job as programmer easier.

What steps are necessary to make your application Unicode-compatible? You need to perform a series of four steps. I have assumed that the application exists and is being converted to Unicode.

1. Include a definition for the symbol **_UNICODE**. Use Visual C++ 2.0's Visual Workbench compiler options (choose Project | Settings and then choose the C/C++ tab). In Category General is an edit box for Preprocessor Definitions. Add **_UNICODE** to this list and remove **_MBCS** (which tells Visual C++ to use MBCS—Multi-Byte Character Set) if **_MBCS** is defined, because it's incompatible with Unicode.

2. Include the Unicode entry point in Visual C++ 2.0's Visual Workbench compiler options (choose Project | Settings and then choose the Link tab). In Category Output is the Entry-Point Symbol edit box. Change this symbol (it should be blank) to **wWinMainCRTStartup**.

3. Use the portable functions and types that support Unicode. The **_TCHAR** macros enable the programmer to specify a single call, and the macro maps that call to the correct function name. For example, **_tcscpy()** will be converted to **_wcscpy()** for Unicode, **_mbscpy()** for MBCS, or **strcpy()** for standard ANSI code.

   Also, when you have to define a character constant (see step 1), prefix the constant with either **_T** or **_TEXT**. These two identifiers (which are identical in function) will, if **_UNICODE** is defined, cause the compiler to create Unicode strings. The compiler interprets any string prefixed with an uppercase L as being a Unicode string. The **_T** or **_TEXT** macros evaluate to either L if **_UNICODE** is defined or to nothing if **_UNICODE** isn't defined.

4. Check your code to determine which functions are expecting a count of bytes in the buffer and which functions expect a count of characters. With Unicode, the number of bytes needed to hold a given string is not equal to the number of characters. Generally, functions that work with characters (such as the string functions) will want a count of characters. Functions that work with buffers or blocks of memory (such as allocation or I/O functions) will want a count of the number of bytes in the buffer.

An easy method to determine the number of bytes in a string, regardless of whether the string is Unicode or not, is to multiply the value returned by the length function (the CString.Length() function or the strlen() function) by the size of the constant **_TCHAR**. For example:

```
TextOut(hDC, szTitle, strlen(szTitle) * sizeof(_TCHAR));
```

In this example, the sizeof(**_TCHAR**) operator evaluates to zero if **_UNICODE** isn't defined.

Generally, following these four steps will enable you to create a Unicode-compatible program. Of course, as with any programming, experience also helps you find the subtle problems that always arise when you're dealing with a new technology.

SUMMARY

This chapter covered the use of Unicode to help develop applications that are more easily converted to languages other than English. Unicode is a character set that consists of more than 65,500 characters. Built into Unicode is support for English, the European Romantic languages (such as French, German, and Italian), and languages based on the Chinese ideographs (the various Chinese dialects, Japanese, and Korean).

At this time, Unicode doesn't offer support for the Indian languages (such as Hindu). However, Unicode does offer support for some of the Southeast Asian languages (such as Thai and Lao), which are derived in part from the Indian languages.

Topics covered in this chapter include the following:

- SBCS, or Single-Byte Character Set, the character format that most Windows programmers are familiar with.
- MBCS, or Multi-Byte Character Set, the original method to support languages that had too large a character set to use the SBCS method.
- Unicode, the new method to support multiple languages. The Unicode method allows the programmer to create a single source for multiple target languages.

MULTITHREADED PROGRAMMING

Both Windows 95 and Windows NT support multi-threaded program execution. Unfortunately, when writing applications for Win32s, you can't take advantage of the multithreaded features. The term *multithreaded* covers two slightly different methods of program execution:

- Threads: Threads share the same address space as their parent process. They also can share the parent process's resources such as global variables, open resources (such as files and pipes), and functions. The system can create a thread more quickly because a separate address space doesn't need to be created for each thread.

- Processes: Processes have an address space separate from their parent process. A process doesn't have access to the parent's resources. Issues of communicating with the parent process must be addressed, usually by using semaphores, pipes (and named pipes), and other shared resources.

Most programmers are familiar with the concept of single-threaded programs because most Windows applications are single-threaded. In a single-threaded program, only one point of execution takes place at any time. In reality, many Windows programs that are designed as single-threaded actually run as multithreaded applications. A program that updates the screen while the user is performing another task within the program (such as working with a dialog box) uses a form of multithreaded execution, because the draw routines are executing while another task is being performed.

This chapter looks at multithreaded programming and how Visual C++ 2.0 and MFC 3.0 support multithreaded processes.

MFC 3.0 AND MULTITHREADED PROGRAMS

MFC 3.0 offers the **AfxBeginThread()** function as the primary function for creating threads. This function enables you to create a thread in an application with a minimum of effort.

The MFC 3.0 class for multithreaded objects is the **CWinThread** class. It offers a number of functions to assist in the management of threads. The main functions that **CWinThread** offers are the **CreateThread()** function, which takes three parameters, and some helper functions such as **GetThreadPriority()**.

When using **AfxBeginThread()**, you must be careful to access the returned **CWinThread** pointer before the thread has completed. Once the thread has completed, the framework will delete the **CWinThread** object unless the **m_bAutoDelete** member is set to **FALSE**. If you want to create a thread with a persistent **CWinThread** class object, you must create the **CWinThread**, then call **CreateThread()** rather than use **AfxBeginThread()**. Never fear—the sample program shows both **AfxBeginThread()** and **CreateThread()**.

Next, let's look at the interface functions that are part of **CWinThread**.

CWinThread();

The **CWinThread()** function is the default constructor. This constructor doesn't set the thread procedure or passed parameter values. When you create your own **CWinThread**-based object, this is the constructor that you will normally use. You can set both the thread procedure and the passed parameter values directly, should you need to do so.

CWinThread(AFX_THREADPROC pfnThreadProc, LPVOID pParam);

The **CWinThread(AFX_THREADPROC** *pfnThreadProc*, **LPVOID** *pParam*) function is the constructor called when **AfxBeginThread()** is called.

There is nothing to prevent you from using this constructor when you create your **CWinThread**-based object. This version of the constructor allows you to set both the thread procedure and the passed parameter value.

void* m_pThreadParams;

The **m_pThreadParams** member variable contains the 32-bit value that will be passed to your thread procedure. The data placed in this member variable is fully application-specific. It could be a pointer, integer value, or any other data.

The **m_pThreadParams** member is valid after construction, and it should be initialized (either by the constructor or by direct manipulation) prior to starting the thread.

AFX_THREADPROC m_pfnThreadProc;

The **m_pfnThreadProc()** member function is a pointer to the function that will launch the thread. This function has the following prototype:

```
UINT ThreadProc(LPVOID pParam);
```

where *ThreadProc* is the name of the function and *pParam* is the passed parameter (from **m_pThreadParams** or **AfxBeginThread()**).

void CommonConstruct();

The **CommonConstruct()** member function is called from both constructors. Its function is to hold a group of initializers that are required by the constructors and by an application that will reuse the **CWinThread** object. See Listing 8.1.

LISTING 8.1. CWinThread::CommonConstruct().

```
void CWinThread::CommonConstruct()
{
        m_pMainWnd = NULL;

        // No HTHREAD until it is created
```

continues

Listing 8.1. continued

```
        m_hThread = NULL;
        m_nThreadID = 0;

        // Initialize message pump
#ifdef _DEBUG
        m_nDisablePumpCount = 0;
#endif
        m_msgCur.message = WM_NULL;
        m_nMsgLast = WM_NULL;
        ::GetCursorPos(&m_ptCursorLast);

        // Most threads are deleted when not needed
        m_bAutoDelete = TRUE;
}
```

See the Threadie program, discussed later, for an example of calling `CommonConstruct()`.

virtual ~CWinThread();

This is the `CWinThread` destructor.

BOOL CreateThread(DWORD dwCreateFlags = 0, UINT nStackSize = 0, LPSECURITY_ATTRIBUTES lpSecurityAttrs = NULL);

`CreateThread()` is used to create a thread. Optional parameters allow setting the following attributes:

- *dwCreateFlags*: Flags that are used to control the thread. Valid values are shown in Table 8.1.

Table 8.1. dwCreateFlags VALUES.

Identifier	Description
`DEBUG_PROCESS`	Debugs this thread or process.
`DEBUG_ONLY_THIS_PROCESS`	Debugs only this thread or process.
`CREATE_SUSPENDED`	Creates but doesn't start this thread or process. The process can then be started using the `ResumeThread()` function.

Identifier	Description
DETACHED_PROCESS	Creates this process as detached (with no parent).
CREATE_NEW_CONSOLE	Creates a console thread.
NORMAL_PRIORITY_CLASS	Creates a normal priority thread or process.
IDLE_PRIORITY_CLASS	Creates a process that is serviced only when there is system idle time.
HIGH_PRIORITY_CLASS	Creates a process that has a very high priority.
REALTIME_PRIORITY_CLASS	Because Windows doesn't support true real-time processing, the results might not be acceptable.
CREATE_NEW_PROCESS_GROUP	Creates a new process group.
CREATE_UNICODE_ENVIRONMENT	Uses the Unicode environment (not available under Windows 95).
CREATE_SEPARATE_WOW_VDM	Creates a separate WOW (Windows on Windows) Virtual Display Manager.
CREATE_DEFAULT_ERROR_MODE	Enables the default error mode.
CREATE_NO_WINDOW	Creates a process that has no window.

All the **dwCreateFlags** can be combined using a logical **OR** as needed.

- *nStackSize*: A value that specifies the stack size for the process. A value of zero selects the default stack size. A thread uses its parent's stack.

- *lpSecurityAttrs*: You can use this pointer to a **SECURITY_ATTRIBUTES** structure to set whether the handle retrieved can be inherited or not. The following code fragment shows the **SECURITY_ATTRIBUTES** structure's definition:

```
typedef struct _SECURITY_ATTRIBUTES { /* sa */

    DWORD  nLength;
    LPVOID lpSecurityDescriptor;
    BOOL   bInheritHandle;
} SECURITY_ATTRIBUTES;
```

CWnd* m_pMainWnd

The **m_pMainWnd** member variable holds the window handle for the main window for the owning process. Generally the value in **m_pMainWnd** will be the same as the return value from **AfxGetApp()->m_pMainWnd**.

BOOL m_bAutoDelete;

If **m_bAutoDelete** is **FALSE**, the **CWinThread** object won't be deleted when the thread or process is terminated. It's the application's responsibility to delete the **CWinThread** object in this case. If **m_bAutoDelete** is **!FALSE**, the framework will delete the **CWinThread** object when the thread or process terminates.

HANDLE m_hThread;

The **m_hThread** data member holds the thread or process's handle.

DWORD m_nThreadID;

The **m_hThreadID** data member holds the thread or process's identifier.

int GetThreadPriority();

The **GetThreadPriority()** function returns the thread or process's current priority. See the next section for more information.

BOOL SetThreadPriority(hThread, nPriority);

The **SetThreadPriority()** function allows the parent process to reset a thread or process's priority. Valid *nPriority* values are listed in Table 8.2.

Whenever a thread or process's priority is increased, you must consider the effect that the change will have on system performance. If you reduce the priority of a thread or process, you also must consider the effect on the thread or process's performance.

	TABLE 8.2. THREAD PRIORITY IDENTIFIERS.	
Identifier	Value	Description
THREAD_PRIORITY_IDLE	THREAD_BASE_PRIORITY_IDLE (-15)	Very lowest priority. Executes only if there is system idle time.
THREAD_PRIORITY_LOWEST	THREAD_BASE_PRIORITY_MIN (-2)	Lowest normal priority.
THREAD_PRIORITY_BELOW_NORMAL	(THREAD_PRIORITY_LOWEST + 1) (-1)	Less-than-normal priority.
THREAD_PRIORITY_NORMAL	0	Normal priority (default).
THREAD_PRIORITY_ABOVE_NORMAL	(THREAD_PRIORITY_HIGHEST - 1) (1)	Slightly-more-than-normal priority.
THREAD_PRIORITY_HIGHEST	THREAD_BASE_PRIORITY_MAX (2)	Highest normal priority.
THREAD_PRIORITY_TIME_CRITICAL	THREAD_BASE_PRIORITY_LOWRT (15)	Very highest priority. Preempts all other processes and threads. Significantly affects system performance.
THREAD_PRIORITY_ERROR_RETURN	(MAXLONG)	A return value that GetThreadPriority() returns when there is an erroneous priority value.

DWORD SuspendThread(hThread);

The `SuspendThread()` function allows the thread or process's owner to (temporarily) pause the thread's execution. To continue a suspended thread or process's execution, use the `ResumeThread()` function.

DWORD ResumeThread(hThread);

The `ResumeThread()` function is used to restart a suspended thread.

virtual BOOL InitInstance();

The default `InitInstance()` function calls the `ASSERT_VALID()` macro. You can override this function and provide your own validation code if necessary.

virtual int Run();

The `Run()` function controls the actual execution of the thread or process.

virtual BOOL PreTranslateMessage(MSG* pMsg);

The `PreTranslateMessage()` function is used to preprocess the messages by calling the parent's `PreTranslateMessage()` function.

virtual BOOL OnIdle(LONG lCount);

The `OnIdle()` function can be overridden to allow you to process things during the thread's idle time. The `OnIdle()` function can be used only for user interface threads (that is, threads that process Windows messages). You can specify that additional idle time is required with the *lCount* parameter.

Be careful not to engage in lengthy actions in the `OnIdle()` processor. When `OnIdle()` is executing, the application can't process any other messages.

virtual int ExitInstance();

The `ExitInstance()` function performs a `delete this` on the `CWinThread` object.

Yes, you can `delete this` from within an object!

virtual LRESULT ProcessWndProcException (CException* e, const MSG* pMsg);

This function is called whenever there is an unhandled exception in the thread or process. The default **ProcessWndProcException()** handler will fail on a **WM_CREATE** and validate the affected window when a **WM_PAINT** fails.

virtual CWnd* GetMainWnd();

This function works like **AfxGetMainWnd()**. It returns the current main window's handle.

void Delete();

The **Delete()** function performs a **delete this**, but only if **m_bAutoDelete** is **!FALSE**.

MSG m_msgCur;

The member variable will contain the current message.

virtual BOOL PumpMessage();

The **PumpMessage()** function is a low-level message pump.

virtual BOOL IsIdleMessage(MSG* pMsg);

The **IsIdleMessage()** function is used to check for special idle messages. **IsIdleMessage()** returns **FALSE** if the message just dispatched shouldn't cause the **OnIdle()** function to be run.

Frequent messages that don't usually affect the state of the user interface are usually checked for.

CWinThread in AFXWIN.H

In Listing 8.2, I have extracted the **CWinThread** definitions from AFXWIN.H. This listing shows the private members, and it also contains comments describing the **CWinThread** object.

LISTING 8.2. CWinThread DEFINITION FROM AFXWIN.H.

```
///////////////////////////////////////////////////////////////////////////
// CWinThread

typedef UINT (*AFX_THREADPROC)(void*);

class CWinThread : public CCmdTarget
{
    DECLARE_DYNAMIC(CWinThread)

public:
// Constructors
    CWinThread();
    BOOL CreateThread(DWORD dwCreateFlags = 0, UINT nStackSize = 0,
        LPSECURITY_ATTRIBUTES lpSecurityAttrs = NULL);

// Attributes
    CWnd* m_pMainWnd;  // Main window (usually same AfxGetApp()->m_pMainWnd)
    BOOL m_bAutoDelete;  // Enables 'delete this' after thread termination

    // Valid only while running
    HANDLE m_hThread;    // This thread's HANDLE
    DWORD m_nThreadID;  // This thread's ID

    int GetThreadPriority();
    BOOL SetThreadPriority(int nPriority);

// Operations
    DWORD SuspendThread();
    DWORD ResumeThread();

// Overridables
    // Thread initialization
    virtual BOOL InitInstance();

    // Running and idle processing
    virtual int Run();
    virtual BOOL PreTranslateMessage(MSG* pMsg);
    virtual BOOL OnIdle(LONG lCount);  // Return TRUE if more idle processing

    // Thread termination
    virtual int ExitInstance();  // Default will 'delete this'

    // Advanced: exception handling
    virtual LRESULT ProcessWndProcException(CException* e, const MSG* pMsg);

    // Advanced: virtual access to m_pMainWnd
    virtual CWnd* GetMainWnd();

// Implementation
public:
    virtual ~CWinThread();
#ifdef _DEBUG
    virtual void AssertValid() const;
    virtual void Dump(CDumpContext& dc) const;
```

```
    int m_nDisablePumpCount;   // Diagnostic trap to detect illegal reentrancy
#endif
    void CommonConstruct();
    void Delete();  // 'delete this' only if m_bAutoDelete == TRUE

    // Message pump for Run
    MSG m_msgCur;                    // Current message
    virtual BOOL PumpMessage();  // Low-level message pump
    virtual BOOL IsIdleMessage(MSG* pMsg);  // Checks for special messages
public:
    // Constructor used by implementation of AfxBeginThread
    CWinThread(AFX_THREADPROC pfnThreadProc, LPVOID pParam);

    // Valid after construction
    void* m_pThreadParams;  // Generic parameters passed to starting function
    AFX_THREADPROC m_pfnThreadProc;

protected:
    CPoint m_ptCursorLast;  // Last mouse position
    UINT m_nMsgLast;        // Last mouse message
};
```

Implementing a **CWinThread** object is easy. Refer to the sample program Threadie later in this chapter for an example of the usage of **CWinThread**.

Thread Termination

Threads can terminate themselves by simply having their main function return. When a thread's owner wants to terminate a thread, the owner must communicate this desire to the thread.

THREADIE'S REVENGE: A MULTITHREADED PROGRAM

I've created a simple thread-based Windows program that implements two helper threads. One helper thread is created with a call to **AfxBeginThread()**, and the other thread is launched by directly using a **CWinThread** object.

To create this project, you should use Visual C++ 2.0's new project facilities. Threadie was created with most of the standard options. (I chose to use the Single document style, and I didn't include support for printing or print preview.) Name your project Threadie.

After you've created the project using the Visual Workbench, do an initial project build. I find that I feel more comfortable with the project when I build it once after it has been created. After Visual Workbench's AppWizard has finished, you will have the files shown in the following:

```
Directory of E:\WEVCPSK\SOURCE\THREADIE

RES             <DIR>           07-03-94  12:50p
MAINFRM  CPP     2,740 07-03-94  12:48p
MAINFRM  H       1,098 07-03-94  12:48p
README   TXT     3,917 07-03-94  12:48p
RESOURCE H         465 07-03-94  12:48p
STDAFX   CPP       206 07-03-94  12:48p
STDAFX   H         284 07-03-94  12:48p
THREADIE CLW     1,857 07-03-94  12:48p
THREADIE CPP     3,324 07-03-94  12:48p
THREADIE H         947 07-03-94  12:48p
THREADIE MAK     8,798 07-03-94  12:48p
THREADIE RC      8,262 07-03-94  12:48p
THREADOC CPP     1,760 07-03-94  12:48p
THREADOC H       1,083 07-03-94  12:48p
THREAVW  CPP     1,741 07-03-94  12:48p
THREAVW  H       1,243 07-03-94  12:48p
        18 file(s)       37,725 bytes
```

The first change that must be made is to create a couple of new menu items. To do this, open the resource file (**THREADIE.RC**) and then open the menu (**IDR_MAINFRAME**). With the menu opened, select the View drop-down menu, and add two new selections, Thread 1 and Thread 2.

After you've added your new menu items, you need to use ClassWizard to add handlers for each one. In Threadie, I've chosen to add them to the mainframe (MAINFRM.CPP and MAINFRM.H). However, where a menu handler is added depends on the application: Don't assume that because Threadie uses a handler in the mainframe that your application must have its handlers in the mainframe. I chose the mainframe as a matter of convenience.

After creating your handlers (ClassWizard will create shell functions and the necessary message map macros), you need to create your thread functions. When a thread is started, you begin with a single function that is called to start the thread. This function will then call whatever other functions are needed to do the job.

The first function, which I call **Thread1Proc()**, is shown in Listings 8.3 (THREAD1.CPP) and 8.4 (THREAD1.H).

Listing 8.3. Thread1Proc() in THREAD1.CPP.

```cpp
// Thread 1 code:
#include "stdafx.h"
#include "Threadie.h"
#include "thread1.h"

UINT    Thread1Proc(LPVOID    pParam)
{
double    dTemp;
int       j;

// Tell the user we're starting to waste time:

    CTime Time = CTime::GetCurrentTime();
    CString TimeString = Time.Format("%c");

    TRACE("In Thread %5.5d start  time: %s\n",
        pParam, (const char *)TimeString);

// Now, kill just a little time:

    for(j = 0; j < 100000; j++)
    {
        dTemp = dTemp * j;
        if (dTemp > 123454)
        {
            dTemp /= j;
        }
    }

// Through wasting time; get on with it...

    CTime Time2 = CTime::GetCurrentTime();
    CString TimeString2 = Time2.Format("%c");

    TRACE("In Thread %5.5d end    time: %s\n",
        pParam, (const char *)TimeString2);

    return(FALSE);
}
```

In **Thread1Proc()**, I first print a message to the programmer (using a **TRACE()** macro) telling what time the thread got started. After the message is printed, I proceed to do some nonsensical mathematical operations (I simulate a spreadsheet recalculation), which takes about 10 seconds to complete on a 386-33.

After the thread function has finished, it prints a second message to the programmer and returns. The return ends the thread, and the **CWinThread** object created when **AfxBeginThread()** started will be deleted.

Listing 8.4 shows how simple the header file for **Thread1Proc()** is—only a function prototype is needed.

LISTING **8.4.** **Thread1Proc()** IN THREAD1.H.

```
// Thread 1 header:

UINT    Thread1Proc(LPVOID pParam = (LPVOID)-1);
```

Listings 8.5 and 8.6 show the code for **Thread2Proc()**. **Thread2Proc()** is very similar to **Thread1Proc()**, except for minor cosmetic changes to the messages.

LISTING **8.5.** **Thread2Proc()** IN THREAD2.CPP.

```
// Thread 2 code:
#include "stdafx.h"
#include "Threadie.h"
#include "thread2.h"

UINT    Thread2Proc(LPVOID    pParam)
{
double    dTemp;
int       j;

//  Tell the user we're starting to waste time:

    CTime Time = CTime::GetCurrentTime();
    CString TimeString = Time.Format("%c");

    TRACE("\nIn Thread2 %5.5d start  time: %s\n",
        pParam, (const char *)TimeString);

// Now, kill just a little time:

    for(j = 0; j < 100000; j++)
    {
        dTemp = dTemp * j;
        if (dTemp > 123454)
        {
            dTemp /= j;
        }
    }

// Through wasting time; get on with it...

    CTime Time2 = CTime::GetCurrentTime();
    CString TimeString2 = Time2.Format("%c");

    TRACE("\nIn Thread2 %5.5d end    time: %s\n",
```

```
        pParam, (const char *)TimeString2);

    return(FALSE);
}
```

As I mentioned, the code in THREAD2.CPP is very similar to that in THREAD1.CPP.

LISTING 8.6. Thread2Proc() IN THREAD2.H.

```
// Thread 2 header:

UINT    Thread2Proc(LPVOID pParam = (LPVOID)-1);
```

We now have two functions that we will run as threads. Next, we must add code to the MAINFRM.CPP file to create the threads. First, let's look in Listing 8.7 at the handler for the Thread 1 menu item.

LISTING 8.7. THREAD 1 MENU HANDLER (FRAGMENT).

```
void CMainFrame::OnViewThread1()
{
    // TODO: Add your command handler code here

    int nThreadID = rand();

    CTime Time = CTime::GetCurrentTime();

    TimeString = Time.Format("%c");

    TRACE("Start #   %5.5d start  time: %s\n",
        nThreadID, (const char *)TimeString);

    AfxBeginThread(Thread1Proc, (LPVOID)nThreadID);

    CTime Time2 = CTime::GetCurrentTime();

    TimeString = Time2.Format("%c");

    TRACE("Start #   %5.5d done   time: %s\n",
        nThreadID, (const char *)TimeString);
}
```

Only one line in this handler is required—the call to **AfxBeginThread()**. All the other lines in the example are simply for housekeeping, such as the lines that tell you when the thread was launched and when the launch process has completed.

With **AfxBeginThread()**, the first parameter is the name of the function that will be the thread's main function. The second parameter is an optional 32-bit value that will be passed to **Thread1Proc()**. If your thread function doesn't require any passed parameters, you can hardcode any arbitrary value because there is no default value.

Thread1 shows a simple, minimum-effort thread launch.

Listing 8.8 shows the code that creates Thread2. This code is a bit more complex than that for Thread1. One major difference is that for Thread2 I have created a static variable (a member of Threadie's **CMainFrame** class), which is used to manage Thread2's creation.

LISTING 8.8. THREAD 2 MENU HANDLER (FRAGMENT).

```
void CMainFrame::OnViewThread2()
{
    // TODO: Add your command handler code here
    int nThreadID = rand();
    int    nReallyBad;
    DWORD    dwReturnCode;

if (Thread2.m_hThread != NULL)
    {// We already have a thread running; warn, then go home!
        AfxMessageBox("Already have a thread2 running");
        return;
    }

    CTime Time = CTime::GetCurrentTime();

    TimeString = Time.Format("%c");

    TRACE("Start #   %5.5d start  time: %s\n",
        nThreadID, (const char *)TimeString);

    Thread2.m_bAutoDelete = FALSE;
    Thread2.m_pfnThreadProc = Thread2Proc;
    Thread2.m_pThreadParams = (LPVOID)nThreadID;

    Thread2.CreateThread();

// Now we just waste time till the thread is done.
// In a more realistic program, we'd be doing something
// worthwhile rather than just tossing CPU cycles!
```

```
    nReallyBad = 0;
    TRACE("\n");
    while((::GetExitCodeThread(Thread2.m_hThread, &dwReturnCode)) &&
        dwReturnCode == STILL_ACTIVE)
    {
        TRACE(".");
        if (++nReallyBad > 75)
        {// Insert a newline after 75 characters written out
            nReallyBad = 0;
            TRACE("\n");
        }
    }

    TRACE("Now Done\n");

// Restore our CWinThread object to its new state:
    Thread2.m_pfnThreadProc = NULL;
    Thread2.m_pThreadParams = NULL;

    Thread2.CommonConstruct();

    CTime Time2 = CTime::GetCurrentTime();
    TimeString = Time2.Format("%c");

    TRACE("Start #   %5.5d done    time: %s\n",
        nThreadID, (const char *)TimeString);
}
```

Let's take a closer look at the Thread2 handler. First, we test to see if the thread is already active. If it is, we simply give the user a message and return. This is necessary because we have only one **CWinThread** object, which supports one execution of the thread at a time.

```
    if (Thread2.m_hThread != NULL)
    {// We already have a thread running; warn, then go home!
        AfxMessageBox("Already have a thread2 running");
        return;
    }
```

Next we set up to launch the thread by initializing our **CWinThread** object:

```
Thread2.m_bAutoDelete = FALSE;
Thread2.m_pfnThreadProc = Thread2Proc;
Thread2.m_pThreadParams = (LPVOID)nThreadID;
```

In this section we tell the **CWinThread** object not to delete itself when the thread ends. This is necessary because we will reuse this object—the user may restart this thread later. Next we fill in the pointer to **Thread2Proc()** and the parameter that will be passed to the function.

Finally, we launch the thread using the **CWinThread** member function **CreateThread()**. This function takes no parameters:

```
Thread2.CreateThread();
```

After the thread has been launched, the **CreateThread()** function returns, and the thread probably is still running. (If whatever the thread has to do is simple and fast, it could finish even before **CreateThread()** returns.)

In our handler, we wait and check to see when the thread completes. We do this by checking the thread's status, which is obtained with a call to **GetExitCodeThread()**. This function takes the thread's handle and a pointer to a **DWORD** object used to hold the thread's return code. **GetExitCodeThread()** returns either the manifest constant **STILL_ACTIVE** (**259**) or the return value of the function. Of course, your application shouldn't return **259** when using a test such as the one shown next, because the **while** loop would never end:

```
nReallyBad = 0;
TRACE("\n");
while((::GetExitCodeThread(Thread2.m_hThread, &dwReturnCode)) &&
    dwReturnCode == STILL_ACTIVE)
{
   TRACE(".");
   if (++nReallyBad > 75)
   {// Insert a newline after 75 characters written out
       nReallyBad = 0;
       TRACE("\n");
   }
}

TRACE("Now Done\n");
```

In my sample code, I print a period each time the **while** loop executes. When 75 periods are printed, I start a new line.

After the thread ends, you need to reset the **CWinThread** object. This reinitialization is done in two steps. First, I clear (set to **NULL**) the function pointer and the passed parameter:

```
Thread2.m_pfnThreadProc = NULL;
Thread2.m_pThreadParams = NULL;
```

Then I call the **CWinThread** member function **CommonConstruct()**, which resets the remaining member variables:

```
Thread2.CommonConstruct();
```

The entire MAINFRM.CPP file is shown in Listing 8.9. The lines I've added or changed (either by hand or by using ClassWizard) appear in bold.

LISTING 8.9. THREADIE'S MAINFRM.CPP.

```cpp
// mainfrm.cpp: implementation of the CMainFrame class
//

#include "stdafx.h"
#include "Threadie.h"

#include "mainfrm.h"
#include <stdlib.h>
#include <time.h>
#include "thread1.h"
#include "thread2.h"

#ifdef _DEBUG
#undef THIS_FILE
static char BASED_CODE THIS_FILE[] = __FILE__;
#endif

/////////////////////////////////////////////////////////////////////////////
// CMainFrame

IMPLEMENT_DYNCREATE(CMainFrame, CFrameWnd)

BEGIN_MESSAGE_MAP(CMainFrame, CFrameWnd)
    //{{AFX_MSG_MAP(CMainFrame)
    ON_WM_CREATE()
    ON_COMMAND(ID_VIEW_THREAD1, OnViewThread1)
    ON_COMMAND(ID_VIEW_THREAD2, OnViewThread2)
    //}}AFX_MSG_MAP
END_MESSAGE_MAP()

/////////////////////////////////////////////////////////////////////////////
// Arrays of IDs used to initialize control bars

// Toolbar buttons - IDs are command buttons
static UINT BASED_CODE buttons[] =
{
    // Same order as in the bitmap toolbar.bmp
    ID_FILE_NEW,
    ID_FILE_OPEN,
    ID_FILE_SAVE,
        ID_SEPARATOR,
    ID_EDIT_CUT,
    ID_EDIT_COPY,
    ID_EDIT_PASTE,
        ID_SEPARATOR,
    ID_FILE_PRINT,
    ID_APP_ABOUT,
};

static UINT BASED_CODE indicators[] =
{
    ID_SEPARATOR,           // Status line indicator
    ID_INDICATOR_CAPS,
    ID_INDICATOR_NUM,
```

continues

Listing 8.9. continued

```
    ID_INDICATOR_SCRL,
};


/////////////////////////////////////////////////////////////////////////////
// CMainFrame construction/destruction

CMainFrame::CMainFrame()
{
    // TODO: Add member initialization code here
    srand((unsigned)time(NULL));

// Initialize Thread2 function pointer:
    Thread2.m_pfnThreadProc = NULL;
}

CMainFrame::~CMainFrame()
{
}

int CMainFrame::OnCreate(LPCREATESTRUCT lpCreateStruct)
{
    if (CFrameWnd::OnCreate(lpCreateStruct) == -1)
        return -1;

    if (!m_wndToolBar.Create(this,
            WS_CHILD ¦ WS_VISIBLE ¦ CBRS_TOP ¦ CBRS_TOOLTIPS ¦ CBRS_FLYBY) ¦¦
        !m_wndToolBar.LoadBitmap(IDR_MAINFRAME) ¦¦
        !m_wndToolBar.SetButtons(buttons,
          sizeof(buttons)/sizeof(UINT)))
    {
        TRACE0("Failed to create toolbar\n");
        return -1;  // Fail to create
    }

    if (!m_wndStatusBar.Create(this) ¦¦
        !m_wndStatusBar.SetIndicators(indicators,
          sizeof(indicators)/sizeof(UINT)))
    {
        TRACE0("Failed to create status bar\n");
        return -1;  // Fail to create
    }

    // TODO: Delete these three lines if you
    // don't want the toolbar to be dockable
    m_wndToolBar.EnableDocking(CBRS_ALIGN_ANY);
    EnableDocking(CBRS_ALIGN_ANY);
    DockControlBar(&m_wndToolBar);

    return 0;
}


/////////////////////////////////////////////////////////////////////////////
// CMainFrame diagnostics
```

```
#ifdef _DEBUG
void CMainFrame::AssertValid() const
{
    CFrameWnd::AssertValid();
}

void CMainFrame::Dump(CDumpContext& dc) const
{
    CFrameWnd::Dump(dc);
}

#endif //_DEBUG

/////////////////////////////////////////////////////////////////////////
// CMainFrame message handlers

CString TimeString;

void CMainFrame::OnViewThread1()
{
    // TODO: Add your command handler code here

int nThreadID = rand();

    CTime Time = CTime::GetCurrentTime();

    TimeString = Time.Format("%c");

    TRACE("Start #   %5.5d start  time: %s\n",
        nThreadID, (const char *)TimeString);

    AfxBeginThread(Thread1Proc, (LPVOID)nThreadID);

    CTime Time2 = CTime::GetCurrentTime();

    TimeString = Time2.Format("%c");

    TRACE("Start #   %5.5d done   time: %s\n",
        nThreadID, (const char *)TimeString);
}

void CMainFrame::OnViewThread2()
{
    // TODO: Add your command handler code here
int nThreadID = rand();
int     nReallyBad;
DWORD   dwReturnCode;

    if (Thread2.m_hThread != NULL)
    {// We already have a thread running; warn, then go home!
        AfxMessageBox("Already have a thread2 running");
        return;
    }

    CTime Time = CTime::GetCurrentTime();

    TimeString = Time.Format("%c");
```

continues

Listing 8.9. continued

```
    TRACE("Start #   %5.5d start  time: %s\n",
        nThreadID, (const char *)TimeString);

    Thread2.m_bAutoDelete = FALSE;
    Thread2.m_pfnThreadProc = Thread2Proc;
    Thread2.m_pThreadParams = (LPVOID)nThreadID;

    Thread2.CreateThread();

// Now we just waste time till the thread is done.
// In a more realistic program, we'd be doing something
// worthwile rather than just tossing CPU cycles!

    nReallyBad = 0;
    TRACE("\n");
    while((::GetExitCodeThread(Thread2.m_hThread, &dwReturnCode)) &&
        dwReturnCode == STILL_ACTIVE)
    {
        TRACE(".");
        if (++nReallyBad > 75)
        {// Insert a newline after 75 characters written out
            nReallyBad = 0;
            TRACE("\n");
        }
    }

    TRACE("Now Done\n");

// Restore our CWinThread object to its new state:
    Thread2.m_pfnThreadProc = NULL;
    Thread2.m_pThreadParams = NULL;

    Thread2.CommonConstruct();

    CTime Time2 = CTime::GetCurrentTime();
    TimeString = Time2.Format("%c");

    TRACE("Start #   %5.5d done   time: %s\n",
        nThreadID, (const char *)TimeString);
}
```

Listing 8.10 contains the MAINFRM.H file, which shows the creation of the **CWinThread** object.

Listing 8.10. Threadie's MAINFRM.H.

```
// mainfrm.h: interface of the CMainFrame class
//
//////////////////////////////////////////////////////////////////////
```

```
class CMainFrame : public CFrameWnd
{
protected:  // Create from serialization only
    CMainFrame();
    DECLARE_DYNCREATE(CMainFrame)

// Attributes
public:

    CWinThread      Thread2;

// Operations
public:

// Overrides
    // ClassWizard generated virtual function overrides
    //{{AFX_VIRTUAL(CMainFrame)
    //}}AFX_VIRTUAL

// Implementation
public:
    virtual ~CMainFrame();
#ifdef _DEBUG
    virtual void AssertValid() const;
    virtual void Dump(CDumpContext& dc) const;
#endif

protected:  // Control bar embedded members
    CStatusBar  m_wndStatusBar;
    CToolBar    m_wndToolBar;

// Generated message map functions
protected:
    //{{AFX_MSG(CMainFrame)
    afx_msg int OnCreate(LPCREATESTRUCT lpCreateStruct);
    afx_msg void OnViewThread1();
    afx_msg void OnViewThread2();
    //}}AFX_MSG
    DECLARE_MESSAGE_MAP()
};
```

///

As Threadie shows, creating a thread in a Windows program is relatively simple. Using **AfxBeginThread()**, you can launch a thread with a single line of code. Using **CWinThread**, you can launch a thread with just a few lines of code. It's usually necessary to use a **CWinThread** object only if you must modify some of the thread's characteristics, or when you must monitor the thread's status.

When you run Threadie, you will see the following debug output (make sure that you have the debug output option enabled in the **AFXTraceOptions** application). The thread marked 29021 was started with Thread1, and the thread marked 01726 was started with Thread2. It's unlikely that your computer will have the same performance as mine, so the times that your run of Threadie produces might differ:

```
Start #   29021 start  time: 07/03/94 13:35:14
Start #   29021 done   time: 07/03/94 13:35:14
In Thread 29021 start  time: 07/03/94 13:35:15
In Thread 29021 end    time: 07/03/94 13:35:23
Thread 0x81166BCC terminated, exit code 0 (0x0).


Start #   01726 start  time: 07/03/94 13:35:30

.

In Thread2 01726 start  time: 07/03/94 13:35:30
In Thread2 01726 end    time: 07/03/94 13:35:40
.Thread 0x81166F40 terminated, exit code 0 (0x0).
Now Done
Start #   01726 done   time: 07/03/94 13:35:40
```

Summary

This chapter covered creating multithreaded programs under Windows NT and Windows 95. Many of the concepts discussed in this chapter aren't available under Win32s, because it doesn't support multithreaded operations.

Topics covered in this chapter include the following:

- Helper threads, threads and processes that don't process Windows messages
- User Interface threads, threads and processes that are designed to interface with users (with a window) and process Windows messages
- **CWinThread**, an MFC object that helps create and manage threads

TABBED DIALOG BOXES

Tabbed dialog boxes (also known as *property sheets*) are a major improvement in the user interface tools that Visual C++ 2.0 offers the programmer. Many high-end programs have offered tabbed dialog boxes for some time (take a look at Word for Windows or Excel). Many programmers want to emulate the user interface features of these high-end products, allowing the user of their programs to more easily navigate through the user interface.

A tabbed dialog box is a dialog box (called the *sheet*) that offers the user a number of other sub-dialog boxes (called *pages*). The user selects a dialog box by clicking on a *tab* at the top of the sheet dialog box.

You, the programmer, can specify which page is topmost on the tabbed dialog sheet, and the user can maneuver through the pages in the tabbed dialog in any order. Optional Apply Now and Help buttons assist the user in making a selection.

The MFC interface to tabbed dialog boxes consists of two new MFC classes. The **CPropertyPage** class is used to create the individual pages in a tabbed dialog box. The **CPropertySheet** class is used to create the final tabbed dialog box. The **CPropertySheet** class object is told of each page that is found in the tabbed dialog box.

After I describe these new MFC classes, I will present a very simple program to demonstrate the creation of a tabbed dialog box.

CPropertyPage

The **CPropertyPage** MFC class is used to construct a single page in a tabbed dialog box. The **CPropertyPage** class has a number of member functions, which I will describe in detail.

I don't describe any member functions or variables that are defined as private because your applications can't access them.

CPropertyPage(UINT nIDTemplate, UINT nIDCaption = 0);

This function is the constructor for the **CPropertyPage** object. When you create a **CPropertyPage** object using ClassWizard, the constructor will be overridden. Your actual **CPropertyPage** object is then created using a simple declaration.

The parameters are provided by the constructor that ClassWizard supplies when it creates a **CPropertyPage**-based object. The ClassWizard-supplied constructor takes no parameters, and it calls the **CPropertyPage** constructor with the correct *nIDTemplate* identifier.

CPropertyPage(LPCTSTR lpszTemplateName, UINT nIDCaption = 0);

This function is an alternative constructor for the **CPropertyPage** object. When you create a **CPropertyPage** object using ClassWizard, the constructor will be overridden. Your actual **CPropertyPage** object is then created using a simple declaration.

When ClassWizard is used to create an object based on **CPropertyPage**, ClassWizard also creates a constructor. The parameters that **CPropertyPage**'s constructor requires are provided by the constructor that ClassWizard supplies when it creates a **CPropertyPage**-based object. The ClassWizard-supplied constructor takes no parameters, and it calls the **CPropertyPage** constructor with the correct *lpszTemplateName* identifier.

void CancelToClose( );

Sometimes the user makes a change that your application can't undo. In this case, it's necessary to change the Cancel button to Close, because Cancel is defined as throwing away the user's selections.

Because a modeless tabbed dialog box normally doesn't have a Cancel button, this member function does nothing when called for a modeless tabbed dialog.

void SetModified(BOOL bChanged = TRUE);

The **SetModified()** member function is used to enable or disable the Apply Now button. This button, which is disabled by default, can be used to allow the user to see the effect of changes to the dialog without actually ending the dialog.

It's up to the application as to how to implement the Apply Now button.

virtual BOOL OnSetActive( );

This overridable function is called by the framework whenever the page becomes the active (topmost) page in the tabbed dialog. You can override this function to perform housekeeping or other services.

After you've done your processing, you should call the default **OnSetActive()** function.

virtual BOOL OnKillActive( );

This overridable function is called by the framework whenever the page ceases to be the active (topmost) page in a tabbed dialog. You can override this function to perform housekeeping or other services.

After you've done your processing, you can call the default **OnKillActive()** function.

virtual void OnOK( );

This overridable function is called by the framework whenever the user presses either OK or Apply Now. It's also called after the **OnKillActive()** function returns. You can override this function to perform housekeeping or other services.

After the default **OnOK()** function has completed its tasks, it marks the page as "clean," indicating that the data has been updated by the **OnKillActive()** function.

virtual void OnCancel();

This overridable function is called by the framework whenever the user presses either Cancel or the Esc key. You can override this function to perform housekeeping or other services. One possible reason to override this function is to display a confirm prompt following extensive changes made by the user.

The default **OnCancel()** function discards all changes made by the user.

virtual BOOL PreTranslateMessage(MSG* pMsg);

This function is used to process the Tab, Enter, and Esc keystrokes. This is done to allow the user to change property sheets using the keyboard.

CPropertyPage in AFXDLGS.H

In Listing 9.1, I have extracted the **CPropertyPage** definitions from AFXDLGS.H. This listing shows the private members, and it also contains comments describing the **CPropertyPage** object.

LISTING 9.1. CPropertyPage DEFINITION FROM AFXDLGS.H.

```
/////////////////////////////////////////////////////////////////////////////
// CPropertyPage: one page of a tabbed dialog

class CPropertyPage : public CDialog
{
    DECLARE_DYNAMIC(CPropertyPage)

// Construction
public:
    CPropertyPage(UINT nIDTemplate, UINT nIDCaption = 0);
    CPropertyPage(LPCTSTR lpszTemplateName, UINT nIDCaption = 0);

// Operations
public:
    void CancelToClose();  // Called when the property sheet should
                           // display Close instead of Cancel
    // Lets the property sheet activate the Apply Now button
```

```
        void SetModified(BOOL bChanged = TRUE);

// Overridables
public:
    virtual BOOL OnSetActive();    // Called when this page gets the focus
    virtual BOOL OnKillActive();   // Perform validation here
    virtual void OnOK();           // OK or Apply Now pressed. KillActive
                                   // is called first.
    virtual void OnCancel();       // Cancel pressed

// Implementation
public:
    virtual ~CPropertyPage();
    virtual BOOL PreTranslateMessage(MSG* pMsg);  // Handle Tab, Enter,
                                                  // and Escape keys
#ifdef _DEBUG
    virtual void AssertValid() const;
    virtual void Dump(CDumpContext& dc) const;
    // EndDialog is provided to generate an assert if it is called
    void EndDialog(int nEndID);
#endif

protected:
    CString m_strCaption;
    BOOL m_bChanged;
    HWND m_hWndDefault;  // Current default pushbutton if there is one

    void CommonConstruct(LPCTSTR lpszTemplateName, UINT nIDCaption);
    HGLOBAL GetDlgTemplateHandle();  // Loads the resource indicated by
                                     // CDialog::m_lpDialogTemplate
    BOOL ProcessTab(MSG* pMsg);  // Handles Tab key from PreTranslateMessage
    BOOL CreatePage();  // Called from CPropertySheet to create the dialog
                        // by loading the dialog resource into memory and
                        // turning off WS_CAPTION before creating
    void LoadCaption();  // Gets the caption of the dialog from the
                         // resource and puts it in m_strCaption
    void CheckDefaultButton(HWND hPre, HWND hPost);  // Makes sure correct
                                                     // default button

    // Generated message map functions
    //{{AFX_MSG(CPropertyPage)
    afx_msg BOOL OnNcCreate(LPCREATESTRUCT lpcs);
    afx_msg int OnCreate(LPCREATESTRUCT lpcs);
    afx_msg HBRUSH OnCtlColor(CDC* pDC, CWnd* pWnd, UINT nCtlColor);
    //}}AFX_MSG
    DECLARE_MESSAGE_MAP()

    friend class CPropertySheet;
};
```

Implementing a **CPropertyPage** object is rather easy. You need to perform the following steps:

1. Create a dialog template for the dialog box for the page. This dialog box should have neither OK nor Cancel buttons, because these

buttons are supplied by the **CPropertySheet** dialog. In the dialog created for the **CPropertyPage** object, do the following:

Lay out your controls in a logical order.

Set the style of the dialog template to Child.

Set the border to thin, and be sure that both the Disabled and Title Bar styles are selected.

Change the dialog's caption to the text that you want on the tab used to select this page.

2. Use ClassWizard and create a **CPropertyPage**-based object for the dialog template that you created in step 1.

3. Again, use ClassWizard and create member variables in your **CPropertyPage** object for each control in the dialog template created in step 1.

Follow the preceding process for each page that will be part of the tabbed dialog. It's not uncommon for a tabbed dialog to have five or more pages, with each page having a specific functionality.

CPropertySheet

The **CPropertySheet** MFC class is used to construct the tabbed dialog. A tabbed dialog is a single **CPropertySheet** and a number of **CPropertyPage** objects. The **CPropertySheet** class has a number of member functions. I will describe each member function in detail.

I don't describe any member functions or variables that are defined as private or protected because your applications can't access these objects. You may create functions to override only member functions that are meant to be overridden.

CPropertySheet(UINT nIDCaption, CWnd* pParentWnd = NULL, UINT iSelectPage = 0);

The **CPropertySheet** constructor **CPropertySheet()** constructs the tabbed dialog object. After the tabbed dialog object is created, the **AddPage()** member function is called to create each individual page in the tabbed dialog.

The only required parameter for the **CPropertySheet()** constructor is a resource string identifier for the string that will be the title for the tabbed dialog. Other parameters to the constructor allow setting the tabbed dialog's parent and setting the initial page that will be displayed.

CPropertySheet(LPCTSTR pszCaption, CWnd* pParentWnd = NULL, UINT iSelectPage = 0);

The **CPropertySheet** constructor **CPropertySheet()** constructs the tabbed dialog object. After the tabbed dialog object is created, the **AddPage()** member function is called to create each individual page in the tabbed dialog.

The only required parameter for the **CPropertySheet()** constructor is a pointer to a string that will be the title for the tabbed dialog. Other parameters to the constructor allow setting the tabbed dialog's parent and setting the initial page that will be displayed.

BOOL Create(CWnd* pParentWnd = NULL, DWORD dwStyle = WS_SYSMENU | WS_POPUP | WS_CAPTION | DS_MODALFRAME | WS_VISIBLE, DWORD dwExStyle = WS_EX_DLGMODALFRAME);

The **Create()** member function is used to create a modeless version of the tabbed dialog. You can specify a number of attributes for the tabbed dialog with the **Create()** function. After the dialog box is created, the **Create()** function returns. This allows your application to modify the tabbed dialog as necessary (adding new pages, and so on).

It's possible to call **Create()** in the constructor for the **CPropertySheet** object. Normally a tabbed dialog that is modeless won't have the OK, Cancel, Apply Now, or Help buttons. If your application requires these buttons, you must create them yourself.

int GetPageCount() const;

This function returns the number of pages in the current tabbed dialog.

CPropertyPage* GetPage(int nPage) const;

You can use the **GetPage()** member function to get a **CPropertyPage** pointer for a specific page in the tabbed dialog. The index *nPage* must be between zero and one less than the value returned by **GetPageCount()**.

int DoModal();

The **DoModal()** function works exactly like a dialog box's **DoModal()** function. This function displays the tabbed dialog, and when the user selects either OK or Cancel, the **DoModal()** function returns.

The return value for **DoModal()** is either **IDOK** or **IDCANCEL**, depending on whether the user selected OK or Cancel.

void AddPage(CPropertyPage* pPage);

The **AddPage()** member function is used to add a new **CPropertyPage** page to the tabbed dialog. This function typically is called prior to calling **Create()** or **DoModal()**; however, **AddPage()** can be called at any time.

When a page is added to a tabbed dialog that has already been created (with **Create()** or **DoModal()**), using **AddPage()**, the tab row will be updated to reflect the new page. The page itself won't be created until the user selects the page.

void RemovePage(CPropertyPage* pPage); and void RemovePage(int nPage);

The **RemovePage()** function performs in the opposite manner of **AddPage()**. You can use **RemovePage()** to remove a page from a tabbed dialog.

The parameter can be either a pointer to a **CPropertyPage** object that has already been added to the tabbed dialog, or a valid integer page number.

void EndDialog(int nEndID);

The **EndDialog()** function is used to terminate the modal tabbed dialog. The parameter *nEndID* should be either **IDOK** or **IDCANCEL**. You would normally call this function whenever an event occurs that implies that the tabbed dialog should be closed.

CPropertySheet in AFXDLGS.H

In Listing 9.2, I have extracted the **CPropertySheet** definitions from AFXDLGS.H. This listing shows the private members, and it also contains comments describing the **CPropertySheet** object.

LISTING 9.2. **CPropertySheet** DEFINITION FROM AFXDLGS.H.

```
//////////////////////////////////////////////////////////////////////////////
// CPropertySheet: a tabbed "dialog" (really a pop-up window)
class CPropertySheet : public CWnd
{
    DECLARE_DYNAMIC(CPropertySheet);

// Construction
public:
    CPropertySheet(UINT nIDCaption, CWnd* pParentWnd = NULL,
        UINT iSelectPage = 0);
    CPropertySheet(LPCTSTR pszCaption, CWnd* pParentWnd = NULL,
        UINT iSelectPage = 0);

    // For modeless creation
    BOOL Create(CWnd* pParentWnd = NULL, DWORD dwStyle =
        WS_SYSMENU | WS_POPUP | WS_CAPTION | DS_MODALFRAME | WS_VISIBLE,
        DWORD dwExStyle = WS_EX_DLGMODALFRAME);

// Attributes
public:
    int GetPageCount() const;
    CPropertyPage* GetPage(int nPage) const;

// Operations
public:
    int DoModal();
    void AddPage(CPropertyPage* pPage);
    void RemovePage(CPropertyPage* pPage);
    void RemovePage(int nPage);

protected:
    void EndDialog(int nEndID);  // Used to terminate a modal dialog

// Implementation
public:
    virtual ~CPropertySheet();
#ifdef _DEBUG
    virtual void AssertValid() const;
    virtual void Dump(CDumpContext& dc) const;
#endif
    virtual BOOL PreTranslateMessage(MSG* pMsg);
    virtual BOOL DestroyWindow();

protected:
    BOOL ProcessCtrlTab(MSG* pMsg);
    BOOL CreateStandardButtons();
    BOOL PreTranslatePageMessage(MSG* pMsg);
    BOOL PumpMessage();
    BOOL SetActivePage(int nPage);
    void PageChanged();
    void CancelToClose();
    void CommonConstruct(CWnd* pParent, UINT iSelectPage);
    void RecalcLayout();
    CPropertyPage* GetActivePage() const;
```

continues

Listing 9.2. continued

```
// Implementation data members
HFONT m_hFont;   // Sizes below dependent on this font
CSize m_sizeButton;
CSize m_sizeTabMargin;
int m_cxButtonGap;
BOOL m_bModeless;

CButton m_buttonOK;   // Standard property sheet buttons
CButton m_buttonCancel;
CButton m_buttonApply;
CButton m_buttonHelp;

int m_nCurPage;
int m_nID;   // ID passed to EndDialog and returned from DoModal

CObArray m_pages;         // Array of CPropertyPage pointers
HWND m_hFocusWnd;         // Focus when you lost activation
CWnd* m_pParentWnd;       // Owner of the tabbed dialog
CString m_strCaption;     // Caption of the pseudo-dialog
CTabControl    m_tabRow;  // Entire row of tabs at top of dialog
BOOL m_bParentDisabled;   // TRUE if parent was disabled by DoModal

// Generated message map functions
//{{AFX_MSG(CPropertySheet)
afx_msg BOOL OnNcCreate(LPCREATESTRUCT lpcs);
afx_msg int OnCreate(LPCREATESTRUCT lpCreateStruct);
afx_msg void OnPaint();
afx_msg void OnActivate(UINT nState, CWnd* pWndOther, BOOL bMinimized);
afx_msg void OnClose();
afx_msg HBRUSH OnCtlColor(CDC* pDC, CWnd* pWnd, UINT nCtlColor);
afx_msg void OnSetFocus(CWnd* pOldWnd);
afx_msg void OnOK();
afx_msg void OnCancel();
afx_msg void OnApply();
afx_msg void OnHelp();
afx_msg LONG OnGetFont(WPARAM, LPARAM);
//}}AFX_MSG
afx_msg LONG OnTabChanged(WPARAM, LPARAM);
afx_msg LONG OnTabChanging(WPARAM wParam, LPARAM);
DECLARE_MESSAGE_MAP()

    friend class CPropertyPage;   // For tab handler
};
```

As Listing 9.2 shows, the **CPropertySheet** class is based on **CWnd** and has a number of **protected** members that may be accessed from member functions that you might write.

THE PROPSHET PROGRAM

Now that you've learned about the two tabbed dialog classes, **CPropertyPage** and **CPropertySheet**, it's time to put that knowledge to work! I looked at tabbed dialogs as being complex and difficult to implement. Also, I really wanted to include them in my program!

There's only one way for me to learn, and that's to just jump in! Jump in I did, and PropShet is the result. I wanted to create the simplest implementation of a tabbed dialog program possible so that the process of creating a tabbed dialog box would be clear.

First, the basics. To create PropShet, you need a program. I won't describe the steps to create an application using AppWizard. Just create a simple SDI or MDI program. If you want to add a tabbed dialog to an existing application, use your program. Don't bother creating a new one. Let's assume that you've planned your tabbed dialog and you know what you want: a tabbed dialog with three sheets—one for line style, one for line width, and one for line color. Here are the steps to follow:

1. Using the resource editor, create the dialog box templates for your tabbed dialog pages. Remember not to include OK or Cancel buttons. (Delete them if the editor creates them by default.) Set the dialog's attributes to Child, Thin Border, Disabled, with Title Bar. Give the dialog a one- or two-word title. It will be used in the tab bar when the tabbed dialog is displayed.

2. For each page in your tabbed dialog, create a **CPropertyPage** object using ClassWizard. Generally ClassWizard's defaults are sufficient, but try to make your class names descriptive. You'll thank yourself in a few months.

3. The user of the application needs a way to call up the new tabbed dialog. You probably will be adding or using an existing menu item, or perhaps the tabbed dialog will be activated by a button in an existing dialog box.

4. With the addition of a place to display the tabbed dialog, you need to add the code to display the dialog box. The following code fragment shows how I implemented this code:

```
CLineColor LineColor;
CLineStyle LineStyle;
CLineWidth LineWidth;
CPropertySheet TabDialog(IDS_TAB_TITLE);
```

```
TabDialog.AddPage(&LineColor);
TabDialog.AddPage(&LineStyle);
TabDialog.AddPage(&LineWidth);

TabDialog.DoModal();
```

First, it was necessary to create **CPropertyPage** objects for each of the pages in the tabbed dialog. Next, I created the **CPropertySheet** object and specified the tabbed dialog's title. After all the necessary objects were created, I added each of the pages to the tabbed dialog. The final step was to display the tabbed dialog.

Let's look at the PropShet program as I wrote it. Figure 9.1 shows each of the member dialog boxes. These dialog boxes are examples only. Put into your dialogs whatever controls your application requires.

Table 9.1 shows the directory that PropShet's source is in, as well as the files that make up PropShet.

TABLE 9.1. PropShet's source directory.		
File Information	*Status*	*Description*
RES	Original	A subdirectory containing the application's resources.
WINDEBUG	Original	The subdirectory that contains the debugging version of the project.
LINECOLO.CPP	New	The source file for the Line Color dialog box's **CPropertyPage** implementation.
LINECOLO.H	New	The header file for the Line Color dialog box's **CPropertyPage** implementation.
LINESTYL.CPP	New	The source file for the Line Style dialog box's **CPropertyPage** implementation.
LINESTYL.H	New	The header file for the Line Style dialog box's **CPropertyPage** implementation.

File Information	Status	Description
LINEWIDT.CPP	New	The source file for the Line Width dialog box's **CPropertyPage** implementation.
LINEWIDT.H	New	The header file for the Line Width dialog box's **CPropertyPage** implementation.
MAINFRM.CPP	Original	The application's mainframe class.
MAINFRM.H	Original	The application's mainframe header file.
PROPSDOC.CPP	Original	The application's document class.
PROPSDOC.H	Original	The application's document header file.
PROPSHET.CLW	Original	The application's ClassWizard control file.
PROPSHET.CPP	Modified	The application's main application class.
PROPSHET.H	Modified	The application's main application header file.
PROPSHET.MAK	Original	The Visual C++ project file (do not modify!).
PROPSHET.RC	Modified	The application's resource file.
PROPSVW.CPP	Original	The application's view class.
PROPSVW.H	Original	The application's view header file.
README.TXT	Original	Information about the application from AppWizard.
RESOURCE.H	Modified	The resource header file.
STDAFX.CPP	Original	The precompiled header source file.
STDAFX.H	Original	The precompiled header include file.

Let's look at the files that are either new or modified. First, all of the LINE????.CPP and LINE????.H files are basically identical (except for the names, which change for each dialog). Listing 9.3 shows the LINECOLO.CPP file, and Listing 9.4 shows the LINECOLO.H file.

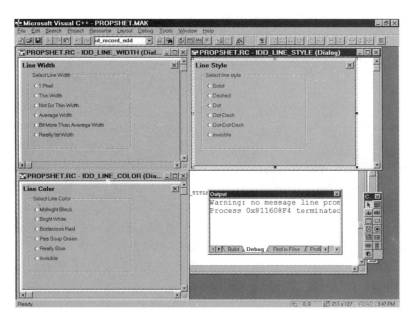

Figure 9.1. PropShet's tabbed dialog page dialog boxes.

LISTING 9.3. LINECOLO.CPP: LINE COLOR DIALOG IMPLEMENTATION.

```
// LINECOLO.CPP: implementation file
//

#include "stdafx.h"
#include "propshet.h"
#include "linecolo.h"

#ifdef _DEBUG
#undef THIS_FILE
static char BASED_CODE THIS_FILE[] = __FILE__;
#endif

/////////////////////////////////////////////////////////////////////////
// CLineColor property page


CLineColor::CLineColor() : CPropertyPage(CLineColor::IDD)
{
    //{{AFX_DATA_INIT(CLineColor)
        // NOTE: ClassWizard will add member initialization here
    //}}AFX_DATA_INIT
}

void CLineColor::DoDataExchange(CDataExchange* pDX)
{
```

```
    CPropertyPage::DoDataExchange(pDX);
    //{{AFX_DATA_MAP(CLineColor)
        // NOTE: ClassWizard will add DDX and DDV calls here
    //}}AFX_DATA_MAP
}

BEGIN_MESSAGE_MAP(CLineColor, CPropertyPage)
    //{{AFX_MSG_MAP(CLineColor)
        // NOTE: ClassWizard will add message map macros here
    //}}AFX_MSG_MAP
END_MESSAGE_MAP()


/////////////////////////////////////////////////////////////////////////////
// CLineColor message handlers
```

Listing 9.4. LINECOLO.H: Line Color dialog header.

```
// LINECOLO.H: header file
//

/////////////////////////////////////////////////////////////////////////////
// CLineColor dialog

class CLineColor : public CPropertyPage
{
// Construction
public:
    CLineColor();

// Dialog data
    //{{AFX_DATA(CLineColor)
    enum { IDD = IDD_LINE_COLOR };
        // NOTE: ClassWizard will add data members here
        // DO NOT EDIT what you see in these blocks of generated code!
    //}}AFX_DATA


// Overrides
    // ClassWizard generates virtual function overrides
    //{{AFX_VIRTUAL(CLineColor)
    protected:
    virtual void DoDataExchange(CDataExchange* pDX);   // DDX/DDV support
    //}}AFX_VIRTUAL

// Implementation
protected:
    // Generated message map functions
    //{{AFX_MSG(CLineColor)
        // NOTE: ClassWizard will add member functions here
    //}}AFX_MSG
    DECLARE_MESSAGE_MAP()
};
```

The actual construction of the tabbed dialog is in the PROPSHET.CPP and PROPSHET.H files.

PROPSHET.CPP was modified in three steps. First, I used the resource editor to add a menu item called Line Stuff to the View menu. Next, I added a command handler using ClassWizard. Finally, I edited the command handler and added the code to create the tabbed dialog. One other modification was to add includes for the three **CPropertyPage** objects—CLineColor, CLineWidth, and CLineStyle.

In Listing 9.5, the lines that I added appear in bold.

LISTING 9.5. PROPSHET.CPP: CREATING A TABBED DIALOG.

```cpp
// PROPSHET.CPP: defines the class behaviors for the application
//

#include "stdafx.h"
#include "propshet.h"

#include "mainfrm.h"
#include "propsdoc.h"
#include "propsvw.h"

#include "linecolo.h"
#include "linestyl.h"
#include "linewidt.h"

#ifdef _DEBUG
#undef THIS_FILE
static char BASED_CODE THIS_FILE[] = __FILE__;
#endif

/////////////////////////////////////////////////////////////////////////////
// CPropshetApp

BEGIN_MESSAGE_MAP(CPropshetApp, CWinApp)
    //{{AFX_MSG_MAP(CPropshetApp)
    ON_COMMAND(ID_APP_ABOUT, OnAppAbout)
    ON_COMMAND(ID_VIEW_LINESTUFF, OnViewLinestuff)
    //}}AFX_MSG_MAP
    // Standard file-based document commands
    ON_COMMAND(ID_FILE_NEW, CWinApp::OnFileNew)
    ON_COMMAND(ID_FILE_OPEN, CWinApp::OnFileOpen)
    // Standard print setup command
    ON_COMMAND(ID_FILE_PRINT_SETUP, CWinApp::OnFilePrintSetup)
END_MESSAGE_MAP()

/////////////////////////////////////////////////////////////////////////////
// CPropshetApp construction

CPropshetApp::CPropshetApp()
```

```
{
    // TODO: Add construction code here
    // Place all significant initialization in InitInstance
}

/////////////////////////////////////////////////////////////////////////////
// The one and only CPropshetApp object

CPropshetApp theApp;

/////////////////////////////////////////////////////////////////////////////
// CPropshetApp initialization

BOOL CPropshetApp::InitInstance()
{
    // Standard initialization
    // If you are not using these features and wish to reduce the size
    //  of your final executable, you should remove from the following
    //  the specific initialization routines you do not need.

    Enable3dControls();

    LoadStdProfileSettings();  // Load standard .INI file
                               // options (including MRU)

    // Register the application's document templates. Document templates
    // serve as the connection between documents, frame windows, and views.

    CSingleDocTemplate* pDocTemplate;
    pDocTemplate = new CSingleDocTemplate(
        IDR_MAINFRAME,
        RUNTIME_CLASS(CPropshetDoc),
        RUNTIME_CLASS(CMainFrame),  // Main SDI frame window
        RUNTIME_CLASS(CPropshetView));
    AddDocTemplate(pDocTemplate);

    // Create a new (empty) document
    OnFileNew();

    if (m_lpCmdLine[0] != '\0')
    {
        // TODO: Add command-line processing here
    }

    return TRUE;
}

/////////////////////////////////////////////////////////////////////////////
// CAboutDlg dialog used for App About

class CAboutDlg : public CDialog
{
public:
    CAboutDlg();

// Dialog data
```

continues

LISTING 9.5. CONTINUED

```
    //{{AFX_DATA(CAboutDlg)
    enum { IDD = IDD_ABOUTBOX };
    //}}AFX_DATA

// Implementation
protected:
    virtual void DoDataExchange(CDataExchange* pDX);   // DDX/DDV support
    //{{AFX_MSG(CAboutDlg)
        // No message handlers
    //}}AFX_MSG
    DECLARE_MESSAGE_MAP()
};

CAboutDlg::CAboutDlg() : CDialog(CAboutDlg::IDD)
{
    //{{AFX_DATA_INIT(CAboutDlg)
    //}}AFX_DATA_INIT
}

void CAboutDlg::DoDataExchange(CDataExchange* pDX)
{
    CDialog::DoDataExchange(pDX);
    //{{AFX_DATA_MAP(CAboutDlg)
    //}}AFX_DATA_MAP
}

BEGIN_MESSAGE_MAP(CAboutDlg, CDialog)
    //{{AFX_MSG_MAP(CAboutDlg)
        // No message handlers
    //}}AFX_MSG_MAP
END_MESSAGE_MAP()

// App command to run the dialog
void CPropshetApp::OnAppAbout()
{
    CAboutDlg aboutDlg;
    aboutDlg.DoModal();
}


/////////////////////////////////////////////////////////////////////////
// CPropshetApp commands

void CPropshetApp::OnViewLinestuff()
{
    // TODO: Add your command handler code here
    CLineColor LineColor;
    CLineStyle LineStyle;
    CLineWidth LineWidth;
    CPropertySheet TabDialog(IDS_TAB_TITLE);

    TabDialog.AddPage(&LineColor);
    TabDialog.AddPage(&LineStyle);
    TabDialog.AddPage(&LineWidth);
```

```
        TabDialog.DoModal();


}
```

As Listing 9.5 shows, the amount of code needed to create a tabbed dialog isn't great. However, there is a catch to the simplicity that I show: You must create code both to initialize the page dialogs and to retrieve the user's input when the dialog ends. This process is identical to that for a standard dialog box.

Listing 9.6 shows the header file PROPSHET.H. All of the changes to this file were done using ClassWizard.

LISTING 9.6. PROPSHET.H.

```
// PROPSHET.H: main header file for the PROPSHET application
//

#ifndef __AFXWIN_H__
    #error include 'stdafx.h' before including this file for PCH
#endif

#include "resource.h"  // Main symbols

/////////////////////////////////////////////////////////////////////////////
// CPropshetApp:
// See PROPSHET.CPP for the implementation of this class
//

class CPropshetApp : public CWinApp
{
public:
    CPropshetApp();

// Overrides
    // ClassWizard generated virtual function overrides
    //{{AFX_VIRTUAL(CPropshetApp)
    public:
    virtual BOOL InitInstance();
    //}}AFX_VIRTUAL

// Implementation

    //{{AFX_MSG(CPropshetApp)
    afx_msg void OnAppAbout();
    afx_msg void OnViewLinestuff();
    //}}AFX_MSG
    DECLARE_MESSAGE_MAP()
};


/////////////////////////////////////////////////////////////////////////////
```

As PROPSHET shows, implementing a tabbed dialog isn't difficult. One nice thing is that because tabbed dialogs are implemented using MFC (not Windows), there are no issues of portability.

Figure 9.2 shows the final tabbed dialog in PROPSHET.

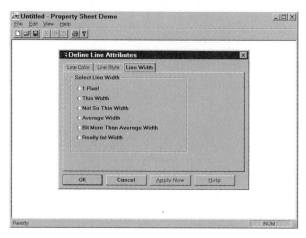

Figure 9.2. PropShet's tabbed dialog box.

Summary

This chapter showed how to create tabbed dialog boxes. Microsoft refers to tabbed dialog boxes as property sheets.

Two new MFC classes are used to support tabbed dialogs:

- **CPropertySheet**, a class to manage the entire tabbed dialog
- **CPropertyPage**, a class to manage a page in a tabbed dialog

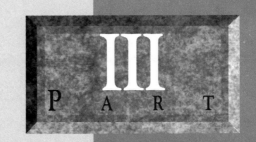

OLE 2

AN INTRODUCTION TO OLE CUSTOM CONTROLS

Part III of this book covers OLE—specifically, OLE Custom Controls. When OLE was first introduced, it was offered as a separate SDK (Software Development Kit). With upcoming versions of Windows, and with Visual C++ 2.0, Microsoft has added OLE Custom Controls to Windows, and the OLE SDK to Visual C++. This means that now there is one less development tool that you, the programmer, must purchase. The OLE Custom Controls Development Kit is called either CDK16 (for 16-bit development) or CDK32 (for 32-bit development). Using the CDK to develop 16-bit controls requires Visual C++ 1.5.01, which includes some fixes and changes to the Visual Workbench and ClassWizard to facilitate developing OLE Custom Controls.

Where has the "2" in "OLE-2" gone? Microsoft has announced its intention to change OLE's name from "OLE-2" to just "OLE." This change was made to allow Microsoft to expand OLE without changing the name, meaning that there will never be an OLE-3 or OLE-4. Actually, OLE is becoming such a large system that Microsoft probably will subdivide it into parts, such as OLE Custom Controls, OLE Linking and Embedding, and so on.

This part of the book looks at OLE Custom Controls. In keeping with this book's objective of introducing the new and changed parts of Visual C++ 2.0, I describe OLE Custom Controls and cover only a minimum of the portions of OLE that have been around for some time.

The term *OLE Custom Controls* is a mouthful. Some publications use the acronym OCX for OLE Custom Controls, but in this book I use the term *OLE Controls*. I refer to the OLE Custom Controls Development Kit as the *CDK*.

It's possible to have some rather nasty accidents when using applications that work with the registration database. On more than one occasion, I've destroyed the registration database, and the results are nothing short of awful. Some versions of Windows will refuse to run; others will run, but not well; and still others will never notice the loss of the registration database.

Make sure that you have a backup of your current registration database. Many versions of RegEdit, the utility that is used to make manual modifications to the registration database, also export the registration database. For Windows 3.x, the file is REG.DAT. For Windows 95, back up the SYSTEM.DAT, SYSTEM.DA0, and USER.* files. Some of these files might have the hidden attribute and therefore won't be visible unless you use the DIR /AH command.

Remember: Back it up or lose it! Generally, losing the registration database means reinstalling Windows and many (if not all) of your Windows applications.

THE CONTROL DEVELOPMENT KIT

The OLE Controls Development Kit is a separate component of the Visual C++ 2.0 system. You can elect to install the CDK only if you're going to create OLE Controls.

The CDK installation makes a number of changes to Visual C++ 2.0, including adding support for the following:

- ControlWizard: This is a new support wizard that works much like AppWizard. You can create a new control easily because the wizard writes the control's shell for you. All OLE Controls are created as DLL files.
- ClassWizard: For Visual C++, the CDK installs a new ClassWizard that offers the necessary support for OLE Controls. Two new extensions are added to ClassWizard: OLE Automation and OLE Events.
- MFC: The CDK adds new classes to MFC to support OLE Controls.
- Sample code: The CDK includes a number of sample controls that you can work with to help learn some of the OLE Control programming techniques.
- CDK Books OnLine: The CDK adds a new help file, CDK Books OnLine, which allows you to easily look up information on OLE Controls.
- Test Container: Also included is a program called Test Container that you can use to test your newly developed OLE Controls. This program enables you to test all of a new control's functionality.

Many of the new tools used to create OLE Controls are placed on the Visual Workbench Tools menu. You'll find the following new items on the Tools menu:

- ControlWizard is the equivalent of AppWizard for controls.
- Register Control enables you to register your OLE Control in the system registry.
- Unregister Control is used to remove your OLE Control from the registry.
- Test Container enables you to test your newly developed OLE Control. It also offers the capability to test all of an OLE Control's features.

- WPS (installed only under 16-bit environments) is a thread/process monitoring utility. WPS enables you to kill a thread or process if necessary. This utility isn't installed with Visual C++ 2.0. However, Windows 95 users might find it useful because it performs many of the same tasks as the PStat and PView utilities that don't run under Windows 95.
- Make Typelib is used to make the typelib required by 16-bit versions of OLE Controls. This utility isn't used with Visual C++ 2.0.

Chapter 11, "OLE Controls Development Tools," describes each of these tools in detail.

The CDK is installed in a directory called either CDK32 (for Visual C++ 2.0) or CDK16 (for the 16-bit versions of Visual C++) under Visual C++'s main directory (MSVC20 in most installations). You should change any references to CDK32 to CDK16 if you're writing OLE Controls using 16-bit versions of Visual C++. Why am I mentioning 16-bit products in a book on the 32-bit compiler Visual C++ 2.0? Simply because it's necessary to maintain compatibility with existing versions of Windows for many applications. One nice thing is that the CDK's utility ControlWizard, regardless of which platform it's executed under, generates code that is compatible with both Visual C++ 2.0 and 16-bit versions of Visual C++. It generates a Visual C++ 2.0-compatible project file and a project file that can be used with 16-bit versions of Visual C++.

Under the CDK32 subdirectory are five additional subdirectories:

- The BIN directory contains the ControlWizard program, the Registration server, and the Test Container application.
- The INCLUDE directory contains the AFXCTL.H, AFXCTL.INL, OLECTL.H, and OLECTLID.H files.
- The LIB directory contains the link libraries for the various OLE Controls' DLL files.
- The SAMPLES directory contains the 11 sample controls that are supplied with the CDK. These include the following:

  BUTTON: A simple pushbutton control.

  CIRC1: A control that implements a custom pushbutton.

  CIRC2: An advanced version of CIRC1.

  CIRC3: A more advanced version of CIRC1.

LICENSED: An example of a licensed control.

LOCALIZE: A control showing localization techniques.

PAL: A color palette control.

PUSH: A custom pushbutton control.

SPINDIAL: An implementation of a spindial control.

TIME: A control that triggers an event at a timer interval.

XLIST: A custom list box control.

- The SRC directory contains the source for the OLE Controls support. This code is used primarily by the debugger to enable you to help debug your applications. You wouldn't normally have to rebuild the OLE Controls MFC support.

OLE Controls are supported by a number of runtime DLL files. These DLL files include the following:

- OC25.DLL contains the release (nondebug) version of the 16-bit OLE Controls.
- OC25D.DLL contains the debug version of the 16-bit OLE Controls.
- OC30.DLL contains the release (nondebug) version of the 32-bit OLE Controls. This 32-bit version of OLE Controls supports ANSI/DBCS.
- OC30D.DLL contains the debug version of the 32-bit OLE Controls. This 32-bit version of OLE Controls supports ANSI/DBCS.
- OC30U.DLL contains the release (nondebug) version of the 32-bit OLE Controls. This 32-bit version of OLE Controls supports Unicode.
- OC30UD.DLL contains the debug version of the 32-bit OLE Controls. This 32-bit version of OLE Controls supports Unicode.

The appropriate DLL files are also installed in the WINDOWS\SYSTEM directory and registered by the CDK setup program. If the registration database becomes corrupted and has to be replaced, you'll need to reinstall the CDK to use OLE Controls.

A Few OLE Definitions

This section attempts to define a few of the more common terms used with OLE. I've included these definitions here because many of these terms aren't defined in a single location. Understanding each of them will greatly help your comprehension of OLE and OLE Controls.

OLE

OLE is an acronym for Object Linking and Embedding. OLE was created as a wrapper to the original concept of DDE (Dynamic Data Exchange).

OLE defines a set of standard interfaces to objects, such as `IUnknown`.

Objects

An object is an item that's being placed in a document. Objects may be either linked, meaning that the object's data is external to the containing document, or embedded, meaning that the object's data is internal to the containing document.

Objects may also be referred to as servers.

Containers

A container is a document into which objects may be embedded or linked. Generally, the term *container* refers to either a container application such as Word, Excel, or Access or a container document such as a Word document, an Excel worksheet, or an Access report or form.

Containers may also be referred to as clients.

Linked Objects

A linked object is an object whose basic data is not part of the containing document. The information that is part of a linked object tells where the actual information is located and includes a view of the object.

When the user elects to change the object, the object's server uses the link information to retrieve the object's data. When a linked object is modified outside the container application, the container's representation of the object's data is also updated.

Embedded Objects

An embedded object's data resides in the container document. Changes to the embedded object's original source data don't affect the embedded object or its data.

An embedded object can be modified if needed.

A document with embedded objects is larger than a document that has linked objects, because the embedded objects' data must be included in the containing document.

Windows Objects

A Windows object is an OLE object that defines at least one interface, `IUnknown`.

Each object must provide a function table for each interface that the object supports. When OLE Controls are developed using ControlWizard, the details of the interface are managed for you.

DDE

DDE (Dynamic Data Exchange) is a method by which two applications can exchange information. With DDE it's necessary for the two applications to agree on the data's format and the method of exchange.

DDE isn't often used, mainly due to its complexity and the availability of other easier-to-use methods of exchanging data, such as OLE and DDEML (Dynamic Data Exchange Management Library).

Automation Servers

An OLE automation server is an application that exposes a programmable object (the server's functionality) to an OLE container application. The exposure is done using the `IDispatch` interface.

For example, my GIS program could expose its zip code validator to other applications for their own use. That way, a mail list program (perhaps part of an Access database) could verify the zip code, city, and state portions of an address prior to printing a mailing label.

Events

Events are simply things that happen (an accurate, but crummy, definition). A Windows event could be an action such as a mouse message (movement or clicking), a keyboard action, or perhaps (as in our digital clock OLE Control) a timer message.

Servers

A server is an application that is the source, or creator, of an object. Even if the preceding sentence says it all, it says nothing! It's simply jargon used to explain more jargon. No wonder Windows programming is getting so complex!

THE RELATIONSHIP AMONG SERVERS, DOCUMENTS, AND CONTAINERS

Let's try to define a server again. Rather than using computer terms, let's try something else: a company picnic. I've planned the picnic because I want to butter up my boss (the chairman of the board) so that I can ask for a raise.

We set up a table, put on a tablecloth, silverware, and napkins, and ask each of our employees to bring something to eat.

The company, which is sponsoring the picnic, is the container application. The table is the document. Actually, the table is a compound document, because it has objects on it. (In OLE terminology, the objects would be embedded or linked; however, be careful how you embed a bowl of potato salad in the table. The results might be less than appealing if the embedding is done too aggressively.)

You could place a bowl on the table with a picture of potato salad and a small card inside, telling those who want potato salad that "the potato salad is in the cooler." This would make the potato salad a linked object because its data (the actual salad) is stored externally to the main document (the picnic table).

However, in keeping with picnic tradition, you place an object full of potato salad on the table. Because you brought the potato salad, you are the server, the potato salad is an object, and the table is a compound document. (Please, don't say I'm nuts...yet.)

When you brought your potato salad, you didn't bring it on a nice plate with the necessary garnishes. You transported it in a plastic Tupperware container. As president of the company, I ask you to present your potato salad, and you do so by putting it on an attractive plate with a little parsley on the side to make it look good. Now that the potato salad is presentable, I put it in the center of the table.

It just so happens that the company's chairman of the board (my boss, the person for whom we're having this picnic) has sampled your potato salad. He thinks he knows everything about salads, and he wants to change yours by adding some pepper. My boss (representing the user) tells me (the application) to get you (the server) to make the change. (He couldn't really tell the table; it's just a document.) You comply by adding the pepper, and you put the potato salad back on the table.

I figured that having you change your salad would satisfy my boss. Not! My boss (the user) tells me (the application) that he thinks the salad would look better at the end of the table, so I move it. Because I'm only moving the salad and not changing it, I can do this myself. Of course, each time I move the salad, you step in and adjust the plate so that it looks just right.

Now you can say I'm nuts, but basically, that's how OLE servers and containers work!

Just like the movies, let's give proper OLE credit to the players (cue the music):

> The Company: The application (the container).
> You: The object's server.
> My Boss: The user.
> The Potato Salad: The object to be embedded.
> The Table: The compound document.

The recipe for a really awesome potato salad is included on the sample source disk. See the Introduction for ordering information.

What Are OLE Controls?

Here we are, well into the introduction to OLE Controls, and we haven't discussed OLE Controls yet. The first question that comes to mind is "What is an OLE Control?" This is perhaps the most interesting question I could think to ask in this chapter.

Microsoft defines an OLE Control as being "implemented as an OLE compound document object with visual editing support. OLE Controls have additional capabilities beyond those of ordinary OLE objects, such as the ability to fire events." Now let's see if we can come up with our own definition for an OLE Control.

To define what an OLE Control is, let's review some of the basic OLE terms such as OLE Server, OLE Container, Embedded Object, and Linked Object.

- An OLE Server is a program that allows objects that it creates to be embedded into OLE Container applications.
- An OLE Container application is a program that may have one or more OLE objects embedded or linked into it.
- An embedded object is stored in the container object. An embedded object's data normally won't change without some form of user inter-action, such as editing.
- A linked object is stored externally to the container object. A linked object's data changes whenever the user changes the original object that was linked.

OLE objects generally are placed into a document using a menu option, usually found in the Edit menu and called Insert Object. You can select the object to be linked or embedded from a list box of available objects.

This still leaves us searching for a definition for OLE Control. An OLE Control is a program that behaves like an object whose working interface with the user is through the OLE Control's user area. An OLE Control's format or layout generally is fixed, but its contents may vary. For example, a programmer could create an OLE Control that looked very similar to the standard list box found in many dialog boxes but that included special properties such as multiple columns.

In Chapter 12, "Creating an OLE Control," we create an OLE Control that is a digital clock. In this OLE Control, we display the current time in a font and style that the end-user can define. In fact, you could use the digital clock control in an Access 2.x form or report to display the current time or embed it into a Word 6 document. (However, Word 6.x and Excel 5.x don't fully support OLE Controls, so the actual performance of the OLE Control in Word 6 probably will be less than satisfactory.) When an OLE Control is embedded into a Word or Excel document, it basically becomes an OLE Automation Server, which might not be the desired effect.

An Automation Server is an application that exposes a programmable object to another application. OLE Controls become Automation Servers in Word and Excel documents because the current versions of Word (6.0) and Excel (5.0) don't support events. Events are responses by an OLE Custom Control to an outside action on the control, such as a mouse click.

One thing to keep in mind is that Microsoft has committed to supporting OLE Controls in its database and development tools. I would be surprised if Microsoft didn't support OLE Controls in future versions of both Word and Excel.

In Chapter 13, "Adding OLE Controls to an Application," we create a simple OLE Container application that works as a container for OLE Controls that you create.

USING OLE CONTROLS IN AN APPLICATION

You can use OLE Controls in many different applications. OLE Controls enable a developer to interface with other applications such as Microsoft Access. Additionally, OLE Controls add functionality to an existing application. A classic example would be adding the OLE Control digital clock, which we develop in Chapter 12, to an Access database program's forms. Another possible OLE Control is a calendar that would display the current month, perhaps with buttons to scroll forward and backward. There are many situations in which a person using an Access database might need to look up a specific date or a date's day of the week.

Applications from Microsoft

As this book was being written in the summer of 1994, the only application that fully supported OLE Controls was Microsoft Access 2.x. In Access 2.0, you can place OLE Controls in both forms and reports.

Access 2.0 can work with OLE Controls that you create, and also with the many aftermarket OLE Controls that will be available for Access.

Word for Windows 6.x and Excel 5.x both allow the insertion of OLE Controls into documents. However, when an OLE Control is subsequently copied to the clipboard, or when the container document is saved, the OLE Control ceases to be an OLE Control and becomes a standard OLE automation server, with a few minor differences.

It's still possible to create OLE Controls that may be used in containers that don't support OLE Controls. What must be taken into consideration is that the control won't receive event notifications (such as mouse actions or certain Windows messages) other than those necessary to manage the embedded control, such as resizing and movement.

SUMMARY

This chapter introduced OLE Controls, the CDK, and the OLE concepts that make up OLE Controls. The following topics were covered:

- OLE Controls, which are OLE Compound objects with additional capabilities such as event support
- CDK, the Control Development Kit
- Definitions of some of the terms commonly used with OLE Controls

OLE CONTROLS DEVELOPMENT TOOLS

This chapter describes the development tools that are supplied with the OLE Control CDK. These tools make the process of developing OLE Controls easy and (hopefully) painless, and they vary depending on the platform that you are developing under. For instance, the Make TypeLib (MKTYPLIB) utility isn't called by the programmer directly, except when running 16-bit versions of Visual C++. The WPS utility isn't used under Windows NT because the PStat and PView utilities are part of the Visual C++ 2.0 package. Both PStat and PView run only under Windows NT.

Unless otherwise noted, the descriptions of the tools are for how they run under Visual C++ 2.0. When a tool works differently under Visual C++ 1.5, I mention the differences.

CONTROLWIZARD

This section introduces you to ControlWizard. We'll use ControlWizard to develop the shell for our digital clock control in Chapter 12, "Creating an OLE Control."

ControlWizard's user interface looks and feels very much like that of AppWizard in Visual C++ 1.5.

To create a new OLE Control, you first start ControlWizard. Once started, ControlWizard displays the main dialog box, as shown in Figure 11.1. This figure shows that I have started to create the clock OLE Control, having entered the name for the control.

Figure 11.1. ControlWizard's main dialog.

Prior to naming the new OLE Control, you must select the directory that the new control will be created in.

When you specify the control's name, that name is used to create the control's directory. If you like, after specifying the control's name, you can edit the contents of the New Subdirectory edit box and rename the directory.

After naming your new control, you can then specify the control's options and configuration. The options and configuration are grouped under three pushbuttons: Project Options, Control Options, and Controls.

Project Options

The following options are available in the Project Options dialog box:

- Context Sensitive Help: This option normally isn't selected, but you can elect to include context-sensitive help if it's appropriate to your control.

- External Makefile: Normally selected, this option tells ControlWizard to create a makefile that can be managed by hand, but not through Visual C++ 2.0's development environment.

- Source Comments: Generally selected, this option tells ControlWizard to create comments in the source and header files to assist you in adding and modifying the code created.

- License Validation: Normally not selected, this option tells Control-Wizard to add calls to enforce licensing and to create an LIC license file for your control.

Figure 11.2 shows the Project Options dialog box. The only option I've selected is Source Comments.

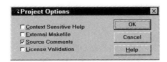

Figure 11.2. ControlWizard's Project Options dialog box.

Make sure that you check the Project Options dialog box to see that the options you want for your new control are correct.

Control Options

The following options are available in the Control Options dialog box:

- Control: This combo box lists the control being configured.

- Activate when visible: This check box tells ControlWizard to create code to activate your control when it's visible.

- Show in Insert Object dialog: This check box tells ControlWizard to make this control (when it's registered) appear in the Insert Object dialog box.

- Invisible at runtime: This check box creates a control that isn't visible when it's run. The control could be a data validation control, for example.

- Simple Frame: This check box tells ControlWizard to create the control with a simple frame style.

- About box: This check box tells ControlWizard to create an About box for the control. You can later customize the About dialog box.

- Subclass Windows control: This check box creates a control that sub-classes a standard Windows control. Windows controls that may be subclassed using this method include the following:

    BUTTON: A pushbutton control.

    COMBOBOX: A combo box control.

    EDIT: An edit control.

    LISTBOX: A list box control.

    SCROLLBAR: A scroll bar control.

    STATIC: A static control.

- Use VBX control as template: This check box tells ControlWizard to create the control based on an existing VBX control.

The Control Options dialog for our clock control is shown in Figure 11.3.

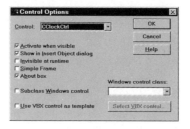

Figure 11.3. ControlWizard's Control Options dialog box.

As with the Project Options dialog, check all the options to ensure that they are correct for your new control.

Controls

The Controls dialog box enables you to define a number of attributes associated with your control. The following attributes may be changed:

- Short Name: The short name for this control, which is usually the same as the control's project name. If your control's project name isn't clear, you should specify a new short name.
- Class: Options in this combo box include Control and Property Page.
- C++ Class Name: The name of the control's main class.
- Header File: The filename of the main header file.

- User Type Name: The name that will appear in the Insert Object dialog box in the container application.
- Implementation File: The name of the main source file.
- Programmatic ID: The name used in programming.

The Controls dialog for our clock control is shown in Figure 11.4.

Figure 11.4. ControlWizard's Controls dialog box.

Again, check all the options to ensure that they are correct for your new control.

Generating Your OLE Control

Once you've defined your new OLE Control, you can click on Save from ControlWizard's main dialog. When you click on OK, you're presented with the New Control Information dialog box, shown in Figure 11.5. This dialog shows the various options, names, and configurations that you selected in the OLE Control creation stage.

Review this dialog box and, if all is in order, click on Create. You can then open the new control in Visual Workbench by selecting the correct .MAK file (for example, CLOCK.MAK for 16-bit or CLOCK32.MAK for 32-bit).

In most cases you'll want to create both 16-bit and 32-bit versions of your OLE Control. Until 16-bit applications such as Access 2.0 cease to be important (we're talking years here), programmers who are creating OLE Controls and other tools must take the 16-bit world into consideration.

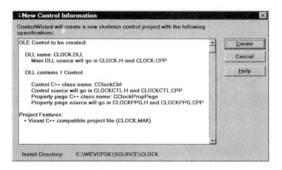

Figure 11.5. ControlWizard's New Control Information dialog box.

REGISTER/UNREGISTER CONTROL

Register Control and Unregister Control are two separate menu options on the Tools menu in Visual C++. However, both options call the registration program (REGSVR.EXE for Windows 3.x and REGSVR32.EXE for Windows NT and Windows 95) found in the CDK's BIN directory.

The REGSVR program takes as an argument the name of the control to be either registered or unregistered. This name generally is the OLE Control's DLL filename with the file extension. REGSVR also takes two optional parameters:

- The /V option tells REGSVR to communicate results back to Visual C++. This option is valid only when an OLE Control project is open.
- The /U option tells REGSVR to unregister the control rather than register it.

REGSVR is a QuickWin program, and as such is both small and efficient. REGSVR doesn't have any features other than those just described.

TEST CONTAINER

Test Container (TSTCON16 or TSTCON32, depending on the version of Windows to which you are targeting your OLE Controls) is a very useful utility that enables you to embed OLE Controls and test their functionality. The Test Container utility doesn't have all the usability of a full-fledged application, but it does allow you to test most of the aspects of your control. However, you still must test your control in its final environment, such as in an Access form.

Test Container runs externally to Visual C++, and therefore doesn't come in a debugging version. Generally, you have your control loaded in Visual C++ when debugging it and start Test Container from Visual C++'s Tools menu.

When Test Container is loaded and running, the first thing that you'll probably do is insert an OLE Control. Once a control is inserted into Test Container's document space, you can work with the OLE Control's interface. (You'll need to test both the user interface and the OLE Control's interface with the container.)

Test Container's user interface is both a menu and a toolbar. The menu offers the options described in Table 11.1.

TABLE 11.1. TEST CONTAINER'S MENU OPTIONS.

Menu	Option	Description
File	Save to Stream	Saves the currently selected OLE Control to a stream. A stream may hold one or more OLE Controls, and an OLE Control may be saved to the stream more than once. After an OLE Control has been saved to a stream, the Save to Substorage selection is disabled until the stream has been cleared.
	Save to Substorage	Saves the currently selected OLE Control to substorage. The substorage may hold one or more OLE Controls, and an OLE Control may be saved to the substorage more than once. After an OLE Control has been saved to substorage, the Save to Stream selection is disabled until the substorage has been cleared.
	Load	Loads the currently saved stream or substorage.
	Save Property Set	Saves the properties of the currently selected OLE Control to a document file.

continues

	TABLE 11.1. CONTINUED	
Menu	Option	Description
	Load Property Set	Creates a new OLE Control and initializes it from the previously saved document file.
	Register Controls	Registers a new OLE Control. Performs the same function as Visual C++'s Tools | Register Control menu option.
	Exit	Ends the Test Container program.
Edit	Insert OLE Control...	Opens the Insert OLE Control dialog and allows you to select a new control to be added to Test Container's document space.
	Delete	Deletes the currently selected OLE Control.
	Delete All	Deletes all the OLE Controls that are in Test Container's document.
	Set Ambient Properties...	Using the Ambient Properties dialog, sets the container properties that affect all OLE Controls. Properties such as UserMode, BackColor, Font, and so on may be set in this dialog.
	View Event List	Enables you to specify the logging of events, such as clicking the mouse button.
	Invoke Methods	Enables you to test the OLE Control's methods. All OLE Controls that are created using ControlWizard have at least an About method, which displays the control's About box.
	Draw Metafile	Draws the control's metafile so that you can see the effects of metafile drawing of your control's client area.

Menu	Option	Description
	Embedded Object Functions	Provides a submenu of choices: Activate calls `COleClientItem::Activate (OLEIVERB_PRIMARY, ...)`. Close calls `COleClientItem::Close()`. Deactivate calls `COleClientItem::Deactivate()`. Also discards the contents of the Undo buffer. Deactivate UI Only calls `COleClientItem::DeactivateUI()`. Hide calls `COleClientItem::Activate(OLEIVERB_HIDE, ...)`. Open calls `COleClientItem::Activate(OLEIVERB_OPEN, ...)`. Reactivate and Undo calls `COleClientItem::ReactivateAndUndo()`. Run calls `COleClientItem::Run()`. Show calls `COleClientItem::Activate(OLEIVERB_SHOW, ...)`.
	Object	Shows the currently active OLE Control's property sheet.
View	Toolbar	Shows or hides the toolbar.
	Status Bar	Shows or hides the status bar.
	Event Log	Displays the event log.
	Notification Log	Displays the notification log.
	Saved Control Stream	Displays a dump of the currently saved stream. This dump is divided into sections, one per saved control.
	Properties	Shows or hides the properties dialog for the selected control.

continues

TABLE 11.1. CONTINUED		
Menu	Option	Description
Options	Passive Container Mode	Tells the container not to automatically change the control's state. Selecting Passive Container Mode automatically deselects Simulated Design Mode.
	Simulated Design Mode	Tells the container to automatically change the control's state. Selecting Simulated Design Mode automatically deselects Passive Container Mode.
	Freeze Events	Freezes or releases on-event firing for all controls.
	Honor ACTI-VATEWHEN-VISIBLE	Turns on or off support for the `OLEMISC_ACTIVATEWHENVISIBLE` flag.
	Honor INVISIBLE-ATRUNTIME	Turns on or off support for the `OLEMISC_INVISIBLEATRUNTIME` flag.
Help	About Test Container	Provides help on Test Container.

Test Container also has a customized toolbar that provides information about the currently selected control and Test Container. The following is a list of the panes in the status bar from left to right:

- Test Container's Status: Provides menu prompts and Test Container's general status.

- OLE Control Name: The name of the currently selected control is displayed in the second pane. If there is no currently selected control, this pane is blank.

- OLE Control Count: Test Container keeps a count of how many instances of each control type are currently loaded. This pane displays the count for the currently selected control. For example, if you loaded three copies of the digital clock control, the Count pane would be either 01, 02, or 03, depending on which copy of the digital clock control was currently selected. If no control is currently selected, this pane is blank.

- OLE Control UI Status: The rightmost pane provides the status of the currently selected control. To change the control's UI status, select Edit | Embedded Object Functions. If no control is currently selected, this pane is blank.

Figure 11.6 shows Test Container's main window and its client area with my digital clock custom control. Notice how the digital clock looks in Test Container, then compare this figure with Figure 12.26 (in Chapter 12, "Creating an OLE Control"), in which the digital clock control is embedded in an Access form.

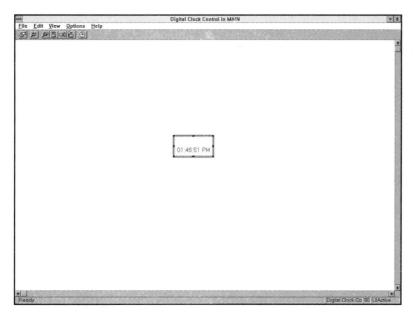

Figure 11.6. Test Container's main window.

Test Container also provides a dialog to configure the logging of events (see Figure 11.7). You can tell Test Container which events you want to log (see the description of the Event Log that follows). You can select each event and elect to have it logged or not logged. Also, there are buttons to turn event logging for all events on or off. Compare the events shown in Figure 11.7 with the Event Log window shown in Figure 11.8 (Test Container's logging windows).

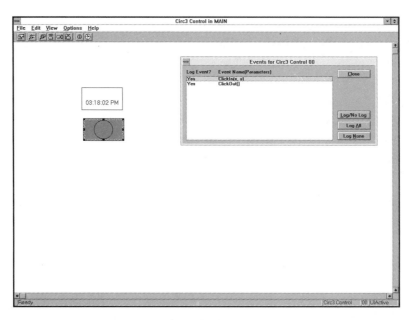

Figure 11.7. Test Container's Events for dialog box.

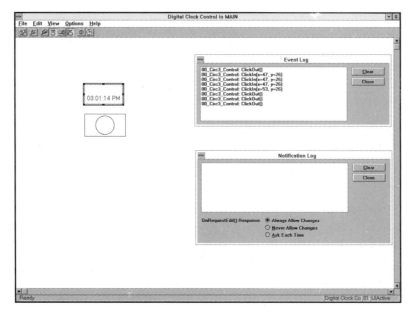

Figure 11.8. Test Container's logging windows.

With Test Container's status windows, you can see the OLE Control's Event Log and Notification Log. Both the Event Log and the Notification Log dialog boxes are modeless and can be left displayed for the entire Test Container session.

The Event Log shows the events for the currently active control. For example, the Circ3 control posts events for mouse clicks, both inside and outside the circle. For mouse clicks inside the circle, the event routines are configured to show the relative coordinates of the mouse cursor.

The Notification Log window notifies you of changes in the controls' properties. Figure 11.9 shows the notifications received when the Circ3 control has had its BackColor and ForeColor properties changed.

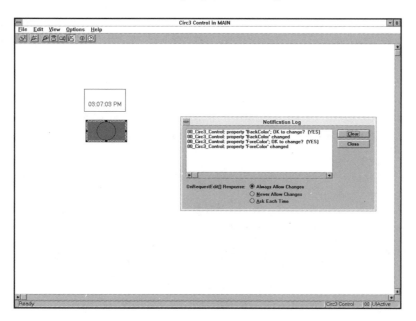

Figure 11.9. Test Container's Notification Log with changes to Circ3.

Also part of the Notification Log dialog box are radio buttons to configure the response to the **OnRequestEdit()** call. Choices include the following:

- Always Allow Changes: The response to the **OnRequestEdit()** call will be yes.

- Never Allow Changes: The response to the `OnRequestEdit()` call will be no.
- Ask Each Time: The user is presented with a confirmation dialog box that lets the user decide whether it's OK to change the property. If the user selects Yes, the property is changed; if the user selects No, the property isn't changed.

WPS

WPS is a utility that enables you to view both running tasks and loaded modules. It's part of the 16-bit version of the CDK. With WPS you can perform a number of functions, such as freeing a task or a module, saving the list of currently running tasks and loaded modules in a file, or forcing the loading of a module. Although this utility is intended for use with Windows 3.x, it also runs under Windows 95.

WPS has several uses for programmers who are developing OLE Controls. First, when a container program (such as Access) uses an OLE Control, the container program won't unload the control when it terminates. You can't make changes to a DLL file while it's loaded, so you must force Windows to unload the DLL prior to rebuilding it.

As a side benefit, WPS is useful as both a general process viewer and as a method to delete an undesirable process.

As with any system-level utility, WPS has the capability to bring Windows to a screeching halt. If you free a module or a task that Windows needs to run, the world as Windows knows it will come to an end!

WPS presents itself as a window split horizontally, with processes in the top third and loaded modules in the lower two thirds. One small flaw is that you can't change the size of the two parts of the window.

WPS offers several menu options, which are listed in Table 11.2.

	TABLE 11.2. WPS MENU OPTIONS.	
Menu	Option	Description
File	Load Module...	Enables you to force the loading of a module (an .EXE or a .DLL file).
	Dump	Allows you to save the main window's contents in a standard text file format. The saved file's contents can then be reviewed later.
	About WPS	Displays the About dialog, giving the authors' names and their company.
	Exit	Ends the current WPS session.
Options	Free Module	Frees the module that is currently selected.
	Free Task	Frees the task that is currently selected.
	Font	Allows you to change the font that WPS uses. Selecting a smaller font allows more lines of information to be displayed.
Edit	Copy	Copies the contents of the WPS window to the clipboard.
Update!		Tells WPS to update its display.

Figure 11.10 shows WPS running on my system. Notice that I have more tasks running than will fit into the Tasks part of the window (the top part), and many more modules loaded than will fit into the Modules part of the window (the bottom part). However, because both of these lists are sorted by name, it isn't difficult to find a specific task or module.

Looking at Figure 11.10, you can see a number of columns. Table 11.3 describes the columns and their usage.

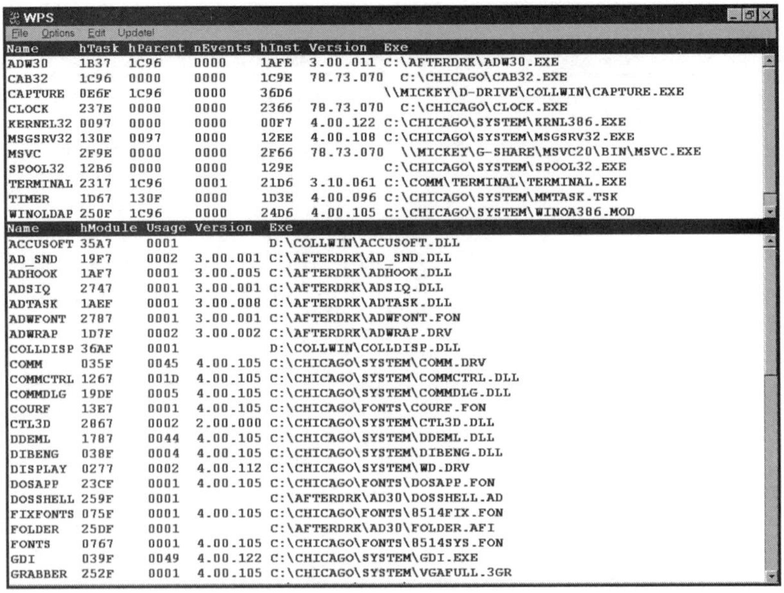

Figure 11.10. The WPS main window.

TABLE 11.3. COLUMNS IN WPS.

Column	Description
	Tasks Section
Name	The name of the running task. Generally, this is the eight-character program name. Often it's the same as the task's eight-character filename.
hTask	The handle for the task (see hParent).
hParent	The hTask for the parent task of this task. If the parent task is zero, the task is a 32-bit task owned by Windows.
nEvents	The count of the hardware resources, such as communications ports, for this task.
hInst	The instance handle for this task.
Version	The version number from the task's version resource (if the task has a version resource). If there is no version resource, this field is blank.

Column	Description
Exe	The fully qualified filename for the task. Some versions of Windows use UIC names for files that are on shared nonlocal network drives.

Modules Section

Name	The name of the loaded module. This name may be the same as the module's filename.
hModule	The handle for the module.
Usage	The usage count (lock count) that indicates the number of references to this module. Most nonsystem modules have a usage count of 1 or 2. System modules may have usage counts of 50 or more.
Version	The version number from the task's version resource (if the task has a version resource). If there is no version resource, this field is blank.
Exe	The fully qualified filename for the task. Some versions of Windows use UIC names for files that are on shared nonlocal network drives.

In all, I've found WPS to be a very useful tool for looking at what's loaded and running under Windows. I find it amazing how much is going on in Windows that I wouldn't be aware of otherwise.

MAKE TYPELIB

Make TypeLib is a utility that is run only as a separate step (by you, the programmer) under 16-bit versions of Visual C++. It isn't used when you're developing OLE Controls using Visual C++ 2.0 under Windows 95 or Windows NT. Rather, Visual C++ 2.0 can create the typelib as part of the project's build process by calling MKTYPLIB directly as part of the project's make process. The Make TypeLib command is found on the Visual Workbench's Tool menu when you're using Visual C++ 1.5. Make TypeLib invokes the MKTYPLIB program.

A typelib allows other applications to determine which properties, methods, and events your OLE Control will support. MKTYPLIB's input files have a file type of ODL, while an output typelib file has a file type of TLB.

When an OLE Control is created using ControlWizard, an initial ODL file is created for you. The ClassWizard program updates this file as you add new properties, methods, or events to your OLE Control. When developing under Visual C++ 1.5, you must use the Make TypeLib option on the Tools menu to update the typelib file.

The MKTYPLIB program has a number of options, which are described in Table 11.4. These options are specified when you start MKTYPLIB from the Visual C++ 1.5 Tools menu. MKTYPLIB can also be started from a DOS prompt, and these options may then be specified in the command line. The current version of MKTYPLIB is 2.01.

TABLE 11.4. MKTYPLIB OPTIONS.

Option	Description
/**help** or /**?**	Displays a message specifying the options for MKTYPLIB.
/**tlb** <*filename*>	Specifies the name of the output type library file. If not specified, the output file defaults to the same name as the input file, with a file type of TLB.
/**h** [*filename*]	Specifies the output .H filename.
/<*system*>	Available in both versions of MKTYPLIB. Use this option to specify which type of TLB is produced. Valid types of typelibs include **WIN16**, **WIN32**, **MAC**, **MIPS**, **ALPHA**, **PPC**, and **PPC32**. Defaults to **WIN32** for the 32-bit version of MKTYPLIB and to **WIN16** for the 16-bit version.
/**align** <#>	Available in the 32-bit version of MKTYPLIB only. Use this option to override the default alignment setting.
/**o** *filename*	Tells MKTYPLIB to redirect its output to the specified file. Normally, MKTYPLIB sends the output to the **stdout** device.
/**nologo**	Tells MKTYPLIB not to display the startup logo or copyright message.
/**w0**	Tells MKTYPLIB to disable all warnings.

Option	Description
/nocpp	Tells MKTYPLIB not to spawn the C preprocessor.
/cpp_cmd <*path*>	Specifies the path for the C preprocessor, which is part of the C/C++ compiler. Defaults to CL.EXE. If MKTYPLIB were to be used with compilers other than Visual C++, this option might have to be changed to reflect the actual name of the preprocessor.
/cpp_opt "<*opt*>"	Specifies the C/C++ preprocessor's options. The default options are **/C** **/E** **/D__MKTYPLIB__**. The actions taken with the default options are as follows: **/C**: Doesn't strip any comments from the preprocessor output. **/E**: Performs a preprocessor pass only, writing the output to **stdout**. **/D__MKTYPLIB__** defines the identifier **__MKTYPLIB__** that is referenced in OLECTL.H.
/D*define*[=*value*]	Defines additional C/C++ preprocessor identifiers. This option is used in addition to the **/cpp_opt** "<*opt*>" option just described.
/I *includepath*	Specifies paths for any include files.

The default installation for Visual C++ 1.5 (as done by the CDK setup program) uses the following option list. I've added comments to each option:

```
/cpp_cmd D:\MSVC15\BIN\cl    // Defines the preprocessor command
/W0                          // Disables all warnings
/I D:\MSVC15\CDK16\INCLUDE   // Sets the include path
/nologo                      // Disables the startup logo
$Proj.odl                    // The input filename
/tlb tlb16\$Proj.tlb         // The output filename (and directory)
```

You could modify these options, but you probably won't need to.

The default commands for MKTYPLIB for Visual C++ 2.0 are shown in the following code fragment. Notice that there are four different calls to MKTYPLIB: ANSI debug and release and Unicode debug and release. This code fragment is set up to create a 32-bit ANSI Windows release version:

```
SOURCE=.\CDKCLOCK.ODL
DEP_CDKCLOCK_O=\
```

```
MTL=MKTYPLIB
CFG=Win32 ANSI Release

!IF   "$(CFG)" == "Win32 ANSI Release"

$(OUTDIR)/CDKCLOCK.tlb : $(SOURCE) $(DEP_CDKCLOCK_O) $(OUTDIR)
   $(MTL) /nologo /D "NDEBUG" /D "_WIN32" /tlb $(OUTDIR)/"CDKCLOCK.tlb" \
   /win32  $(SOURCE)

!ELSEIF   "$(CFG)" == "Win32 ANSI Debug"

$(OUTDIR)/CDKCLOCK.tlb : $(SOURCE) $(DEP_CDKCLOCK_O) $(OUTDIR)
   $(MTL) /nologo /D "_DEBUG" /D "_WIN32" /tlb $(OUTDIR)/"CDKCLOCK.tlb" \
   /win32  $(SOURCE)

!ELSEIF   "$(CFG)" == "Win32 Unicode Release"

$(OUTDIR)/CDKCLOCK.tlb : $(SOURCE) $(DEP_CDKCLOCK_O) $(OUTDIR)
   $(MTL) /nologo /D "NDEBUG" /D "_UNICODE" /D "_WIN32" /tlb \
   $(OUTDIR)/"CDKCLOCK.tlb" /win32 $(SOURCE)

!ELSEIF   "$(CFG)" == "Win32 Unicode Debug"

$(OUTDIR)/CDKCLOCK.tlb : $(SOURCE) $(DEP_CDKCLOCK_O) $(OUTDIR)
   $(MTL) /nologo /D "_DEBUG" /D "_UNICODE" /D "_WIN32" /tlb \
   $(OUTDIR)/"CDKCLOCK.tlb" /win32 $(SOURCE)

!ENDIF
```

With Visual C++ 2.0, you set the typelib options by accessing the Project Settings dialog box. In this dialog, select the .ODL file in the Settings For: list box. You see two tabs, General and OLE Types.

Under the General tab, you can choose to exclude the typelib from the build. If you do so, you must build the typelib manually if you make any changes to the control's properties, methods, or events.

Visual C++ 2.0's Project Settings for CDKCLOCK's typelib generation, General tab, is shown in Figure 11.11.

Under the OLE Types tab, you can specify the output TBL filename, output header filenames, additional include directories, and preprocessor definitions. You also can specify whether MKTYPLIB's startup banner is displayed. In addition, there is a Reset button so that you can reset the typelib options to their default values. Visual C++ 2.0's Project Settings for CDKCLOCK's typelib generation, OLE Types tab, is shown in Figure 11.12.

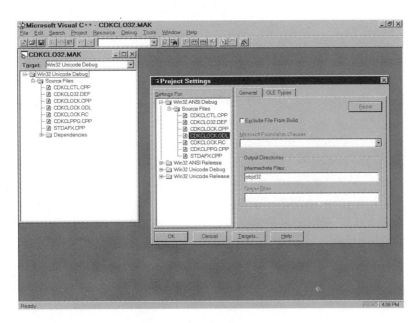

Figure 11.11. CDKCLOCK.ODL Project settings, General tab.

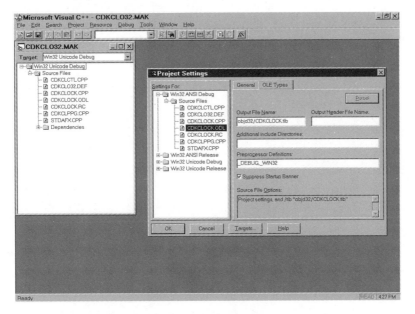

Figure 11.12. CDKCLOCK.ODL Project settings, OLE Types tab.

SUMMARY

This chapter introduced the CDK tools, which enable the developer to create OLE Controls with a minimum of effort. The following topics were covered:

- ControlWizard: A program to create an OLE Control program shell. The programmer can define a number of the control's attributes.

- Register/Unregister: You can register or unregister controls using REGSVR or REGSVR32.

- Test Container: A program that enables the developer to test the OLE Control that is being developed.

- WPS: A utility that shows the processes and modules that are currently loaded. WPS allows the killing of a process or module if necessary.

- Make TypeLib: The MKTYPLIB utility is used in the 16-bit environment to create type libraries.

CREATING AN OLE CONTROL

In this chapter we create an OLE Control and demonstrate how an OLE Custom Control handles various events, properties, and methods. The control created in this chapter can be embedded in an Access 2.0 form or report or in any other container that supports OLE Controls.

There is little reason to create an OLE Control without using ControlWizard. If you were to create an OLE Control manually, you couldn't use ClassWizard to manage the control's classes and you'd have difficulty creating a project file that was compatible with Visual C++. If you convert an existing VBX control to an OLE Control, ControlWizard offers an option to assist in automating the conversion process.

UNICODE REMINDER

Remember, Windows NT and OLE are Unicode-compatible. You should always code string literals using the `_T()` macro. For example, the string "Peter D. Hipson" should be written as `_T("Peter D. Hipson")`. The `_T()` macro takes care of the conversions to Unicode when necessary.

To create an OLE Control, you must have the OLE Control CDK installed. If you haven't installed the CDK, you should do so now. If you're developing using versions of Visual C++ other than 2.0, make sure that the versions into which you're planning to install the CDK are compatible with the CDK. Versions of Visual C++ earlier than 1.50.01 (including 1.5) must be upgraded before you install the CDK.

CREATING AN OLE CONTROL SHELL

To create our new OLE Control, which we'll call Clock, we first must start ControlWizard, which is located on Visual C++'s Tools menu.

Our new OLE Control project can be created using a series of steps:

1. Select the directory that the new OLE Control's project directory will be created under. Make sure that there isn't already a subdirectory with the same name in this directory.

2. Name your new project in the Project Name edit box. For our clock OLE Control, we'll use the name *clock*. Note that you're restricted to lowercase letters.

3. Click on the Project Options button to display the Project Options dialog box. In this dialog box, make sure that the only option selected is Source Comments. The other three options (Context Sensitive Help, External Makefile, and License Validation) shouldn't be selected.

4. Click on OK in the Project Options dialog box.

5. Click on the Control Options button to display the Control Options dialog box. In this dialog box, make sure that Activate when visible, Show in Insert Object dialog, and About box are selected. The other four options (Invisible at runtime, Simple Frame, Subclass Windows

control, and Use VBX control as template) shouldn't be selected. In the Control combo box, **CClockCtrl** should be selected. The Windows control class combo box should be blank. Figure 12.1 shows the Control Options dialog box with the correct options selected.

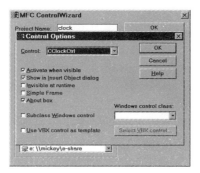

Figure 12.1. ControlWizard's Control Options dialog for Clock.

6. Click on OK in the Control Options dialog box.
7. Click on the Controls button to display the Controls dialog box. In this dialog box, make sure that the Short Name is Clock and that the class is Control. Change the User Type Name to Digital Clock Control. Accept the default names for the Header and Implementation filenames and the Programmatic ID. Figure 12.2 shows the Controls dialog box with the correct options and names selected.

Figure 12.2. ControlWizard's Controls dialog for Clock.

8. Click on OK in the Controls dialog box.

9. Click on OK in the MFC ControlWizard dialog box.

10. You're presented with the New Control Information dialog box. Compare the results in your session with those shown in Figure 12.3. The only difference should be the Install Directory field (located at the bottom of the dialog box).

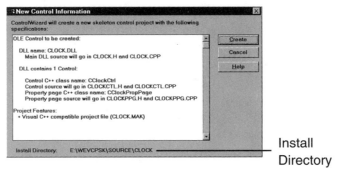

Figure 12.3. The New Control Information dialog box.

11. Click on Create in this dialog box.

In 11 simple steps, you've created your OLE Control. You didn't have to know a single thing about OLE, controls, containers, embedding, or linking to create the control.

After you've created your OLE Control, you should perform a full rebuild of it. If you're building a Windows 95 control, you need to select the Win32 ANSI Debug version. If you're building a Windows NT control, use the default Win32 Unicode Debug version. Rebuilding a new project ensures that, after making some changes, you know that the project would have built before the changes were made. When the build completes successfully, you should register your control and test it using Test Container. Because your control has no real functionality, it simply displays in Test Container as an ellipse inside the control's user area.

Your Clock control should look like the one shown in Figure 12.4. This figure shows Clock running in Test Container.

Now that we have a basic OLE Control that can be used, the next step in the development process is to add some properties.

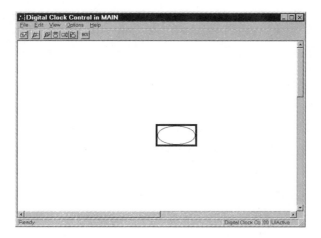

Figure 12.4. Clock, fresh from ControlWizard, in Test Container.

In this chapter, I add properties, events, and methods—in that order. It isn't necessary to follow a certain order when you add features to your OLE Control. I followed the order described simply because it made this chapter easier to write!

ADDING PROPERTIES TO AN OLE CONTROL

Properties are divided into two categories: stock (which are part of the OLE Control system) and custom (which are specific to a given OLE Control).

I cover stock properties first. After creating our stock properties, we will add a custom property to our clock.

Stock Properties: Colors

The OLE Custom Control system lets you rely on a set of stock properties for your control. With stock properties, you don't have to design a dialog box to set the property, because the stock property dialog boxes are already included in the OLE Control support DLL file.

OLE supports the stock properties shown in Table 12.1.

TABLE 12.1. STOCK PROPERTIES SUPPORTED BY OLE.	
Property	*Description*
BackColor	The control's background color. The default is white.
BorderStyle	The style of the border around the control.
Caption	The control's caption.
Enabled	The control's enabled state.
Font	The font used for text in the control.
ForeColor	The foreground color for the control.
hWnd	The control's **hWnd**.
Text	The control's text.

The first properties that we add are for foreground and background colors. These properties are supported with a stock color selection dialog.

The process to add a stock property in an OLE Control isn't too difficult.

DIFFERENCES BETWEEN VISUAL C++ 1.5 (16-BIT) AND VISUAL C++ 2.0

In Visual C++ 1.5, you must manually call the Make TypeLib utility (MKTYPLIB) to build the type library prior to rebuilding your project. In Visual C++ 2.0, the Visual Workbench takes care of building the type library. When building OLE Controls in Visual C++ 1.5, you should always select Tools | Make TypeLib after you've changed properties, events, or methods and before you rebuild the OLE Control.

The following is the process to add a stock property:

1. Start ClassWizard (press Ctrl-W). Select the OLE Automation tab (see Figure 12.5). Make sure that the class listed in the Class Name combo box is the OLE Control class (**CClockCtrl** in the Clock control).

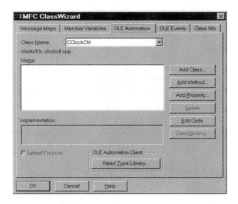

Figure 12.5. The OLE Automation tab in ClassWizard.

2. Click on the Add Property button to display the Add Property dialog box, shown in Figure 12.6. In this dialog box you must provide the external name for the property. The External Name combo box lets you select one of the stock property names (see Table 12.1), or you can enter the name of a custom property (see the section titled "Custom Properties").

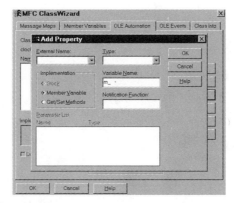

Figure 12.6. The Add Property dialog.

In our Clock OLE Control, the first stock property that we will add is **BackColor**. This property can be found in the External Names combo box. After you've selected the name of a stock property, you must make sure that the Stock radio button in the Implementation group is selected. You can override a stock property by changing the Implementation if desired.

3. When you're done with the Add Property dialog box, click on OK. You're returned to the OLE Automation tab, where in the Name list box you see the new property that you've added (**BackColor**), with an S symbol preceding it to indicate that **BackColor** is a stock property.

4. The changes that you've made with ClassWizard have added an interface to allow the background color to be changed. However, there still is no code in the control's drawing function to actually implement this.

At this stage, you must make whatever changes are necessary to implement your stock property. For example, the **BackColor** property is the background for the control (most Windows applications' controls are a light gray color).

To fill the OLE Control's background, you must add a few lines to the OLE Control's **OnDraw()** function. This function exists as a basic shell that you modify to draw whatever the control must display for the user. The original **OnDraw()** as supplied by ControlWizard is as follows:

```
/////////////////////////////////////////////////////////////////
// CClockCtrl::OnDraw - Drawing function

void CClockCtrl::OnDraw(
      CDC* pdc, const CRect& rcBounds, const CRect& rcInvalid)
{
    // TODO: Replace the following code
    // with your own drawing code
    pdc->FillRect(rcBounds, CBrush::FromHandle(
       (HBRUSH)GetStockObject(WHITE_BRUSH)));
    pdc->Ellipse(rcBounds);
}
```

This function must be modified because it has been hardcoded to fill the OLE Control's background using the stock **WHITE_BRUSH**. This raises a question: ClassWizard added the interface to set the background color, but how does the program find out what color the user selected? It's a good thing that there is a set of functions we can call to obtain the necessary attributes for a given property!

To obtain the color of the background, we use the **GetBackColor()** function, which retrieves the current background color. The format that **GetBackColor()** returns must then be processed by the

TranslateColor() function, after which the value from **TranslateColor()** can be used to create a new brush. The following code shows in bold the changes necessary to implement a background color property:

```
////////////////////////////////////////////////////////////////
// CClockCtrl::OnDraw - Drawing function

void CClockCtrl::OnDraw(
     CDC* pdc, const CRect& rcBounds, const CRect& rcInvalid)
{
    // TODO: Replace the following code
    // with your own drawing code
//   pdc->FillRect(rcBounds,
//   CBrush::FromHandle((HBRUSH)GetStockObject(WHITE_BRUSH)));
     CBrush  bkBrush(TranslateColor(GetBackColor()));
     pdc->FillRect(rcBounds, &bkBrush);

     pdc->Ellipse(rcBounds);
}
```

We must also add the necessary property page information to the **BEGIN_PROPPAGEIDS()** section. This change tells OLE which dialogs to display. Originally, the **BEGIN_PROPPAGEIDS()** section looked like this:

```
////////////////////////////////////////////////////////////////
// Property pages

// TODO: Add more property pages as needed.
// Remember to increase the count!
BEGIN_PROPPAGEIDS(CClockCtrl, 1)
    PROPPAGEID(CClockPropPage::guid)
END_PROPPAGEIDS(CClockCtrl)
```

We must add a new property page to the list. This necessitates making two changes. First, the number of property page sheets will change from 1 (the default page for the Clock control) to 2 (the default page and a color page). The count of pages is in the opening macro:

```
BEGIN_PROPPAGEIDS(CClockCtrl, 1)
```

In the **BEGIN_PROPPAGEIDS()** macro, the second parameter specifies the count and must be changed from 1 to 2:

```
BEGIN_PROPPAGEIDS(CClockCtrl, 2)
```

Second, we must add a new **PROPPAGEID()** macro to the list, making the
BEGIN_PROPPAGEIDS() block as follows:

```
//////////////////////////////////////////////////////////////////
// Property pages


// TODO: Add more property pages as needed.
// Remember to increase the count!
BEGIN_PROPPAGEIDS(CClockCtrl, 2)
    PROPPAGEID(CClockPropPage::guid)
    PROPPAGEID(CLSID_CColorPropPage)
END_PROPPAGEIDS(CClockCtrl)
```

5. After making these changes, you must rebuild the OLE Control. If
   you're using Visual C++ 1.5, you must rebuild the typelib by selecting
   Tools | Make Typelib. After rebuilding the typelib, you must rebuild
   your OLE Control.

6. After successfully rebuilding your control, try it out in the Test Container application. You should be able to select the control's property
   sheets, and there should be two tabs: General and Colors. If you select
   the Colors tab, you'll see a dialog box similar to the one shown in
   Figure 12.7.

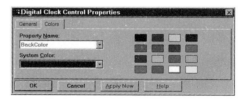

Figure 12.7. The Digital Clock Control Properties dialog (Colors tab).

Adding Functionality to the Clock Control

Now that we've added a stock property, it's time to add some functionality to
our clock control. We need to do the following:

1. Set up a timer loop with a one-second resolution.

2. Add code in our **OnDraw()** function to display the time.

3. Add code to kill the timer when the control ceases to run.

Setting up the timer isn't too difficult. We need to add code to the **OnCreate()** function (which we will create with ClassWizard) to start the timer. To create our timer, we follow these steps:

1. Start ClassWizard and go to the Message Maps tab. Select the **CClockCtrl** class and select the **CClockCtrl ObjectID**. You will see the Messages list box filled with the various **WM_** messages. Select **WM_CREATE** and then click on the Add Function button.

2. The Member Functions list box shows a new member, **OnCreate**, which will have the handler **ON_WM_CREATE**.

3. Click on the Edit Code button, which ends ClassWizard and places the cursor in the **OnCreate()** member function in CLOCKCTL.CPP.

We must add some code to **OnCreate()**. The following code fragment shows in bold the changes that are needed in the **OnCreate()** function:

```
int CClockCtrl::OnCreate(LPCREATESTRUCT lpCreateStruct)
{
        TRACE(_T("OnCreate() called\n"));

        if (COleControl::OnCreate(lpCreateStruct) == -1)
                return -1;

    m_IDTimer = SetTimer(999, 1000, NULL);
    if (m_IDTimer == 0)
    {
        AfxMesssageBox(_T("Couldn't set the timer in OnCreate()\n"));
    }

        return 0;
}
```

Notice that in **OnCreate()** we reference a new member variable, m_IDTimer. This member variable is used to hold the timer's ID, which **SetTimer()** returns. The timer ID is needed later to kill the timer, and it should be checked whenever a timer interrupt occurs so that we know which timer's interval has expired. In CLOCKCTL.H, we must add a declaration for m_IDTimer:

```
class CClockCtrl : public COleControl
{
        DECLARE_DYNCREATE(CClockCtrl)

// Constructor
public:
        CClockCtrl();

// Overrides

        // Drawing function
        virtual void OnDraw(
```

```
                              CDC* pdc, const CRect& rcBounds, const CRect& rc

        // Persistence
        virtual void DoPropExchange(CPropExchange* pPX);

        // Reset control state
        virtual void OnResetState();

// Implementation
protected:
        ~CClockCtrl();

        int  m_IDTimer;
```

As with any member function, in the constructor for the **CClockCtl** object we must initialize our member variable m_IDTimer:

```
CClockCtrl::CClockCtrl()
{
        InitializeIIDs(&IID_DClock, &IID_DClockEvents);

        // TODO: Initialize your control's instance data here
        m_IDTimer = -1;
}
```

Now we have the code to create a timer. We also need code to kill the timer when the OLE Control ends execution. This is important, because timers are a limited system resource (especially under 16-bit versions of Windows). We get rid of our timer in the **WM_DESTROY** message handler. We need to create this handler in the same manner that we did when we created the **WM_CREATE** handler: Start ClassWizard, select **WM_DESTROY**, then select Add Function to create the function handler. When creation is complete, select Edit Code to end ClassWizard and begin editing your function.

The following is the changed **OnDestroy()** function. The changes to kill the timer are in bold:

```
void CClockCtrl::OnDestroy()
{
        COleControl::OnDestroy();

        // TODO: Add your message handler code here

        KillTimer(m_IDTimer);
        m_IDTimer = -1;
}
```

Let's take a moment to take stock of what we've done. We now have a timer that is started when the OLE Control starts and that ends when the OLE Control ends. It's up to us to make use of this timer. To do so, we must make two more changes. First, we need a handler for the **WM_TIMER** messages that will be sent to the application whenever the timer's interval expires. Again, with

ClassWizard we need to create a handler, this time for **WM_TIMER**. In our **OnTimer()** function we need to tell the control to update its display:

```
void CClockCtrl::OnTimer(UINT nIDEvent)
{
        // TODO: Add your message handler code here and/or call default

        if (m_IDTimer == 999)
                InvalidateControl();

        COleControl::OnTimer(nIDEvent);
}
```

The process of telling a control to update itself is very similar to the process of telling a window to update itself: A window is updated whenever a call is made to **InvalidateRect()**, and a control is updated whenever a call is made to **InvalidateControl()**. We check to see if the timer message is correct so that we don't do more updates than we need to.

Finally, it's necessary to update the control's display of the time. Until now, our clock OLE Control has simply displayed the default ellipse. We now want to delete the ellipse drawing code and add whatever functionality is needed to display the time.

With the advent of **strftime()**, formatting a time value has become trivial. However, because an OLE Control is in a DLL, we can't call the **strftime()** function. We must format the time for display ourselves. Fortunately, this isn't too difficult. First, we add an include to the CLOCKCTL.CPP file to include the TIME.H file.

Once we have the header file for the standard time functions, we can add the time display code to the **OnDraw()** function:

```
void CClockCtrl::OnDraw(
                CDC* pdc, const CRect& rcBounds, const CRect& rcInvalid)
{
    // TODO: Replace the following code with your own drawing code
//  pdc>FillRect(rcBounds,
//      CBrush::FromHandle((HBRUSH)GetStockObject(WHITE_BRUSH)));
    CBrush bkBrush(TranslateColor(GetBackColor()));
    pdc->FillRect(rcBounds, &bkBrush);

//  pdc->Ellipse(rcBounds);

    struct  tm *newtime;
    char    am_pm[] = _T("AM");
    time_t long_time;
    char    szBuffer[80];

    time(&long_time);
    newtime = localtime(&long_time);
```

```
if (newtime->tm_hour > 12)
{
    strcpy(am_pm, _T("PM"));
    newtime->tm_hour -= 12;
}

sprintf(szBuffer, _T("%2.2d:%2.2d:%2.2d %s"),
    newtime->tm_hour,
    newtime->tm_min,
    newtime->tm_sec,
    am_pm);

pdc->SetTextAlign(TA_LEFT | TA_TOP);

pdc->ExtTextOut(rcBounds.left, rcBounds.top,
    ETO_CLIPPED, rcBounds,
    szBuffer, strlen(szBuffer), NULL);

}
```

When you've made these changes, you should rebuild your control and test it. If all goes well, you'll get a display like the one shown in Figure 12.8.

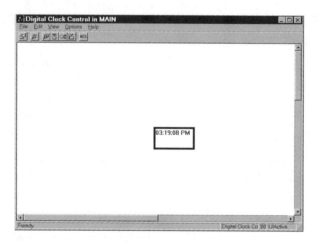

Figure 12.8. Test Container with Clock showing the time.

We still need one more stock color property. We can set the background color; wouldn't it be nice if we could set the color of the text? No sooner said than done! Again, we must follow a process very similar to the one we followed to add the **BackColor** property. The main difference is that we don't have to add a stock dialog page because we have one already, created for the **BackColor** property.

In ClassWizard, select the OLE Automation tab. Click on Add Property and, in the External Name combo box, select **ForeColor**. Make sure that the Stock Implementation is selected, and then click on OK. Close ClassWizard by clicking on OK in the main ClassWizard dialog.

Next, we must modify the **OnDraw()** function to utilize the new color. We're going to use the **ForeColor** property for the text that will display the time:

```
void CClockCtrl::OnDraw(
                CDC* pdc, const CRect& rcBounds, const CRect& rcInvalid)
{
    // TODO: Replace the following code with your own drawing code
//  pdc>FillRect(rcBounds,
//      CBrush::FromHandle((HBRUSH)GetStockObject(WHITE_BRUSH)));
    CBrush  bkBrush(TranslateColor(GetBackColor()));
    pdc->FillRect(rcBounds, &bkBrush);

//  pdc->Ellipse(rcBounds);

    struct  tm *newtime;
    char    am_pm[] = _T("AM");
    time_t long_time;
    char    szBuffer[80];

    time(&long_time);
    newtime = localtime(&long_time);

    if (newtime->tm_hour > 12)
    {
        strcpy(am_pm, _T("PM"));
        newtime->tm_hour -= 12;
    }

    sprintf(szBuffer, _T("%2.2d:%2.2d:%2.2d %s"),
        newtime->tm_hour,
        newtime->tm_min,
        newtime->tm_sec,
        am_pm);

    pdc->SetTextAlign(TA_LEFT | TA_TOP);

    pdc->SetTextColor(TranslateColor(GetForeColor()));
    pdc->SetBkMode(TRANSPARENT);

    pdc->ExtTextOut(rcBounds.left, rcBounds.top,
        ETO_CLIPPED, rcBounds,
        szBuffer, strlen(szBuffer), NULL);

}
```

We added only two new lines to set the text color! Now rebuild your clock control and give it a try. When you do so, you see that the colors' property page now has two selections: **BackColor** and **ForeColor**. When you change the **ForeColor** property, the color of the displayed time changes to match!

More Stock Properties: Fonts

The OLE Custom Control system lets you rely on a set of stock properties for
your control. With stock properties, you don't have to design a dialog box to
set the property, because the stock property dialog boxes are already included
in the OLE Control support DLL file.

Now that our clock has color, the next logical addition is the capability to
change the font of the time display. Many digital clock users will appreciate the
capability to change the font—nothing beats having a digital clock in a font
that looks digital.

To add a font property, first start ClassWizard. Select the OLE Automation tab,
then click on the Add Property button. You're presented with the Add Property
dialog. In the External Name combo box, select Font. Make sure that Stock
Implementation is also selected, then click on OK to close the Add Property
dialog. Click on OK again to close ClassWizard.

We haven't yet installed a stock property dialog box for fonts. We can fix this
by making an addition to the **BEGIN_PROPPAGEIDS()** block:

```
// TODO: Add more property pages as needed. Remember to increase the count!
BEGIN_PROPPAGEIDS(CCdkclockCtrl, 3)
        PROPPAGEID(CCdkclockPropPage::guid)
        PROPPAGEID(CLSID_CColorPropPage)
        PROPPAGEID(CLSID_CFontPropPage)
END_PROPPAGEIDS(CCdkclockCtrl)
```

Don't forget to change the number of property page IDs from two to three
(`BEGIN_PROPPAGEIDS (CCdkclockCtrl, 3)`).

Next, we must again make a change to the **OnDraw()** function to utilize the
correct font. In the previous version, we simply used the default font that was
already selected. Now, we want to use the font that the user selects, draw the
text, and then restore the original default font.

```
void CClockCtrl::OnDraw(
                    CDC* pdc, const CRect& rcBounds, const CRect& rcInvalid)
{
    // TODO: Replace the following code with your own drawing code.
//  pdc>FillRect(rcBounds,
//      CBrush::FromHandle((HBRUSH)GetStockObject(WHITE_BRUSH)));
    CBrush  bkBrush(TranslateColor(GetBackColor()));
    pdc->FillRect(rcBounds, &bkBrush);

//  pdc->Ellipse(rcBounds);

    struct  tm *newtime;
    char    am_pm[] = _T("AM");
    time_t long_time;
```

```
char    szBuffer[80];

time(&long_time);
newtime = localtime(&long_time);

if (newtime->tm_hour > 12)
{
    strcpy(am_pm, _T("PM"));
    newtime->tm_hour -= 12;
}

sprintf(szBuffer, _T("%2.2d:%2.2d:%2.2d %s"),
    newtime->tm_hour,
    newtime->tm_min,
    newtime->tm_sec,
    am_pm);

pdc->SetTextAlign(TA_LEFT | TA_TOP);

pdc->SetTextColor(TranslateColor(GetForeColor()));
pdc->SetBkMode(TRANSPARENT);

CFont* pOldFont;
pOldFont = SelectStockFont(pdc);

pdc->ExtTextOut(rcBounds.left, rcBounds.top,
    ETO_CLIPPED, rcBounds,
    szBuffer, strlen(szBuffer), NULL);

pdc->SelectObject(pOldFont);
}
```

Notice that we've added a call to **SelectStockFont()**, a function that inserts into the specified device context the font that the user selected. The **SelectStockFont()** function returns a **CFont** pointer to the previous font that was selected. After drawing our text, we restore the original font by calling **SelectObject()** with the pointer that was returned by **SelectStockFont()**.

Figure 12.9 shows the stock Fonts property tab. This dialog enables you to select any installed font available on the system. The Effects group box allows strikeout and underline fonts, and you also can select bold, italic, or both.

Again, rebuild the clock control. When the rebuild is done (without errors), try the clock control again. You'll notice an immediate change—the default font is now different! This is caused by the call to **SelectStockFont()**, which returns a different font than was originally selected into the device context. Using the clock's properties sheet, change to a new font. To see the effect of the change, look at our clock control, shown in Figure 12.10, for an example of the clock with a different font.

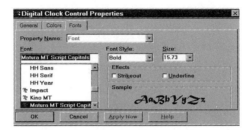

Figure 12.9. Digital Clock Control Properties dialog (Fonts tab).

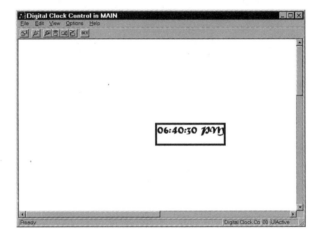

Figure 12.10. A new font in Clock.

You should keep several things in mind when working with stock properties. First, whenever a new stock property page is selected, the changes made on the previous property page are implemented. When the stock property pages exit (when you click on OK or a different tab), an **InvalidateControl()** call is made.

As you can see, it's very easy to add stock properties to an OLE Control. Next, we will add a few customized properties.

Custom Properties

Not everything in an OLE Control can be configured with the stock properties. Some things (sometimes many things) can only be set using a custom properties sheet.

Fortunately, Microsoft decided to make custom properties easy. First, the ControlWizard applet creates a default properties dialog box for you, to which you can add dialog controls that may be used to customize the operation of your OLE Control.

For the clock control, the first change that I want is the ability to configure the time display format. In our original format for Clock, the time was formatted with the string "%2.2d:%2.2d:%2.2d %s". There is always a leading zero when the time is earlier than 10 o'clock. Also, you might want to display the hours, minutes, and seconds, separated by dashes rather than colons.

We need to have an edit control in our default properties page with which we can edit the display format. This could be a difficult change, but ClassWizard does most of the work for us.

Here are the few simple steps to follow to create a custom property:

1. Start ClassWizard and click on the OLE Automation tab.

2. Click on the Add Property button.

3. In the External Name combo box, enter the name TimeFormat. The Implementation should be Member Variable. In the Variable Name field, the default name of m_timeFormat is displayed. In the Notification Function field, the default name of OnTimeFormatChanged is displayed. The Type box should have CString selected.

4. When you're satisfied with the names for the name, variable, and function, click on OK. Figure 12.11 shows the Add Property dialog with the TimeFormat property.

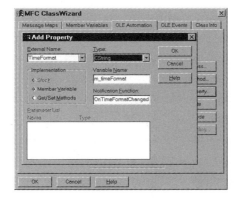

Figure 12.11. TimeFormat in the Add Property dialog.

Figure 12.12 shows ClassWizard's main dialog and the implementation of the `TimeFormat` property. Notice that the `TimeFormat` property is prefixed with a C symbol. This shows that `TimeFormat` is a custom property. When you're done reviewing the `TimeFormat` property, click on OK to end ClassWizard.

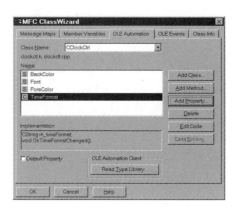

Figure 12.12. ClassWizard showing the `TimeFormat` property.

5. After you end ClassWizard, you must implement whatever code is necessary to make the `TimeFormat` property work. ClassWizard has created a member variable in **CClockCtrl** called m_timeFormat. This variable must be initialized and used where necessary. To initialize m_timeFormat, you must change the **CClockCtrl()** constructor, adding an assignment for the m_timeFormat variable:

```
CClockCtrl::CClockCtrl()

{
        InitializeIIDs(&IID_DClock, &IID_DClockEvents);


        // TODO: Initialize your control's instance data here
        m_IDTimer = -1;


        m_timeFormat = _T("%2.2d:%2.2d:%2.2d %s");
}
```

Now that we have our default format in the m_timeFormat variable, we must use it. This means changing our **OnDraw()** function so that the **sprintf()** function that we use to format the time uses m_timeFormat rather than a character constant. Notice the cast on m_timeFormat.

This casting is necessary because **sprintf()** expects a pointer to a character string, and just passing m_timeFormat would pass a **CString** object, making **sprintf()** very confused:

```
if (newtime->tm_hour > 12)
{
        strcpy(am_pm, _T("PM"));
        newtime->tm_hour -= 12;
}


sprintf(szBuffer, (const char *)m_timeFormat,
        newtime->tm_hour,
        newtime->tm_min,
        newtime->tm_sec,
        am_pm);


pdc->SetTextAlign(TA_LEFT | TA_TOP);
```

At this point we've done everything except allow the user to actually change the time format. We still need to add an edit control to the default property page dialog box and connect this edit control to the m_timeFormat variable in **CClockCtrl**.

6. To add an edit control to our default property page dialog box, we must edit the dialog box by selecting the IDD_PROPPAGE_CLOCK dialog into an edit window. Next, locate a group box at the left side of the property page dialog and label it Display Format. Inside this group box, add an edit control named IDC_TIME_FORMAT (or some other meaningful name). When you're done, the IDD_PROPPAGE_CLOCK dialog box will look like the one shown in Figure 12.13.

> There is a subtle inconsistency in the Visual Workbench in that an added control in a dialog box isn't always visible to ClassWizard until the dialog box is saved. After adding the IDC_TIME_FORMAT control, make sure that you manually save the dialog box (by pressing Ctrl-S) before invoking ClassWizard.

7. When you've added the IDC_TIME_FORMAT control to the default property page dialog (and saved the dialog box), you must link the control to the m_timeFormat variable that's in **CClockCtrl**.

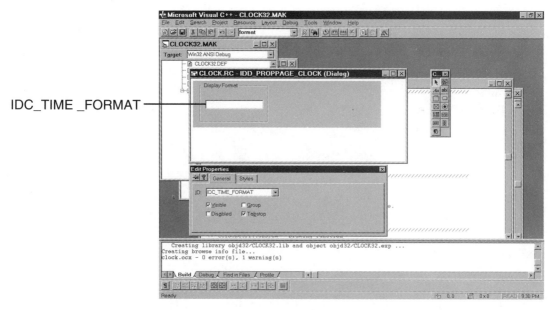

IDC_TIME_FORMAT

Figure 12.13. IDD_PROPPAGE_CLOCK *with* IDC_TIME_FORMAT.

8. Again, start ClassWizard. Click on the Member Variables tab, and then select the IDC_TIME_FORMAT line in the Controls IDs list box. Click on the Add Variable button. You're presented with the Add Member Variable dialog box.

9. In the Add Member Variable dialog box, you must supply a variable name. You can reuse the name m_timeFormat, because this class (**CClockPropPage**) can't see the m_timeFormat variable in **CClockCtrl**. In the Category combo box, select Value. In the Variable Type combo box, select **CString**. To link this control in the property page dialog box with the m_timeFormat variable in **CClockCtrl**, you must provide the Optional OLE Property Name. This is the name you entered in the Name field when you created the custom property in step 3. With this information, ClassWizard can create all the necessary linkages to manage the time display format. Your Add Member Variable dialog should look like the one shown in Figure 12.14. Click on OK.

There's no need in our clock control to have length validation for our format string. In a more finished project, you would want to make sure that the results from using the format string would fit in the buffers. However, in our clock control we will omit this error checking for clarity.

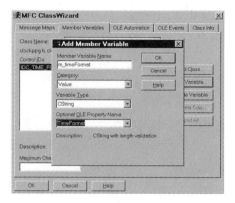

Figure 12.14. The Add Member Variable dialog in ClassWizard.

10. After closing ClassWizard's main dialog, you must rebuild your clock control. Visual C++ should build the control for you (with no errors—if you have errors, find and correct them). Next, try the control in the Test Container application. After embedding the clock control, select Properties. Your dialog should look like the one in Figure 12.15, in which I've set a new format string and clicked on Apply Now.

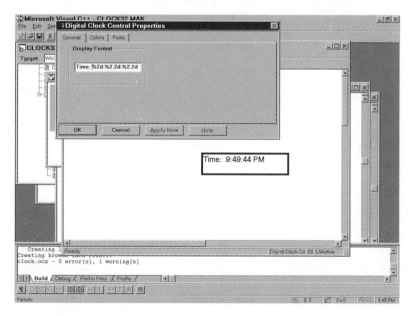

Figure 12.15. Test Container showing custom properties for Clock.

I would like to make one final change to our clock control before we move on to other things (like events). I like my clock to have a 24-hour format in which 6 p.m. is displayed as 18:00. Let's add a check box to change the format of the displayed time.

To make this change, we first must add a set of radio buttons to our dialog. I chose radio buttons because they seem to convey more information about the exclusive nature of the a.m./p.m. versus 24-hour display format than a check box could.

To enclose the radio buttons, I used the group box that we created when we added the TimeFormat property. I followed these steps to make changes to the clock control:

1. In ClassWizard, I created a new custom property called Display24Hour, which is created as a type short.

2. To the IDD_PROPPAGE_CLOCK dialog, I added two radio buttons, IDC_AM_PM and IDC_24_HOUR. Figure 12.16 shows these two new dialog controls. When you're done with the IDD_PROPPAGE_CLOCK dialog, select File | Save.

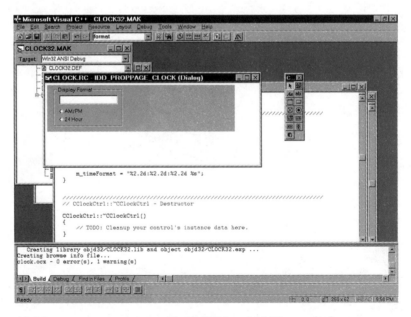

Figure 12.16. *IDD_PROPPAGE_CLOCK* with AM/PM and 24 Hour radio buttons.

3. Again, invoke ClassWizard and select the Member Variables tab. Select the IDD_AM_PM control and Add Member Variable. Use the name m_display24Hour for the variable, and make the variable's type int. In Optional OLE Property Name, use the name you entered in step 1. Click on OK in the Add Member Variable dialog, and then click on OK in ClassWizard's main dialog.

4. Next, you must add code to the **OnDraw()** function to change the format of the time being displayed. First, in the **CClockCtrl** constructor, you must add an initializer for the m_display24Hour variable. Initialize this variable to zero. Next, modify the **OnDraw()** function to test the m_display24Hour variable. Replacing an **if()** block with a **switch()** block is easy, as the following code fragment shows:

```
void CClockCtrl::OnDraw(
            CDC* pdc, const CRect& rcBounds, const CRect& rcInvalid)
{
    // TODO: Replace the following code with your own drawing code
//    pdc->FillRect(rcBounds,
//        CBrush::FromHandle((HBRUSH)GetStockObject(WHITE_BRUSH)));
    CBrush  bkBrush(TranslateColor(GetBackColor()));
    pdc->FillRect(rcBounds, &bkBrush);
//    pdc->Ellipse(rcBounds);

    struct    tm *newtime;
    char    am_pm[] = _T("AM");
    time_t long_time;
    char    szBuffer[80];

    time(&long_time);
    newtime = localtime(&long_time);

// REPLACE if (newtime->tm_hour.... with a switch()
//    if (newtime->tm_hour > 12)
//    {
//        strcpy(am_pm, _T("PM"));
//        newtime->tm_hour -= 12;
//    }

    switch (m_display24Hour)
    {// Shows how to handle radio buttons:
        case 0:  // First radio button, AM/PM format, being used
            if (newtime->tm_hour > 12)
            {
                strcpy(am_pm, _T("PM"));
                newtime->tm_hour -= 12;
            }
            break;
        case 1:  // Second radio button, 24 Hour format
            am_pm[0] = '\0';
            break;
        default:  // ERROR: An unhandled radio button selected!
```

```
        break;
    }

    sprintf(szBuffer, (const char *)m_timeFormat,
        newtime->tm_hour,
        newtime->tm_min,
        newtime->tm_sec,
        am_pm);

    pdc->SetTextAlign(TA_LEFT | TA_TOP);

    pdc->SetTextColor(TranslateColor(GetForeColor()));
    pdc->SetBkMode(TRANSPARENT);

    CFont* pOldFont;
    pOldFont = SelectStockFont(pdc);

    pdc->ExtTextOut(rcBounds.left, rcBounds.top,
        ETO_CLIPPED, rcBounds,
        szBuffer, strlen(szBuffer), NULL);

    pdc->SelectObject(pOldFont);
}
```

Now our clock has all the properties that we need. We can add more properties (such as an alarm function) later by simply following the preceding steps as a guideline.

Next, we will add some events to our clock control.

ADDING EVENTS TO AN OLE CONTROL

Your birthday, my birthday, the day the cow jumped over the moon—all are examples of events, but not the events that OLE Controls are interested in. When we talk about events with OLE Controls, we're referring to the process in which the control notifies the container that an event of some significance has occurred. This event may be as simple as the user clicking in the control's user area or (using our clock control as an example) as complex as a time period having expired.

When a container is notified that an event has occurred, it's said that the event has been *fired*. All event functions are called *firing functions* and usually are prefixed with the word Fire, as in **FireClick()**.

Like properties, events come in two flavors: stock and custom. I will cover stock events first, and then we will add a custom event to our clock.

Stock Events

The stock events that are available to an OLE Control are listed in Table 12.2. You can add these events by simply selecting Add Event in ClassWizard's OLE Events tab. The stock events have default functions defined for them. Each function has zero or more parameters and never has a return value.

TABLE 12.2. OLE CONTROL STOCK EVENTS.

Event	Firing Function	When It Gets Fired
Click	void FireClick(), which has no parameters	The mouse has been captured by the control, and any button-up message (WM_LBUTTONUP, WM_RBUTTONUP, or WM_MBUTTONUP) is received when the mouse is located over the control's user area. Prior to this event, the stock MouseDown and MouseUp events are fired (if defined).
DblClick	void FileDblClick(), which has no parameters	The mouse has been captured by the control, and any button has been double-clicked. A WM_LDBLCLICK, WM_RDBLCLICK, or WM_MDBLCLICK message is received when the mouse is located over the control's user area. Prior to this event, the stock Click, MouseDown, and MouseUp events are fired (if defined).

continues

	TABLE 12.2. CONTINUED	
Event	*Firing Function*	*When It Gets Fired*
Error	**void FireError(SCODE** *scode*, **LPCSTR** *lpcszErrorDescription*, **UINT** *nHelpID* = **0)**	This event is fired whenever an error condition occurs in the control. The **FireError()** function has parameters to describe the actual error.
KeyDown	**void FireKeyDown(short** *nChar*, **short** *nShiftState*)	This event is fired whenever a key (either **WM_SYSKEYDOWN** or **WM_KEYDOWN**) is pressed and the control has input focus. The **FireKeyDown()** function has parameters to tell which key was pressed and the state of the Shift keys.
KeyPress	**void FireKeyPress(short *** *pnChar*)	This event is fired whenever a **WM_CHAR** message has been received. The **FireKeyPress()** function has a parameter that points to the character for the key that was pressed.
KeyUp	**void FireKeyUp(short** *nChar*, **short** *nShiftState*)	This event is fired whenever a key (either **WM_SYSKEYUP** or **WM_KEYUP**) is pressed and the control has input focus. The **FireKeyUp()** function has parameters to tell which key was pressed and the state of the Shift keys.

Event	Firing Function	When It Gets Fired
MouseDown	void FireMouseDown(short nButton, short nShiftState, float x, float y)	This event is fired when a WM_LBUTTONDOWN, WM_RBUTTONDOWN, or WM_MBUTTONDOWN message is received. The mouse is captured just prior to the MouseDown event being fired. The FireMouseDown() function has parameters to indicate which mouse button was pressed, the state of the Shift keys, and the mouse's x and y coordinates. Note that the x and y coordinates are floating-point values.
MouseMove	void FireMouseMove(short nButton, short nShiftState, float x, float y)	This event is fired when a WM_MOUSEMOVE message is received. The FireMouseDown() function has parameters to indicate which mouse button was pressed, the state of the Shift keys, and the mouse's x and y coordinates. Note that the x and y coordinates are floating-point values.

continues

	TABLE 12.2. CONTINUED	
Event	Firing Function	When It Gets Fired
MouseUp	void FireMouseUp(short nButton, short nShiftState, float x, float y)	This event is fired when a WM_LBUTTONUP, WM_RBUTTONUP, or WM_MBUTTONUP message is received. The mouse is released from capture just prior to the MouseUp event being fired. The FireMouseUp() function has parameters to indicate which mouse button was pressed, the state of the Shift keys, and the mouse's x and y coordinates. Note that the x and y coordinates are floating-point values.

Our control can't offer a great deal of functionality in implementing a stock event. We'll add the stock event DblClick to our clock control as an exercise in adding stock events.

To add a stock event, start ClassWizard, then click on the OLE Events tab. You will see a dialog in which you can view currently defined events and add new events. To add an event, click on the Add Event button. ClassWizard displays the Add Event dialog (see Figure 12.17), which enables you to select the event's external name. The External Name combo box lets you select stock events from the dropdown list box or create a custom event by entering the event name in the External Name combo box's edit field.

From the dropdown list box, select DblClick. Stock implementation should be selected. The Internal Name field changes to FireDblClick and becomes read-only so that the name of the event firing function can't be changed. If we were defining the DblClick event as a Custom implementation, we could edit the function's name if we wanted to.

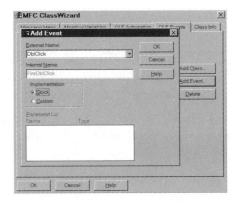

Figure 12.17. Add Event in ClassWizard's OLE Events tab.

The Parameter List list box is also disabled because the stock **DblClick** event doesn't take any parameters. Figure 12.17 shows the Add Event dialog box.

After you've defined the **DblClick** event, click on OK in the Add Event dialog box. You're returned to the OLE Events tab in ClassWizard. You should see a single event defined—**DblClick**, which is prefixed with an S symbol. This indicates that **DblClick** is a stock event. See Figure 12.18.

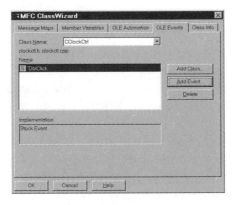

*Figure 12.18. OLE Events in ClassWizard with the **DblClick** event displayed.*

After you've reviewed your stock event, close ClassWizard by clicking on OK, and rebuild the control. When you've successfully rebuilt the control, you can test it using Test Container, in which you can view the event log by selecting View | Event Log. Double-clicking on the clock control causes an event notification to be logged in the Event Log dialog box.

Custom Events

Stock events are defined for you, but a custom event is totally up to your imagination. Let's take a trip back to the days of the first digital watches. Almost as soon as digital watches appeared, some smart engineer designed one with an alarm. Hey, what a concept—a digital alarm clock!

If we added a field to our clock's property page for the alarm time (a simple edit field, for example), which we could then parse out to an alarm time, we could compare this alarm time with the current time whenever we received a **WM_TIMER** message.

First, let's add a set alarm section to our property page. Adding a set alarm time field presents a minor problem: We really could use a custom time control that would validate our alarm time. However, to keep our clock custom control simple, we will use a set of simple combo box fields with the hours, minutes, and seconds entered in three separate combo boxes. Using combo boxes, we can force the user to enter a valid time value.

> The MFC implementation of **IDispatch** allows for a maximum of 15 parameters (our alarm function uses three). Be careful not to exceed this limitation.

I won't describe the process of defining the alarm property. It's exactly the same as adding the properties that we added earlier. After adding the necessary code for an alarm property, we have three new property variables: m_alarmHours, m_alarmMinutes, and m_alarmSeconds. When the clock control starts, we initialize the alarm to the current time:

```
CClockCtrl::CClockCtrl()
{
        InitializeIIDs(&IID_DClock, &IID_DClockEvents);

        // TODO: Initialize your control's instance data here
        m_IDTimer = -1;

        m_timeFormat = _T("%2d:%2.2d:%2.2d %s");

        m_display24Hour = 0;


        struct  tm *newtime;
        time_t long_time;
```

```
        time(&long_time);
        newtime = localtime(&long_time);

        m_alarmHours   = newtime->tm_hour;
        m_alarmMinutes = newtime->tm_min;
        m_alarmSeconds = newtime->tm_sec;
}
```

The properties dialog box is shown in Figure 12.19.

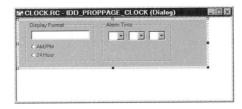

Figure 12.19. IDD_PROPPAGE_CLOCK with alarm feature added.

After the clock control has started, each time the **WM_TIMER** message is received in the **OnTimer()** function, the time is checked with the alarm time. If they match, our alarm event is fired.

What happens when the alarm event fires is up to the container application. Were the clock control to be embedded in an Access form, the alarm might serve to remind the user that a task must be performed (such as a backup or saving data).

Next, we must add the alarm event handler. To add a custom event handler, we use ClassWizard's OLE Events tab. Click on the Add Event button after selecting **CClockCtrl** in the Class Name combo box.

In the Add Event dialog, specify an external name for Alarm. The internal name should be FireAlarm (I couldn't have picked a better name if I tried!). In the Parameter List combo box, double-click on the left side of the top (current) line. You're presented with an edit field in which you can enter a variable name. Enter the first variable as *nHour*. Next, either tab forward or double-click on the right side of the current line. You're presented with a dropdown list from which you can select *nHour*'s variable type. Use short. After creating *nHour*, create *nMinute* (double-click on the line under *nHour*) and *nSecond* (double-click on the line under *nMinute*).

When you're finished with the Add Event dialog and it looks like the one in Figure 12.20, click on OK.

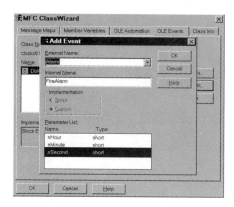

Figure 12.20. Add Event under OLE Events in ClassWizard.

The final part of adding our alarm event is to add the actual alarm code. There are several factors to take into consideration when comparing the alarm time with the current time. First and foremost is that there is no guarantee that there will be a **WM_TIMER** message every second. If Windows is busy, there might be one (or more) skipped **WM_TIMER** messages. This presents a problem, because we're testing for an exact time. What seems best here is to find out if the alarm time has passed and, if an alarm hasn't yet been sounded, fire the alarm. We do this by setting a flag signaling that an alarm is set and hasn't been sounded. Of course, if the user sets an alarm time that's earlier than the current time, this generates an immediate alarm, which is a minor problem in this sample program.

First, let's take a look at our final **OnDraw()** function. We've added code to **OnDraw()** to find out if the alarm has been set (if m_Alarmed is **TRUE**) and if the current time is later than the alarm time. If both tests are true, an alarm event is triggered.

```
void CClockCtrl::OnDraw(
          CDC* pdc, const CRect& rcBounds, const CRect& rcInvalid)
{
    // TODO: Replace the following code with your own drawing code
    CBrush bkBrush(TranslateColor(GetBackColor()));
    pdc->FillRect(rcBounds, &bkBrush);

    struct    tm *newtime;
    char     am_pm[] = _T("AM");
    time_t long_time;
    char     szBuffer[80];

    time(&long_time);
    newtime = localtime(&long_time);
```

```
//    Check for alarms. If past alarm time, sound it!

    if (m_Alarmed &&
        m_alarmHours   <= newtime->tm_hour &&
        m_alarmMinutes <= newtime->tm_min &&
        m_alarmSeconds <= newtime->tm_sec)
    {//    It's an alarming event!
        m_Alarmed = FALSE;
        FireAlarm(m_alarmHours, m_alarmMinutes, m_alarmSeconds);
    }

//   Format time for display

    switch (m_display24Hour)
    {// Shows how to handle radio buttons:
        case 0:  // First radio button, AM/PM format, being used
            if (newtime->tm_hour > 12)
            {
                strcpy(am_pm, _T("PM"));
                newtime->tm_hour -= 12;
            }
            break;
        case 1:  // Second radio button, 24 Hour format
            am_pm[0] = '\0';
            break;
        default:  // ERROR: An unhandled radio button selected!
            break;
    }

    sprintf(szBuffer, (const char *)m_timeFormat,
        newtime->tm_hour,
        newtime->tm_min,
        newtime->tm_sec,
        am_pm);

//   Set up display of time

    pdc->SetTextAlign(TA_LEFT | TA_TOP);

    pdc->SetTextColor(TranslateColor(GetForeColor()));
    pdc->SetBkMode(TRANSPARENT);

    CFont* pOldFont;
    pOldFont = SelectStockFont(pdc);

    pdc->ExtTextOut(rcBounds.left, rcBounds.top,
        ETO_CLIPPED, rcBounds,
        szBuffer, strlen(szBuffer), NULL);

//   Restore device context

    pdc->SelectObject(pOldFont);
}
```

When the alarm time has passed, a call is made to `FireAlarm()` with the alarm time. The `FireAlarm()` function is created by ClassWizard in the CLOCKCTL.H file as a single-line function that calls the OLE Controls function `FireEvent()` with the correct parameters.

```
// Event maps
   //{{AFX_EVENT(CClockCtrl)
   void FireAlarm(short nHour, short nMinute, short nSecond)
      {FireEvent(eventidAlarm,EVENT_PARAM(VTS_I2  VTS_I2  VTS_I2),
         nHour, nMinute, nSecond);}
   //}}AFX_EVENT
   DECLARE_EVENT_MAP()
```

The `m_Alarmed` variable is tied to a property that is, in turn, mapped to a check box in Clock's property page dialog. This enables the user to turn the alarm function on or off.

ADDING METHODS TO AN OLE CONTROL

Along with properties, methods are another way that a control's container can communicate with the control. Like properties, there are both stock methods and custom methods.

A method can do everything a property can do, plus the following:

- Simulate user interface actions such as mouse clicks.
- Send commands such as Refresh to the control.
- Send control-specific commands to the control.

In the next two sections, we will add both a stock method and a custom method to our clock control. First, we will add the stock method, Refresh, which tells the control to update its user area. Because the implementation of a stock method is performed by the OLE Control's base class implementation, most of the work is performed using ClassWizard.

ADDING A STOCK METHOD

To add a method to an OLE Control, you must start ClassWizard, choose the OLE Automation tab, and click on the Add Method button.

Clicking on the Add Method button displays the Add Method dialog box. In this dialog box, you define the method's external name. For a stock method, you must select one of the names available in the External Name combo box: **DoClick** or **Refresh**.

For our stock method, let's choose the **Refresh** method. Note that the implementation must be Stock and that all other data entry controls in the Add Method dialog box are disabled. When you've selected the method name of Refresh and the Stock implementation, the Add Method dialog should look like the one shown in Figure 12.21.

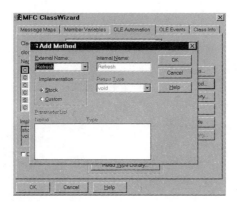

Figure 12.21. Add Method in ClassWizard.

Click on OK in the Add Method dialog to add the new method. You're returned to ClassWizard's main dialog, which should look like Figure 12.22. The new method, **Refresh** (which is highlighted), is preceded by the M symbol, indicating that **Refresh** is a method.

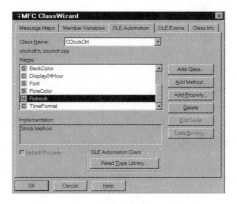

*Figure 12.22. ClassWizard showing the **Refresh** method.*

Next, rebuild the clock control. After the control has been built, you can test your new method. Start the Test Container program and load the clock control into it. In Test Container, select Edit | Invoke Methods... to display the Invoke Control Method dialog box. Our clock control actually has two methods—our new stock **Refresh** method and the preexisting AboutBox method that was created by ControlWizard when the control was first created. Figure 12.23 shows Test Container's Invoke Control Method dialog.

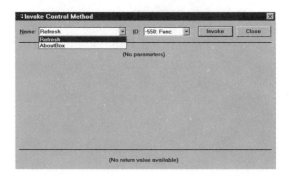

Figure 12.23. Test Container's Invoke Control Method dialog.

With **Refresh** selected, you can click on the Invoke button to update the clock's display. The effects of the **Refresh** method probably will be a bit difficult to see, because the clock is updated automatically. However, if you set the timer interrupt interval from one second to one minute, the effect of the **Refresh** method is much more visible.

Next, we will create a custom method for our clock control.

ADDING A CUSTOM METHOD

In addition to stock methods, there are custom methods, which allow your control to be manipulated in ways that are unique to it. For example, we'll create a method to allow the container to set the alarm.

First, let's make a minor modification to our alarm function. Until now, the alarm function simply fired an event. Let's also tell the user that the alarm is ringing. To do this, we simply add a call to **MessageBeep()** in our alarm handler, as the following code fragment shows:

```
//    Check for alarms. If past alarm time, sound it!

   if (m_Alarmed &&
       m_alarmHours    <= newtime->tm_hour &&
       m_alarmMinutes <= newtime->tm_min &&
       m_alarmSeconds <= newtime->tm_sec)
   {//    It's an alarming event!
       m_Alarmed = FALSE;
       FireAlarm(m_alarmHours, m_alarmMinutes, m_alarmSeconds);
       MessageBeep(MB_ICONEXCLAMATION);
   }
```

With this audible alarm, the user will know when a container sets an alarm.

Now, let's design our custom method. This method (let's call it `SetAlarm`) takes four parameters: `hours`, `minutes`, `seconds`, and a flag that specifies whether the alarm is on or off.

To create our custom method, we must start ClassWizard. Click on the Add Methods button in ClassWizard's OLE Automation tab to display the Add Method dialog box.

In the Add Method dialog box, you must specify the external name (`SetAlarm`). ClassWizard provides the internal name, which you may modify if you like. You also can specify a return value for the method. In `SetAlarm`, I specified the return value as a short, which is the previous value for the alarm on/off flag.

You also need to specify the parameters for your method. As just described, `SetAlarm` has four properties. They are shown in Figure 12.24.

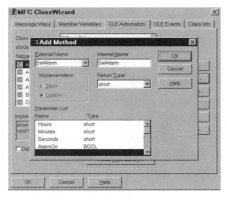

Figure 12.24. Add Method in ClassWizard with the `SetAlarm` method shown.

When you're finished with the Add Method dialog, click on OK to add the new method, and then click on OK to end ClassWizard.

ClassWizard then adds a member to the **DISPATCH_MAP**, describing the new method, and also creates an empty function that you, the programmer, can fill with whatever code is necessary to perform the method's function.

In Clock, we must set the alarm's time and the flag that specifies whether the alarm is on or off. The following code fragment is an example of how this might be done. My changes appear in bold:

```
short CClockCtrl::SetAlarm(short Hours, short Minutes,
    short Seconds, BOOL AlarmOn)
{
    // TODO: Add your dispatch handler code here
    short nReturnCode = m_Alarmed;

    m_alarmHours   = Hours;
    m_alarmMinutes = Minutes;
    m_alarmSeconds = Seconds;
    m_Alarmed = AlarmOn;

//  return 0;

    return(nReturnCode);
}
```

It's only necessary to save the new alarm time and the state of the alarm on/off flag. After you've added the SetAlarm method and the preceding changes to your SetAlarm() function, rebuild the clock control.

Figure 12.25 shows Test Container with the clock control installed. The Invoke Methods dialog enables the user to set the alarm time and turn the alarm on or off.

A custom method allows the container application to set virtually any possible attribute or to control almost any aspect of an OLE Control's operation. Don't be limited by my examples. Let your imagination run wild.

A Few More Bells and Whistles

What else could our clock OLE Control have? One enhancement that comes to mind is to expand what the user sees when the clock is running. First, it would be nice to display both the current time and the alarm time. It also might be a good idea to have some visual indicator that there is an active alarm.

Perhaps a digital clock isn't the best display. After all, this is a graphical environment: You could make the time display an analog format.

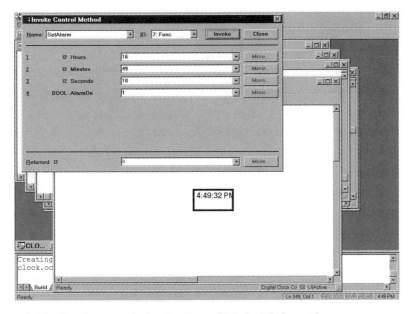

Figure 12.25. Test Container's Invoke Control Method dialog with SetAlarm.

Only a few digital clocks don't offer some kind of date display. Our clock control might benefit from having a date display with the time. Perhaps the date display could be optional, or the time could change to the date whenever the mouse button is pressed over the control.

A dynamic calendar display, in which previous and future months could be viewed, would enhance the clock control. Perhaps the date could be displayed when the left mouse button is pressed and the calendar could be displayed when the right mouse button is pressed.

Enhancements to the clock control are almost limitless. Adding a simple reminder system isn't difficult. Of course, you would want multiple reminders and multiple alarms. If you have reminders and multiple alarms, why not add an address book feature as well? The possibilities are endless, and all within a single OLE Control!

LICENSE VALIDATION

The OLE Control system includes a feature called license validation. With license validation you can determine who can distribute or use your OLE Control.

To use license validation, you would ship your control with the .LIC license file to other developers. These other developers would then ship the control embedded in their application but wouldn't ship the .LIC license file with their application. This prevents the users of the application in which your control is embedded from reusing the control on their own.

However, you must make sure that the people you've licensed to use your control and to whom you've given the .LIC license file never distribute the .LIC license file.

Adding License Validation to a New Control

To add license validation to a new OLE Control, you simply select the License validation check box in ControlWizard. This adds the necessary code to check the license validation.

License validation works by looking for a specific string in the .LIC license file. For example, the clock OLE Control's license file is shown in Listing 12.1.

LISTING 12.1. LICENSE FILE FOR CLOCK, CLOCK.LIC.

```
Copyright (c) 1994 Peter Hipson

Warning:  This product is licensed to you pursuant to the terms of the
license agreement included with the original software, and is
protected by copyright law and international treaties.  Unauthorized
reproduction or distribution may result in severe civil and criminal
penalties, and will be prosecuted to the maximum extent possible under
the law.
```

The actual check to verify the license file looks at the first line in the file. This line is compared with the license string that's contained in the program.

Adding License Validation to Clock

To add licensing to an existing control, you need to make several changes to the control. First, you must have a .LIC license file. If you can't come up with your own, you can copy the file from Listing 12.1 and change its name to the name you're using.

Next, in the control's ?????CTL.H file, you must change the class factor and GUID macro to include license checking. The following code fragment shows the necessary change:

```
// DECLARE_OLECREATE_EX(CClockCtrl)   // Class factory and GUID

BEGIN_OLEFACTORY(CClockCtrl)          // Class factory and GUID
      virtual BOOL VerifyUserLicense();
      virtual BOOL GetLicenseKey(DWORD, BSTR FAR*);
   END_OLEFACTORY(CClockCtrl)
```

You must comment out the original class factory line:

```
// DECLARE_OLECREATE_EX(CClockCtrl)   // Class factory and GUID
```

and add a new class factor macro:

```
BEGIN_OLEFACTORY(CClockCtrl)          // Class factory and GUID
      virtual BOOL VerifyUserLicense();
      virtual BOOL GetLicenseKey(DWORD, BSTR FAR*);
   END_OLEFACTORY(CClockCtrl)
```

The final change is to add a single parameter to the control's .ODL file. This file contains the control's typelib information.

The change is simply the addition of the keyword licensed to the help file line. In the following code fragment, I've replaced the control's name and **uuid** with question marks. In your control, the control's name and the correct **uuid** will be present in these fields. The keyword that must be added is shown in bold:

```
//   Class information for C????????Ctrl

      [ uuid(????????-????-????-????-????????????), licensed,
        helpstring("???????? Control") ]
      coclass ????????
```

Gotcha! When Visual C++ 2.0 compiles a project, it creates subdirectories for the output. Creating subdirectories allows you to have both debugging and release versions of the same project at the same time. In Visual C++ 1.5 and earlier versions, creating a release version when a debugging version exists overwrites the debugging version, and vice versa. Visual C++ 2.0 creates a separate subdirectory for each executable type. (An OLE Control will have four types: Unicode release, Unicode debug, ANSI release, and ANSI debug.)

The .LIC file must be in the same directory as the executable for the control. This means that you must manually copy the .LIC file to the directory that the control's .OCX file is in. If you don't have the .LIC file in the same directory as the control's executable file, the license verification will fail.

Time lost finding this problem: two hours.

How does licensing work? The call to **AfxVerifyLicFile()** opens the specified license file and reads the first line. If the first line in the license file matches the provided license string, the license verification is deemed a success.

Now that you know this, there are a few issues that you need to keep in mind:

- For each new control that you develop, you should modify the license check line in both the .LIC file and the _szLicString[] variable of the application so that each control's licensing is unique. If you don't do this, all controls that you develop will have the same license string, and an unscrupulous user or developer could misuse your controls.
- You must resist the urge to peek at the license string in a licensed control and not create a new (bogus) license validation file. Be honest, and don't misappropriate someone else's OLE Controls.
- If you don't need to license your controls, don't add license validation. For controls that are distributed using shareware distribution techniques, license validation has no real use.

Overall, license validation provides a weak method of ensuring that a user or developer has actually licensed your control. It's easily defeated by anyone who is reasonably skilled, so it shouldn't be depended on for absolute security.

USING OUR OLE CONTROL

Using our OLE Control is relatively easy. First, you must have an application that can use an OLE Control. When this book was being written, only one application could use an OLE Control: Access 2.0.

Inserting an OLE Control in an Access form or report is simple. When designing the form, decide where you want to insert the OLE Control. Then, from Access, select Insert | Object.

Figure 12.26 shows our clock control installed in an Access 2.0 form. I've set an appropriate font, the digits are colored dark blue, and the background is set to match the form's background. Notice how well the custom control blends in with the form.

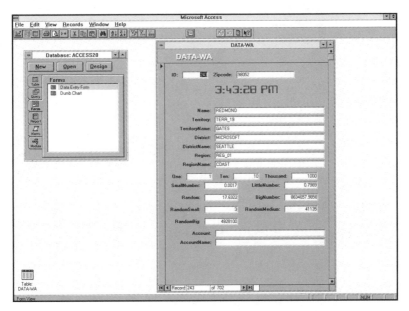

Figure 12.26. Our clock control in an Access 2.0 form.

SHIPPING YOUR OLE CONTROL

Once you've developed your new OLE Control, you must distribute the control to your users. The installation process can be either a separate step (in which your product is only the OLE Control) or part of another application's installation process.

For the 16-bit versions of your OLE Controls, you should change the extension of the control's file from .DLL to .OCX. This will cause all the OLE Controls to have the same file extension. Make this change to the DLL's name prior to registering the control, because the system won't find a control that is renamed after registration. OLE Controls that are created using Visual C++ 2.0 are already named with the .OCX extension.

Microsoft recommends that your OLE Controls be installed in the Windows system directory on the user's machine. Your OLE Control installation program can obtain the name of the system directory by using the **GetSystemDirectory()**

function. Make sure that you don't install your OLE Controls in the main Windows directory.

A number of redistributable DLL files should be available with your OLE Control. These files should be placed on the target system if either of the following is true:

- No DLL file with this name exists on the target system.
- An existing DLL of the same name has an earlier version number.

You don't have to distribute the entire OLE set of DLL files. Your OLE Control will be used only in an OLE container application that will already have installed the necessary OLE DLL files. Your OLE Control won't need DLL files other than those listed in Table 12.3.

TABLE 12.3. DLL FILES TO BE DISTRIBUTED WITH OLE CONTROLS.

DLL Name	Description
OC25.DLL	The OLE Control 16-bit runtime DLL file.
OC30.DLL	The OLE Control 32-bit runtime DLL file. This DLL supports the ANSI character set.
OC30U.DLL	The OLE Control 16-bit runtime DLL file. This DLL supports the Unicode character set.
REGSVR.EXE	This utility is used to register an OLE Control. This version of the registration server is used only with 16-bit versions of Windows.
REGSVR32.EXE	This utility is used to register an OLE Control. This version of the registration server is used with 32-bit versions of Windows, including Windows NT and Windows 95.

It's also possible that you might need to distribute the Visual C++ 2.0 files listed in Table 12.4. The requirement to distribute these files depends on the C/C++ functions that are called by the OLE Control.

TABLE 12.4. OPTIONAL C/C++ FILES TO BE DISTRIBUTED WITH OLE CONTROLS.	
DLL Name	Description
MSVCRT20.DLL	The C runtime library is contained within this DLL file.
MSCANS32.DLL	This DLL contains the ANSI-to-Unicode wrapper code. This file is required only with OLE Controls that are built to use the ANSI character set (that is, for OLE Controls that are not Unicode).

As a matter of safety, you should always create your distribution disk versions of these DLL files using the copies found on the CD-ROM, which has the OLE Custom Control Developer's Kit. This helps minimize the possibility of distributing an incorrect version or a corrupted DLL.

Before a user may use your OLE Control, it must be registered. Although some OLE Control container applications have a method for registering an OLE Control, you shouldn't depend on such a feature being available. You can register a control by calling either REGSVR.EXE or REGSVR32.EXE (as appropriate for the target version of Windows).

If you install the OLE Control DLL files (OC25.DLL, OC30.DLL, and/or OC30U.DLL), you also should register the DLL. This is necessary to make the stock font and color property pages active. You don't need to register these DLL files if they're already installed on the target system: You can assume that whatever installed them has already registered them. At some point you might get a customer support call saying "I can't see my font and color property sheets." If this happens, you should simply have the customer reregister the OC25.DLL, OC30.DLL, and/or OC30U.DLL files.

If your control is licensed, you must make sure that the license control file (the .LIC file) is available to any developers who will use your control. You shouldn't inadvertently distribute the .LIC file to end-users if you intend to enforce licensing!

SUMMARY

In this chapter, we learned that developing OLE Controls isn't too difficult. OLE Controls can be developed, without any prior experience in using OLE, by using the ControlWizard and ClassWizard applets that are supplied with Visual C++ 2.0. We also developed the clock OLE Control in this chapter. The clock OLE Control can be embedded into any container application that supports OLE Controls. It also can be embedded into an OLE container application, where it will function as an OLE Automation Server.

The following topics were covered in this chapter:

- Events: OLE Control events are the method by which the OLE Control can communicate events and information to the container application.
- Properties: OLE Control properties allow the container application to communicate information to the control.
- Methods: OLE Control methods are a way for the container application to communicate with the control.
- Licensing: OLE Controls can be protected with a simple form of license validation. This validation lets the programmer control who can embed the control into applications.
- Using the ControlWizard applet.
- Customizing the control.
- Packaging and shipping your OLE Control.

ADDING OLE CONTROLS TO AN APPLICATION

Three different groups are involved with an OLE Control, each with different objectives, desires, and needs.

First, there is the OLE Control developer, which is what you and I were when we developed the clock control in Chapter 12, "Creating an OLE Control." An OLE Control developer creates a control that he or she might (or might not) use in an application. An OLE Control developer knows how the OLE Control works but might have only anecdotal information about how the application's developer will actually use the OLE Control.

Second, there is the application's developer. This person develops applications, perhaps using a system such as Microsoft Access. If using Access, this person will develop data entry forms, tables, reports, and so on. In the forms and reports, there probably will be a need for OLE Controls to perform special functions. Just look at our clock control, which can be embedded in an Access data entry form. The application's developer might have some understanding of how the OLE Control works internally but need not fully understand the inner workings of an OLE Control to use it.

Finally, there is the end-user, who has his or her own needs, wants, and desires. Often, developers try to guess what the user will want and like. Successful developers, more often than not, listen to the user and provide the features the user needs. If the user says that he or she needs a clock in the data entry form, then it's needed. However, the user is rarely interested in the mechanics of the OLE Control, as long as it works as intended.

THE APPLICATION USER

The application user wants an application that's easy to use and that works well. Microsoft can't provide all the types of controls that a typical application might need. Typical custom controls might include the following:

- Clocks and timer controls
- Spreadsheet-type controls for data display
- Specialty pushbutton controls (which typically have bitmap images)

THE APPLICATION DEVELOPER

The application developer creates applications for the application user. It's possible that the application developer is also the OLE Control developer, but that isn't always the case.

If the application developer is restricted to using just the controls that are supplied with Windows, many applications won't present a user interface with the functionality that is desired.

When the application developer must use an OLE Control, the control must be easy to use and have an attractive appearance. The control's look and feel must match both Windows and the application being created.

THE OLE CONTROL DEVELOPER

The OLE Control developer is responsible for creating OLE Controls that can be used by both the application developer and the application user.

It's necessary for the OLE Control developer to work with the application developer to create controls that are capable of performing the desired tasks.

ACCESS 2.0 AND OLE CONTROLS

At the time this book was being written, Access 2.0 (which was released by Microsoft in early 1994) was the only application that offered support of OLE Controls.

With Access, you can create an application that has OLE Controls in forms and reports. As shown in Chapter 12, a control can easily be integrated into an Access form.

> Because this isn't an Access 2.0 book, I've skipped a number of minor details about custom controls in the following discussion of using our clock OLE Control in an Access form. The skipped details are self-evident when you add an OLE Control to an Access form.

Now, let's see what we can do with our OLE Control in an Access form. First, as Chapter 12 showed, I've included our clock OLE Control in an Access form. Figure 13.1 reminds you what this form looks like.

Figure 13.1 shows our clock control in an Access form that's currently in user mode. There are two modes: user mode, in which the user interacts with the form, and design mode, in which the form is designed or modified. Notice that the time is displayed on the form.

You might remember that when we designed the clock control, we added a few bells and whistles. One such addition was the inclusion of an alarm function. Now, our Access user wants to implement the alarm function to display a message box on the screen at a certain time. To do this, two things must be present:

1. A way to display the message when the clock control sends an alarm event.
2. A way to set the alarm attributes, such as the time for the alarm to go off.

Figure 13.1. Our clock OLE Control in an Access 2.0 form.

To display a message or take any other action when an OLE Control fires an event, you must add an event handler for the OLE Control. As the application developer, you should first open the form in design mode, then follow these steps to add an event handler:

1. Single-click on the OLE Control with the right mouse button. A pop-up menu is shown, which includes the selection Build Event.... When you select Build Event..., you're presented with an event handler shell, as shown in Figure 13.2.

2. The Events window has an empty implementation of the OLE Control's registered events. You can scroll through each of the event handlers using the Page Up and Page Down keys. Figure 13.2 shows the alarm event handler.

   Notice how the alarm event handler already has the three parameters (nHour, nMinute, and nSecond) that we defined when we created the clock control. Our function will be able to determine which alarm occurred if we decide to allow for multiple alarms in our handler.

   For our handler, we want a simple message box that displays a message saying that the alarm has occurred. To display a message box in Access Basic, we can use the **MsgBox()** function, as shown in Figure 13.3.

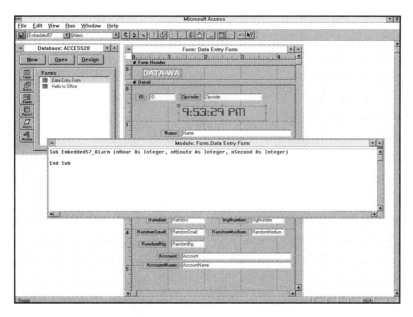

Figure 13.2. Clock's event handler for the Alarm event.

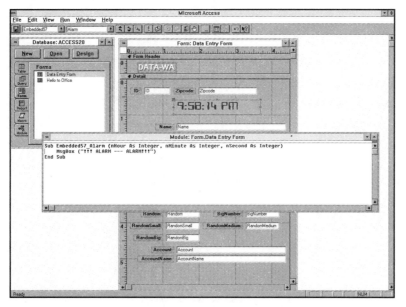

Figure 13.3. Clock's alarm function showing the **MsgBox( )** *call.*

After you've written your handler for the OLE Control event, you can compile it by selecting Run | Compile Loaded Modules from Access. When it's compiled, save the code and test the clock's alarm function.

To test the alarm function you must become the user, then set the clock's alarm time and enable the alarm. First, close the Design Form window to save the changes you've made to the form.

Next, to set the alarm time and enable the alarm, we use the control's property page. We included the necessary controls in the property sheet dialog for just such an occasion. In order to access the clock's property page dialog, the user must do the following:

1. Make the clock control the current, active control. You do this by simply clicking on one of the clock's digits. The clock OLE Control doesn't provide any feedback to tell the user that it has input focus, but Access knows which control has focus.

2. From Access, the user must select Edit | Digital Clock Control Object | Properties (see Figure 13.4). This displays the clock's property page dialog, shown in Figure 13.5.

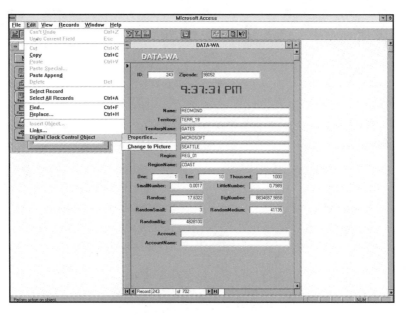

Figure 13.4. Menu selections to activate the clock's property page dialog.

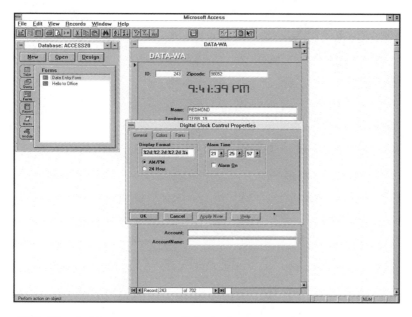

Figure 13.5. The clock's property page dialog in Access.

When the alarm time has been set and the alarm has been enabled, simply wait for the alarm to occur. When this happens, the alarm message box is displayed, as shown in Figure 13.6. Needless to say, it's an alarming experience!

With an OLE Control, you can emulate many of the functions that are provided with other Access forms' objects. For example, you could have a custom button that supports animation (actually, the clock control is just such a control) or an OLE Control button that displays information in a format that isn't possible using a standard control. An example of an OLE Control that provides a unique display of information might be a "gas gauge" type of control that could be used to show the quantity of an item in stock for an inventory database system. Many cars now have a "low fuel" light, so perhaps this control should have a "low inventory level" light!

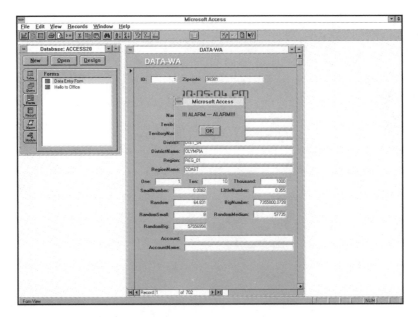

Figure 13.6. Our clock control: it's alarming!

SUMMARY

This chapter covered the process for adding an OLE Control to an existing application. Controls are added in the container application's design mode, usually by selecting Insert | Object. Many applications also have a design toolbar that might have a button for OLE Controls.

The following topics were covered in this chapter:

- Shipping OLE Controls to other developers
- Using OLE Controls from other developers
- Installing an OLE Control: the control developer, the application developer, and the user

PART

IV

ODBC

AN INTRODUCTION TO ODBC

For many Windows users and virtually all Windows programmers, the term *ODBC* doesn't mean much. Although ODBC was released in the summer of 1993, it received little attention for some time, and even a year later few Windows programs support ODBC features.

WHAT IS ODBC?

ODBC stands for Open Database Connectivity. ODBC does exactly what it says: It makes it possible for Windows applications to openly access a vast array of DataSources without having to know the format or structure of the data contained in the DataSource being used.

ODBC works as a set of shell routines called the *driver manager*. Each of the routines that an ODBC application would call starts with the letters SQL, such as `SQLFetch(hstmt);`. The ODBC driver manager routines then call functions that are found in one of the ODBC drivers. Figure 14.1 shows the relationship between an ODBC application, the ODBC driver manager, the ODBC drivers, and the actual DataSources.

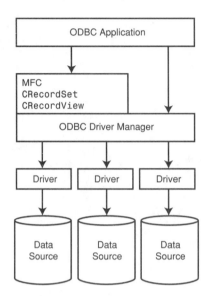

Figure 14.1. ODBC relationships.

Note that an ODBC application can use either the MFC ODBC classes or direct calls to the ODBC driver manager. There is no restriction on mixing MFC ODBC class functions and direct calls to the driver manager, but applications written with the MFC ODBC classes generally can use the class member functions.

ODBC works as both a standardized interface layer that interfaces with your Windows application and as a set of DLLs that interface with various DataSources. Figure 14.2 shows this relationship.

ODBC supports a wide array of DataSources, including the basic set of ODBC drivers listed in Table 14.3 (near the end of this chapter). This table shows the ODBC drivers that are available from Microsoft. Most ODBC applications include this basic set of ODBC drivers.

ODBC FUNCTIONS

ODBC offers a wide array of functions. For general database work, you'll have to work with only a few ODBC functions. The process of using ODBC can be divided into the following three stages:

- Initialization, in which allocations and connections are made
- DataSource access, in which the DataSource's data is read, updated, or added to
- Termination, in which the connections are broken and allocations are freed

For many ODBC applications, the initialization (in which allocations and the connection to the DataSource are made) is often completed in the application's initialization stage. One compelling reason for this is that often these steps take some time. Depending on the DataSource's format, it can take several seconds to open a connection.

The DataSource access can be as simple and straightforward as using the records in the order provided (keeping in mind that SQL's SELECT statement allows you to specify a sort field and order). Or, you may use a more complex set of constraints, including JOINs. (For more information on JOINs, see Chapter 16, "An Introduction to SQL.")

ODBC should be terminated at the same level at which it was initialized. In other words, if ODBC was initialized at program startup time, it should be terminated when the program is being closed. However, if ODBC is initialized later in the application's execution, its termination should take place at the corresponding level.

Figure 14.2 shows the process that an application follows when using ODBC. This figure is divided into three parts—the initialization, data access, and termination stages.

Initialization

In the initialization stage, it is first necessary to allocate an ODBC environment. This is done using the **SQLAllocEnv()** function, which performs the necessary memory allocation for the ODBC structures that are needed and returns a **HENV** handle. You need to save this handle for use with other **SQL...()** function calls.

After your application allocates the environment, it is then necessary to set up the connection. This is done using the **SQLAllocConnect()** function. This function allocates the memory necessary for the connection under the environment allocated using the **SQLAllocEnv()** function. For this reason, **SQLAllocConnect()** is called after **SQLAllocEnv()**.

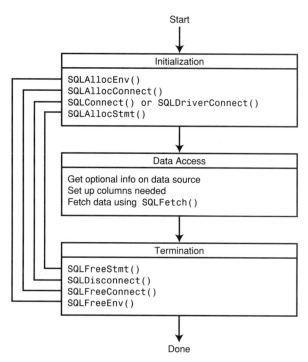

Figure 14.2. Steps to utilize ODBC.

Either **SQLConnect()** or **SQLDriverConnect()** is called after the environment and the connection have been allocated. The call to **SQLConnect()** or **SQLDriverConnect()** actually performs the necessary linkage to enable your application to access a particular DataSource. The main difference between **SQLDriverConnect()** and **SQLConnect()** is that **SQLDriverConnect()** supports the parameters needed to provide the user interface necessary to make connections to DataSources, including those that are part of a network topology.

Accessing the Data

Once a connection between your application and a DataSource has been established, your application can access the data contained in the DataSource. This process is initiated using the **SQLAllocStmt()** function, which allocates memory for the actual SQL statement handle.

> Whenever a character string parameter is passed to an **SQL...()** function, the length of the string must also be passed. However, when the string is a **NULL**-terminated C/C++ character string, it's possible to pass the predefined constant **SQL_NTS**, which tells the SQL functions to determine the string's length based on the standard C/C++ rules. This is especially useful when passing constants, because you don't have to count the characters by hand.

The actual accessing of the DataSource's data tells ODBC which variables (as defined in your application) are to be used to store data from the DataSource. This is done using the **SQLBindCol()** function. You don't need to assign a variable to each column. Simply determine which columns in the DataSource are needed, then assign variables to them. Columns without an assigned variable will be ignored. Once your columns have been assigned to variables, your application can access each row of data in the DataSource. The accessing of data on a row-by-row basis is done using the **SQLFetch()** function, which fetches one row of data at a time. The variables that are assigned to the desired columns will have the column's value placed in them. You then access the row's data by using the assigned variables. **SQLFetch()** returns one of the defined constants **SQL_SUCCESS** or **SQL_SUCCESS_WITH_INFO**. As long as **SQLFetch()** returns one of these constants, it can be safely assumed that there are more rows of data that may be fetched. When **SQLFetch()** returns one of the other predefined constants that it can return (such as **SQL_ERROR**), your application can assume that there are no more rows of data to be returned.

Many **SQL...()** functions return one of the predefined constants described in Table 14.1. This table also lists the return values that can be expected. Of course, your application should check each function's return value to determine whether the function has succeeded or failed.

TABLE 14.1. SQL PREDEFINED RETURN VALUES.		
Name	Value	Description
SQL_ERROR	−1	An error occurred and the function failed. Call the SQLError() function to get more information regarding the error that occurred.
SQL_INVALID_HANDLE	−2	The handle passed wasn't valid. It's likely that the allocation failed and that the allocation call's return value wasn't checked.
SQL_NEED_DATA	99	Additional data is required.
SQL_NO_DATA_FOUND	100	No data met the specified criterion.
SQL_SUCCESS	0	The function succeeded.
SQL_SUCCESS_WITH_INFO	1	The function probably succeeded, but there is additional information that should be checked. Call the SQLError() function to get more information regarding the problem.
SQL_STILL_EXECUTING	2	An asynchronous function is still executing.

As you can see from Table 14.1, whenever a function returns either **SQL_ERROR** or **SQL_SUCCESS_WITH_INFO**, you need to call **SQLError()** to determine the error condition. Because none of the **SQL...()** functions returns an actual error code, it's necessary to call **SQLError()** to obtain the actual error code. For many programs, it's sufficient to display an error message and end the ODBC access. This can be done by creating a generic error handler, such as the one shown in Listing 14.1.

LISTING 14.1. A GENERIC SQL ERROR HANDLER (SQLERR.C).

```
void     SQLPrintError(HENV henv, HDBC hdbc, HSTMT hstmt)
{
RETCODE RC;
char    szSqlState[256];
char    szErrorMsg[256];
SDWORD  pfNativeError;
```

```
SWORD    pcbErrorMsg;

    RC = SQLError(henv, hdbc, hstmt,
        szSqlState,
        &pfNativeError,
        szErrorMsg,
        sizeof(szErrorMsg),
        &pcbErrorMsg);

    if (RC == SQL_SUCCESS ¦¦ RC == SQL_SUCCESS_WITH_INFO)
    {
        AfxMessageBox(szErrorMsg);
    }
    else
    {
        if (RC != SQL_NO_DATA_FOUND)
        {
            AfxMessageBox("SQLError() returned an error!!!");
        }
    }
}
```

SQLError() returns **SQL_SUCCESS** when error information is available or **SQL_NO_DATA_FOUND** when no error information is available. Pay particular attention to the fact that many of the **SQL...()** functions can have multiple errors—normally you will need to call **SQLError()** more than once. For example, you might want to place the call to **SQLError()** in a loop, such as the one shown in this code fragment:

```
RETCODE RC = SQL_SUCCESS;

    do
    {// Will give message box for each and every error:
        RC = SQLError(henv, hdbc, hstmt,
            szSqlState,
            &pfNativeError,
            szErrorMsg,
            sizeof(szErrorMsg),
            &pcbErrorMsg);

        if (RC == SQL_SUCCESS ¦¦ RC == SQL_SUCCESS_WITH_INFO)
        {
            AfxMessageBox(szErrorMsg);
        }
        else
        {
            if (RC != SQL_NO_DATA_FOUND)
            {
                AfxMessageBox("SQLError() returned an error!!!");
            }
        }
    } while (RC == SQL_SUCCESS ¦¦ RC == SQL_SUCCESS_WITH_INFO)
```

It's important to use discretion when displaying error messages when an **SQL...()** function returns with the **SQL_SUCCESS_WITH_INFO** return code. In this case, the function might have executed correctly, requiring your error handler to determine which errors constitute a fatal error and which errors are benign and may be safely ignored.

> One common error occurs when a returned field's length is insufficient. An example would be a variable that receives the returned data from a DataSource column. If the field isn't sufficiently large, **SQL_SUCCESS_WITH_INFO** is returned, and as much data as will fit is placed in the returned field. In fact, your application might not need the data that didn't fit (for example, a field that's padded with blanks), and the truncation error could possibly be ignored.

Terminating the Connection

Once your application has completed its accessing of the DataSource's data, it must break the connections and free whatever memory has been allocated. This is done by calling **SQLFreeStmt()**, **SQLDisconnect()**, **SQLFreeConnect()**, and **SQLFreeEnv()**, in that order.

The **SQL...()** functions can be divided into a number of broad categories. This book covers two:

- Connecting to a DataSource (Chapter 19)
- Obtaining information about a driver and a DataSource (Chapter 20)

MFC AND ODBC

One of the nice things about ODBC is the MFC wrappers that allow easy access to the ODBC functions while programming in C++. These streamline the accessing of data in a DataSource, allowing you to concentrate on your application rather than on the details of ODBC usage.

Two main MFC classes are used in ODBC access—**CRecordSet** and **CRecordView**. **CRecordSet** is the main class that deals with actual ODBC access, and (as might be apparent) **CRecordView** is a class that assists you in displaying the records in a data set. A **CRecordView** class always has a **CRecordSet** attached to it. If your implementation doesn't attach a **CRecordSet** object, the **virtual CRecordset* OnGetRecordset()** member function in the **CRecordView** class attaches one automatically. ClassWizard will override this function for you (if you're using ClassWizard).

The *CDatabase* Class

The **CDatabase** class is the basic building block in ODBC usage. The **CRecordSet** class objects use a **CDatabase** class object to implement the interface with an actual recordset.

Most programs don't need to explicitly create a **CDatabase** object. If the **CRecordSet**'s constructor is passed a **NULL** for the **CDatabase** class's pointer, the **CRecordSet** derived class will create a new **CDatabase** object.

Data Members
There is one data member in the **CDatabase** object.

m_hdbc
m_hdbc is the ODBC connection handle to a DataSource that is created with a call to **SQLAllocConnect()**. Member variable **m_hdbc** is of type **HDBC**.

Function Members
There are a number of member functions in the **CDatabase** object.

Construction, Destruction, Opening, and Closing
The **CDatabase** object's constructor, destructor, open, and close functions are presented in this section.

CDatabase( )
```
CDatabase();
```

The **CDatabase()** member function is the constructor. It's called when the class is being created. You must call the **Open()** function after creating the **CDatabase** derived class.

Open( )
```
BOOL Open(LPCSTR lpszDSN, BOOL bExclusive = FALSE,
    BOOL bReadOnly = FALSE, LPCSTR lpszConnect = "ODBC;",
        BOOL bUseCursorLib=TRUE);
```

The **Open()** member function opens a connection to a DataSource. The *lpszDSN* parameter is required (**Open()** needs to know what to open), but all the other parameters for this function are optional. If **Open()** fails, it will throw a **CDBException** or a CMemoryException.

Close()

```
virtual void Close();
```

This function, called after a DataSource open (using **Open()**), closes the DataSource.

~CDatabase()

```
virtual ~CDatabase();
```

This is the default destructor for a **CDatabase** object.

Database Attributes

The database attribute functions allow the application to obtain information about the current DataSource (if there is an open DataSource). There are also functions to set the DataSource's attributes.

GetConnect()

```
const CString& GetConnect() const;
```

The **GetConnect()** function returns a **CString** pointer to the ODBC connect string. The connect string was used to connect the DataSource with the **CDatabase** object. If **Open()** hasn't been called, this string is empty.

IsOpen()

```
BOOL IsOpen() const;
```

The **IsOpen()** function returns a nonzero value if a DataSource is connected to the **CDatabase** object. If no DataSource is connected to the **CDatabase** object, **IsOpen()** returns **FALSE**.

GetDatabaseName()

```
CString GetDatabaseName() const;
```

The **GetDatabaseName()** function returns a **CString** pointer to the currently connected database. The name returned isn't the DataSource name as defined in the **Open()** function's *lpszDSN* parameter. The actual string returned depends on ODBC. Most databases are collections of data tables, and ODBC returns the name of the database (and not the currently open table). If no name is available, **GetDatabaseName()** returns an empty string.

CanUpdate()

```
BOOL CanUpdate() const;
```

The **CanUpdate()** function returns a nonzero value if the DataSource connected to the **CDatabase** object can be updated. A DataSource that is read-only can't be updated.

Many of the standard ODBC drivers can't update DataSources (the Access driver is an exception).

CanTransact()

```
BOOL CanTransact() const;
```

The **CanTransact()** function returns a nonzero value if the DataSource supports transaction mode updates.

By updating using transactions, you can make multiple updates to the DataSource as a single operation. That way, you can avoid the problems of concurrency, in which two or more records must be updated and it would therefore be an error not to update all the records simultaneously.

InWaitForDataSource()

```
static BOOL PASCAL InWaitForDataSource();
```

The **InWaitForDataSource()** function helps update the user interface. It's usually desirable to disable the user interface (the menu and toolbar buttons) for database commands when the DataSource is not yet available.

SetLoginTimeout()

```
void SetLoginTimeout(DWORD dwSeconds);
```

The **SetLoginTimeout()** function is used to set the time before a DataSource times out. This function must be called before **Open()** is called for the DataSource. The default wait is 15 seconds. Specifying zero tells the DataSource to wait indefinitely. Not all DataSources support the specification of a login time-out period.

SetQueryTimeout()

```
void SetQueryTimeout(DWORD dwSeconds);
```

The **SetQueryTimeout()** function is used to set the time that is waited prior to a timeout on a connected DataSource.

Timeouts may occur due to network access failures, a query that takes too long, and so on. The default wait is 15 seconds. Specifying zero tells the DataSource to wait indefinitely. Not all DataSources support the specification of a login timeout period. This function must be called before **Open()** is called for the DataSource.

SetSynchronousMode( )

```
void SetSynchronousMode(BOOL bSynchronous);
```

The **SetSynchronousMode()** function is used to control whether ODBC returns control to the calling application while SQL functions are being processed. If asynchronous processing is enabled (the default), the calling application regains control prior to the completion of the ODBC function.

Database Operations

CDatabase supports a number of database operations. They are divided into two categories—those supporting transactions, and all other functions.

BeginTrans( )

```
BOOL BeginTrans();
```

The **BeginTrans()** function lets you begin a series of reversible operations. *Reversible* means that the entire group, not single operations, may be reversed. Reversible calls include **AddNew()**, **Edit()**, **Delete()**, and **Update()**. The DataSource must support transactions (see the section titled "**CanTransact()**").

The **BeginTrans()** function should be called after opening a recordset. Calling **BeginTrans()** prior to opening a recordset might cause problems with ODBC. It is an error to call **BeginTrans()** without a corresponding call to either **CommitTrans()** or **Rollback()**.

CommitTrans( )

```
BOOL CommitTrans();
```

The **CommitTrans()** function causes the DataSource to be modified when updating (adding, editing, or deleting) the DataSource. **CommitTrans()** is called after **BeginTrans()** is called, and any intervening updating is completed. **CommitTrans()** then updates the DataSource with the updated records. It is an error to call **CommitTrans()** if you haven't called **BeginTrans()**. It's also an error to call **CommitTrans()** after a call to **Rollback()**. All updates are applied to the DataSource when **CommitTrans()** is called.

Rollback( )

```
BOOL Rollback();
```

The **Rollback()** function is used to tell ODBC to discard all updates made after the previous **BeginTrans()** call. All updates are discarded.

Cancel( )

```
void Cancel();
```

The **Cancel()** function is used to cancel any pending asynchronous operations.

ExecuteSQL( )

```
BOOL ExecuteSQL(LPCSTR lpszSQL);
```

ExecuteSQL() provides a method to directly execute SQL commands. Even though the **CRecordSet** object normally provides the necessary SQL interface, there might be times when you need to issue an SQL command directly. If the **ExecuteSQL()** function fails, it throws a **CDBException**.

Database Overridable Functions

Several functions in the **CDatabase** class are overridden in derived classes. This section describes them.

OnSetOptions( )

```
virtual void OnSetOptions(HSTMT hstmt);
```

The **OnSetOptions()** function is called when the **ExecuteSQL()** function and **CRecordSet::OnSetOptions()** are called. **OnSetOptions()** sets a number of standard options, such as the timeout value and processing mode.

OnWaitForDataSource( )

```
virtual void OnWaitForDataSource(BOOL bStillExecuting);
```

The **OnWaitForDataSource()** function is called to yield processor time to any other applications whenever there is a lengthy ODBC operation.

The CRecordSet Class

The **CRecordSet** class is a complete wrapper for the **SQL...()** functions. It offers other ODBC features and enhancements to allow an application to easily interface with ODBC.

Let's take a look at **CRecordSet**'s members. We will look at the variable members first. I will cover only variable members that are marked as public. There are a number of private variable members, but your derived classes and your applications shouldn't try to use any private class members.

Note that each of the member variables is prefixed with **m_**, in keeping with MFC class standards. I recommend that you follow the same practice with member variables that you create.

Member Variables

There are five member data variables. Most of these member variables can be modified by your application, but the **m_hstmt** member variable must be treated as a constant.

In many simpler applications, you don't need to modify any of these member variables. More complex and demanding applications might require that you set these member variables to values other than their default values.

m_hstmt

The **m_hstmt** member variable contains the ODBC statement handle for this class's statement. This member has a type of **HSTMT**. Typical uses include calls to **SQLError()** to determine error codes and calls to other **SQL...()** functions that might offer functionality not offered in **CRecordSet**. The **m_hstmt** member is valid only after the **Open()** function has been called. Of course, this member should only be read, not modified directly by your application.

m_nFields

The **m_nFields** member variable contains a count of the number of field data members in the DataSource's table. Generally, this count is equal to the number of columns in the table. Your derived class defines variables for these columns as needed. If you use ClassWizard to create your derived class, ClassWizard creates the necessary variables for each of the columns. If your **CRecordSet** derived class dynamically binds columns, you'll have to modify the **m_nFields** member to accurately reflect the number of **RFX** calls in the **DoFieldExchange()** function. The **m_nFields** member is of type **UINT**.

m_nDatabase

The **m_pDatabase** member variable is a pointer to the **CDatabase** class used by this **CRecordSet** derived class. If the constructor for the **CRecordSet** derived object is called with a null **CDatabase** pointer, a **CDatabase** class object is created. The **m_pDatabase** member is a pointer to a **CDatabase** object and can be used to access the **CDatabase** object's members.

m_nParams

The **m_nParams** member variable contains the number of parameter data members in the DataSource's recordset. The **m_nParams** member must correspond to the number of "params" registered in **DoFieldExchange**, after a call to **SetFieldType()** with the parameter **CFieldExchange::**_param_. The **m_nParams** member is of type **UINT**.

m_strFilter

The **m_strFilter** member is a **CString** object that specifies the SQL WHERE clause for this **CRecordSet**. The WHERE clause is used to limit the records that will be returned to those that meet certain specified criteria. The **m_strFilter** member is used when you call the **CRecordSet** member **Open()**, which builds the SQL SELECT statement. It's possible to directly access and modify this member, but you must set it prior to calling **Open()**.

m_strSort

The **m_strSort** member variable is a **CString** object that specifies an SQL ORDER BY clause. This member is used with the **m_strFilter** member to build the SQL SELECT clause. The **m_strSort** member is used when you call the **CRecordSet** member **Open()**, which builds the SQL SELECT statement. It's possible to directly access and modify this member, but you must set it prior to calling **Open()**.

Member Functions

The **CRecordSet** member functions are divided into the following six broad groups:

- Construction, destruction, open, and close functions
- Recordset attribute functions
- Recordset updating functions
- Recordset movement (navigation) functions
- Other recordset functions
- Overridable public member functions

As with all of the MFC classes, your application probably won't use all of the available member functions. However, many complex ODBC applications benefit from the member functions that are available.

Each member function is described in the following sections. The first line after the header is the prototype. It's followed by a description of the member function.

Construction, Destruction, Open, and Close Functions

The constructor and destructor for the **CRecordSet**-derived classes are typical for MFC class objects. In addition, there are functions to open (connect to) and close (break the connection to) a DataSource connection.

CRecordSet( )

```
CRecordSet( CDatabase* pDatabase );
```

The **CRecordSet** member constructs a **CRecordSet** object. When you create a derived class, you must provide a constructor that calls this one. The **pDatabase** parameter should be either a pointer to a **CDatabase** object or **NULL**. In many applications, **NULL** will be used.

~CRecordSet( )

```
~CRecordSet();
```

The **~CRecordSet** member destroys a **CRecordSet** object. This member is called automatically at the destruction phase of the **CRecordSet** object.

Open( )

```
virtual BOOL Open( UINT nOpenType = snapshot, LPCSTR lpszSql = NULL,
DWORD dwOptions = defaultOptions );
```

The **Open()** member opens a recordset and retrieves the table or performs the query that the recordset specifies.

This function throws exceptions of type **CDBException**, **CMemoryException**, and **CFileException**. Although the **Open()** member function doesn't require any parameters, it's common to specify both the type of open (an enumerated value) and the SQL string. The type of open (*nOpenType*) can be any of the following:

- **CRecordset::dynaset**: A dynamic recordset that allows bidirectional scrolling. Useful where the recordset is being used by more than one application or user.

- **CRecordset::snapshot**: A static recordset that allows bidirectional scrolling. Useful when the current application is the only user of this recordset, or when changes to the recordset aren't significant to this application.

- **CRecordset::forwardOnly**: A dynaset that allows forward scrolling and is read-only. This dynaset enables faster access while taking into consideration the possibility of modifications by other applications or users.

The SQL string is a pointer to a standard **NULL**-terminated string constant. This string is used to specify the SQL SELECT statement that will be used to generate the query. When the **m_strFilter** and/or **m_strSort** member variables have been assigned a value, these are appended to the SQL SELECT statement.

Close()

```
virtual void Close();
```

The **Close()** member function closes the recordset and the ODBC **HSTMT** associated with it. Your application should always call the **Close()** function when it's done using the recordset. It's acceptable to call **Open()/Close()** more than once, but each intervening **Open()** must have a matching **Close()**.

Recordset Attribute Functions

The attribute functions allow your application to query a number of important recordset attributes.

CanAppend()

```
BOOL CanAppend() const;
```

The **CanAppend()** function returns a nonzero value if you can add new records to the recordset. To add new records, your application would call the **AddNew()** member function.

CanRestart()

```
BOOL CanRestart() const;
```

The **CanRestart()** function returns a nonzero value if the **Requery()** member function can be called to run the recordset's query again.

CanScroll()

```
BOOL CanScroll() const;
```

The **CanScroll()** function returns a nonzero value if you can scroll through the records in the recordset.

CanTransact()

```
BOOL CanTransact() const;
```

The **CanTransact()** function returns a nonzero value if the DataSource supports transactions.

CanUpdate()

```
BOOL CanUpdate() const;
```

The **CanUpdate()** function returns a nonzero value if the recordset can be updated by either adding, updating, or deleting records.

GetRecordCount( )

```
long GetRecordCount() const;
```

The **GetRecordCount()** member function returns a count of the number of records in the recordset. It returns 0 if the recordset contains no records and –1 if the record count can't be determined.

You must be careful when using **GetRecordCount()**. This function maintains the count based on the highest-numbered record that has been accessed. The total number of records in a recordset is unknown until the user has moved through the recordset. It's not possible to use the **MoveLast()** member function to assist in determining the count of records in a recordset; **GetRecordCount()** will return –1 if called after a call to **MoveLast()**. To determine the number of records in a recordset, call **MoveNext()** until the **IsEOF()** function returns a non-**FALSE** value.

Although the **CRecordView::AddNew()** and **CRecordView::Delete()** functions update this count, the **CRecordSet::AddNew()** and **CRecordSet::Delete()** functions don't modify the count. If you need an accurate count under these circumstances, you must avoid using the **CRecordSet::AddNew()** and **CRecordSet::Delete()** functions.

GetStatus( )

```
void GetStatus(CRecordsetStatus& rStatus) const;
```

The **GetStatus()** member function passes a pointer to a **CRecordsetStatus** structure, which is used to return the status of the current recordset. This function has no return value.

The **CRecordsetStatus** structure has the following members:

```
struct CRecordsetStatus
{
long m_lCurrentRecord;
    BOOL m_bRecordCountFinal;
};
```

This structure contains the following two members:

- The **m_lCurrentRecord** variable is a long integer that contains the record number of the current record in the recordset. If **GetStatus()** can't determine the current record number (generally when it is before the first record or after the last record), this variable contains –1.

- The **m_bRecordCountFinal** variable is nonzero when **CRecordSet** has been able to accurately determine the total number of records in the record set. See the section titled "**GetRecordCount()**" for a discussion of the process to determine the total number of records in a recordset.

GetTableName( )

```
const CString& GetTableName() const;
```

A call to **GetTableName()** returns the name of the table on which the recordset is based. This name is valid only if the recordset is based on a table. The **GetTableName()** function should be called only when the recordset is open (after a call to **Open()**).

GetSQL( )

```
const CString& GetSQL() const;
```

The **GetSQL()** member function is used to retrieve the SQL string that is used to select the records in the recordset. This function should be called only when the recordset is open (after a call to **Open()**).

IsOpen( )

```
BOOL IsOpen() const;
```

The **IsOpen()** function returns a nonzero value when the recordset is open. This function is useful when calling member functions (such as **GetTableName()** and **GetSQL()**), which require that the recordset be open.

IsBOF( )

```
BOOL IsBOF() const;
```

The **IsBOF()** function returns a nonzero value if the recordset is positioned prior to the first record. It's unacceptable to call **MovePrev()** when **IsBOF()** returns a nonzero value. When **IsBOF()** returns a nonzero value, there is no current record.

IsEOF( )

```
BOOL IsEOF() const;
```

The **IsEOF()** function returns a nonzero value if the recordset is positioned after the last record. It's unacceptable to call **MoveNext()** when **IsEOF()** returns a nonzero value. When **IsBOF()** returns a nonzero value, there is no current record.

IsDeleted( )

```
BOOL IsDeleted() const;
```

The **IsDeleted()** function returns a nonzero value if the current record has been deleted. You can't perform any operations on a deleted record; you must select a new (nondeleted) record.

Recordset Updating Functions

Four functions deal with updating records. These functions allow you to add, edit, or delete records in a recordset. The **AddNew()** and **Edit()** functions both require that you call **Update()** to write the record to the recordset. The **Delete()** function doesn't require a call to **Update()**; its action is immediate.

> Once you have deleted a record, it can be difficult to restore. DataSources generally are updated automatically, without any further user interaction.

Not all DataSources can be updated. You should call **CanUpdate()** to see if the recordset supports updating. When you're using the default ODBC drivers (which are supplied with the ODBC developer's kit), only Access databases support updating, but many third-party ODBC drivers support updating as well.

AddNew( )

```
void AddNew();
```

The **AddNew()** function prepares the **CRecordSet** object to add a new record. After calling **AddNew()**, you must update the column variables, then call **Update()**.

The **AddNew()** function can throw both **CDBException** or **CFileException** on errors.

Delete( )

```
BOOL Delete();
```

The **Delete()** member function deletes the current record from the recordset. After deleting the current record, your application must explicitly scroll to another record. If you attempt to delete a record that is already deleted, this function throws a **CDBException**.

Edit( )

```
void Edit();
```

The **Edit()** function prepares the current record for editing. You call **Edit()**, make the desired changes to the column variables, then call **Update()** to write the changes to the dataset. If there is an error, **Edit()** can throw a **CDBException**, **CMemoryException**, or **CFileException**.

Update()

```
BOOL Update();
```

The **Update()** function is called after either an **AddNew()** or **Edit()** function call. **Update()** writes the added or edited record to the dataset. If an error occurs, **Update()** throws a **CDBException**.

Recordset Movement (Navigation) Functions

It is unlikely that the record you need from a recordset is the current record. In most cases it will be necessary to move through the records in the recordset and present them to the user either one at a time or in some form of list.

The movement from one record to another is always done sequentially, one or more records at a time, relative to the current record. Remember, if the **CRecordSet Open()** function was called with the **CRecordset::forwardOnly** type, you can move only in a forward direction. Once you're past a record, you can't return to it without closing the recordset and reopening it.

Move()

```
virtual void Move(long lRows);
```

The **Move()** function allows the application to move one or more records relative to the current record. To move forward, specify a positive value for **lRows**; to move backward, specify a negative value for **lRows**. Remember, for **CRecordset::forwardOnly**-type recordsets, you can move only in a forward direction.

With an **lRows** parameter value of 1, **Move()** behaves like **MoveNext()**. If **lRows** is –1, **Move()** behaves like **MovePrev()**. If errors occur, **Move()** throws either a **CDBException**, **CFileException**, or **CMemoryException**.

MoveFirst()

```
void MoveFirst();
```

The **MoveFirst()** function moves you to the first record in the recordset. This function must not be called if the recordset has no records. To determine if a recordset has no records, and to call **MoveFirst()** if there are records, you can use the following code:

```
if (!IsBOF() || !IsEOF())
    MoveFirst();
```

In this code fragment, if both **IsBOF()** and **IsEOF()** return **TRUE**, the recordset has no records. If an error occurs, **MoveFirst()** can throw a **CDBException**, **CMemoryException**, or **CFileException**.

MoveLast()

```
void MoveLast();
```

The **MoveLast()** function moves you to the last record in the recordset. Note that the **MoveLast()** function doesn't update the count of records. This function must not be called if the recordset has no records. To determine if a recordset has no records, and to call **MoveLast()** if there are records, you can use the following code:

```
if (!IsBOF() || !IsEOF())
    MoveLast();
```

In this code fragment, if both **IsBOF()** and **IsEOF()** return **TRUE**, the recordset has no records. If an error occurs, **MoveLast()** can throw a **CDBException**, **CMemoryException**, or **CFileException**.

MoveNext()

```
void MoveNext();
```

The **MoveNext()** function moves to the next record in the recordset. Note that the **MoveNext()** function updates the count of records. This function must not be called if the recordset has no records, or if the current record is past the last record in the recordset. To determine if a recordset has no records, and to call **MoveNext()** if you aren't past the last record, you can use the following code:

```
if (!IsEOF())
    MoveLast();
```

In this code fragment, we only need to test whether **IsEOF()** returns **FALSE**, and if so, we can move to the next record. If there are no records in the recordset, or the current record is past the last record, **IsEOF()** returns **TRUE**. If an error occurs, **MoveNext()** can throw a **CDBException**, **CMemoryException**, or **CFileException**.

MovePrev()

```
void MovePrev();
```

The **MovePrev()** function moves to the previous record in the recordset. Note that the **MovePrev()** function doesn't update the count of records. This function must not be called if the recordset has no records, or if the current record is before the first record in the recordset. To determine if a recordset has no records, and to call **MovePrev()** if you aren't past the last record, you can use the following code:

```
if (!IsBOF())
    MovePrev();
```

In this code fragment, we only need to test to see if **IsBOF()** returns **FALSE**, and if so, we can move to the previous record. If there are no records in the recordset, or the current record is before the first record, **IsBOF()** returns **TRUE**. If an error occurs, **MovePrev()** can throw a **CDBException**, **CMemoryException**, or **CFileException**.

Other Recordset Functions

A number of general-purpose member functions are part of the **CRecordSet** class. These functions enable you to perform various functions that aren't otherwise categorized.

Cancel()

```
void Cancel();
```

The **Cancel()** function is used to cancel an asynchronous operation that is already in progress.

IsFieldDirty()

```
BOOL IsFieldDirty(void* pv);
```

The **IsFieldDirty()** function enables you to determine whether a specified data field of a dynaset has been marked as changed. It is possible to unmark a field as changed prior to calling **Update()**, so that that field will not be updated in the recordset. If the parameter pv is **NULL**, **IsFieldDirty()** returns a nonzero value if any field has changed. Should an error occur, **IsFieldDirty()** throws a **CMemoryException** exception.

IsFieldNull()

```
BOOL IsFieldNull(void* pv);
```

The **IsFieldNull()** function enables you to determine whether a specified data field of a dynaset has no value assigned to it. If the parameter pv is **NULL**, **IsFieldNull()** returns a nonzero value if any field is null. If an error occurs, **IsFieldNull()** throws a **CMemoryException**.

WHEN IS *NULL* NOT NULL?

In database terminology, the term *null* has a different meaning than the C/C++ **NULL**. In C/C++, **NULL** signifies a pointer that hasn't been assigned (typically a zero is used), while in database terminology, null is an object that has nothing in it—not even a zero.

> Don't ask me how they do it!
>
> In this chapter, I use **NULL** (uppercase) for the C/C++ context. When referring to databases, I use null (lowercase).

IsFieldNullable( )

```
BOOL IsFieldNullable( void* pv );
```

The **IsFieldNullable()** function is called to determine whether a given field can be set to null (that is, can the field be specified as having no value). Should this function fail, it can throw a **CDBException** exception.

Requery( )

```
virtual BOOL Requery();
```

The **Requery()** function is used to refresh the recordset when the current mode is not a dynaset. For recordsets that are created with **CRecordset::dynaset**, it's not necessary to call **Requery()**. The **Requery()** function can throw a **CDBException**, **CMemoryException**, or **CFileException** when errors occur.

SetFieldDirty( )

```
void SetFieldDirty(void* pv, BOOL bDirty = TRUE);
```

The **SetFieldDirty()** function is used to set or clear, depending on the **bDirty** parameter, the flag that marks a field (column) in the current record as having been changed. This function must only be called after calling either the **AddNew()** or **Edit()** functions. If the parameter pv is **NULL**, then the dirty flags for all fields in the record are either set or cleared.

Marking fields as unchanged can significantly improve the performance of ODBC updating transactions by reducing the number of ODBC/SQL messages that must be passed. Whenever you change a field variable, the dirty flag is set automatically; your application doesn't have to set it.

SetFieldNull( )

```
void SetFieldNull(void* pv, BOOL bDirty = TRUE);
```

The **SetFieldNull()** function is used to clear a field, setting it to null. This function must be called only after calling either the **AddNew()** function or the **Edit()** function. If the parameter pv is **NULL**, all fields in the record are set to null.

When you create a new record using **AddNew()**, all fields are initially set to null and marked as being dirty. Prior to setting a field to null, check to see that it will accept a null value by calling **IsFieldNullable()**, as shown in this code fragment:

```
if (IsFieldNullable(&m_Field1))
    SetFieldNull(&m_Field1);
```

SetLockingMode( )

```
void SetLockingMode( UINT nMode );
```

The **SetLockingMode()** function enables you to control how record locking is handled. The locking of records can affect other applications or users of a dataset if they also want to update a specific record. Not having properly locked a record for updates also can result in a loss of data if the following things occur:

1. User A (Paul) and User B (Ann) set record locking to **CRecordSet::optimistic**.
2. Paul selects a record for updating, using **Edit()**.
3. While Paul is changing the record (but before his calling **Update()**), Ann selects the same record for updating, using **Edit()** again.
4. Using **Update()**, Paul updates the dataset's record with his changes.
5. Using **Update()**, Ann updates the dataset's record with her changes.
6. Paul's changes are lost!

When calling **SetLockingMode()**, specify either **CRecordset::pessimistic** or **CRecordset::optimistic**, like this:

```
SetLockingMode(CRecordSet::pessimistic);
```

The two acceptable locking modes allow for either a more- or less-restrictive locking of records.

The **CRecordSet::optimistic** mode locks the record being updated only during the call to **Update()**.

The **CRecordSet::pessimistic** locking mode locks the record as soon as **Edit()** is called and keeps it locked until the **Update()** function call updates the record. During this time, no other application or user can modify the record.

The default mode is optimistic, meaning that it generally assumes that the DataSource is being used by a single user. You can change that to a more cautious, pessimistic locking mode in which the DataSource can be modified by more than one user or application. Make sure that you change the locking mode prior to calling **Edit()**.

Overridable Public Member Functions

A number of public functions may be overridden in a typical definition of a **CRecordSet**-derived object. When you're using ClassWizard to create your **CRecordSet** objects, ClassWizard provides the necessary overridden functions for you.

DoFieldExchange( )

```
virtual void DoFieldExchange(CFieldExchange* pFX) = 0;
```

The **DoFieldExchange()** function is used to do the actual transfer between the current record and the class member variables that hold each column's data. If an error occurs, **DoFieldExchange** throws a **CDBException**.

The pFX parameter contains a pointer to a **CFieldExchange**-type object. The framework will already have set up this object to specify a context for the field exchange operation. The **DoFieldExchange()** function is called automatically to exchange data between the member variables and their corresponding columns in the current record. Generally, for most **CRecordSet**-derived objects that are created using ClassWizard, you can use the ClassWizard-created **DoFieldExchange()** function.

A typical ClassWizard-created **DoFieldExchange()** function would be similar to the one shown in the following code fragment:

```
void CTestSet::DoFieldExchange(CFieldExchange* pFX)
{
        //{{AFX_FIELD_MAP(CTestSet)
        pFX->SetFieldType(CFieldExchange::outputColumn);
        RFX_Long(pFX, "ID", m_ID);
        RFX_Text(pFX, "Geocode", m_Geocode);
        RFX_Text(pFX, "GeocodeName", m_GeocodeName);
        RFX_Int(pFX, "[State FIPS]", m_State_FIPS);
        RFX_Int(pFX, "[County FIPS]", m_County_FIPS);
        RFX_Double(pFX, "[Previous In Family]", m_Previous_In_Family);
        RFX_Byte(pFX, "[Account Symbol]", m_Account_Symbol);
        RFX_Bool(pFX, "[Is An Account]", m_Is_An_Account);
        RFX_Bool(pFX, "[Is A Point]", m_Is_A_Point);
        RFX_Bool(pFX, "[Has Been Built]", m_Has_Been_Built);
        RFX_Bool(pFX, "[Build Invalid]", m_Build_Invalid);
        //}}AFX_FIELD_MAP
}
```

GetDefaultConnect( )

```
virtual CString GetDefaultConnect();
```

The **GetDefaultConnect()** function is used to return the default connect string. When ClassWizard is used to create your **CRecordSet** object, ClassWizard creates a **GetDefaultConnect()** function for you. An example of a ClassWizard-created **GetDefaultConnect()** is shown in the following code fragment:

```
CString CTestSet::GetDefaultConnect()
{
        return "ODBC;DSN=StarDatabase files;";
}
```

GetDefaultSQL()

```
virtual CString GetDefaultSQL() = 0;
```

The **GetDefaultSQL()** function is used to get the default SQL string to execute.

> The name of the table returned will be empty if a table name can't be identified, if multiple table names are supplied, or if a supplied CALL statement couldn't be interpreted correctly.

An example of a ClassWizard-created **GetDefaultSQL()** is shown in the following code fragment:

```
CString CTestSet::GetDefaultSQL()
{
        return "BASEMAP";
}
```

OnSetOptions()

```
virtual void OnSetOptions( HSTMT hstmt );
```

The **OnSetOptions()** function is used to set initial options for a recordset. Generally, you use **OnSetOptions()** to set options that are specific for a given ODBC driver. Some options, such as the query timeout value or the processing mode, can be set with other functions (which are called prior to calling **Open()**). For example, to set the query timeout mode, call **SetQueryTimeout()**, and to set the processing mode, call **SetSynchronousMode()**. For both of these options, the values set using **SetQueryTimeout()** and **SetSynchronousMode()** apply to subsequent operations on all recordsets or direct SQL calls.

Whenever you override this function, make sure that you call the base class (**CRecordSet**) **OnSetOptions()** function. This is necessary to ensure that all default options are set.

OnWaitForDataSource()

```
virtual void OnWaitForDataSource(BOOL bStillExecuting);
```

The **OnWaitForDataSource()** function is used to yield the processor to other applications while waiting for an asynchronous operation. Make sure that you don't write applications that stop the system while waiting for asynchronous events!

The CRecordView Class

The **CRecordView** class is used to display records from a recordset for the user. This class is derived from the **CFormView** class, and it has all of **CFormView**'s member functions. For more information about **CFormView**, use Visual C++'s help and search for **CFormView**.

Member Variables

CFormView has no member variables. There are member variables in the classes that **CRecordView** is derived from (look at the **CWnd** class for an example).

Member Functions

Four member functions are part of the **CRecordView** class. These functions fall into the three categories described next.

Construction and Destruction

There is only a constructor for the **CRecordView** class.

CRecordView( )

```
CRecordView(LPCSTR lpszTemplateName);
CRecordView(UINT nIDTemplate);
```

The **CRecordView()** function serves as the default constructor. This member function constructs the **CRecordView** object.

The **CRecordView()** constructor requires either a dialog box template name or the identifier for a dialog box template. By default, dialog box templates are created with identifiers, but this behavior can be overridden. If the dialog box template can't be found, this function will fail.

Attributes

Attribute functions return information about a recordset or a specific record. The **OnGetRecordset()** function is used to return a pointer to a **CRecordSet** class-derived object.

OnGetRecordset( )

```
virtual CRecordset* OnGetRecordset() = 0;
```

The **OnGetRecordset()** function returns a pointer to an object of a class derived from **CRecordSet**. ClassWizard creates a function that overrides the **CRecordView OnGetRecordset()** function.

In your **OnGetRecordset()** function, don't create a new recordset. Simply pass a pointer to a **CRecordSet** that already exists. This pointer generally is one created when the **CRecordView**-derived class was created, or perhaps it was created by the **CRecordView**-derived class's constructor.

IsFirstRecord( )

```
BOOL IsFirstRecord();
```

IsFirstRecord() returns a nonzero value if the current record is the first record in the recordset. If the first record is the current one, it's necessary to disable the user interface controls that allow the user to move to the previous record (which is logical, because the first record has no previous record). For applications created using Visual C++'s application creation tools, the support for the user interface is created automatically.

IsLastRecord( )

```
BOOL IsLastRecord();
```

IsLastRecord() returns a nonzero value if the current record is the last record in the recordset. If the last record is the current one, it's necessary to disable the user interface controls that allow the user to move to the next record (again, this is logical, because the last record has no next record). For applications created using Visual C++'s application creation tools, the support for the user interface is created automatically.

Operations

There is one operation member function. This function assists in the updating of records in the recordset.

OnMove( )

```
virtual BOOL OnMove( UINT nIDMoveCommand );
```

The **OnMove()** function moves to the record specified by **nIDMoveCommand**. The following are valid values for **nIDMoveCommand**:

- **ID_RECORD_FIRST**, which moves to the first record in the recordset
- **ID_RECORD_LAST**, which moves to the last record in the recordset
- **ID_RECORD_NEXT**, which moves to the next record in the recordset
- **ID_RECORD_PREV**, which moves to the previous record in the recordset

If an error occurs, the **OnMove()** function throws a **CDBException**.

In an ODBC application created using Visual C++'s tools, this function performs the same functions as the toolbar buttons that enable the user to move to the first, last, next, or previous records.

If the current record has changed, **OnMove()** updates the record in the recordset.

The ODBC Process

To understand the ODBC process, you need to understand each of the components. As Microsoft has currently configured ODBC, each ODBC application is supplied with a standard set of ODBC components. At this time, ODBC isn't part of a standard Windows installation, but this might change. As ODBC becomes more popular, Microsoft might start including it with Windows. If Microsoft begins shipping the standard ODBC components with Windows, it will become unnecessary for each ODBC application to include the ODBC components.

The standard ODBC system consists of the components listed in Table 14.2.

Table 14.2. ODBC system components.	
Part	*Description*
Setup	Used to install the ODBC system. Must be customized by the application developer.
ODBC Driver Manager	This DLL file contains the code to implement the **SQL...()** functions. Calls the individual DataSource drivers.
ODBC Drivers	A number of drivers supplied by Microsoft may be redistributed by developers. The DataSource drivers that are supplied by Microsoft are listed in Table 14.3.
Help Files	Microsoft supplies a help file for each of the components of ODBC. Many applications suppliers, in an attempt to conserve distribution disk space, don't ship the help files. Whenever possible, you should make it a practice to ship the help files, because this enables users to solve their problems with ODBC without having to call for support.
Initialization Files	The ODBC system includes shell .INI files to allow the setup program to configure a working ODBC system.

Part	Description
ODBC Administration	The ODBC Administration system consists of a DLL that is installed in the Windows Control Panel, as well as a number of ancillary supporting files. There is also a stand-alone administration program for use with Windows 3.0.
Misc. Files	There are several files (such as ORACLE.TXT) that you should ship with your ODBC installation set.

Table 14.3 shows the ODBC drivers and DataSources that the standard ODBC installation supports. If you want your application to support a DataSource that is not supported by the standard ODBC driver set, there is a good chance that an aftermarket driver is available. Microsoft produces an ODBC driver catalog.

TABLE 14.3. STANDARD ODBC DRIVERS.

DataSource	Notes
Access Data (*.MDB)	The ODBC driver for files created using Microsoft Access. This driver permits a wide range of operations, including updating.
dBASE Files (*.DBF)	The ODBC driver for files that are in dBASE format. Many programs support dBASE format files, and the ODBC driver allows applications to access these files.
FoxPro Files (*.DBF)	The ODBC driver for files that are in FoxPro format. The ODBC driver allows applications to access these files, but not to update them.
Paradox Files (*.DB)	The ODBC driver for files that are in Paradox format. The ODBC driver allows applications to access these files, but not to update them.

continues

	TABLE 14.3. CONTINUED	
DataSource	Notes
Btrieve Data (FILE.DDF)	The ODBC driver for files that are in Btrieve format. The ODBC driver allows applications to access these files, but not to update them.
Excel Files (*.XLS)	The ODBC driver for files that are in Excel database (not spreadsheet) format. The ODBC driver allows applications to access these files, but not to update them.
Text Files (*.TXT, *.CSV)	The ODBC driver for files that are in any of a number of text formats. Formats supported include comma/quote-delimited, delimited, and columnar data files. At application runtime, ODBC can open many of the text file formats correctly. The ODBC driver allows applications to access these files, but not to update them.
SQL Server	The ODBC driver for files that are provided by an SQL server.
Oracle	The ODBC driver for files that are provided by an Oracle server. The Oracle server can be remote.

As described at the beginning of this chapter, ODBC is an arrangement of DLL files. The first, the driver manager, interfaces with your application (using a known, standard interface) and with the ODBC drivers (with a common interface that the drivers know). The ODBC drivers are DLL files that interact with the driver manager using the known common interface and with the DataSource using an interface that is unique to that DataSource.

Your application calls the ODBC driver manager and initializes the connection to the desired DataSource. Initialization typically consists of allocating memory that the ODBC driver manager uses to store information specific to this connection.

Once there is a connection between your application and the desired DataSource, the application can manipulate the actual data from the DataSource. Data is always presented in columns, row by row. Different DataSources allow different degrees of freedom in how the rows are accessed, but most allow both forward and backward scrolling through the data.

When your application no longer requires the DataSource's data, it drops the connection. Dropping the connection frees any memory that was allocated by the ODBC driver manager (and the driver, if it needed to allocate memory) and releases the DataSource. For shared DataSources such as those found on networks, any records that were locked for updating and not properly unlocked would also be unlocked.

Summary

This chapter introduced ODBC as part of the Visual C++ 2.0 product. ODBC is also available as a separate product, the ODBC SDK 2.0.

Topics covered in this chapter include the following:

- The Microsoft Foundation Classes (MFC) for ODBC, which allow the C++ programmer easy access to the ODBC interface
- The **CDatabase** class, used to work with various ODBC DataSources
- The **CRecordSet** class, which can be used directly by the programmer or included by AppWizard when an ODBC application is created
- The **CRecordView** class, used to allow display of and navigation through records in a DataSource
- The process that takes place when an ODBC DataSource is being used

MFC support makes ODBC access an easy process for the programmer. It's rather easy to create an ODBC class that can then be used to access a particular ODBC DataSource.

ODBC Servers

Microsoft offers a number of ODBC drivers that the application's driver is allowed to redistribute without any royalty. Many other companies also write drivers. For more information on available aftermarket drivers, contact Microsoft and request its ODBC drivers catalog. For those with fax machines, Microsoft also maintains a fax-back service that provides information about driver availability.

Looking at the Drivers

This chapter looks at the drivers that Microsoft provides with both the Visual C++ package and the ODBC SDK 2.0. As with anything in the microcomputer market, things change. Microsoft might add new drivers at any time. If the DataSource driver that your application needs isn't listed in this chapter, you should contact Microsoft to see if it has one available.

Table 15.1 lists the standard Microsoft ODBC drivers. Although nine drivers are listed, there are actually only three. Microsoft decided to include a number of DataSources in a single driver (SIMBA), which works with a number of other drivers (RED110.DLL and TXTISAM.DLL).

	TABLE 15.1. STANDARD ODBC DRIVERS.	
DataSource	*Driver (DLL) Name*	*Description*
Access Data (*.MDB)	SIMBA	The ODBC driver for files created using Microsoft Access. This driver permits a wide range of operations, including updating.
dBASE Files (*.DBF)	SIMBA	The ODBC driver for files that are in dBASE format. Many programs support dBASE format files, and the ODBC driver allows applications to access these files.
FoxPro Files (*.DBF)	SIMBA	The ODBC driver for files that are in FoxPro format. The ODBC driver allows applications to access these files, but not to update them.
Paradox Files (*.DB)	SIMBA	The ODBC driver for files that are in Paradox format. The ODBC driver allows applications to access these files, but not to update them.
Btrieve Data (FILE.DDF)	SIMBA	The ODBC driver for files that are in Btrieve format. The ODBC driver allows applications to access these files, but not to update them.

DataSource	Driver (DLL) Name	Description
Excel Files (*.XLS)	SIMBA	The ODBC driver for files that are in Excel database (not spreadsheet) format. The ODBC driver allows applications to access these files, but not to update them.
Text Files (*.TXT, *.CSV)	SIMBA	The ODBC driver for files that are in any of a number of text formats. Formats supported include comma/quote-delimited, delimited, and columnar data files. ODBC can, at application runtime, open many of the text-file formats correctly. The ODBC driver allows applications to access these files, but not to update them.
SQL Server	SQLSRVR	The ODBC driver for files that are provided by an SQL Server.
Oracle	SQORA	The ODBC driver for files that are provided by an Oracle server. The Oracle server can be remote.

Even though many of the DataSources are served with the SIMBA driver, each DataSource is considered to be separate. This allows us to discuss the driver and DataSource without having to take into consideration the driver's packaging.

Access Data (*.MDB)

The Microsoft Access database driver allows ODBC applications to access and update data found in Microsoft Access databases. This powerful driver offers a great deal of flexibility to the ODBC programmer.

Driver Parameters

The Access driver enables the user to set up several parameters that will affect the driver's performance. These parameters include System Database, Page Timeout, Buffer Size, and Exclusive mode.

System Database

You can specify the path to the Microsoft Access system database that will be used with the Access database that you specify. You can click on the None button to access the database as the Admin user. Accessing as the Admin user doesn't require that a system database be used.

You can get more information about using the system database by referring to the *Microsoft Access User's Guide.*

Page Timeout

The Page Timeout option enables the user to specify (in tenths of a second) how long a page that isn't being used will remain in memory. Setting this parameter for one Access DataSource affects all other Access DataSources. The default value is 60 seconds (Page Timeout = 600).

Buffer Size

The Buffer Size option tells the Access driver what size to allocate for its internal buffer. The value is in kilobytes. The Access driver uses the internal buffer to transfer data to and from the DataSource. The default value is 256 kilobytes (Buffer Size = 256).

Exclusive

Microsoft Access DataSources may be opened in either the exclusive mode, in which only one application or user is currently accessing the DataSource, or in the nonexclusive mode, in which the DataSource may be shared between more than one user at a time.

If the Exclusive box is selected, the DataSource is limited to only one user at a time. When a DataSources is opened in the exclusive mode, the performance of the Access driver is enhanced, because it doesn't have to deal with the issues locking the DataSource.

The exclusive mode is enabled by default. For most single-user situations, the exclusive mode should be turned off.

Good Things to Know

The Microsoft Access driver has a number of other limitations. These limitations usually don't pose serious problems to the typical ODBC application, but it's still useful to know them. Here is a list of the Microsoft Access driver's limitations:

- Column names can't be longer than 64 characters. If they are, an error condition is generated.

- A column name may contain any of the characters that are valid in Microsoft Access. This includes spaces, as in Column One. However, any column name that contains characters other than letters, numbers, underscores, or spaces must be surrounded by double quotes (" "). It's an error to put in quotation marks a name that doesn't contain these special characters.

- Column names are expected to be in the first row of the database.

- A maximum of 255 columns are supported whenever a table is created.

- Tables aren't locked automatically, but they can be locked using Microsoft Access. Because of this, multiple users can read a table but not update it.

- Table names can't be longer than 64 characters. If a table name is longer than 64 characters, an error condition is generated.

- A table name may contain any of the characters that are valid in Microsoft Access. This includes spaces, as in Column One. However, any table name that contains characters other than letters, numbers, underscores, or spaces must be surrounded by double quotes (" "). It's an error to put in quotation marks a name that doesn't contain these special characters.

- A literal, such as a string, can have a length of up to 1,000 characters.

- Character strings may include any valid ANSI character (in other words, the character may range in value from 0x01 to 0xFF). Use two consecutive single quotes to insert one single quote.

- Your applications can support these character sets: English, French, German, Portuguese, Italian, Spanish, Nordic, and Dutch.

- The user can control system security by using Microsoft Access and modifying the Admin user. Modifications include the changing of the Admin user's password (the default is blank) and replacing the Admin user with a new user name.

Connecting to an Access DataSource

Whenever a DataSource is opened using ODBC, a connect string is required. Applications build this string at runtime in most cases. When developing your application, you can predict which keywords in the connect string will be required. For Access DataSources, the following keywords are used:

- The **DSN** parameter is the name of the Microsoft Access DataSource.

- The **UID** parameter provides the login ID for the user.

- The **PWD** parameter provides the password for the user.

- The **DBQ** parameter is the database being opened.

- The **FIL** parameter is the file type. In the case of Access, **RedISAM** is used.

For example, if you open an Access DataSource that has a DataSource name of MACTRI, and the actual database is in the file E:\ODBC\ACCESS.MDB, the connect string might look like this:

```
DSN=MACTRI;DBQ=e:\odbc\access.mdb;FIL=RedISAM;
```

In this example, I have coded neither a **UID** nor a **PWD** keyword. The MACTRI DataSource is opened in the exclusive mode, and no system database or users are defined. I could have defined the connect string like this:

```
DSN=MACTRI;DBQ=e:\odbc\access.mdb;FIL=RedISAM;UID=Admin;PWD=;
```

This example covers the situation in which there is userid and password checking and the default **UID** and **PWD** are acceptable.

SQL Functions Support

The Access driver supports all the Core and Level-1 functions. It also supports the Level-2 functions listed in Table 15.2.

ODBC defines a core grammar that roughly corresponds to the X/Open and SQL Access Group SQL CAE specification (1992). ODBC also defines a minimum grammar, to meet a basic level of ODBC conformance, and an extended grammar, to provide for common DBMS extensions to SQL. The following summarizes the grammar included in each conformance level.

TABLE 15.2. LEVEL-2 FUNCTIONS SUPPORTED BY THE ACCESS DRIVER.	
Function	*Description*
SQLDataSources()	Used to enumerate DataSource names. The **SQLDataSources()** function is implemented by the ODBC driver manager.
SQLMoreResults()	Used to determine whether the **hstmt** has more statement results. If there are more statement results, this function initializes processing for the next available result set.

The ODBC functions listed in Table 15.3 include Level-1 functions that have limitations or specifications in the Access driver.

TABLE 15.3. LEVEL-1 FUNCTIONS WITH LIMITATIONS WHEN SUPPORTED BY THE ACCESS DRIVER.	
Function	*Description*
SQLDriverConnect()	Supports the **DSN**, **UID**, **PWD**, **DBQ**, and **FIL** keywords.
SQLGetConnectOption(), **SQLSetConnectOption()**	Support **SQL_ACCESS_MODE**, **SQL_CURRENT_QUALIFIER**, **SQL_OPT_TRACE**, and **SQL_OPT_TRACEFILE**. The **SQLGetConnectOption()** function also supports the **SQL_AUTOCOMMIT** option.
SQLGetCursorName(), **SQLSetCursorName()**	Supported except for positioned updates or deletions.

continues

TABLE 15.3. CONTINUED	
Function	*Description*
`SQLGetData()`	Can be used to obtain data from any column, regardless of whether or not there are any bound columns after the column. It doesn't matter in which order the columns are retrieved.
`SQLGetInfo()`	Supports `SQL_FILE_USAGE`, a parameter that is specific to the Access driver. The return value (a 16-bit int) can be one of the following: `== 0` (`SQL_FILE_NOT_SUPPORTED`): The driver is not a single-tier driver. `== 1` (`SQL_FILE_TABLE`): A single-tier driver treats files in a DataSource as tables. `== 3` (`SQL_FILE_QUALIFIER`): A single-tier driver treats files in a DataSource as qualifiers. When `SQL_FILE_USAGE` is used with the Access driver, the return value from `SQLGetInfo()` is always `SQL_FILE_QUALIFIER` because an Access database is completely contained within a single file.
`SQLGetStmtOption()`, `SQLSetStmtOption()`	Support the `SQL_MAX_LENGTH`, `SQL_MAX_ROWS`, `SQL_LOCK_TABLES`, and `SQL_NOSCAN` options.
`SQLGetTypeInfo()`	Returns the data type names that can be used to create tables using the CREATE statement.
`SQLMoreResults()`	Always returns `SQL_NO_DATA_FOUND`.
`SQLTables()`	Doesn't return information on tables that are attached to an Access database.
`SQLTransact()`	Supports COMMIT but not ROLLBACK.

The Microsoft Access ODBC driver offers more features than many of the other supplied drivers. The primary disadvantage of the ODBC Access driver is that it's slow when updating, especially when used in the nonexclusive mode.

dBASE Files (*.DBF)

The ODBC dBASE driver supports both dBASE III and dBASE IV file formats. This driver allows Microsoft Windows applications to access files created by many different applications that utilize the dBASE file formats.

Driver Parameters

The dBASE driver enables the user to set up several parameters that will affect the driver's performance. These parameters include Collating Sequence, Page Timeout, Exclusive mode, Show Deleted Rows, and Approximate Page Count.

Collating Sequence

You can select either the ASCII collating sequence or the International collating sequence. Generally, for applications used in the U.S., the ASCII collating sequence is the correct choice. Users who are outside the U.S. or who are working with something other than the standard ANSI character sets might benefit from using an International collating sequence. Setting this parameter for one dBASE DataSource affects all other dBASE DataSources.

An indicator that the wrong collating sequence is being used is when an SQL ORDER BY clause doesn't produce the correct sorting of the records.

Page Timeout

The Page Timeout option enables the user to specify (in tenths of a second) how long a page that isn't being used will remain in memory. Setting this parameter for one dBASE DataSource affects all other dBASE DataSources. The default value is 60 seconds (Page Timeout = 600).

Exclusive

dBASE DataSources may be opened in either the exclusive mode, in which only one application or user is currently accessing the DataSource, or in the nonexclusive mode, in which the DataSource may be shared between more than one user at a time. This option affects only the DataSource being defined.

If the Exclusive box is selected, the DataSource is limited to only one user at a time. When the DataSource is opened in the exclusive mode, the performance of the dBASE driver is enhanced, because it doesn't have to deal with the issues locking the DataSource.

The exclusive mode is enabled by default. For most single-user situations, the exclusive mode should be turned off.

Show Deleted Rows

You can tell the driver to show rows that have been marked as deleted. In a dBASE database, the first character in a record is reserved as a status field. If the status field contains an asterisk (*), the record has been deleted. Setting this parameter for one dBASE DataSource affects all other dBASE DataSources.

Although it's technically easy to undelete a record, the ODBC dBASE driver doesn't provide this option.

Approximate Row Count

This option enables you to tell the ODBC dBASE driver to guess the number of rows in the DataSource. This is done by taking the size of the database file's data area and dividing it by the size of a record (the record size is fixed).

If the DataSource has deleted records, approximating the row count often provides an inaccurate number because the ODBC driver might not know about all deleted records at any given time.

Good Things to Know

The Microsoft ODBC dBASE driver has a number of other limitations. These limitations usually don't pose serious problems to the typical ODBC application, but it's useful to know about them. Here's a list of the Microsoft ODBC dBASE driver's limitations:

- When working with dBASE III files, you must select indexes using the ODBC control panel. This is because indexes for dBASE III files are external and the ODBC dBASE driver doesn't know about the connection between a given index and the dBASE DataSource.

- When a reserved word is used as an identifier such as a column or table name, it must be placed in double quotes, as in `"TIME"`.

- A column or table name may contain any characters that are valid in dBASE. A column name that contains characters other than letters, numbers, or underscores must be surrounded by double quotes (`" "`). It's an error to put in quotation marks a name that doesn't contain these special characters.

- Clipper .NTX index files aren't supported by the Microsoft ODBC dBASE driver.

- You can significantly improve performance when dealing with large dBASE DataSources by creating an index (an .MDX or .NDX file, depending on the version of dBASE being used) on the column that is the subject of the WHERE clause of a SELECT statement. When an .MDX index exists, it's automatically used when Boolean operations are performed in the WHERE clause, the LIKE clause, and in JOIN predicates.

When dealing with dBASE IV DataSources that have index files, or dBASE III DataSources where you have indicated that there is an index (.NDX) file, the ODBC dBASE driver automatically updates the index file.

There are several limitations when dealing with indexes to dBASE files:

- The dBASE DataSource's column names must all be valid.
- The dBASE columns must be in the same ascending or descending order.
- When a single text column is being indexed, the column's length must be less than 100 bytes.
- The total length of text columns being indexed must be less than 100 bytes. When more than one column is being used for indexing, each column must be text.
- You can't index logical or memo fields.
- You can't have duplicate index fields.
- Index files must be named according to dBASE standards. For dBASE III files, each index is in a separate file that has an .NDX extension. For dBASE IV files, all indexes are in a single index file with the same filename as the DataSource and an extension of .MDX.

Connecting to a dBASE DataSource

Whenever a DataSource is opened using ODBC, a connect string is required. Applications build this string at runtime in most cases. When developing your applications, you can predict which keywords in the connect string will be required. For dBASE DataSources, the following keywords are used:

- The **DSN** parameter is the name of the dBASE DataSource.
- The **DBQ** parameter is the directory of the dBASE DataSource being opened.
- The **FIL** parameter is the file type, which, in the case of dBASE, is either **DBASE3** or **DBASE4**.

For example, if you open a dBASE III DataSource that has a DataSource name of MACTRI, and the actual database is in the directory E:\DBASEODBC, the connect string might look like this:

```
DSN=MACTRI;DBQ=e:\dbaseodbc;FIL=DBASE3;
```

This example covers the accessing of most dBASE files.

SQL Functions Support

The ODBC dBASE driver supports the entire minimum grammar specification. It also supports all the Core and Level-1 functions, as well as the Level-2 functions listed in Table 15.4.

TABLE 15.4. LEVEL-2 FUNCTIONS SUPPORTED BY THE dBASE DRIVER.

Function	Description
SQLDataSources()	Used to enumerate DataSource names. The SQLDataSources() function is implemented by the ODBC driver manager.
SQLMoreResults()	Used to determine whether the hstmt has more statement results. If there are more statement results, this function initializes processing for the next available result set.

The ODBC functions listed in Table 15.5 include Level-1 functions that have limitations or specifications in the dBASE driver.

TABLE 15.5. LEVEL-1 FUNCTIONS WITH LIMITATIONS WHEN SUPPORTED BY THE dBASE DRIVER.

Function	Description
SQLDriverConnect()	Supports the DSN, DBQ, and FIL keywords.
SQLGetConnectOption(), SQLSetConnectOption()	Support SQL_ACCESS_MODE, SQL_CURRENT_QUALIFIER, SQL_OPT_TRACE, and SQL_OPT_TRACEFILE. The SQLGetConnectOption() function also supports the SQL_AUTOCOMMIT option.

Function	Description
SQLGetCursorName(), **SQLSetCursorName()**	Supported except for positioned updates or deletions.
SQLGetData()	Can be used to obtain data from any column, regardless of whether or not there are any bound columns after the column. It doesn't matter in which order the columns are retrieved.
SQLGetInfo()	Supports **SQL_FILE_USAGE**, a parameter that is specific to the Access driver. The return value (a 16-bit int) can be one of the following: **== 0** (**SQL_FILE_NOT_SUPPORTED**): The driver is not a single-tier driver. **== 1** (**SQL_FILE_TABLE**): A single-tier driver treats files in a DataSource as tables. **== 3** (**SQL_FILE_QUALIFIER**): A single-tier driver treats files in a DataSource as qualifiers. When **SQL_FILE_USAGE** is used with the Access driver, the return value from **SQLGetInfo()** will always be **SQL_FILE_TABLE** because each dBASE table is a DOS file.
SQLGetStmtOption(), **SQLSetStmtOption()**	Support the **SQL_MAX_LENGTH**, **SQL_MAX_ROWS**, and **SQL_NOSCAN** options.
SQLGetTypeInfo()	Returns the data type names that can be used to create tables using the CREATE statement.
SQLMoreResults()	Always returns **SQL_NO_DATA_FOUND**.
SQLTables()	Returns table names (which are actual dBASE filenames) that don't have file extensions.
SQLTransact()	Because the dBASE driver doesn't support transactions, the **SQLTransact()** function returns **SQL_SUCCESS** when called for a COMMIT and **SQL_ERROR** for a ROLLBACK.

The Microsoft ODBC dBASE driver offers reasonable support for dBASE files. Support for indexes is available.

FoxPro Files (*.DBF)

The ODBC FoxPro driver supports FoxPro file formats for FoxPro 2.0 and 2.5. This driver allows Microsoft Windows applications to access files created by many different applications that utilize the FoxPro file formats. The internal format of FoxPro files is very similar to that of dBASE files.

Driver Parameters

The FoxPro driver enables the user to set up several parameters that will affect the driver's performance. These parameters include Collating Sequence, Page Timeout, Exclusive mode, Show Deleted Rows, and Approximate Row Count.

Collating Sequence

You can select either the ASCII collating sequence or the International collating sequence. Generally, for applications that are used in the U.S., the ASCII collating sequence is the correct choice. Users outside the U.S., or who are working with something other than the standard ANSI character sets, might benefit from using an International collating sequence. Setting this parameter for one FoxPro DataSource affects all other FoxPro DataSources.

An indicator that the wrong collating sequence is being used is when an SQL ORDER BY clause doesn't produce the correct sorting of the records.

Page Timeout

The Page Timeout option enables the user to specify (in tenths of a second) how long a page that isn't being used will remain in memory. Setting this parameter for one FoxPro DataSource affects all other FoxPro DataSources. The default value is 60 seconds (Page Timeout = 600).

Exclusive

FoxPro DataSources may be opened in either the exclusive mode, in which only one application or user is currently accessing the DataSource, or in the nonexclusive mode, in which the DataSource may be shared between more than one user at a time. This option affects only the DataSource being defined.

If the Exclusive box is selected, the DataSource is limited to only one user at a time. When the DataSource is opened in the exclusive mode, the performance of the FoxPro driver is enhanced, because it does not have to deal with the issues locking the DataSource.

The exclusive mode is enabled by default. For most single-user situations, the exclusive mode should be turned off.

Show Deleted Rows

You can tell the driver to show rows that have been marked as deleted. In a FoxPro database, the first character in a record is reserved as a status field. If the status field contains an asterisk (*), the record has been deleted. Setting this parameter for one FoxPro DataSource affects all other FoxPro DataSources.

Although it's technically easy to undelete a record, the ODBC FoxPro driver doesn't provide this option.

Approximate Row Count

This option enables you to tell the ODBC FoxPro driver to guess the number of rows in the DataSource. This is done by taking the size of the database file's data area and dividing it by the size of a record (the record size is fixed).

If the DataSource has deleted records, approximating the row count often provides an inaccurate number because the ODBC driver might not know about all deleted records at any given time.

Good Things to Know

The Microsoft FoxPro ODBC driver has a number of other limitations. These limitations usually don't pose serious problems to the typical ODBC application, but it's useful to know about them. Here's a list of the Microsoft ODBC FoxPro driver's limitations:

- When working with FoxPro 2.0 files, you must select indexes using the ODBC control panel. This is because indexes for FoxPro 2.0 files are external, and the ODBC FoxPro driver doesn't know about the connection between a given index and the FoxPro DataSource.

- When a reserved word is used as an identifier such as a column or table name, it must be placed in double quotes, as in `"TIME"`.

- A column or table name may contain any of the characters that are valid in FoxPro. Any column name that contains characters other than letters, numbers, or underscores must be surrounded by double quotes (`" "`). It's an error to put in quotation marks a name that doesn't contain these special characters. Any character that has a value greater than 0x7F is converted to an underscore.

- Clipper .NTX index files aren't supported by the Microsoft ODBC FoxPro driver.
- You can significantly improve performance when dealing with large FoxPro DataSources by creating an index (a .CDX or .IDX file) on the column that is the subject of the WHERE clause of a SELECT statement. When an .MDX index exists, it's used automatically when Boolean operations are performed in the WHERE clause, the LIKE clause, and in JOIN predicates.

There are several limitations when you're dealing with indexes to FoxPro files:

- The FoxPro DataSource's column names must all be valid.
- The FoxPro columns must be in the same ascending or descending order.
- When a single text column is being indexed, the column's length must be less than 100 bytes.
- The total length of text columns being indexed must be less than 100 bytes. When more than one column is being used for indexing, each column must be text.
- You can't index logical or memo fields.
- You can't have duplicate index fields.
- Index files must be named according to FoxPro standards. For FoxPro 2.0 files, each index is in a separate file that has a .IDX extension. For FoxPro 2.5 files, all indexes are in a single index file with the same filename as the DataSource and an extension of .CDX.

Connecting to a FoxPro DataSource

Whenever a DataSource is opened using ODBC, a connect string is required. Applications build this string at runtime in most cases. When developing your application, you can predict which keywords in the connect string will be required. For FoxPro DataSources, the following keywords are used:

- The **DSN** parameter is the name of the FoxPro DataSource.
- The **DBQ** parameter is the directory of the FoxPro DataSource being opened.
- The **FIL** parameter is the file type, which, in the case of FoxPro, is either **FoxPro 2.0** or **FoxPro 2.5**.

For example, if you open a FoxPro 2.0 DataSource that has a DataSource name of MACTRI, and the actual database is in the directory E:\FOXPROODBC, the connect string might look like this:

```
DSN=MACTRI;DBQ=e:\FXPRODBC;FIL=FoxPro 2.0;
```

This example covers the accessing of most FoxPro files.

SQL Functions Support

The ODBC FoxPro driver supports the entire minimum grammar specification. It also supports all the Core and Level-1 functions, as well as the Level-2 functions listed in Table 15.6.

TABLE 15.6. LEVEL-2 FUNCTIONS SUPPORTED BY THE FOXPRO DRIVER.	
Function	Description
SQLDataSources()	Used to enumerate DataSource names. The SQLDataSources() function is implemented by the ODBC driver manager.
SQLMoreResults()	Used to determine whether the hstmt has more statement results. If there are more statement results, this function initializes processing for the next available result set.

The ODBC functions listed in Table 15.7 include Level-1 functions that have limitations or specifications in the FoxPro driver.

TABLE 15.7. LEVEL-1 FUNCTIONS WITH LIMITATIONS WHEN SUPPORTED BY THE
FOXPRO DRIVER.

Function	Description
SQLDriverConnect()	Supports the DSN, DBQ, and FIL keywords.
SQLGetConnectOption(), SQLSetConnectOption()	Support SQL_ACCESS_MODE, SQL_CURRENT_QUALIFIER, SQL_OPT_TRACE, and SQL_OPT_TRACEFILE. The SQLGetConnectOption() function also supports the SQL_AUTOCOMMIT option.
SQLGetCursorName(), SQLSetCursorName()	Supported except for positioned updates or deletions.
SQLGetData()	Can be used to obtain data from any column, regardless of whether or not there are any bound columns after the column. It doesn't matter in which order the columns are retrieved.
SQLGetInfo()	Supports SQL_FILE_USAGE, a parameter that is specific to the Access driver. The return value (a 16-bit int) can be one of the following: == 0 (SQL_FILE_NOT_SUPPORTED): The driver is not a single-tier driver. == 1 (SQL_FILE_TABLE): A single-tier driver treats files in a DataSource as tables. == 3 (SQL_FILE_QUALIFIER): A single-tier driver treats files in a DataSource as qualifiers. When SQL_FILE_USAGE is used with the Access driver, the return value from SQLGetInfo() is always SQL_FILE_TABLE because each FoxPro table is a DOS file.
SQLGetStmtOption(), SQLSetStmtOption()	Support the SQL_MAX_LENGTH, SQL_MAX_ROWS, and SQL_NOSCAN options.
SQLGetTypeInfo()	Returns the data type names that can be used to create tables using the CREATE statement.
SQLMoreResults()	Always returns SQL_NO_DATA_FOUND.
SQLTables()	Returns table names (which are actual FoxPro filenames) that don't have file extensions.

Function	Description
SQLTransact()	Because the FoxPro driver doesn't support transactions, the SQLTransact() function returns SQL_SUCCESS when called for a COMMIT and SQL_ERROR for a ROLLBACK.

The Microsoft ODBC FoxPro driver offers reasonable support for FoxPro files. Support for indexes also is available.

PARADOX FILES (*.DB)

The ODBC Paradox driver supports Paradox file formats for Paradox 3.5. This driver allows Microsoft Windows applications to access files created by many different applications that utilize the Paradox file formats. Unlike FoxPro, the internal format of Paradox files differs from that of dBASE files.

Driver Parameters

The Paradox driver enables the user to set up several parameters that will affect the driver's performance. These parameters include Collating Sequence, Page Timeout, Exclusive mode, Network Directory, and User Name.

Collating Sequence

You can select either the ASCII collating sequence or the International collating sequence. Generally, for applications that are used in the U.S., the ASCII collating sequence is the correct choice. Users who are outside the U.S., or who are working with something other than the standard ANSI character sets, might benefit from using an International collating sequence. Setting this parameter for one Paradox DataSource affects all other Paradox DataSources.

An indicator that the wrong collating sequence is being used is when an SQL ORDER BY clause doesn't produce the correct sorting of the records.

Page Timeout

The Page Timeout option enables the user to specify (in tenths of a second) how long a page that isn't being used will remain in memory. Setting this parameter for one Paradox DataSource affects all other Paradox DataSources. The default value is 60 seconds (Page Timeout = 600).

Exclusive

Paradox DataSources may be opened in either the exclusive mode, in which only one application or user is currently accessing the DataSource, or in the nonexclusive mode, in which the DataSource may be shared between more than one user at a time. This option affects only the DataSource being defined.

If the Exclusive box is selected, the DataSource is limited to only one user at a time. When a DataSource is opened in the exclusive mode, the performance of the Paradox driver is enhanced, because it doesn't have to deal with the issues locking the DataSource.

The exclusive mode is enabled by default. For most single-user situations, the exclusive mode should be turned off.

Network Directory

You can specify the full pathname for the directory containing the PARADOX.NET file. This file must exist in this directory, or the Paradox ODBC will create it. This option requires that a user name be supplied (see the next section).

User Name

You can provide a Paradox user name. It's required if you're using network support.

Good Things to Know

The Microsoft Paradox ODBC driver has a number of other limitations. These limitations usually don't pose serious problems to the typical ODBC application, but it's useful to know about them. Here's a list of the Microsoft Paradox ODBC driver's limitations:

- When working with Paradox 2.0 files, you must select indexes using the ODBC control panel. This is because indexes for Paradox 2.0 files are external, and the ODBC Paradox driver doesn't know about the connection between a given index and the Paradox DataSource.
- When a reserved word is used as an identifier (such as a column or table name), it must be placed in double quotes, as in `"TIME"`.
- A column or table name may contain any of the characters that are valid in Paradox. A column name that contains characters other than letters, numbers, or underscores must be surrounded by double quotes (`" "`). It's an error to put in quotation marks a name that doesn't

contain these special characters. Any character that has a value greater than 0x7F is converted to an underscore.

- Clipper .NTX index files aren't supported by the Microsoft ODBC Paradox driver.

- You can significantly improve performance when dealing with large Paradox DataSources by creating an index (a .CDX or .IDX file) on the column that is the subject of the WHERE clause of a SELECT statement. When an .MDX index exists, it's automatically used when Boolean operations are performed in the WHERE clause, the LIKE clause, and in JOIN predicates.

There are several limitations when dealing with indexes to Paradox files:

- The Paradox DataSource's column names must all be valid.

- The Paradox columns must be in the same ascending or descending order.

- When a single text column is being indexed, the column's length must be less than 100 bytes.

- The total length of text columns being indexed must be less than 100 bytes. When more than one column is being used for indexing, each column must be text.

- You can't index logical or memo fields.

- You can't have duplicate index fields.

- The Paradox ODBC driver requires that 4096 (and preferably more than 6144) bytes of stack be available after the driver is called.

- Index files must be named according to Paradox standards. For Paradox 2.0 files, each index is in a separate file that has an .IDX extension. For Paradox 2.5 files, all indexes are in a single index file with the same filename as the DataSource and an extension of .CDX.

Connecting to a Paradox DataSource

Whenever a DataSource is opened using ODBC, a connect string is required. Applications build this string at runtime in most cases. When developing your application, you can predict which keywords in the connect string will be required. For Paradox DataSources, the following keywords are used:

- The **DSN** parameter is the name of the Paradox DataSource.
- The **DBQ** parameter is the directory of the Paradox DataSource being opened.
- The **UID** parameter provides the login ID for the user.
- The **PWD** parameter provides the password for the user.
- The **FIL** parameter is the file type, which, in the case of Paradox, is **PARADOX.**

For example, if you open a Paradox 3.5 DataSource that has a DataSource name of MACTRI, and the actual database is in the directory E:\PARADOX, the connect string might look like this:

```
DSN=MACTRI;UID=NAME;PWD=PASSWORD;DBQ=e:\PARADOX\MACTRI;FIL=PARADOX;
```

This example covers the accessing of Paradox files.

SQL Functions Support

The ODBC Paradox driver supports the entire minimum grammar specification. It also supports all the Core and Level-1 functions, as well as the Level-2 functions listed in Table 15.8.

TABLE 15.8. LEVEL-2 FUNCTIONS SUPPORTED BY THE PARADOX DRIVER.

Function	Description
SQLDataSources()	Used to enumerate DataSource names. The **SQLDataSources()** function is implemented by the ODBC driver manager.
SQLMoreResults()	Used to determine whether the **hstmt** has more statement results. If there are more statement results, this function initializes processing for the next available result set.

The ODBC functions listed in Table 15.9 include Level-1 functions that have limitations or specifications in the Paradox driver.

TABLE 15.9. LEVEL-1 FUNCTIONS WITH LIMITATIONS WHEN SUPPORTED BY THE PARADOX DRIVER.	
Function	Description
SQLDriverConnect()	Supports the **DSN**, **DBQ**, and **FIL** keywords.
SQLGetConnectOption(), SQLSetConnectOption()	Support **SQL_ACCESS_MODE**, **SQL_CURRENT_QUALIFIER**, **SQL_OPT_TRACE**, and **SQL_OPT_TRACEFILE**. The **SQLGetConnectOption()** function also supports the **SQL_AUTOCOMMIT** option. The Paradox ODBC driver supports an additional connection option, 0x47E (1150), and no identifier is defined. The *vParam* argument is a 32-bit **HWND**, or **NULL**. If *vParam* is **NULL**, the Paradox ODBC driver doesn't display any dialog boxes other than those used by **SQLDriverConnect()**. If *vParam* is a **HWND**, it should be the **HWND** of the application's parent. When *vParam* is a valid **HWND**, the driver uses it to display dialog boxes.
SQLGetData()	Can be used to obtain data from any column, regardless of whether or not there are any bound columns after the column. It doesn't matter in which order the columns are retrieved.
SQLGetInfo()	Supports **SQL_FILE_USAGE**, a parameter that is specific to the Access driver. The return value (a 16-bit int) can be one of the following: == **0** (**SQL_FILE_NOT_SUPPORTED**): The driver is not a single-tier driver. == **1** (**SQL_FILE_TABLE**): A single-tier driver treats files in a DataSource as tables. == **3** (**SQL_FILE_QUALIFIER**): A single-tier driver treats files in a DataSource as qualifiers. When **SQL_FILE_USAGE** is used with the Access driver, the return value from **SQLGetInfo()** is always **SQL_FILE_TABLE** because each Paradox table is a DOS file.

continues

TABLE 15.9. CONTINUED	
Function	*Description*
SQLGetStmtOption(), SQLSetStmtOption()	Support the SQL_MAX_LENGTH, SQL_MAX_ROWS, and SQL_NOSCAN options. The Paradox ODBC driver also supports the driver-specific option SQL_LOCK_TABLES. Support for passwords is provided by passing a value of 1151 in *fOption*, and a pointer to a password string in *vParam*.
SQLGetTypeInfo()	Returns the data type names that can be used to create tables using the CREATE statement.
SQLMoreResults()	Always returns SQL_NO_DATA_FOUND.
SQLTransact()	Because the Paradox driver doesn't support transactions, the SQLTransact() function returns SQL_SUCCESS when called for a COMMIT and SQL_ERROR for a ROLLBACK.

The Microsoft Paradox ODBC driver offers reasonable support for Paradox files. Support for indexes is available.

BTRIEVE DATA (FILE.DDF)

The Microsoft Btrieve ODBC database driver allows ODBC applications to access and update data found in Btrieve databases. This is a powerful driver that offers a great deal of flexibility to the ODBC programmer.

Driver Parameters

The Btrieve driver enables the user to set up several parameters that affect the driver's performance. These parameters include Collating Sequence, Page Timeout, and Exclusive mode.

Collating Sequence

You can select either the ASCII collating sequence or the International collating sequence. Generally, for applications that are used in the U.S., the ASCII collating sequence is the correct choice. Users who are outside the U.S., or who are working with something other than the standard ANSI character sets, might benefit from using an International collating sequence. Setting this parameter for one Btrieve DataSource affects all other Btrieve DataSources.

An indicator that the wrong collating sequence is being used is when an SQL ORDER BY clause doesn't produce the correct sorting of the records.

Page Timeout

The Page Timeout option enables the user to specify (in tenths of a second) how long a page that isn't being used will remain in memory. Setting this parameter for one Btrieve DataSource affects all other Btrieve DataSources. The default value is 60 seconds (Page Timeout = 600).

Exclusive

Btrieve DataSources may be opened in either the exclusive mode, in which only one application or user is currently accessing the DataSource, or in the nonexclusive mode, in which the DataSource may be shared between more than one user at a time.

If the Exclusive box is selected, the DataSource is limited to only one user at a time. When a DataSource is opened in the exclusive mode, the performance of the Btrieve driver is enhanced, because it doesn't have to deal with the issues locking the DataSource.

The exclusive mode is enabled by default. For most single-user situations, the exclusive mode should be turned off.

Good Things to Know

The Microsoft Btrieve ODBC driver has a number of other limitations. These limitations usually don't pose serious problems to the typical ODBC application, but it's useful to know about them. Here's a list of the Microsoft Btrieve ODBC driver's limitations:

- When a Btrieve DataSource is opened and the .DDF files aren't found, the Btrieve ODBC driver creates them. These files contain only information about tables that are created after they are created. Any existing table information isn't included in these created files.

- A column name may contain any character. This includes spaces, as in `Column One`. However, any column name that contains characters other than letters, numbers, underscores, or spaces must be surrounded by double quotes (" "). It's an error to put in quotation marks a name that doesn't contain these special characters.

- If a column name contains an SQL reserved word, it must be placed in double quotes, as in "TIME".

- The Btrieve ODBC driver is unable to access data from password-protected files.

- Characters strings may be any valid ANSI character (in other words, the character may range in value from 0x01 to 0xFF). Use two consecutive single quotes to insert one single quote.

- Your applications can support the ASCII and International character sets.

Connecting to a Btrieve DataSource

Whenever a DataSource is opened using ODBC, a connect string is required. Applications build this string at runtime in most cases. When developing your application, you can predict which keywords in the connect string will be required. For Btrieve DataSources, the following keywords are used:

- The **DSN** parameter is the name of the Btrieve DataSource.
- The **DBQ** parameter is the database being opened.
- The **FIL** parameter is the file type, which, in the case of Btrieve, is **BTRIEVE**.

For example, if you open a Btrieve DataSource that has a DataSource name of MACTRI, and the actual database is in the directory E:\BTRIEVE\STUFF, the connect string might look like this:

```
DSN=MACTRI;DBQ=e:\BTRIEVE\STUFF;FIL=BTRIEVE;
```

This example covers all Btrieve DataSource opening.

SQL Functions Support

The Btrieve driver supports all the Core and Level-1 functions. It also supports the Level-2 functions listed in Table 15.10.

TABLE 15.10. LEVEL-2 FUNCTIONS SUPPORTED BY THE BTRIEVE DRIVER.

Function	Description
SQLDataSources()	Used to enumerate DataSource names. The SQLDataSources() function is implemented by the ODBC driver manager.
SQLMoreResults()	Used to determine whether the hstmt has more statement results. If there are more statement results, this function initializes processing for the next available result set.

The ODBC functions listed in Table 15.11 include Level-1 functions that have limitations or specifications in the Btrieve driver.

TABLE 15.11. LEVEL-1 FUNCTIONS WITH LIMITATIONS WHEN SUPPORTED BY THE BTRIEVE DRIVER.

Function	Description
SQLDriverConnect()	Supports the DSN, DBQ, and FIL keywords.
SQLGetConnectOption(), SQLSetConnectOption()	Support SQL_ACCESS_MODE, SQL_CURRENT_QUALIFIER, SQL_OPT_TRACE, and SQL_OPT_TRACEFILE. The SQLGetConnectOption() function also supports the SQL_AUTOCOMMIT option.
SQLGetCursorName(), SQLSetCursorName()	Supported except for positioned updates or deletions.
SQLGetData()	Can be used to obtain data from any column, regardless of whether or not there are any bound columns after the column. It doesn't matter in which order the columns are retrieved.
SQLGetInfo()	Supports SQL_FILE_USAGE, a parameter that is specific to the Btrieve driver. The return value (a 16-bit int) can be one of the following:

continues

TABLE 15.11. CONTINUED	
Function	Description
	== **0** (**SQL_FILE_NOT_SUPPORTED**): The driver is not a single-tier driver. == **1** (**SQL_FILE_TABLE**): A single-tier driver treats files in a DataSource as tables. == **3** (**SQL_FILE_QUALIFIER**): A single-tier driver treats files in a DataSource as qualifiers. When **SQL_FILE_USAGE** is used with the Btrieve driver, the return value from **SQLGetInfo()** is always **SQL_FILE_QUALIFIER** because a Btrieve database is completely contained within a single file.
SQLGetStmtOption() **SQLSetStmtOption()**	Support the **SQL_MAX_LENGTH**, **SQL_MAX_ROWS**, and **SQL_NOSCAN** options.
SQLGetTypeInfo()	Returns the data type names that can be used to create tables using the CREATE statement.
SQLMoreResults()	Always returns **SQL_NO_DATA_FOUND**.
SQLTransact()	Because the Btrieve driver doesn't support transactions, the **SQLTransact()** function returns **SQL_SUCCESS** when called for a COMMIT and **SQL_ERROR** for a ROLLBACK.

The Btrieve driver enables you to access Novell Btrieve files. This driver has reasonable performance, and it supports most of the Btrieve functionality, except for passwords.

Excel Files (*.XLS)

The Microsoft Excel ODBC database driver allows ODBC applications to access data found in Excel spreadsheet databases. This driver offers some limited access to Excel spreadsheets. To use the Excel ODBC driver, the user must save the spreadsheet in the database format. Because of this, the Excel ODBC driver is unable to access an Excel spreadsheet directly.

Driver Parameters

The Excel driver enables the user to set up one parameter, Rows to Scan, that affects the driver's performance.

Rows to Scan

You must tell the Excel ODBC driver how many rows to scan to determine what the data type is for each column. To tell the Excel ODBC driver to scan the entire file, enter a value of zero.

Scanning more rows than necessary can slow the driver's performance.

Good Things to Know

The Microsoft Excel ODBC driver has a number of other limitations. These limitations usually don't pose serious problems to the typical ODBC application, but it's useful to know about them. Here's a list of the Microsoft Excel ODBC driver's limitations:

- A column name must be 64 or fewer characters long. If the column name is more than 64 characters long, an error will occur.

- A column name may contain any character. This includes spaces, as in `Column One`. However, any column name that contains characters other than letters, numbers, underscores, or spaces must be surrounded by double quotes (`" "`). It's an error to put in quotation marks a name that doesn't contain these special characters.

- An Excel DataSource may not have more than 255 columns.

- There may not be more than 1,000 characters in a literal.

- All Excel DataSources are opened in shared mode. No exclusive mode is available.

- If a column name contains an SQL reserved word, it must be placed in double quotes, as in `"TIME"`.

- The Excel ODBC driver is unable to access data from password-protected files.

- Characters strings may be any valid ANSI character (in other words, the character may range in value from 0x01 to 0xFF). Use two consecutive single quotes to insert one single quote.

- Applications can create Excel tables that, once closed, can't be modified. When you're creating an Excel table, no other operations can be performed on the table.
- Once created, all Excel tables are read-only and can't be modified.

Connecting to an Excel DataSource

Whenever a DataSource is opened using ODBC, a connect string is required. Applications build this string at runtime in most cases. When developing your application, you can predict which keywords in the connect string will be required. For Excel DataSources, the following keywords are used:

- The **DSN** parameter is the name of the Microsoft Excel DataSource.
- The **DBQ** parameter is the database being opened.
- The **FIL** parameter is the file type. In the case of Excel, **EXCEL** is used.

For example, if you open an Excel DataSource that has a DataSource name of MACTRI, and the actual database is in the directory E:\EXCEL\STUFF, the connect string might look like this:

```
DSN=MACTRI;DBQ=E:\EXCEL\STUFF;FIL=EXCEL;
```

This example covers all Excel DataSource opening.

SQL Functions Support

The Excel driver supports all the Core and Level-1 functions. It also supports the Level-2 functions listed in Table 15.12.

	TABLE 15.12. LEVEL-2 FUNCTIONS SUPPORTED BY THE EXCEL DRIVER.
Function	Description
SQLDataSources()	Used to enumerate DataSource names. The SQLDataSources() function is implemented by the ODBC driver manager.
SQLMoreResults()	Used to determine whether the hstmt has more statement results. If there are more statement results, this function initializes processing for the next available result set.

The ODBC functions listed in Table 15.13 include Level-1 functions that have limitations or specifications in the Excel driver.

TABLE 15.13. LEVEL-1 FUNCTIONS WITH LIMITATIONS WHEN SUPPORTED BY THE EXCEL DRIVER.

Function	Description
`SQLDriverConnect()`	Supports the **DSN**, **DBQ**, and **FIL** keywords.
`SQLGetConnectOption()`, `SQLSetConnectOption()`	Support **SQL_ACCESS_MODE**, **SQL_CURRENT_QUALIFIER**, **SQL_OPT_TRACE**, and **SQL_OPT_TRACEFILE**. The `SQLGetConnectOption()` function also supports the **SQL_AUTOCOMMIT** option.
`SQLGetCursorName()`, `SQLSetCursorName()`	Supported except for positioned updates or deletions.
`SQLGetData()`	Can be used to obtain data from any column, regardless of whether or not there are any bound columns after the column. It doesn't matter in which order the columns are retrieved.
`SQLGetInfo()`	Supports **SQL_FILE_USAGE**, a parameter that is specific to the Excel driver. The return value (a 16-bit int) can be one of the following: `== 0` (**SQL_FILE_NOT_SUPPORTED**): The driver is not a single-tier driver. `== 1` (**SQL_FILE_TABLE**): A single-tier driver treats files in a DataSource as tables. `== 3` (**SQL_FILE_QUALIFIER**): A single-tier driver treats files in a DataSource as qualifiers. When **SQL_FILE_USAGE** is used with the Excel driver, the return value from `SQLGetInfo()` is always **SQL_FILE_TABLE** because an Excel database is completely contained within a single file.
`SQLGetStmtOption()`, `SQLSetStmtOption()`	Support the **SQL_MAX_LENGTH**, **SQL_MAX_ROWS**, and **SQL_NOSCAN** options.

continues

TABLE 15.13. CONTINUED	
Function	*Description*
SQLGetTypeInfo()	Returns the data type names that can be used to create tables using the CREATE statement.
SQLMoreResults()	Always returns SQL_NO_DATA_FOUND.
SQLTables()	Table names returned by the Excel ODBC driver don't have filename extensions.
SQLSpecialColumns()	An empty result set is always returned, with a return code of SQL_SUCCESS.
SQLTransact()	The Excel driver supports transactions for COMMIT, but not for ROLLBACK.

The Excel driver enables you to access Microsoft Excel files. This driver has reasonable performance, but it requires that Excel spreadsheets be converted to database format.

Text Files (*.TXT, *.CSV)

The text-file driver allows ODBC applications to access data found in a number of flat text-file formats. These formats include the following:

- Comma-delimited format, in which the input file usually has a .CSV extension and each column is delimited with commas. Text fields that contain blanks, tabs, or the delimiting character must be enclosed in quotation marks.

- Tab-delimited, in which the fields are delimited with tabs. Text fields that contain blanks, tabs, or the delimiting character must be enclosed in quotation marks.

- Custom-delimited, in which the delimiting character is specified. The delimiter must not be a double quote. Text fields that contain the delimiting character must be enclosed in quotation marks.

- Columnar data, in which the width of the columns is fixed.

Also, a text file may optionally have column names as the first record in the file.

Driver Parameters

The text-file driver enables the user to set up parameters that affect the driver's performance. These parameters include the Extensions list and Define Format.

Extensions List

You can tell the driver which extensions are to be used when prompting the user for the file to open in the dialog box's Extensions list.

Define Format

The Define Format option enables the user to define the file type and how it is delimited, how many rows to scan to determine the column's data type, and what the delimiter is (if the file is delimited with a custom character). You can select the character set used (ANSI or OEM).

The Define Format option also enables you to define the column names. For each column, the user may provide a name, define the data type, and (optionally, for columnar data) define the column's width.

Good Things to Know

The Microsoft text-file ODBC driver has a number of other limitations. These limitations usually don't pose serious problems to the typical ODBC application, but it's useful to know about them. Here's a list of the Microsoft text-file ODBC driver's limitations:

- A column name must be 30 or fewer characters long. If the column name is more than 30 characters long, it will be truncated.
- The default column names are **Col***n*, where *n* is a number starting at 1 that is incremented for each column.
- Table names may be any valid ANSI character (in other words, the character may range in value from 0x01 to 0xFF). Use two consecutive single quotes to insert one single quote. A table name must be a valid filename.
- A column name may contain any character. This includes spaces, as in `Column One`. However, any column name that contains characters other than letters, numbers, underscores, or spaces must be surrounded by double quotes (`" "`). It's an error to put in quotation marks a name that doesn't contain these special characters.
- A column of type LONGCHAR may be a maximum of 65,500 characters long.

- An empty (or null) column is represented by a set of delimiters with nothing between them, or by a blank string for a columnar file. All columns may have leading spaces.

- There may not be more than 1,000 characters in a literal.

- All text-file DataSources are opened in shared mode. No exclusive mode is available. The only exception is that tables opened for insertion are opened in exclusive mode only and may be modified by only one user at a time.

- A table's data may not be updated or deleted. Tables are read-only (except for tables opened for insertion).

- Applications can create text-file tables that, once closed, can't be modified. When you're creating a text-file table, no other operations can be performed on the table.

- Once created, all text-file tables are read-only and can't be modified.

Connecting to a Text-File DataSource

Whenever a DataSource is opened using ODBC, a connect string is required. Applications build this string at runtime in most cases. When developing your application, you can predict which keywords in the connect string will be required. For text-file DataSources, the following keywords are used:

- The **DSN** parameter is the name of the text-file DataSource.

- The **DBQ** parameter is the database being opened.

- The **FIL** parameter is the file type. In the case of text files, **TEXT** is used.

For example, if you open a text-file DataSource that has a DataSource name of MACTRI, and the actual text file is in the directory E:\DATA\STUFF, the connect string might look like this:

```
DSN=MACTRI;DBQ=E:\DATA\STUFF;FIL=TEXT;
```

This example covers all text-file DataSource opening.

SQL Functions Support

The text-file driver supports all the Core and Level-1 functions. It also supports the Level-2 functions listed in Table 15.14.

TABLE 15.14. LEVEL-2 FUNCTIONS SUPPORTED BY THE TEXT-FILE DRIVER.

Function	Description
SQLDataSources()	Used to enumerate DataSource names. The SQLDataSources() function is implemented by the ODBC driver manager.
SQLMoreResults()	Used to determine whether the hstmt has more statement results. If there are more statement results, this function initializes processing for the next available result set.

The ODBC functions listed in Table 15.15 include Level-1 functions that have limitations or specifications in the text-file driver.

TABLE 15.15. LEVEL-1 FUNCTIONS WITH LIMITATIONS WHEN SUPPORTED BY THE TEXT-FILE DRIVER.

Function	Description
SQLDriverConnect()	Supports the DSN, DBQ, and FIL keywords.
SQLGetConnectOption(), SQLSetConnectOption()	Support SQL_ACCESS_MODE, SQL_CURRENT_QUALIFIER, SQL_OPT_TRACE, and SQL_OPT_TRACEFILE. The SQLGetConnectOption() function also supports the SQL_AUTOCOMMIT option.
SQLGetCursorName(), SQLSetCursorName()	Supported except for positioned updates or deletions.
SQLGetData()	Can be used to obtain data from any column, regardless of whether or not there are any bound columns after the column. It doesn't matter in which order the columns are retrieved.
SQLGetInfo()	Supports SQL_FILE_USAGE, a parameter that is specific to the text-file driver. The return value (a 16-bit int) can be one of the following:

continues

TABLE 15.15. CONTINUED	

Function	Description
	== **0** (**SQL_FILE_NOT_SUPPORTED**): The driver is not a single-tier driver. **== 1** (**SQL_FILE_TABLE**): A single-tier driver treats files in a DataSource as tables. **== 3** (**SQL_FILE_QUALIFIER**): A single-tier driver treats files in a DataSource as qualifiers. When **SQL_FILE_USAGE** is used with the text-file driver, the return value from **SQLGetInfo()** is always **SQL_FILE_TABLE** because a text file is completely contained within a single file.
SQLGetStmtOption(), SQLSetStmtOption()	Support the **SQL_MAX_LENGTH**, **SQL_MAX_ROWS**, and **SQL_NOSCAN** options.
SQLGetTypeInfo()	Returns the data type names that can be used to create tables using the CREATE statement.
SQLMoreResults()	Always returns **SQL_NO_DATA_FOUND**.
SQLSpecialColumns()	Always returns **SQL_SUCCESS** as the return code. This function doesn't return a result set.
SQLTables()	Table names returned by the text-file ODBC driver don't have filename extensions. The application must either determine or return column file types.
SQLTransact()	The text-file driver supports transactions for COMMIT, but not for ROLLBACK.

The text-file driver enables you to access text files. This driver has reasonable performance, but it limits the ability to update a text-type file.

SQL SERVER

The SQL Server driver allows ODBC applications to access data found on an SQL Server. An SQL Server is a multiuser relational database system that runs on LANs. SQL Servers are available from a number of sources, including

Microsoft and Sybase. SQL Servers normally are found only on multiuser LAN-based systems.

The discussion of using an SQL Server is beyond the scope of this book; therefore, only a broad overview of the SQL Server ODBC driver is provided.

Driver Parameters

The SQL Server driver enables the user to set up parameters that affect the driver's operation. With SQL Servers, you must provide information about the server, the network address, and the network library. You also must provide login information, including the database name and the language that will be used.

Good Things to Know

The Microsoft SQL ODBC Server driver supports named procedures.

Connecting to an SQL Server DataSource

Whenever a DataSource is opened using ODBC, a connect string is required. Applications build this string at runtime in most cases. When developing your application, you can predict which keywords in the connect string will be required. For SQL Server DataSources, the following keywords are used:

- The **DSN** parameter is the name of the SQL Server DataSource.
- The **SERVER** parameter is the name of the computer where the DataSource is.
- The **UID** parameter is the user's name.
- The **PWD** parameter is the user's password.
- The **APP** parameter is the name of the calling program. This parameter is optional.
- The **WSID** parameter is the workstation ID. **WSID** often is the same as the network name of the computer on which the ODBC application is running.
- The **DATABASE** parameter is an optional parameter that specifies the name of the SQL Server database.
- The **LANGUAGE** parameter, used with SQL Server versions 4.2 and later, is the national language to be used.

For example, if you open an SQL Server DataSource that has a DataSource name of MACTRI, a userid of HIPSON, and a password of ICECREAM, the connect string might look like this:

```
DSN=MACTRI;UID=HIPSON;PWD=ICECREAM;SERVER=MICKEY;
```

This example is just one of many possible SQL Server connect strings.

SQL Functions Support

The SQL Server driver supports all the Core and Level-1 functions. It also supports the Level-2 functions listed in Table 15.16.

TABLE 15.16. LEVEL-2 FUNCTIONS SUPPORTED BY THE SQL SERVER DRIVER.

Function	Description
SQLDataSources()	Used to enumerate DataSource names. The SQLDataSources() function is implemented by the ODBC driver manager.
SQLMoreResults()	Used to determine whether the hstmt has more statement results. If there are more statement results, this function initializes processing for the next available result set.
SQLBrowseConnect()	Used to enumerate attributes required to connect to DataSources.
SQLColumnPrivileges()	Returns a list of columns and their associated privileges.
SQLDataSources()	Used to enumerate DataSource names.
SQLForeignKeys()	Returns a list of column names that comprise foreign keys if they exist in the specified table.
SQLMoreResults()	Used to determine whether more statement results are available.
SQLNativeSql()	Returns a driver-translated SQL string.
SQLNumParams()	Returns the number of parameters in an SQL statement.
SQLProcedureColumns()	Returns a list of input and output parameters and columns that make up the result set.

Function	Description
SQLProcedures()	Returns a list of procedure names that have been stored in a specified DataSource.
SQLParamOptions()	Allows the application to specify multiple values for parameters set using SQLSetParam().
SQLPrimaryKeys()	Returns the column name(s) of the primary key(s).
SQLSetScrollOptions()	Used to set options that control the behavior of cursors that are associated with the specified HSTMT.
SQLTablePrivileges()	Returns a list of tables and their associated privileges.

The ODBC functions listed in Table 15.17 include Level-1 functions that have limitations or specifications in the SQL Server driver.

TABLE 15.17. LEVEL-1 FUNCTIONS WITH LIMITATIONS WHEN SUPPORTED BY THE SQL SERVER DRIVER.

Function	Description
SQLDriverConnect()	Supports the DSN, SERVER, UID, PWD, APP, WSID, DATABASE, and LANGUAGE keywords.
SQLColAttributes()	If called after an SQL SELECT statement has been prepared but not executed, this function causes the SQL Server to generate an empty result set to obtain the desired information.
SQLDescribeCol()	If called after an SQL SELECT statement has been prepared but not executed, this function causes the SQL Server to generate an empty result set to obtain the desired information.
SQLNumResultCols()	If called after an SQL SELECT statement has been prepared but not executed, this function causes the SQL Server to generate an empty result set to obtain the desired information.

continues

TABLE 15.17. CONTINUED	
Function	Description
SQLColumns()	If the *szTableQualifier* is a null string rather than a **NULL** pointer, the driver returns an error.
SQLStatistics()	If the *szTableQualifier* is a null string rather than a **NULL** pointer, the driver returns an error.
SQLConnect()	Used to retrieve the language from the ODBC.INI file.
SQLPrepare()	The SQL Server doesn't support statement preparation and execution. The SQL Server driver stores a statement as a procedure, then compiles it for future execution.

The SQL Server driver enables you to access Microsoft SQL Server and Sybase SQL Server files.

ORACLE

The Oracle Server driver allows ODBC applications to access data found on an Oracle Server, a multiuser relational database system that runs on LANs. Oracle Servers are available from Oracle Corporation. They normally are found only on multiuser LAN-based systems.

The discussion of using an Oracle Server is beyond the scope of this book; therefore, only a broad overview of the Oracle Server ODBC driver is provided.

Driver Parameters

The Oracle Server driver enables the user to set up parameters that affect the driver's operation. With Oracle Servers, you must provide information about the server, the network address, and the network library. You also must provide information regarding the network connection and the DataSource.

Good Things to Know

The Oracle Server driver supports named procedures.

Connecting to an Oracle Server DataSource

Whenever a DataSource is opened on an Oracle server, the SQL*Net driver must be installed on the application's computer, and the SQL*Net listener must be installed on the Oracle server machine.

For information about the SQL*Net drivers, refer to the documentation supplied with SQL*Net.

SQL Functions Support

The Oracle Server driver supports all the Core and Level-1 functions. It also supports the Level-2 functions listed in Table 15.18.

TABLE 15.18. LEVEL-2 FUNCTIONS SUPPORTED BY THE ORACLE SERVER DRIVER.

Function	Description
SQLDataSources()	Used to enumerate DataSource names. The SQLDataSources() function is implemented by the ODBC driver manager.
SQLMoreResults()	Used to determine whether the hstmt has more statement results. If there are more statement results, this function initializes processing for the next available result set.
SQLNativeSql()	Returns a driver-translated SQL string.

The ODBC functions listed in Table 15.19 include Level-1 functions that have limitations or specifications in the Oracle Server driver.

TABLE 15.19. LEVEL-1 FUNCTIONS WITH LIMITATIONS WHEN SUPPORTED BY THE ORACLE SERVER DRIVER.	
Function	*Description*
SQLConnect()	When the CONFIG.ORA file contains the LOCAL keyword, only the userid and password are required.
SQLDriverConnect()	Supports the DSN, DBQ, UID, and PWD keywords.
SQLColAttributes()	If called after an SQL SELECT statement has been prepared but not executed, this function causes the Oracle Server to generate an empty result set to obtain the desired information.
SQLMoreResults()	Oracle doesn't support multiple result sets. SQLMoreResults() always returns SQL_NO_DATA_FOUND.
SQLSpecialColumns()	When called with the SQL_BEST_ROWID option set, this function returns the ROWID column.

The Oracle Server driver enables you to access an Oracle Server.

SUMMARY

This chapter outlined each of the ODBC drivers that Microsoft supplies with the ODBC SDK and with Visual C++ 2.0. Drivers are available for the following types of files:

- Microsoft Access databases
- dBASE III and dBASE IV format files
- FoxPro 2.0 format files
- Paradox format files
- Btrieve (Novell) databases
- Excel files saved in database format
- Text files, either delimited (comma-delimited, blank-delimited, or custom-delimited) or fixed-column
- Files from an SQL Server
- Oracle databases (from an Oracle server)

The drivers included with Visual C++ 2.0 can be redistributed without any further royalties. The complete terms of the redistribution license can be found in the file REDISTRB.WRI in the \REDIST directory.

For situations in which you need to access files from a DataSource that is not part of those supplied by Microsoft, aftermarket ODBC drivers are available.

AN INTRODUCTION TO SQL

The purpose of this chapter is to introduce you to SQL. Visual C++ 2.0 and ODBC (32-bit) can be used together to enable you to create 32-bit database-aware applications. SQL is a language used to interface with databases.

ODBC was introduced in Chapter 14. ODBC consists of a set of functions that enable the programmer to implement an interface with a number of DataSources. Drivers for these DataSources are available from both Microsoft and independent sources.

THINGS CHANGE

No book can remain current because technology changes so quickly. Support of SQL by ODBC and Microsoft is in a period of flux. ODBC 2.0 is just being completed, and already, not too far in the future, a new version of ODBC (fully 32-bit) is looming! In addition, not all ODBC drivers support all the different SQL commands. For this reason, your application must determine whether a given SQL command is supported by a given DataSource at runtime. It might be useful to make this determination at runtime and offer the user whatever support the current DataSource driver has to offer.

Now that you have been exposed to the basic ODBC statements, it's time to learn about the second half of database access—SQL.

So many questions arise: What is SQL? If I have ODBC, why do I need SQL?

What is SQL? The quick answer is that SQL is an acronym for Structured Query Language. SQL was derived from IBM's SEQUEL (Structured English Query Language) database language that was developed for IBM's mainframe computers. IBM also produced SEQUEL/2, which is the true predecessor of SQL.

SQL was originally developed and specified by IBM. However, when SQL became popular with other companies, it became apparent that a standard was needed. The main standard for SQL is ANSI X.3.135-1992 (usually referred to as SQL-92), which is the current SQL standard. An earlier standard was published in 1989 (usually referred to as SQL-89). In addition to the ANSI standard, the ISO also has published the standard for SQL (in ISO/IEC 9075:1992) as an international standard. The existence of these standards makes it possible to create SQL applications with a minimum amount of customization for different platforms. A minimum amount of customization? OK, let's face it. Most SQL systems (and Microsoft Access in particular) don't totally follow the standards. For example, there are minor differences between the standard as written and Access's implementation of SQL. Some of the information presented in this chapter is from Transact-SQL.

If I have ODBC, why do I need SQL? Knowing and having ODBC calls in your application might be sufficient for simple applications. For more complex applications, however, there are a number of functions that are available only with SQL and for which there are no direct ODBC calls. A typical simple application, such as a Rolodex-type PIM (Personal Information Manager), would simply use the Visual C++ AppWizard-created ODBC code, with minimum modification. A complex program that must do selective queries has to create SQL statements (generally at runtime) to implement these queries. Also, many database management functions, such as table creation, are implemented only in the SQL interface and there are no ODBC functions available to perform these functions.

SQL Statement Components

SQL can be considered a simple computer language that is used to define the methodology for accessing a database. Not all databases support SQL, but with ODBC you can use SQL on any ODBC-supported database regardless of whether the database supports SQL in its native mode.

An SQL statement is made up of various parts. For example, a typical query is composed of three, four, or five components: the verb (**SELECT**), the object (table and field names), a preposition clause (**FROM**), an optional qualifier (**WHERE**), and an optional order qualifier (**ORDER BY**).

Although the various parts of a given SQL statement aren't always required, their order is predetermined. For example, the **SELECT** statement must be in this order: **SELECT...FROM...WHERE...ORDER BY...**

You can't put the **ORDER BY** clause before the **WHERE** clause, or the **FROM** clause after the **WHERE** clause. The order of the parts of the SQL statement is fixed.

The ALTER DATABASE Command

The **ALTER DATABASE** command alters the amount of space allocated for a given database. Some database systems require a fixed, predetermined amount of disk storage, which **ALTER DATABASE** is used to modify.

The ALTER TABLE Command

The **ALTER TABLE** command is used to add new columns to an existing table. This command's syntax is as follows:

```
ALTER TABLE table ADD new_column_name datatype NULL ...
```

You should not exceed the maximum number of columns per table. You also can't add bit-type columns to an existing table.

The BEGIN...END Keywords

The **BEGIN...END** keywords are used to enclose a group of SQL commands so that they will be acted on as a group. They work very much like the C programming language's { and } keywords.

The BEGIN TRANSACTION Statement

The **BEGIN TRANSACTION** statement is used to mark the beginning of a user-specified transaction. This statement is used with **COMMIT TRANSACTION**, **ROLLBACK TRANSACTION**, and **SAVE TRANSACTION**.

The BREAK Command

The **BREAK** command is used to terminate a **WHILE** block. You usually execute the **BREAK** SQL command based on a conditional test (using an **IF...ELSE** statement).

A **BREAK** command ends the current execution block. If there are nested blocks, the next higher block will be the current block.

The CHECKPOINT Command

The **CHECKPOINT** command causes all pages in the result set that have been modified to be written back to the dataset. Generally, SQL makes sure that changes are written, but on some occasions you will want to ensure that changes have taken effect.

The COMMIT TRANSACTION Command

The **COMMIT TRANSACTION** command is used to mark the end of a transaction block. See the section titled "The **BEGIN TRANSACTION** Statement" for more information.

The COMPUTE Keyword

The **COMPUTE** keyword is used to generate control break summary values. You use **COMPUTE** with the **SUM**, **AVG**, **MIN**, **MAX**, and **COUNT** data aggregating functions. The **COMPUTE** keyword isn't compatible with **SELECT INTO**.

The CONTINUE Command

The **CONTINUE** command works much like the C language's **continue** command. Execution of statements following the **CONTINUE** statement is skipped, and the **WHILE** loop is re-executed starting at the first statement following the **WHILE** statement. You usually execute the **CONTINUE** SQL command based on a conditional test (using an **IF...ELSE** statement).

The CONVERT Command

The **CONVERT** command is used to convert expressions from one data type to another.

The CREATE DATABASE Command

The **CREATE DATABASE** command is used to create a new database. To use **CREATE DATABASE** you must have the necessary permissions (such as being in the master database).

The CREATE DEFAULT Command

The **CREATE DEFAULT** command is used to define a default value for a column when no value is specified.

The CREATE INDEX Command

The **CREATE INDEX** command is used to create an index for a given table, based on the specified column. With **CREATE INDEX** you can specify whether or not the key column must be unique, whether the column is sorted, and whether duplicate rows should be allowed.

The CREATE PROCEDURE Command

The **CREATE PROCEDURE** command is used to create a stored procedure.

The CREATE RULE Command

The **CREATE RULE** command allows the specification of rules that control which new or edited records are acceptable to the system. For example, it's not meaningful for a salary value to be less than zero, so a rule can be created that will catch this error.

The CREATE TABLE Command

The **CREATE TABLE** command is used to create a new table in the DataSource. The **CREATE TABLE** command requires the table name and the names, data types, and null status of each of the columns to be created in the new table.

The CREATE TRIGGER Command

When a data integrity constraint is violated, a trigger procedure is executed. Data integrity constraints might be a date that is outside a predetermined range, or a dollar value that is too low or too high. Triggers usually are used with **RULE**s (see the section titled "The **CREATE RULE** Command").

The CREATE VIEW Command

A view is an alternative way of looking at a specified table. You use the **CREATE VIEW** command to create a new view of the table.

The DECLARE Keyword

The **DECLARE** keyword is used to declare local variables. After a local variable is declared, its value can be assigned using a **SELECT** statement.

The DELETE Command

The **DELETE** command is used to delete (selectively, based on a condition) one or more rows from a DataSource. It's often necessary to delete rows from a DataSoruce, such as when the row will be replaced with a new row. The **DELETE** command is entered with a qualifier that indicates which row or rows are to be deleted.

The EXECUTE Command

The **EXECUTE** command is used to run either a system procedure, a user-defined procedure, or an extended stored procedure.

The GOTO Command

The SQL **GOTO** command works like the C language **goto** statement. Execution continues at the line following the label specified in the **GOTO** command.

The GRANT Command

The GRANT command is used to assign permissions for other users. You must have the necessary privilege to use this command.

The GROUP BY Keyword

The GROUP BY keyword allows the record set returned to be grouped by the *aggregate_expression*. Expressions include those shown in Table 16.1. Where the qualifier [ALL ¦ DISTINCT] is shown, the default is ALL. The ALL qualifier returns information based on all rows, while the DISTINCT qualifier returns information based only on unique rows.

TABLE 16.1. `aggregate_expression`S.	
Function	*Description*
SUM([ALL ¦ DISTINCT] *expression*)	Evaluates to the total of the column's values.
AVG([ALL ¦ DISTINCT] *expression*)	Evaluates to the average of the column's values.
COUNT([ALL ¦ DISTINCT] *expression*)	Evaluates to the count of all non-null rows.
COUNT(*)	Evaluates to the count of all rows selected.
SUM([ALL ¦ DISTINCT] *expression*)	Evaluates to the total of the column.
MIN(*expression*)	Evaluates to the smallest value in the column.
MAX(*expression*)	Evaluates to the largest value in the column.

The HAVING Keyword

The HAVING keyword, which doesn't require the GROUP BY clause, works like the WHERE keyword. For more information, see the section titled "The WHERE Keyword."

The *IF...ELSE* Commands

Using the **IF...ELSE** commands is much like using the C language **if...else** commands. The **IF** command requires a Boolean expression. The statement (or block of statements if a **BEGIN...END** block is defined) following the **IF** command is executed if the Boolean expression is true. If the Boolean expression is false, the statement (or block of statements if a **BEGIN...END** block is defined) following the **ELSE** command is executed.

The *INSERT* Command

The **INSERT** command is used to add a new row to the table or view specified. You can specify the columns to be assigned values, along with the values to assign to these columns.

The *ORDER BY* Command

The **ORDER BY...ASC ¦ DESC** command is used to specify the sort order of the records in the returned record set. You can specify the column to sort by, and whether the column will be sorted in either **ASC** (ascending, the default) or **DESC** (descending, which must be specified if used).

The *RETURN* Statement

The **RETURN** statement is used to return from a procedure. **RETURN** works just like its C language counterpart.

The *REVOKE* Command

The **REVOKE** command is used to cancel the permissions that have been granted using the **GRANT** command.

The *ROLLBACK TRANSACTION* Command

The **ROLLBACK TRANSACTION** command is used to cancel any transaction. Also see the sections titled "The **BEGIN TRANSACTION** Statement," "The **COMMIT TRANSACTION** Command," and "The **SAVE TRANSACTION** Command."

The SAVE TRANSACTION Command

The **SAVE TRANSACTION** command is used to set a save point in a transaction so that a selective rollback can be done.

The SELECT Statement

In a query statement, the verb **SELECT** is an SQL keyword. The **SELECT** keyword tells the system (the DataSource) that the application is attempting to retrieve records from the DataSource. When the DataSource sees the **SELECT** keyword, it knows that the next item in the query is the definition of which columns, which may be table-qualified, to select. Table qualification is required if there is to be a **JOIN**.

The following is an all-inclusive syntax of Transact-SQL's **SELECT** statement:

```
SELECT [ALL ¦ DISTINCT] select_list
[INTO [[database.]owner.]table_name]
[FROM [[database.]owner.]{table_name ¦ view_name}
[HOLDLOCK][,[[database.]owner.]{table_name ¦ view_name} [HOLDLOCK]]...]
[WHERE search_conditions]
[GROUP BY [ALL] aggregate_free_expression[, aggregate_free_expression]...]
[HAVING search_conditions]
[ORDER BY {[[[database.]owner.]{table_name. ¦ view_name.}]
column_name ¦ select_list_number ¦ expression} [ASC ¦ DESC][,
{[[[database.]owner.]{table_name ¦ view_name.}]
column_name ¦ select_list_number ¦ expression} [ASC ¦ DESC]]...]
[COMPUTE row_aggregate(column_name)[, row_aggregate(column_name)...]
[BY column_name [, column_name]...]]
[FOR BROWSE]
```

In the preceding **SELECT** statement, the following keywords are used:

- **ALL ¦ DISTINCT**: The **ALL** keyword (the default) tells SQL to retrieve all rows, and the **DISTINCT** keyword tells SQL to retrieve only those rows from the table that are unique.

- select_list: One of the following values:

  An asterisk (*) to signify that all columns in the table are to be retrieved.

  A list of columns in the order that they are to be retrieved. You must bind variables to each column to be retrieved.

  A replacement column heading in the format
  column_heading=column_name or *column_heading column_name*. If the column heading contains spaces, it must have quotation marks.

- **INTO**: Tells SQL to create a new table containing the records that meet the specified criteria. You can create an empty table if the **WHERE** clause doesn't allow any records to be selected. The **INTO** keyword requires that a table name be specified.

- **FROM**: Specifies the table from which the records will be extracted. A valid table name must be specified.

- **HOLDLOCK**: Specifies that sharing won't be allowed on the selected table until the transaction is completed. **HOLDLOCK** can't be specified for a **SELECT** that has the **FOR BROWSE** option.

- **WHERE**: The **WHERE** keyword specifies the search conditions. Keywords that can be used in the **WHERE** keyword's *search_conditions* are listed in Table 16.3, found in the section titled "The **WHERE** Keyword."

- **GROUP BY**: Used to group records retrieved based on the *aggregate_free_expression*, which includes the values shown in Table 16.3, in the section titled "The **GROUP BY** Keyword."

- **HAVING**: The **HAVING** keyword, which doesn't require the **GROUP BY** clause, works like the **WHERE** keyword. For more information, see the section titled "The **WHERE** Keyword."

- **ORDER BY...ASC ¦ DESC**: Use the **ORDER BY** clause to specify the order of the records in the returned record set. You can specify the column, and whether the column will be sorted in **ASC** (ascending, the default) or **DESC** (descending, which must be specified if used).

- **COMPUTE...BY**: The **COMPUTE** keyword is used to generate control break summary values. You use **COMPUTE** with the **SUM**, **AVG**, **MIN**, **MAX**, and **COUNT** data aggregating functions. The **COMPUTE** keyword isn't compatible with **SELECT INTO**.

- **FOR BROWSE**: The **FOR BROWSE** keyword enables the user to perform updates while viewing the data set retrieved. This keyword can be used only for applications that use the **DB_Library**, a separate system that is used to integrate applications with databases.

Columns to be retrieved in an SQL query are specified in one of several ways. The simplest query retrieves all columns in the DataSource. This is done by using an asterisk (*), which is a wildcard specifier for all columns in the table:

```
SELECT *
```

You can explicitly specify the columns you want. Some tables have many columns, perhaps several hundred, but your application might need to use only a few of them. If the query is based on a single table, you don't need to qualify the column names with table names. However, if the query is multitable (a join), the column names must be qualified with table names. The format of a column name is as follows:

```
Table.Column
```

When an identifier contains non-alphanumeric characters, that identifier must be enclosed in delimiters. The standard delimiters in an Access DataSource are the [and] characters. Here's an example of a column name with an embedded blank:

```
Product.[Item Price]
```

In this example, the [and] delimiters are required. The same rule applies to any identifier, whether it's used for a table, column, or other name.

The source (table) of the columns being selected must also be specified. This specification is in addition to the specification of table in the column descriptions, as described earlier. For example, selecting the [Item Price] and [Stock Quantity] columns from the Product table might be specified like so:

```
SELECT Product.[Item Price] Product.[Stock Quantity] FROM Product
```

This SQL query selects the two specified columns (Item Price and Stock Quantity) from the Product table. This SQL statement is executable as shown, and it illustrates the minimum required to retrieve these two columns from the Product table.

In most applications, the data retrieved from a DataSource needs to be limited to a certain number of records, and the order (sort) in which the records are retrieved needs to be specified.

Specifying which records are retrieved is done by using a **WHERE** clause in the SQL statement. The **WHERE** clause gives the programmer a great deal of flexibility. Taking our **SELECT** statement from earlier and restricting the search to products with a price greater than $10.00 is done by adding the **WHERE** clause like this:

```
SELECT Product.[Item Price] Product.[Stock Quantity] FROM Product
WHERE Product.[Item Price] > 10.00
```

When using a **WHERE** clause, you can include multiple conditions. For example, assume that you want all products with a price greater than $10.00, and more than 10 items are in stock:

```
SELECT Product.[Item Price] Product.[Stock Quantity] FROM Product
WHERE Product.[Item Price] > 10.00 and Product.[Quantity] > 10
```

The preceding **SELECT** returns only those records in which the Item Price is greater than $10.00 and the Quantity is greater than 10 units. As expected, using the or keyword provides basically the same results as if you were programming in C:

```
SELECT Product.[Item Price] Product.[Stock Quantity] FROM Product
WHERE Product.[Item Price] > 10.00 or Product.[Quantity] > 10
```

This example returns records in which either the Item Price is greater than $10.00 *or* the Quantity is greater than 10.

Finally, you might need to have the records returned in descending order by Item Price. The ordering of the returned record set is specified using the **ORDER BY** clause. The following **SELECT** has a single **ORDER BY** clause:

```
SELECT Product.[Item Price] Product.[Stock Quantity] FROM Product
WHERE Product.[Item Price] > 10.00 and Product.[Quantity] > 10
ORDER BY Product.[Item Price] DESC
```

Notice that I have used the **DESC** qualifier for the **ORDER BY** operand to tell SQL that we want the records in descending order (highest to lowest). You can specify more than one column to sort on and receive the expected results. For example, it's possible to order by both the Item Price (in descending order) and the Quantity (in ascending order). Because ascending order is the default, you don't need to specify it explicitly, but you can do so without casuing an error:

```
SELECT Product.[Item Price] Product.[Stock Quantity] FROM Product
WHERE Product.[Item Price] > 10.00 and Product.[Quantity] > 10
ORDER BY Product.[Item Price] DESC, Product.[Quantity]
```

There are many different variations of the SQL **SELECT** statement. **SELECT** is the most-used SQL statement because it actually retrieves the information from the DataSource.

The SET Command

The **SET** command is used to set various options for the current session. Options that can be set are listed in Table 16.2.

Table 16.2. Common set table options.	

Option	Description
`ARITHABORT ¦ ARITHIGNORE`	Controls what happens when an overflow or divide-by-zero error occurs. `ARITHABORT` terminates the query; `ARITHIGNORE` sets the offending item to null and displays a message.
`NOCOUNT`	Disables the message that shows how many records were affected by a change.
`NOEXEC`	Compiles the queries but doesn't execute them.
`OFFSETS`	Returns offsets to specified keywords in an SQL statement.
`PARSEONLY`	Checks the query's syntax but doesn't take any other action.

The *TRUNCATE TABLE* Command

The `TRUNCATE TABLE` command deletes all rows in a table using the fastest method possible. For more information about deleting rows, see the section titled "The `DELETE` Command."

The *UNION* Operator

The `UNION` operator is used to combine two or more queries into a single record set.

The *UPDATE* Command

The `UPDATE` command changes data in existing rows in a DataSource or adds new rows.

The *USE* Command

The `USE` command allows the current database to be set.

The WAITFOR Command

The **WAITFOR** command causes the system to wait for a specified period of time.

The WHERE Keyword

The **WHERE** keyword is used to restrict which records are retrieved using a **SELECT** statement and from any other statements that allow the **WHERE** keyword. The valid conditions for the **WHERE** keyword are listed in Table 16.3.

TABLE 16.3. WHERE CONDITIONS.	
Condition	*Description*
!<	Not less than.
!=	Not equal to.
!>	Not greater than.
%	Modulo.
&	Bitwise **AND** (specify two operands).
*	Multiplication.
+	Addition.
-	Subtraction.
/	Division.
<	Less than.
<=	Less than or equal to.
<>	Not equal to.
=	Equal to.
>	Greater than.
>=	Greater than or equal to.
^	Bitwise exclusive **OR** (specify two operands).
¦	Bitwise **OR** (specify two operands).
~	Bitwise **NOT** (specify one operand).
ALL	All records from a subquery.
AND	Logical condition **AND** logical condition.
ANY	Any record from a subquery.

Condition	Description
BETWEEN	Selects records that have a value between the two specified values. For example, **BETWEEN** abc **AND** def.
EXISTS	Where a column exists (based on a subquery).
IN	Value **IN** column.
IS NULL	Selects records that are null only.
LIKE	Like the example.
NOT	Logical negation.
OR	Logical condition **OR** logical condition.

Table 16.4 shows the wildcard characters that can be used when specifying a character-based search. Some of the items in the Condition column contain sample information.

TABLE 16.4. CHARACTER SEARCH WILDCARD CHARACTERS.	
Condition	Description
%	Matches any number of characters, zero or more.
_	Matches a single character.
[a-z]	Matches a range of characters. The example shown matches any character a to z.
[abc]	Matches a set of characters. The example shown matches a, b, or c.
[^a-z]	Matches any character that is not in the range of characters. The example shown matches any character except for a to z.
[^abc]	Matches any character that is not in the set of characters. The example shown matches any character except for a, b, or c.

The **WHERE** clause is the main method by which SQL determines which records are to be returned. When used carefully, it can greatly enhance your program's performance by limiting the number of undesirable records retrieved.

The WHILE Command

The **WHILE** command is used to define the beginning of a conditional block that will be executed one or more times, as long as the conditional clause is true.

Summary

This chapter covered SQL, the ANSI standard, and Transact-SQL. Topics discussed include the following:

- SQL standards
- Some common SQL commands, keywords, clauses, and statements

CREATING AN ODBC SHELL APPLICATION

Creating an ODBC application under Visual C++ 2.0 is the same as creating an ODBC application under earlier versions of Visual C++. You start AppWizard and select the level of database support that you want to include. The differences between Visual C++ 2.0 applications and those created using earlier versions of Visual C++ are relatively minor, as shown in the next section.

> **NOTE**
>
> Because the new 32-bit ODBC drivers weren't complete when this book was written, the sample programs in this chapter were tested using Visual C++ 1.5.

DIFFERENCES BETWEEN VISUAL C++ 2.0 32-BIT ODBC PROGRAMS AND THOSE CREATED WITH EARLIER VERSIONS OF VISUAL C++

There are only a few minor differences between applications created with Visual C++ 2.0 and those created with earlier versions of Visual C++. Most of the differences are hidden in the MFC library and the new 32-bit ODBC drivers. Listing 17.1 shows (in bold) the minimum change necessary to convert to Visual C++ 2.0 an application created with an earlier version of Visual C++. Of course, this example assumes that whatever code you've written is also compatible with 32-bit programming.

To convert to 32-bit versions of Windows, you must make modifications to the main source file in the project. In the main source file is a section of initialization code including a function called **InitInstance()**, which is called when the application first starts. You can make the changes shown in the following code fragment to make this application compatible with either Visual C++ 1.x (for 16-bit Windows) or Visual C++ 2.0 (for both 32-bit versions of Windows). For example, this code fragment was created using Visual C++ 1.5, and then was converted to be 32-bit–compliant.

LISTING 17.1. InitInstance() FOR BOTH 16-BIT AND 32-BIT WINDOWS.

```
BOOL CCardfileApp::InitInstance()
{
        // Standard initialization
        // If you are not using these features and wish to reduce the size
        // of your final executable, you should remove from the following
        // the specific initialization routines you do not need.

// Add test; if 16-bit, keep SetDialogBkColor() call:
#ifndef WIN32  // Only 16-bit Windows
        SetDialogBkColor();          // Set dialog background color to gray
#endif
#ifdef WIN32  // It's 32-bit Windows with 3D controls
```

```
        Enable3dControls();        // Use 3D controls in dialogs
#endif
        LoadStdProfileSettings();  // Load standard .INI file options
                                   // (including MRU)

        // Register the application's document templates. Document templates
        // serve as the connection between documents, frame windows, and views.

        CSingleDocTemplate* pDocTemplate;
        pDocTemplate = new CSingleDocTemplate(
                IDR_MAINFRAME,
                RUNTIME_CLASS(CCardfileDoc),
                RUNTIME_CLASS(CMainFrame),  // Main SDI frame window
                RUNTIME_CLASS(CCardfileView));
        AddDocTemplate(pDocTemplate);

        // Create a new (empty) document
        OnFileNew();

        if (m_lpCmdLine[0] != '\0')
        {
                // TODO: Add command-line processing here
        }


        return TRUE;
}
```

This simple change enables the 3D controls that will be part of future versions of Windows. The call to **Enable3dControls()** replaces the call to **SetDialogBkColor()**.

CARDFILE: HASN'T SOMEONE ELSE USED THIS NAME?

OK, I'll confess that Windows already has a program called CardFile. Actually, the original Windows CardFile application is nearing the end of its life, and it probably will be replaced with a new program when future versions of Windows are released.

> CardFile is also 16-bit–compatible. You can create a Visual C++ 1.5 project with CardFile that will compile and run under Windows 3.1. For that matter, many 32-bit programs that are written with the idea that they might need to be compiled and run in a 16-bit environment are easy to convert.

The version of CardFile that is found in Windows is very limited when used as a form of Rolodex, in which you build a database of names, addresses, and information about people.

For many years I have used a traditional Rolodex system. A large Rolodex sits on top of my monitor, and I update the cards by hand. This can be inconvenient because I can't create mailing labels, and it's really difficult to look up someone when I don't know how I filed that person. (Was it by name or by company? It must have been by company. Was the company the one he works for now, or the one he worked for when I first added him to the Rolodex?)

A standard Rolodex is suitable for some people, but not for me. When visitors enter my office, they expect to see a high-tech, fully computerized office. The time has come to computerize my Rolodex file system.

Now we have the idea: Create a program that will hold information about all the people who are currently in my Rolodex file.

First, let's determine which information we want to keep in our database. I want the CardFile program to give me the information that I have generally been keeping on the cards in my Rolodex. This information is shown in Table 17.1. I used Microsoft Access to create a database called CardFile. Table 17.1 shows names and descriptions of each column, including the column's data type.

TABLE 17.1. COLUMNS IN THE CARDFILE DATABASE.

Column Name	Data Type	Description
ID	Auto-increment number	This column is an auto-incrementing counter used to hold the record number. ODBC and Microsoft Access take care of assigning a value to ID, which must always contain a unique value.
First Name	Character	This column is for the person's first name. You also can place a middle initial here if needed.
Last Name	Character	Using a separate last-name column allows us to sort on last name.

Column Name	Data Type	Description
Classification	Character	This column contains a one- or two-word classification of the person (such as Hardware Expert, Windows Developer, Editor, Bail Bondsman, Lawyer, or Insurance Agent).
Misc Info	Character	This column is used to hold a description of the person, which usually includes much more than the two words found in Classification.
Title	Character	This column holds the person's title if she has one.
Company	Character	Not everybody has a company name, but if he does, it's stored here.
Company Type	Character	This column tells us what type of company the person works for. Not all software developers work for software companies.
Address 1	Character	This column contains the first line of address information.
Address 2	Character	This column contains the second line of address information.
City	Character	This column holds the person's city. The City column usually is the city of the two Address lines.
State	Character	This column holds the state in which City is located.
ZipCode	Character	This column holds the city's zip code. It can be five characters, nine characters, or any other format. If it's for a foreign country, the country name is in this field too.

continues

	TABLE 17.1. CONTINUED	
Column Name	Data Type	Description
Phone: Voice	Character	This column holds the person's voice phone. I keep this as a pure number whenever possible. For example, I place extension numbers in the Misc Info column.
Phone: Fax	Character	This column holds the person's business fax number.
Phone: Home	Character	This column holds the person's home phone number.
Phone: Home Fax	Character	Hey, some people have fax machines at home too!
Phone: Data	Character	A few people have BBS systems, either at home or as part of their work.
OnLine: E-Mail	Character	This column holds the person's preferred e-mail address. It could be CI$, Internet, or an internal mail system address.
E-Mail: Internet	Character	This column holds the person's Internet address.
E-Mail: CI$	Character	This column holds the person's CompuServe address.
E-Mail: AOL	Character	This column holds the person's America OnLine address.
E-Mail: MCI	Character	This column holds the person's MCI-Mail address.
E-Mail: Prodigy	Character	This column holds the person's Prodigy address.
E-Mail: Ours	Character	This column holds the person's e-mail address if the person is on our e-mail system.

Column Name	Data Type	Description
Description/Notes	Character	This column includes a detailed description of the person and company. It can contain information about calls or letters as well.
Date Entered	Date	This column holds the date the person's card was first added to the CardFile database. Once added, this date is fixed. Our CardFile program automatically inserts this date for us.
Date Updated	Date	This column contains the date of the last change to any column in the person's record in the database. Just scrolling through the database won't update this date column—a column must be changed. Our CardFile program automatically updates this date for us.

After I decided what information was needed in the CardFile program, I needed to decide how to implement it. First and foremost, it was important that CardFile be able to work alone, without any external supporting programs such as Microsoft Access. If the database used by CardFile could be accessed by other programs, all the better.

A second consideration was that CardFile must be an ODBC program. There were several reasons: I needed a program in this chapter to illustrate ODBC, I have some really nice ODBC utilities (report generators) that I wanted to try out, and I thought it would be nice to be able to access my program's data from other programs such as Microsoft Access and MS-Query.

Choosing the best ODBC-compliant format wasn't difficult. With the 16-bit versions of ODBC, only the Access driver can update records. It was a basic consideration that the program be able to access data, but to be able to update the database in my ODBC program was an added advantage. This functionality would make the program self-sufficient.

If you don't have Microsoft Access, you might wonder how you'll create the initial database. Fortunately, the ODBC driver manager offers a solution: You can either attach an existing database or create a new one. In the case of CardFile, I simply ran Access and created the table from within Access; I didn't add any records to the new database. To make things easy for readers who don't have Microsoft Access, I've included copies of the CardFile database files on the source code disk. (See the Introduction for ordering information.)

After creating the database (using Access), I needed to create the CardFile program. The process to create an ODBC application is simple:

1. Create (or somehow get your hands on) a DataSource. The Data-Source must be of a format that is supported by the 32-bit version of ODBC. If you want your application to be able to update the Data-Source, make sure that the ODBC driver is capable of updating a DataSource.

2. Register the DataSource with ODBC. Remember, when you use Access or any other database program to create a database, that database is unknown to ODBC until it's registered. Use the ODBC administrator program, 32-bit ODBC (found in Control Panel), to add the database as an ODBC DataSource. For our sample program, you should name the DataSource CardFile.

3. From within Visual C++ 2.0, select File | New | Project. You're placed in AppWizard, where you can work on creating your new program. AppWizard presents a series of dialog boxes, each numbered step 1 of n, step 2 of n, and so on. The total number of dialog boxes (n) depends on the type of program you're going to create.

4. In the first step, the first option presented is whether the program will be a multiple-document interface (MDI) or a single-document inter-face (SDI). Microsoft recommends that applications be created using the SDI model because the SDI model works much better with the OLE support (objects). Because Windows is on its way to becoming an object-oriented operating system, it's perhaps best to stick with an SDI if possible. Select Single Document from the list of options provided in AppWizard's Step 1 dialog box.

5. In step 2 of 6, you must set the option to make your application an ODBC application. This option entails selecting the level of database support, which comes in four flavors:

- None: Selecting this option (the default) tells AppWizard not to include any database support in your application.

- Only Include Header Files: Selecting this option tells AppWizard to include (in the STDAFX file) an include for the standard ODBC header file. This enables you to later create and use one of the MFC ODBC class objects (**CRecordSet**, **CRecordView**, and/or **CDatabase**) in your application.

- A Database View Without File Support: Selecting this option tells AppWizard to create a program that has ODBC support but that doesn't support files. The File menu doesn't have Save, Open, or any other file-based commands.

- Both a Database View and Support: Selecting this option tells AppWizard to create a program that supports both ODBC and external files. When I created CardFile, I chose this option. I then removed the File menu options Open, Save, and Save As. By choosing this option, I can later add file support if needed.

For CardFile we'll select Both a Database View and File Support, after which AppWizard prompts us to select the DataSource that this program will be used with. You must select a DataSource so that AppWizard can bind variables to each of the columns in the DataSource. If the DataSource that you'll be using isn't installed yet, you need to use Control Panel's 32-bit ODBC applet to add the DataSource. You can do this while Visual C++ is running. When the DataSource is installed, you can return to AppWizard to continue creating your ODBC application.

6. In step 3 of 6, you must select the level of OLE support. Your choices include the following:

- None: No OLE support is included. For our sample ODBC program, this is the level of OLE support that we'll choose (it's also the default).

- Container: Support for containers allows objects to be embedded into this application's documents but doesn't allow this application's documents to be embedded in other application's documents.

- Miniserver: A miniserver allows its objects to be embedded (but not linked) into other applications. A miniserver can't run as an application.

- Full server: A full server allows its objects to be embedded or linked into other applications. A full server can run as an application.
- Both container and server: Combines container support and full server support.

In addition to container and server support, the application also can support OLE automation when you click on the "Yes, please" button under the prompt for OLE Automation.

7. In step 4 of 6, you select the application's appearance. You can choose to include the following six options and set advanced options as desired:

- Dockable toolbar support
- Initial status bar support
- Printing and print preview support
- Context-sensitive help support
- Use of 3D controls
- The number of filenames maintained in the MRU (Most Recently Used) file list

The advanced options enable you to customize the document template, specifying the document type name, the new filename, the document file extension and filter, and registry information. You also can specify the style of the main window, the main window's caption, frame styles (discussed later), and whether the main window will be based on a splitter window.

8. In step 5 of 6, you specify some of the project's build options. These options include the makefile type, whether there will be source file comments, and whether the MFC support is statically linked or dynamically linked at runtime from MFC30.DLL.

9. Finally, in step 6 of 6, you can customize the classes created for your project. The names of each class can be changed (they are initially based on the name of the project). For the view class, you can select which base view class is used: **CEditView**, **CFormView**, **CScrollView**, or **CView**. Because you're creating an ODBC application, your program is based on **CRecordView**, and you shouldn't change that class.

10. When you've finished the project definition stage, click on the Finish button. (You can go back to any step and make changes by using the Back button.) The Finish button causes the project's files to be created and saved.

After AppWizard has created the project, you should build the project. Although I've never had a problem with a project created by AppWizard, I always feel better when I see the project built prior to making changes.

We've Got Our ODBC Shell Program. Now What?

When you've saved your AppWizard-created ODBC shell application and done a build of the initial project, you can start making the changes that will make this program a useful application.

The first necessary change is to get the DataSource's data displayed so that the user can view it. This is relatively simple, because the major change here is to design a dialog box template that will be used by **CRecordView** to display the data. Remember, **CRecordView** is based on **CFormView**, which also uses a dialog box template to display data for the user.

I've laid out CardFile's dialog as shown in Figure 17.1. (Figure 17.4 shows the finished CardFile application.) I managed to include all the information that is found in the DataSource in a relatively small dialog box. This layout is particular to my needs; you could easily modify this layout to suit whatever needs you have for the CardFile program.

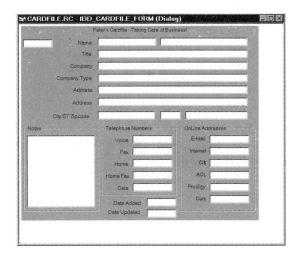

Figure 17.1. CardFile's dialog box template.

Once the dialog template has been developed, you can attach variables for each of the DataSource's columns to the dialog template's controls. AppWizard needs to know which DataSource the ODBC program will be using in order to create variables for each column. The only thing that the programmer must do is tell Visual C++ (by using ClassWizard) which variable is to be attached to which control on the template.

The connecting (or *binding*) of these variables to controls is done by selecting the **CRecordView**-based class (**CCardfileView** in CardFile) in ClassWizard's Member Variables tab. When you select the Member Variables tab, you're presented with a dialog that has a list of the various dialog template controls. Each control must be selected and the Add Variable button clicked on.

When the Add Variable button is clicked on, the Add Member Variable dialog is displayed. Unlike other dialog boxes, a dialog template used with a **CRecordView** class object should have the controls attached to variables contained in the **CRecordSet** class object. To make this process easier, simply click the drop-down button in the Member Variable Name combo box and select the correct variable. Each column variable (except for the **CTime** columns; we'll take care of them later) is listed in the Member Variable Name combo box. Select the correct name from the combo box and click on OK when you're done.

With the Add Member Variable dialog, you can bind variables for all the columns in the DataSource except for the two time variables. This is a minor inconvenience that is easily fixed, as you'll see later in this chapter. For the time being, simply don't add any variable to the two date fields (**ID_DATE_ADDED** and **ID_DATA_UPDATED**).

After you've bound **CRecordSet**'s variables to **CRecordView**'s controls, you should again rebuild the CardFile project and run it. Once CardFile is running, you can see the effects of the changes you made. But you don't see anything! What's going on here?

Actually, you're seeing exactly what you should be seeing. There are no records in the CardFile DataSource yet, so CardFile can't show any! Now we have a problem: We must add records to the DataSource so that CardFile can show them. If you don't have Microsoft Access, this could present a problem. How will you add records? More important, because CardFile is intended to be a stand-alone application, it too must have the capability to add (and delete) records in the database. Looking at the menu (and the toolbar), we can see that there are buttons for moving from record to record and for jumping to the first or last record, but there is no way of adding a record to the DataSource.

ADDING AND DELETING RECORDS

Because AppWizard doesn't add the code to either add or delete records contained in a DataSource, it's up to the programmer to add the necessary code. First, however, let's do a few simple housekeeping tasks.

One thing that we did when we created our project was to include support for files. In this version of CardFile, we don't need Open, Save, or Save As, which are found on the File menu. We also don't need the buttons on the toolbar that perform these functions. To change the menu, open the CardFile.RC file and select the Menu resource by clicking on the + symbol in the tree view of the project's resources. The Menu resource presents you with a list of the menus that are defined for this project. You should select only one menu—**IDR_MAINFRAME**. Make the following changes to the **IDR_MAINFRAME** menu:

1. Delete all items except Exit from the Files submenu.
2. Add the following new menu selections, in order, to the Record submenu:
   - A separator bar (after Last Record)
   - A new selection, &Add Record (after the separator)
   - A new selection, &Delete Record (after Update Record)
3. Add a new top-level menu selection called &Sorted by. Under Sorted by, add the following new menu selections:
   - A new selection, &Last Name (as the first item)
   - A new selection, &Company (after Last Name)
   - A new selection, C&ity (after Company)
   - A new selection, Cl&assification (after City)
4. When you've made these changes, you can save the menu by selecting the CardFile.RC window and pressing Ctrl-S. A smart programmer saves work often. This is preferable to saying, "Wow, the computer crashed and I just lost the whole thing. Boy, am I really dumb!" (I won't say how many times I've said just that.)

After you've completed the changes to the menu, you need to change the toolbar bitmaps. We'll delete all the buttons except for the ones used to navigate through the DataSource, and the About button. We'll also create buttons to add and delete records in the DataSource.

To change a bitmap, open the CardFile.RC file and select the Bitmap resource section by clicking on the + symbol in the tree view of the project's resources. The Bitmap resource presents you with a list of the bitmaps that are defined for this project. In an application just created using AppWizard, you should select only one bitmap—**IDR_MAINFRAME**. When you have the bitmap displayed, press the m key to zoom into (blow up) the bitmap so that it's easier to work with. Also, select Image | Grid Settings, which causes the Grid Settings dialog to appear. In this dialog, select both Pixel Grid and Tile Grid. Tile Grid should have the same dimensions as the bitmap height (15) and the standard toolbar width of 16. Click on OK to exit the Grid Settings dialog.

Make the following changes to the **IDR_MAINFRAME** bitmap:

1. First, copy into the clipboard the four record movement buttons (the first four buttons in Table 17.2). Next, copy the clipboard contents to the beginning of the **IDC_MAINFRAME** bitmap. When this is done, the record movement buttons are the first four buttons. As an alternative to using the clipboard, you can move the buttons using the block define and move functions.

2. In the bitmap block following the fourth record movement button bitmap, create a new bitmap. Base this bitmap's image on an X character. This will be our Delete Record button.

3. In the bitmap block following the Delete Record bitmap, create a new bitmap. Base this bitmap's image on a + character. This will be our Add Record button.

4. Finally, after the Add Record bitmap, copy the About button's bitmap (a ? character). Use one of the techniques described in step 1.

5. You can get fancy and add color to the buttons if you like. I've filled each with yellow, but you can make changes to suit your tastes.

After you've made these changes, your toolbar bitmap's first seven buttons should be First Record, Previous Record, Next Record, Last Record, Delete Record, Add Record, and About (see Table 17.2). The button images following the About button image aren't used and can be ignored or deleted as you wish.

TABLE 17.2. TOOLBAR BUTTONS.	
Button	*Description*
⏮	Moves to the first record.
◀	Moves to the previous record.
▷	Moves to the next record.
⏭	Moves to the last record.
✗	Deletes a record.
✚	Adds a record.
?	Displays the application's About box.

Now that we've made the cosmetic changes to the CardFile program, let's get down to some "real" programming. First, we must map our toolbar bitmaps to their corresponding menu selections. Every toolbar button should have a corresponding menu selection so that users who have turned off the toolbar won't lose functionality. In CardFile, the first six buttons map (one-to-one) to the menu items found in the Record menu. The final button matches the Help menu's About selection.

Toolbar buttons are assigned identifiers in the application's **CMainFrame** object constructor. The buttons are assigned as identifiers in an array of integer values called buttons[]. This array must be changed to look like the one shown in the following code fragment:

```
/////////////////////////////////////////////////////////////////////
// Arrays of IDs used to initialize control bars

// Toolbar buttons. IDs are command buttons
static UINT BASED_CODE buttons[] =
{
        // Same order as in the bitmap toolbar.bmp
        ID_RECORD_FIRST,
        ID_RECORD_PREV,
        ID_RECORD_NEXT,
        ID_RECORD_LAST,
                ID_SEPARATOR,
        ID_RECORD_DELETE,
        ID_RECORD_ADD,
                ID_SEPARATOR,
        ID_APP_ABOUT,
};
```

The **ID_RECORD...** and **ID_APP_ABOUT** identifiers are simply the identifiers for their corresponding menu options. The identifier **ID_SEPARATOR** tells Windows to add a small blank space between the two buttons surrounding the **ID_SEPARATOR** identifier. In the preceding code fragment, we have our seven buttons arranged as a group of four (the record movement buttons), a group of two (the Delete Record and Add Record buttons), and a single button that displays the application's About box (see Table 17.2).

Now that we have buttons and menu selections to navigate through add and delete records in the DataSource, we now must add functionality to make these buttons work.

First, the easy part. The record navigation functionality has already been done for us through the magic of MFC, in which Microsoft has provided default handlers for these functions in the **CRecordView** class. You don't have to make any changes to this code either because the default handler functions well in most ODBC applications.

This leaves us with having to add the handler for the Delete Record and Add Record functions. Let's start with the Add Record function.

Adding a Record

To add a record to a DataSource, perform the following steps:

1. Call the **CRecordSet** member **AddRecord()**. This function prepares the **CRecordSet** object to add a record to the DataSource by creating a record that has no data.

2. Add data to the record created by the call to **AddRecord()**.

3. When the record has been filled in, call **Update()** to write the changes to the DataSource.

Unfortunately, this process looks simpler than it really is. In our CardFile program, when the user selects Add Record from the menu or the toolbar button, a new, blank record must be created and displayed. Then the user must fill in the new record. After the user has filled in the record, selecting another record causes CardFile to save the record to the DataSource.

It's necessary to add two new handlers to the **CCardfileView** class to handle the Add Record and Delete Record functions. These handlers can't be added using ClassWizard. Instead, you must add them by hand, by following these steps:

1. In CARDFVW.CPP is a block of code that defines which functions will handle which messages and controls. Each message and control to be handled is defined using macros. For a menu item, the **ON_COMMAND()** macro is used. You must add a new **ON_COMMAND()** macro for the new menu item (Add Records):

```
/////////////////////////////////////////////////////////////
// CCardfileView

IMPLEMENT_DYNCREATE(CCardfileView, CRecordView)

BEGIN_MESSAGE_MAP(CCardfileView, CRecordView)
        //{{AFX_MSG_MAP(CCardfileView)
            // NOTE: ClassWizard will add and remove
            // mapping macros here
            // DO NOT EDIT what you see in these blocks
            // of generated code!
        //}}AFX_MSG_MAP
        // Standard printing commands
        ON_COMMAND(ID_FILE_PRINT, CRecordView::OnFilePrint)
        ON_COMMAND(ID_FILE_PRINT_PREVIEW,
                CRecordView::OnFilePrintPreview)

        // Added by hand...
        ON_COMMAND(ID_RECORD_ADD, OnRecordAdd)
END_MESSAGE_MAP()
```

2. After the **ON_COMMAND()** handlers are added, you need to add a function prototype to the CARDFVW.H file. This prototype can be placed in the Generated message map functions section:

```
// Generated message map functions
protected:
        //{{AFX_MSG(CCardfileView)
            // NOTE: ClassWizard will add and remove member
            // functions here
            // DO NOT EDIT what you see in these blocks
            // of generated code!
        //}}AFX_MSG
        // Added by hand...
        afx_msg void OnRecordAdd();
DECLARE_MESSAGE_MAP()
};
```

3. Finally, you must write the actual code for the Add Record function. This code is a bit complex. It requires that you write the `OnRecordAdd()` function and modify two of the existing **CRecordView** functions (we'll write override functions). First, we'll take a look at the new `OnRecordAdd()` function, which is shown in the following code fragment:

```
void CCardfileView::OnRecordAdd()
{
        // TODO: Add your command handler code here

    if (m_bAddMode)
        OnMove(ID_RECORD_FIRST);

    m_pSet->AddNew();
    m_pSet->SetFieldNull(&(m_pSet->m_ID));
    m_bAddMode = TRUE;
    UpdateData(FALSE);
}
```

In the `OnRecordAdd()` function, we need to find out if we're already adding a record. Creating a new variable called m_bAddMode tells us, if **TRUE**, that we're in the process of adding a new record. I've added code to the **OnMove()** function to complete the necessary steps to the Add Record process. Now, if we're adding a record, we can call **OnMove()** to complete the existing addition prior to starting a new record addition.

As the preceding steps show, to add a record you call **CRecordSet:: AddNew()**, modify the record, then call **CRecordSet::Update()**. The first step, creating the new record using **CRecordSet::AddNew()**, is performed, then we make sure that the DataSource's ID column is set to null. It's necessary to set ID to null because it's the primary key for the Access database and must be a unique number. Because we don't know what the next ID value would be, we set the column to null. In our Access database we've defined this column as auto-increment; therefore, the ODBC Access driver fills in the correct value when the record is added. When we add records to a DataSource, all fields are first set to null, so this explicit step isn't strictly required. However, I included it to show that a record with an auto-increment column being added must have the auto-increment column set to null.

Once we've set the record ID to null, we then set the member variable m_bAddMode to **TRUE** so that other member functions will know that we're in the Add Record mode.

Finally, we call **UpdateData(FALSE)** to tell MFC to update the contents of **CRecordView**'s dialog. Because **CRecordSet::AddNew()** sets all the new columns to null, this effectively clears all the fields in the dialog.

With the code in OnRecordAdd(), we've prepared a new record, set the fields in the new record to null, and updated the user interface to show the new (but empty) record. What's next?

The next step in the Add Record process is to have the user fill in the necessary fields in the record. When the user has added the information to the record, the new record must be added to the DataSource. This addition process can take place when one of two conditions happens: the user moves to a new record, or the user attempts to add a new record. In the case of attempting to add a new record, we took care of the situation in which a record is being added at the same time that Add Record is selected again. The course of action is to do a dummy move to a new record, which forces the write of the original added record.

When the user attempts to move to a new record after electing to add a record, it's necessary to complete the record addition process by calling **CRecordSet::Update()** prior to performing the move.

We need to modify one of the routines that is part of **CRecordSet** by adding the code necessary to save the record that the user is adding. The new **OnMove()** function calls **CRecordSet::OnMove()** if the move wasn't for an added record:

```
BOOL CCardfileView::OnMove(UINT nIDMoveCommand)
{
    if (m_bAddMode)
    {
        if (!UpdateData())
            return FALSE;

            TRY
        {
            m_pSet->m_Date_Entered = CTime::GetCurrentTime();
            m_pSet->m_Date_Updated = CTime::GetCurrentTime();
            m_pSet->Update();
        }
        CATCH(CDBException, e)
        {
            AfxMessageBox(e->m_strError);
            return FALSE;
        }
        END_CATCH
```

```
        m_pSet->Requery();
        UpdateData(FALSE);
        m_bAddMode = FALSE;
        return TRUE;
        }
    else
    {
        return CRecordView::OnMove(nIDMoveCommand);
    }
}
```

Of course, it's necessary to add function prototypes for these functions in the appropriate header file.

Deleting a Record

"I don't want that company in my CardFile anymore! It's gone out of business!" We need a method to get rid of records that are no longer needed.

Adding a Delete Record function is easy. **CRecordSet** is set up to allow the deletion of the current record with a single call to the **CRecordSet::Delete()** function. To implement this function, you must add a menu item handler.

Adding the menu item handler involves adding an **ON_COMMAND()** handler and a prototype in the CARDFVW.H file.

The following code fragment shows the handler for the Delete command:

```
void CCardfileView::OnRecordDelete()
{
    // TODO: Add your command handler code here

// First delete the record, and give a message if the delete
// fails: (go home if the delete fails...)

    TRY
    {
        m_pSet->Delete();
    }
    CATCH(CDBException, e)
    {
        AfxMessageBox(e->m_strError);
        return;
    }
    END_CATCH

// Since we have no current record (we just deleted
// it), we must move to the next record

    if (!m_pSet->IsEOF())
            m_pSet->MoveNext();

// If the new record selected was at the end
// of the file, we must back up one record
```

```
    if (m_pSet->IsEOF())
        m_pSet->MoveLast();

// If there are no more records in the recordset,
// we must clear the current record

    if (m_pSet->IsBOF())
        m_pSet->SetFieldNull(NULL);

// Finally, we show the user the new record:

    UpdateData(FALSE);
}
```

There's more code to display the next record (if there is one—and that's part of the problem) than there is for the actual deleting of the record.

SORTING THE RECORDS

The next major change is the addition of code to support sorting. Nothing is worse than having to look through a bunch of records that aren't in the order you wanted. Imagine looking up a number in a telephone book if the names were listed in order by telephone number! For this reason, I've added code to sort on any of the four fields: Last Name, Company, City, and Classification.

The adding of a sort criterion to a returned record set isn't difficult, but it does present one problem. You can set the sort field only before a DataSource has been opened. For this reason, it's necessary to first close the DataSource and set the sort conditions, then reopen the DataSource. The following code fragment shows how the sorting parameters are specified:

```
void CCardfileView::OnSortedbyLastname()
{
        TRY
    {
            m_pSet->Close();
            m_pSet->m_strSort = " CARDFILE.\"Last Name\"";
            m_pSet->Open();
            m_pSet->Requery();
    }
    CATCH(CDBException, e)
    {
        AfxMessageBox(e->m_strError);
        return;
    }
    END_CATCH

        UpdateData(FALSE);
}
```

```cpp
void CCardfileView::OnSortedbyCompany()
{
        TRY
    {
        m_pSet->Close();
            m_pSet->m_strSort = " CARDFILE.Company";
            m_pSet->Open();
            m_pSet->Requery();
    }
    CATCH(CDBException, e)
    {
        AfxMessageBox(e->m_strError);
        return;
    }
    END_CATCH

    UpdateData(FALSE);
}
void CCardfileView::OnSortedbyCity()
{
        TRY
    {
            m_pSet->Close();
            m_pSet->m_strSort = " CARDFILE.City";
            m_pSet->Open();
            m_pSet->Requery();
    }
    CATCH(CDBException, e)
    {
        AfxMessageBox(e->m_strError);
        return;
    }
    END_CATCH

    UpdateData(FALSE);
}
void CCardfileView::OnSortedbyClassification()
{
        TRY
    {
            m_pSet->Close();
            m_pSet->m_strSort = " CARDFILE.Classification";
            m_pSet->Open();
            m_pSet->Requery();
    }
    CATCH(CDBException, e)
    {
        AfxMessageBox(e->m_strError);
        return;
    }
    END_CATCH

    UpdateData(FALSE);
}
```

For each of the sort menu items, you must add an **ON_COMMAND()** handler and a prototype in the CARDFVW.H file. These prototypes can be placed in the `Generated message map functions` section, along with the other prototypes.

USING DATE FIELDS IN CARDFILE

Earlier, I mentioned that ClassWizard wouldn't map a **CTime** class object to a control. This is a minor problem that's easily fixed. We have two considerations: First, when we update the user interface, we need to display both the Date Created and Date Last Updated time stamps. However, when we retrieve information from the dialog, we want to return only the date updated. That way, if a record is being updated, the updated time stamp reflects the current time, while the creation time stamp doesn't change.

The time stamps are managed using a set of **if** statements. The first **if** tests to see if we're setting the values into the **CRecordView**'s dialog controls. If we are setting the controls, we format the time using the **CTime::Format()** function, saving the formatted time in a **CString** object created to hold the formatted time values (this variable is part of the **CRecordSet** derived class). Once we've formatted the time string and placed it into a **CString** object, we can display the **CString** object using the **DDX_FieldText()** function.

Second, if we're retrieving data from the **CRecordView** dialog, the process is different. We never return the creation date (**IDC_DATE_ADDED**), because this date was set when the record was first added to the DataSource and never changes. We must return the updated date, because we don't know if we're updating or not. In order to have the returned **CTime** object, m_Date_Updated, contain the current date, simply call the **CTime::GetCurrentTime()** function. This function updates the **CTime** object to contain the current time:

```
if (!pDX->m_bSaveAndValidate)
    {// Display date (and time...) of creation...
        m_pSet->m_Date_Updated_Str = m_pSet->m_Date_Updated.Format("%c");
        m_pSet->m_Date_Entered_Str = m_pSet->m_Date_Entered.Format("%c");
        DDX_FieldText(pDX, IDC_DATE_UPDATED, m_pSet->m_Date_Updated_Str,
                    m_pSet);
        DDX_FieldText(pDX, IDC_DATE_ADDED, m_pSet->m_Date_Entered_Str, m_pSet);
    }
    else
    {// We are getting Date(s). (Re)set only the updated time
        if (m_pSet->IsFieldDirty(NULL))
        {// A field has changed, so update the time stamp!
            m_pSet->m_Date_Updated = CTime::GetCurrentTime();
        }
    }
```

Making CardFile Fit the Dialog Template

One final change is to make CardFile's main window fit the dialog template that we created. It looks tacky to have a form-based application with scroll bars!

Telling a program to resize itself is a simple process that can be done in the view class using a simple bit of code placed in the **OnInitialUpdate()** function. This code, shown in the following code fragment, tells Windows to resize the application's window to the size of the dialog template:

```
void CCardfileView::OnInitialUpdate()
{
        m_pSet = &GetDocument()->m_cardfileSet;
        m_pSet->m_strSort = " CARDFILE.\"Last Name\"";
        CRecordView::OnInitialUpdate();

//      The next two lines size window to fit dialog box:
        GetParentFrame()->RecalcLayout();
        ResizeParentToFit(FALSE);
//   End resize of dialog box
}
```

As this code fragment shows, resizing the window is a simple two-step process. First, tell the parent frame window to recompute its size (using the **RecalcLayout()** member function), then force the parent window to fit the frame.

That's fine, but the CardFile program still has a wide resizing border. With a resizing border, the user can change the size of CardFile's main window, making it either too small for the dialog or much too large. How do we change this border to a nonsizing, narrow border? When AppWizard creates an application's shell, the border type can be specified, or you can add code later to make this change if you forgot to specify the nonsizing border. This technique also works for any application created with Visual C++ 1.5 or earlier. This code is found in the mainframe file (mainfrm.CPP in our example) and requires that you override the **CFrameWnd::PreCreateWindow()** function and turn off the **WS_THICKFRAME** window style attribute. After the window style has been modified, the **CFrameWnd::PreCreateWindow()** function is called:

```
/////////////////////////////////////////////////////////////////////////////
// CMainFrame Override Handlers

BOOL CMainFrame::PreCreateWindow(CREATESTRUCT &cs)
{// Remove resizing frame so window can't be resized!
      cs.style &= ~WS_THICKFRAME;
      return(CFrameWnd::PreCreateWindow(cs));
}
```

When AppWizard creates a project with a customized window frame, it creates the **PreCreateWindow()** function using a slightly different format:

```
BOOL CMainFrame::PreCreateWindow(CREATESTRUCT& cs)
{
        cs.style = WS_OVERLAPPED | WS_CAPTION | FWS_ADDTOTITLE
                | WS_SYSMENU | WS_MINIMIZEBOX | WS_MAXIMIZEBOX;
        return CFrameWnd::PreCreateWindow(cs);
}
```

Notice that when AppWizard creates the **PreCreateWindow()** function, it explicitly sets all the window attributes. In my example, only the **WS_THICKFRAME** attribute is cleared (if it's set) and any other attributes are left unchanged.

COMPLETING CARDFILE

With these changes, we now have support for adding, deleting, and controlling the sort order of the records in CardFile.

We've seen the details of the changes made to create the CardFile program. Let's take a look at these changes as complete files. First, as in other listings, changes that I've made either manually or using ClassWizard appear in bold. Second, I've made changes to resources such as the **CRecordView** dialog, the menu, and the toolbar bitmap, which I show as figures.

Virtually all the changes were made to two files. First, in CARDFVW.CPP, is the addition of routines to do most of the work. In CARDFVW.H, header information for the new functions was added. CARDFVW.CPP is shown in Listing 17.2.

LISTING 17.2. CARDFVW.CPP.

```
// CARDFVW.CPP: Implementation of the CCardfileView class
//

#include "stdafx.h"
#include "cardfile.h"

#include "cardfset.h"
#include "cardfdoc.h"
#include "Cardfvw.h"

#ifdef _DEBUG
#undef THIS_FILE
static char BASED_CODE THIS_FILE[] = __FILE__;
#endif
```

continues

LISTING 17.2. CONTINUED

```
//////////////////////////////////////////////////////////////////////////
// CCardfileView

IMPLEMENT_DYNCREATE(CCardfileView, CRecordView)

BEGIN_MESSAGE_MAP(CCardfileView, CRecordView)
    //{{AFX_MSG_MAP(CCardfileView)
        // NOTE: ClassWizard will add and remove mapping macros here
        // DO NOT EDIT what you see in these blocks of generated code!
    //}}AFX_MSG_MAP
    // Standard printing commands
    ON_COMMAND(ID_FILE_PRINT, CRecordView::OnFilePrint)
    ON_COMMAND(ID_FILE_PRINT_PREVIEW, CRecordView::OnFilePrintPreview)

//    Added by hand...
    ON_COMMAND(ID_RECORD_ADD, OnRecordAdd)
    ON_COMMAND(ID_RECORD_DELETE, OnRecordDelete)
    ON_COMMAND(ID_SORTEDBY_LASTNAME, OnSortedbyLastname)
    ON_COMMAND(ID_SORTEDBY_COMPANY, OnSortedbyCompany)
    ON_COMMAND(ID_SORTEDBY_CITY, OnSortedbyCity)
    ON_COMMAND(ID_SORTEDBY_CITY, OnSortedbyClassification)
END_MESSAGE_MAP()

//////////////////////////////////////////////////////////////////////////
// CCardfileView construction/destruction

CCardfileView::CCardfileView()
    : CRecordView(CCardfileView::IDD)
{
    //{{AFX_DATA_INIT(CCardfileView)
    m_pSet = NULL;
    //}}AFX_DATA_INIT
    // TODO: Add construction code here
    m_bAddMode = FALSE;
}

CCardfileView::~CCardfileView()
{
}

void CCardfileView::DoDataExchange(CDataExchange* pDX)
{
    CRecordView::DoDataExchange(pDX);
    //{{AFX_DATA_MAP(CCardfileView)
    DDX_FieldText(pDX, IDC_ADDRESS_1, m_pSet->m_Address_1, m_pSet);
    DDX_FieldText(pDX, IDC_ADDRESS_2, m_pSet->m_Address_2, m_pSet);
    DDX_FieldText(pDX, IDC_CITY, m_pSet->m_City, m_pSet);
    DDX_FieldText(pDX, IDC_COMPANY, m_pSet->m_Company, m_pSet);
    DDX_FieldText(pDX, IDC_COMPANY_TYPE, m_pSet->m_Company_Type, m_pSet);
    DDX_FieldText(pDX, IDC_F_NAME, m_pSet->m_First_Name, m_pSet);
    DDX_FieldText(pDX, IDC_L_NAME, m_pSet->m_Last_Name, m_pSet);
    DDX_FieldText(pDX, IDC_ONLINE_AOL, m_pSet->m_E_Mail__AOL, m_pSet);
    DDX_FieldText(pDX, IDC_ONLINE_CIS, m_pSet->m_E_Mail__CI_, m_pSet);
    DDX_FieldText(pDX, IDC_ONLINE_INTERNET, m_pSet->m_E_Mail__Internet,
                  m_pSet);
```

```
    DDX_FieldText(pDX, IDC_ONLINE_OURS, m_pSet->m_E_Mail__Ours, m_pSet);
    DDX_FieldText(pDX, IDC_ONLINE_PROTEGY, m_pSet->m_E_Mail__Prodigy, m_pSet);
    DDX_FieldText(pDX, IDC_PHONE_DATA, m_pSet->m_Phone__Data, m_pSet);
    DDX_FieldText(pDX, IDC_PHONE_FAX, m_pSet->m_Phone__Fax, m_pSet);
    DDX_FieldText(pDX, IDC_PHONE_HOME, m_pSet->m_Phone__Home, m_pSet);
    DDX_FieldText(pDX, IDC_PHONE_VOICE, m_pSet->m_Phone__Voice, m_pSet);
    DDX_FieldText(pDX, IDC_PNONE_HOME_FAX, m_pSet->m_Phone__Home_Fax, m_pSet);
    DDX_FieldText(pDX, IDC_STATE, m_pSet->m_State, m_pSet);
    DDX_FieldText(pDX, IDC_TITLE, m_pSet->m_Title, m_pSet);
    DDX_FieldText(pDX, IDC_ZIP, m_pSet->m_ZipCode, m_pSet);
    DDX_FieldText(pDX, IDC_ONLINE_E_MAIL, m_pSet->m_OnLine__E_Mail, m_pSet);
    DDX_FieldText(pDX, IDC_NOTES, m_pSet->m_Description_Notes, m_pSet);
    DDX_FieldText(pDX, IDC_RECORD_NUMBER, m_pSet->m_ID, m_pSet);
    //}}AFX_DATA_MAP

    if (!pDX->m_bSaveAndValidate)
    {// Display date (& time...) of creation...
        m_pSet->m_Date_Updated_Str = m_pSet->m_Date_Updated.Format("%c");
        m_pSet->m_Date_Entered_Str = m_pSet->m_Date_Entered.Format("%c");
        DDX_FieldText(pDX, IDC_DATE_UPDATED, m_pSet->m_Date_Updated_Str,
                    m_pSet);
        DDX_FieldText(pDX, IDC_DATE_ADDED, m_pSet->m_Date_Entered_Str, m_pSet);
    }
    else
    {// We are getting Date(s). (Re)set only the updated time.
        if (m_pSet->IsFieldDirty(NULL))
        {// A field has changed, so update the time stamp!
            m_pSet->m_Date_Updated = CTime::GetCurrentTime();
        }
    }
}

void CCardfileView::OnInitialUpdate()
{
    m_pSet = &GetDocument()->m_cardfileSet;
    m_pSet->m_strSort = " CARDFILE.\"Last Name\"";
    CRecordView::OnInitialUpdate();

//    The next two lines size window to fit dialog box:
    GetParentFrame()->RecalcLayout();
    ResizeParentToFit(FALSE);
//  End resize of dialog box
}


/////////////////////////////////////////////////////////////////////////////
// CCardfileView printing

BOOL CCardfileView::OnPreparePrinting(CPrintInfo* pInfo)
{
    // Default preparation
    return DoPreparePrinting(pInfo);
}

void CCardfileView::OnBeginPrinting(CDC* /*pDC*/, CPrintInfo* /*pInfo*/)
{
    // TODO: Add extra initialization before printing
```

continues

LISTING 17.2. CONTINUED

```
}

void CCardfileView::OnEndPrinting(CDC* /*pDC*/, CPrintInfo* /*pInfo*/)
{
    // TODO: Add cleanup after printing
}


/////////////////////////////////////////////////////////////////////////////
// CCardfileView diagnostics

#ifdef _DEBUG
void CCardfileView::AssertValid() const
{
    CRecordView::AssertValid();
}

void CCardfileView::Dump(CDumpContext& dc) const
{
    CRecordView::Dump(dc);
}

CCardfileDoc* CCardfileView::GetDocument() // Nondebug version is inline
{
    ASSERT(m_pDocument->IsKindOf(RUNTIME_CLASS(CCardfileDoc)));
    return (CCardfileDoc*)m_pDocument;
}
#endif //_DEBUG

/////////////////////////////////////////////////////////////////////////////
// CCardfileView database support

CRecordset* CCardfileView::OnGetRecordset()
{
    return m_pSet;
}

/////////////////////////////////////////////////////////////////////////////
// CCardfileView message handlers


void CCardfileView::OnRecordAdd()
{
    // TODO: Add your command handler code here

    if (m_bAddMode)
        OnMove(ID_RECORD_FIRST);

    m_pSet->AddNew();
    m_pSet->SetFieldNull(&(m_pSet->m_ID));
    m_bAddMode = TRUE;
    UpdateData(FALSE);
}

void CCardfileView::OnRecordDelete()
{
```

```
    // TODO: Add your command handler code here

    TRY
    {
        m_pSet->Delete();
    }
    CATCH(CDBException, e)
    {
        AfxMessageBox(e->m_strError);
        return;
    }
    END_CATCH

// Move to the next record after the one just deleted
    if (!m_pSet->IsEOF())
        m_pSet->MoveNext();

// If we moved off the end of file, move back to last record
    if (m_pSet->IsEOF())
        m_pSet->MoveLast();

// If the recordset is now empty, clear the
// fields left over from the deleted record
    if (m_pSet->IsBOF())
        m_pSet->SetFieldNull(NULL);
    UpdateData(FALSE);
}

BOOL CCardfileView::OnMove(UINT nIDMoveCommand)
{
    if (m_bAddMode)
    {
        if (!UpdateData())
            return FALSE;

        TRY
        {
            m_pSet->m_Date_Entered = CTime::GetCurrentTime();
            m_pSet->m_Date_Updated = CTime::GetCurrentTime();
            m_pSet->Update();
        }
        CATCH(CDBException, e)
        {
            AfxMessageBox(e->m_strError);
            return FALSE;
        }
        END_CATCH

        m_pSet->Requery();
        UpdateData(FALSE);
        m_bAddMode = FALSE;
        return TRUE;
    }
    else
    {
        return CRecordView::OnMove(nIDMoveCommand);
    }
```

continues

LISTING 17.2. CONTINUED

```
}

void CCardfileView::OnSortedbyLastname()
{
    TRY
    {
        m_pSet->Close();
        m_pSet->m_strSort = " CARDFILE.\"Last Name\"";
        m_pSet->Open();
        m_pSet->Requery();
    }
    CATCH(CDBException, e)
    {
        AfxMessageBox(e->m_strError);
        return;
    }
    END_CATCH

    UpdateData(FALSE);
}

void CCardfileView::OnSortedbyCompany()
{
    TRY
    {
        m_pSet->Close();
        m_pSet->m_strSort = " CARDFILE.Company";
        m_pSet->Open();
        m_pSet->Requery();
    }
    CATCH(CDBException, e)
    {
        AfxMessageBox(e->m_strError);
        return;
    }
    END_CATCH

    UpdateData(FALSE);
}
void CCardfileView::OnSortedbyCity()
{
    TRY
    {
        m_pSet->Close();
        m_pSet->m_strSort = " CARDFILE.City";
        m_pSet->Open();
        m_pSet->Requery();
    }
    CATCH(CDBException, e)
    {
        AfxMessageBox(e->m_strError);
        return;
    }
    END_CATCH
```

```
    UpdateData(FALSE);
}
void CCardfileView::OnSortedbyClassification()
{
    TRY
    {
        m_pSet->Close();
        m_pSet->m_strSort = " CARDFILE.Classification";
        m_pSet->Open();
        m_pSet->Requery();
    }
    CATCH(CDBException, e)
    {
        AfxMessageBox(e->m_strError);
        return;
    }
    END_CATCH

    UpdateData(FALSE);
}
```

Listing 17.3 shows CARDFVW.H, the header file for CardFile's view class.

Listing 17.3. CARDFVW.H.

```
// CARDFVW.H: Interface of the CCardfileView class
//
///////////////////////////////////////////////////////////////////////

class CCardfileSet;

class CCardfileView : public CRecordView
{
protected: // Create from serialization only
    CCardfileView();
    DECLARE_DYNCREATE(CCardfileView)

public:
    //{{AFX_DATA(CCardfileView)
    enum { IDD = IDD_CARDFILE_FORM };
    CCardfileSet* m_pSet;
    //}}AFX_DATA

// Attributes
public:
    CCardfileDoc* GetDocument();

// Operations
public:
    virtual CRecordset* OnGetRecordset();
    virtual void OnInitialUpdate();
```

continues

LISTING 17.3. CONTINUED

```
private:
    BOOL      m_bAddMode;

// Implementation
public:
    virtual ~CCardfileView();
#ifdef _DEBUG
    virtual void AssertValid() const;
    virtual void Dump(CDumpContext& dc) const;
#endif

protected:
    virtual void DoDataExchange(CDataExchange* pDX);   // DDX/DDV support

    virtual BOOL OnMove(UINT nIDMoveCommand);

    // Printing support
    virtual BOOL OnPreparePrinting(CPrintInfo* pInfo);
    virtual void OnBeginPrinting(CDC* pDC, CPrintInfo* pInfo);
    virtual void OnEndPrinting(CDC* pDC, CPrintInfo* pInfo);

// Generated message map functions
protected:
    //{{AFX_MSG(CCardfileView)
        // NOTE: ClassWizard will add and remove member functions here
        // DO NOT EDIT what you see in these blocks of generated code!
    //}}AFX_MSG
//      Added by hand...
    afx_msg void OnRecordAdd();
    afx_msg void OnRecordDelete();
    afx_msg void OnSortedbyLastname();
    afx_msg void OnSortedbyCompany();
    afx_msg void OnSortedbyCity();
    afx_msg void OnSortedbyClassification();
    DECLARE_MESSAGE_MAP()
};

#ifndef _DEBUG  // Debug version in CARDFVW.CPP
inline CCardfileDoc* CCardfileView::GetDocument()
   { return (CCardfileDoc*)m_pDocument; }
#endif
```

//

Notice in Listing 17.3 that we added seven function prototypes and a single variable (m_bAddMode).

Figures 17.2 and 17.3 show CardFile's menu and toolbar template. Each of these resources can be used as I've shown them, or you can make changes to suit your own needs.

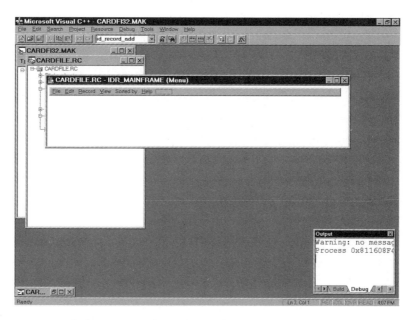

Figure 17.2. CardFile's menu in the resource editor.

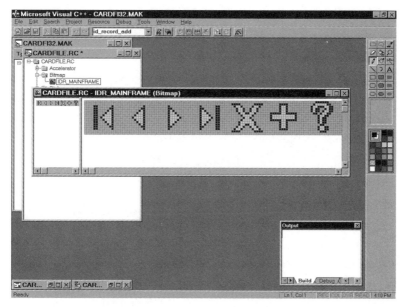

Figure 17.3. CardFile's toolbar bitmap in the resource editor.

Figure 17.4 shows an example of CardFile running.

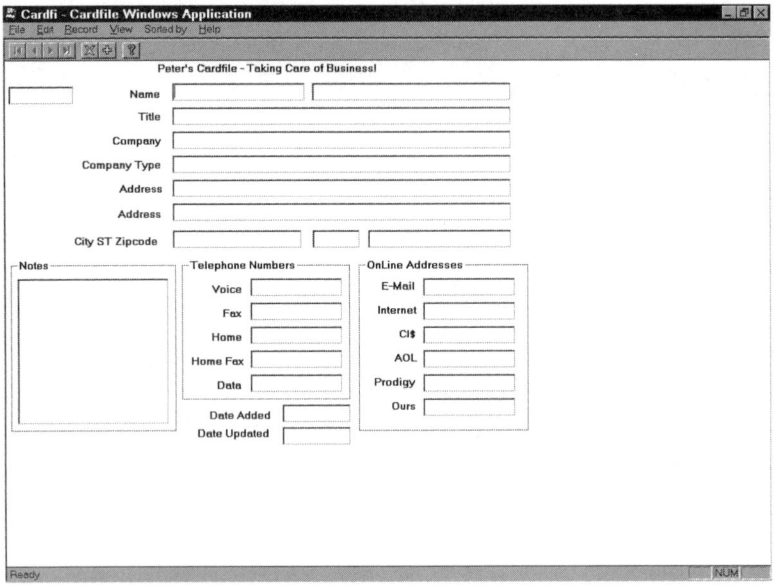

Figure 17.4. CardFile up and running.

No program is perfect, and CardFile is far from optimal. You could add some of the following functionality:

- Searching in any of the fields. The search routine should also allow wildcard-type searches as defined by SQL.

- An index toolbar. This toolbar would have buttons for each letter of the alphabet (or as many buttons as practical). Clicking on a button would cause the DataSource to be searched, finding only those entries that start with the specified letter or letters.

- OLE support to allow embedding and linking of CardFile objects (cards) into other applications.

- OLE support to make CardFile a container program so that CardFile cards could have information from other applications embedded or linked. (For the truly ambitious, allowing embedded and linked objects in CardFile's cards would be a rather challenging project!)

- A hook into the MAPI system so that CardFile could dial telephone numbers. For that matter, hooks for fax numbers so that AtWork Fax could use entries in CardFile would be nice.

Of course, if I were to write all of the preceding enhancements, I'd have a marketable product (albeit low-value but usable). I'll leave it up to you to make your own changes and additions to CardFile. I won't object if you send me your version of the program. Let me know what you can do with it.

Summary

This chapter covered the creation of a simple ODBC shell program that demonstrates the use of the **CRecordSet**, **CRecordView**, and **CDatabase** MFC classes.

Topics discussed include the following:

- Using AppWizard to create an ODBC application
- Modifying an ODBC application created by AppWizard
- Stock ODBC applications based on **CRecordView** and **CRecordSet** classes

Adding ODBC to an Existing Windows Application

Sometimes, when we want to add new technology to our existing applications, we meet with frustration and a resulting application that really doesn't live up to our expectations. This chapter shows how, with ODBC and MFC, you can add ODBC to virtually any Windows application to produce a database-aware program that is easy to understand, maintain, and use.

> Because the new 32-bit ODBC drivers weren't complete when this book was written, the sample programs were tested using Visual C++ 1.5.

There are two distinct methods to add ODBC support to an existing application. You can use the C++ MFC database classes if your original program is compatible with C++ (yes, you can mix C and C++ in a single application). If your program is a C-only program (and you don't want to dive into C++ just yet), you can use the native ODBC `SQL...()` functions that allow full access to the ODBC interface.

USING THE MFC DATABASE CLASSES

Chapter 14, "An Introduction to ODBC," discussed the three classes that make up the ODBC interface. In this chapter, we learn how to use these classes in our program. The following three MFC classes make up the ODBC interface:

- `CRecordView`
- `CDatabase`
- `CRecordSet`

You can create an application from scratch using the Visual C++ 2.0 application builder AppWizard. Using AppWizard to create an ODBC application creates a shell program that has all the linkage to interface with the DataSource and most of the user interface, including toolbar buttons to navigate through the DataSource. The only thing missing is the application's screen layout, which you'll design as a dialog box, and whatever routines are needed to print the user's information, such as a report generator.

The process for creating a shell ODBC application was covered in Chapter 17, "Creating an ODBC Shell Application," so I won't cover this topic any further in this chapter.

This part of the chapter is intended to show a number of examples of what you need to do in order to use the MFC database classes in existing applications.

Figure 18.1 shows relationships between each of the MFC database classes. This figure shows how the three classes work together to form the interface with both the ODBC DataSource and the application's user.

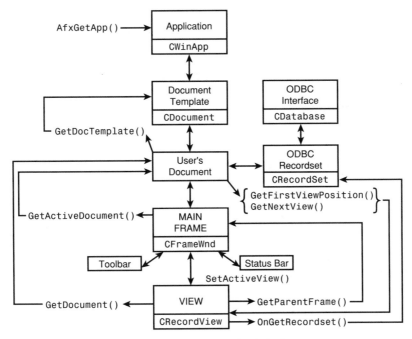

Figure 18.1. The relationships between the MFC ODBC classes.

The CRecordView Class

The MFC **CRecordView** class is derived from the **CFormView** class (which is logical, considering that both classes present information to the user based on a form). The **CFormView** class has the necessary code to allow the user to navigate through the DataSource. It supplies code for the toolbar's database-specific buttons (Next Record, Previous Record, First Record, and Last Record).

If you're planning to use the **CRecordView** class to display information from a DataSource, you must also include a **CRecordSet**-derived object and maintain the necessary pointers to the **CRecordSet**-derived object. The necessary changes are as follows:

1. In your **CDocument** class, include a member class (perhaps called **m_RecordSet**). This class will be derived from **CRecordSet**, and you should use ClassWizard to create it.

2. In your view class (let's assume that the view class is called **COurRecordView**), include a pointer called **m_pSet** to your **CRecordSet**

derived class. In the view class's constructor, initialize this pointer to **NULL**.

3. Override the view class's **OnInitialUpdate()** function if you haven't already done so. In the **OnInitialUpdate()** function, set the **m_pSet** pointer to the address of the **CRecordSet** object (see step 1). A typical **OnInitialUpdate()** function might look like this:

```
void COurRecordView::OnInitialUpdate()
{
    m_pSet = &GetDocument()->m_RecordSet;
    CRecordView::OnInitialUpdate();

}
```

4. Also in your view class, include a member function called **OnGetRecordset()**. This function returns a pointer to your **CRecordSet** derived class. The following is an example of an **OnGetRecordset()** member function:

```
CRecordset* COurRecordView::OnGetRecordset()
{
    return m_pSet;
}
```

5. Base your application's view class on **CRecordView**.

Perhaps the quickest way to convert an application to support ODBC, where you'll be using **CRecordView**, is to create a new application that has the necessary support for **CRecordView**, and use that application as an example.

The CDatabase Class

The **CDatabase** class is the base class for accessing database objects. This class serves as the interface between the **CRecordSet** class and the ODBC DataSource. Please understand, however, that **CRecordSet** isn't derived from **CDatabase**; rather, there is a **CDatabase** object member in **CRecordSet**.

When a **CRecordSet** class object is created, you can pass either a pointer to a **CDatabase** object or a **NULL** pointer. If you pass a **NULL** pointer and your **CRecordSet** object is created using ClassWizard, the constructor for the **CRecordSet** object creates a **CDatabase** object for you.

Generally, if you're using ClassWizard to create your **CRecordSet** class objects, you don't have to define the **CDatabase** class object. Just let **CRecordSet**'s constructor do the hard work for you!

The CRecordSet Class

We've covered the first two MFC ODBC classes in just a few pages. Next we'll cover the remaining class, **CRecordSet**, which is the most important ODBC MFC class. An object derived from the **CRecordSet** class is the only MFC ODBC object that must be defined in an MFC application.

Creating a CRecordSet-Derived Class

Although you can define a class based on the **CRecordSet** class, it really makes no sense not to use ClassWizard to create the class. With ClassWizard you must know which DataSource the **CRecordSet** object will be used with (you need a copy of the DataSource for ClassWizard to use when creating the **CRecordSet** object).

When ClassWizard creates the **CRecordSet** object, it prompts you for the DataSource. It then creates a .CPP source file and an .H header file.

Let's create a sample **CRecordSet**-derived object. First we need a DataSource. It's rather impractical to include a binary file in this book and expect readers to type it in. However, because ODBC supports text files, it's easy to include a comma-delimited file that can be typed in. (I really think you should get the source code disk, though! See the Introduction for details.) Listing 18.1 shows our input data file.

LISTING 18.1. THE ODBC INPUT FILE (STATE.CSV).

```
FIPS,Name,D1,D2,D3,D4,D5,D6,D7
01,ALABAMA,0.0090,0.7446,90.8133,3745572.8195,4,99947,79490296
02,ALASKA,0.0022,0.5828,10.5784,6105901.8293,3,13761,78284208
04,ARIZONA,0.0068,0.4400,28.6371,1614972.8982,24,75358,15271648
05,ARKANSAS,0.0030,0.2418,28.9158,5896080.4893,14,87611,41327044
06,CALIFORNIA,0.0045,0.9360,17.8098,6052240.3659,21,81589,72341056
08,COLORADO,0.0075,0.3436,50.5084,3386909.7253,4,68757,49134380
09,CONNECTICUT,0.0006,0.9139,87.7555,3476772.6215,16,8346,
10,DELAWARE,0.0099,0.0244,35.4088,2503167.9186,16,28580,32985092
11,WASHINGTON_DC,0.0098,0.4736,28.3169,3054250.1330,3,7559,53735176
12,FLORIDA,0.0010,0.2526,21.7849,4444842.9905,20,27055,30938272
13,GEORGIA,0.0015,0.0679,43.4248,2765273.3964,5,28068,99290408
```

continues

LISTING 18.1. CONTINUED

```
15,HAWAII,0.0067,0.0617,2.8885,4240268.1227,5,60082,57632640
16,IDAHO,0.0026,0.9025,96.7416,2529533.7805,3,64228,54501628
17,ILLINOIS,0.0016,0.1827,59.8045,2037419.6963,21,82476,74735264
18,INDIANA,0.0037,0.1033,53.9631,940417.1096,11,66390,49874304
19,IOWA,0.0035,0.8986,89.1301,7523678.8387,15,41363,95827256
20,KANSAS,0.0047,0.8418,68.7994,3487138.0246,21,35695,89691488
21,KENTUCKY,0.0037,0.8249,89.9989,3568.1232,9,11565,21029194
22,LOUISIANA,0.0091,0.3905,0.3974,7072243.2405,7,76405,22577716
23,MAINE,0.0070,0.5837,1.2568,2976451.7984,11,5893,96008624
24,MARYLAND,0.0095,0.8914,40.8306,8397030.8068,8,42862,9181460
25,MASSACHUSETTS,0.0003,0.9819,64.1982,4064390.6173,7,59595,21971886
26,MICHIGAN,0.0009,0.3039,5.0832,333372.9225,23,99885,62916400
27,MINNESOTA,0.0027,0.5148,27.0879,8338561.5175,5,25934,53580256
28,MISSISSIPPI,0.0007,0.0204,50.2479,8610546.0733,17,85585,40042880
29,MISSOURI,0.0018,0.8789,90.6047,2639918.8877,20,39780,53763536
30,MONTANA,0.0002,0.6986,73.0619,7415148.4426,17,67993,82483392
31,NEBRASKA,0.0015,0.9856,72.9229,5630359.7553,21,39697,29002164
32,NEVADA,0.0020,0.9775,42.0143,2418810.7488,13,34348,45303172
33,NEW_HAMPSHIRE,0.0028,0.6344,96.4917,1144564.0588,27466,46216196
34,NEW_JERSEY,0.0030,0.6941,17.4912,2771669.5272,14,49976,14461514
35,NEW_MEXICO,0.0081,0.4498,98.6702,7723409.5255,0,13934,45596292
36,NEW_YORK,0.0054,0.5546,30.8871,2508419.7546,13,21919,16651488
37,NORTH_CAROLINA,0.0019,0.9491,88.0965,6104848.7206,0,66452,74032216
38,NORTH_DAKOTA,0.0027,0.1405,77.1168,3092141.1885,1,86817,11860060
39,OHIO,0.0077,0.9770,11.3818,2354730.8394,24,47799,99152320
40,OKLAHOMA,0.0041,0.9518,77.8327,6512558.5520,0,76003,53208388
41,OREGON,0.0016,0.1045,44.1854,697.0846,19,42062,46918904
42,PENNSYLVANIA,0.0046,0.2930,56.9112,6889691.2785,0,90663,53085596
44,RHODE_ISLAND,0.0055,0.7764,70.8299,4028547.3726,17,13564,41300216
45,SOUTH_CAROLINA,0.0051,0.6030,6.7548,7595802.1866,0,63058,32825774
46,SOUTH_DAKOTA,0.0020,0.9820,5.4907,6150430.3903,2,53833,15249154
47,TENNESSEE,0.0096,0.7180,33.1683,8717507.8320,17,13964,25594872
48,TEXAS,0.0099,0.4226,92.0004,9325105.6908,7,32483,50309480
49,UTAH,0.0053,0.7378,33.6140,4540489.9390,15,75148,88687208
50,VERMONT,0.0047,0.1799,97.1086,5064418.9929,17,21404,24961008
51,VIRGINIA,0.0025,0.1230,27.8656,3822837.1498,11,41660,36181320
53,WASHINGTON,0.0036,0.8333,85.9140,6253767.9530,2,10049,56090144
54,WEST_VIRGINIA,0.0062,0.4255,54.9415,6843368.7971,4,69281,81704416
55,WISCONSIN,0.0090,0.9301,29.4578,3372252.6208,21,69229,75957160
56,WYOMING,0.0006,0.6351,2.6614,8201001.1983,14,65913,12669835
72,PUERTO_RICO,0.0038,0.4634,39.1217,7982612.5474,14,98094,41746440
```

The file shown in Listing 18.1 has CSV (comma-separated, variable-length fields) format. (Notice that the character column **Name** doesn't need to be in quotation marks because it has no imbedded blanks.) Each column in this file is separated with a comma. The first line in this file contains the names of the columns. This is optional, but it allows easier configuration of an ODBC text DataSource.

When you've created this file or copied it from the source disk, you'll need to install it as an ODBC DataSource. To do this (assuming that you're using

Windows 3.1 or later), start Control Panel and select the ODBC applet. This program enables you to configure ODBC drivers and DataSources. Set up this file as an ODBC DataSource. When ODBC sets up the STATE.CSV file, ODBC creates or updates the SCHEMA.INI file found in the same directory as the data file. ODBC creates a SCHEMA.INI file for each directory that contains TEXT formatted DataSources. The contents of the SCHEMA.INI file for STATE.CSV are shown in Listing 18.2.

LISTING 18.2. THE ODBC-CREATED SCHEMA.INI FILE.

```
[state.csv]
ColNameHeader=True
Format=CSVDelimited
MaxScanRows=25
CharacterSet=OEM
Col1=FIPS Integer Width 2
Col2=Name Char Width 13
Col3=D1 Float Width 6
Col4=D2 Float Width 6
Col5=D3 Float Width 7
Col6=D4 Float Width 12
Col7=D5 Integer Width 2
Col8=D6 Integer Width 5
Col9=D7 Integer Width 8
```

The SCHEMA.INI file defines the format of the file (**Format=CSVDelimited**) and specifies the following: that there is a header row (**ColNameHeader=True**); that, when columns are scanned, ODBC will read the first 25 rows (**MaxScanRows=25**); and that the character set for this file is the OEM (**CharacterSet=OEM**)—DOS's (not Windows') character set.

Also included in the SCHEMA.INI file are the definitions for each of the columns in the file. The first column, FIPS (Federal Information Processing Standard) code, contains a numeric designator for each state. The second column, Name, contains the state's name. The final seven columns are data, the first four having floating-point data and the last three having integer (long or 32-bit int) values.

Notice that each column has a width parameter. This field is filled out by the ODBC TEXT DataSource setup program, but the width parameter is useful only for columnar text files. In noncolumnar files, the Width parameter indicates the maximum size for a field in the number of rows scanned (see the earlier description of **MaxScanRows=25**).

When your DataSource is installed and configured, you can create the **CRecordSet** class. The program that will include your ODBC support need not have been created using the ODBC options. However, if database support wasn't included, you must add to the STDAFX.H file the include for the MFC ODBC support. The include file is shown in Listing 18.3.

LISTING 18.3. STDAFX.H WITH DATABASE SUPPORT ADDED.

```
// STDAFX.H: Include file for standard system include files
// or project-specific include files that are used frequently
// but changed infrequently
//

#include <afxwin.h>          // MFC core and standard components
#include <afxext.h>          // MFC extensions (including VB)
#include <afxdb.h>           // MFC database classes
```

If you created your original application with ODBC support, this include file will already be in your STDAFX.H file.

Next, using ClassWizard, create a **CRecordSet**-derived object. I use the name **CStateSet** because my DataSource is data about states.

Listing 18.4 shows the .CPP file that ClassWizard created for our DataSource. Notice that I've accepted ClassWizard's default name for the file.

LISTING 18.4. THE CLASSWIZARD-CREATED DATABASE CLASS CStateSet FILE (STATESET.CPP).

```
// STATESET.CPP: Implementation file
//

#include "stdafx.h"
#include "odbctest.h"   // Our main program
#include "stateset.h"

#ifdef _DEBUG
#undef THIS_FILE
static char BASED_CODE THIS_FILE[] = __FILE__;
#endif

/////////////////////////////////////////////////////////////////////////////
// CStateSet

IMPLEMENT_DYNAMIC(CStateSet, CRecordset)
```

```
CStateSet::CStateSet(CDatabase* pdb)
    : CRecordset(pdb)
{
    //{{AFX_FIELD_INIT(CStateSet)
    m_FIPS = 0;
    m_Name = "";
    m_D1 = 0.0;
    m_D2 = 0.0;
    m_D3 = 0.0;
    m_D4 = 0.0;
    m_D5 = 0;
    m_D6 = 0;
    m_D7 = 0;
    m_nFields = 9;
    //}}AFX_FIELD_INIT
}


CString CStateSet::GetDefaultConnect()
{
    return "ODBC;DSN=States;";
}

CString CStateSet::GetDefaultSQL()
{
    return "STATE.CSV";
}

void CStateSet::DoFieldExchange(CFieldExchange* pFX)
{
    //{{AFX_FIELD_MAP(CStateSet)
    pFX->SetFieldType(CFieldExchange::outputColumn);
    RFX_Long(pFX, "FIPS", m_FIPS);
    RFX_Text(pFX, "Name", m_Name);
    RFX_Double(pFX, "D1", m_D1);
    RFX_Double(pFX, "D2", m_D2);
    RFX_Double(pFX, "D3", m_D3);
    RFX_Double(pFX, "D4", m_D4);
    RFX_Long(pFX, "D5", m_D5);
    RFX_Long(pFX, "D6", m_D6);
    RFX_Long(pFX, "D7", m_D7);
    //}}AFX_FIELD_MAP
}
```

The STATESET.CPP file contains an include for the STATESET.H file, STDAFX.H, and for the header for the main program. Because I generated this class in a program called ODBCTEST, there is an include for ODBCTEST.H. In your application, the name of this include file would be the same as the name of the main application's include file.

After including the necessary header files, ClassWizard creates the initializer function. Notice the inclusion of code to initialize each of the member fields (shown in bold):

```
CStateSet::CStateSet(CDatabase* pdb)
    : CRecordset(pdb)
{
    //{{AFX_FIELD_INIT(CStateSet)
    m_FIPS = 0;
    m_Name = "";
    m_D1 = 0.0;
    m_D2 = 0.0;
    m_D3 = 0.0;
    m_D4 = 0.0;
    m_D5 = 0;
    m_D6 = 0;
    m_D7 = 0;
    m_nFields = 9;
    //}}AFX_FIELD_INIT
}
```

After the initialization of the variables that will hold the dataset's column data, the *m_nFields* member variable that is found in **CRecordSet** is initialized. The *m_nFields* member variable tells **CRecordSet** and its derived class **CStateSet** how many columns are found in the dataset.

The two member functions **GetDefaultConnect()** and **GetDefaultSQL()**, which must be found in a derived class, are used to establish the connection to the DataSource. Notice that both of these functions have "hardwired" return values that can't be altered at runtime. It's possible to rewrite these functions to prompt the user for which DataSource to open, but keep in mind that the columns are hardwired and must be made dynamic as well:

```
CString CStateSet::GetDefaultConnect()
{
    return "ODBC;DSN=States;";
}

CString CStateSet::GetDefaultSQL()
{
    return "STATE.CSV";
}
```

The **GetDefaultConnect()** function is used by the framework to get the default connect string for the DataSource.

The **GetDefaultSQL()** function is used to return the default SQL statement that the recordset is based on. Note that this string isn't a full and correct SQL string. To get the full SQL string, use the **GetSQL()** function. The **GetSQL()** function returns the full select used to create the recordset:

```
void CStateSet::DoFieldExchange(CFieldExchange* pFX)
{
    //{{AFX_FIELD_MAP(CStateSet)
    pFX->SetFieldType(CFieldExchange::outputColumn);
    RFX_Long(pFX, "FIPS", m_FIPS);
```

```
    RFX_Text(pFX, "Name", m_Name);
    RFX_Double(pFX, "D1", m_D1);
    RFX_Double(pFX, "D2", m_D2);
    RFX_Double(pFX, "D3", m_D3);
    RFX_Double(pFX, "D4", m_D4);
    RFX_Long(pFX, "D5", m_D5);
    RFX_Long(pFX, "D6", m_D6);
    RFX_Long(pFX, "D7", m_D7);
    //}}AFX_FIELD_MAP
}
```

The final function created by ClassWizard is the **DoFieldExchange()** function, which tells the framework which member variable is mapped to which column in the dataset. You need to map a variable to each column that your application will use. ClassWizard will map all columns in the specified dataset.

The **RFX_...** functions, listed in Table 18.1, are used to tell the framework what the variable and its type are. Remember, the type specified in the **RFX_...** function is the type of the receiving variable, not the DataSource column. ODBC takes care of converting the data types.

TABLE 18.1. RFX_... FUNCTIONS AND DATA TYPES.

Function	Data Type Expected
RFX_Bool	**BOOL**
RFX_Byte	**BYTE**
RFX_Binary	**CByteArray**
RFX_Double	**double**
RFX_Single	**float**
RFX_Int	**int**
RFX_Long	**long**
RFX_LongBinary	**CLongBinary**
RFX_Text	**CString**
RFX_Date	**CTime**

The **DoFieldExchange()** function manages the transfer of data both from the DataSource and, when updating, to the DataSource. The transfer process is invisible to the programmer, because the calls to the **CRecordSet** member functions that fetch and update make the actual calls to the ODBC SQL functions to move the data to and from the column variables.

The header file that ClassWizard created for the **CStateSet** object that was derived from **CRecordSet** is shown in Listing 18.5. This header file defines **CStateSet**'s variables and member functions.

LISTING 18.5. THE HEADER FILE FOR THE CStateSet CLASS (STATESET.H).

```
// STATESET.H: Header file
//

/////////////////////////////////////////////////////////////////////////////
// CStateSet recordset

class CStateSet : public CRecordset
{
public:
    CStateSet(CDatabase* pDatabase = NULL);

// Field/param data
    //{{AFX_FIELD(CStateSet, CRecordset)
    long m_FIPS;
    CString m_Name;
    double m_D1;
    double m_D2;
    double m_D3;
    double m_D4;
    long m_D5;
    long m_D6;
    long m_D7;
    //}}AFX_FIELD


// Implementation
protected:
    virtual CString GetDefaultConnect();  // Default connection string
    virtual CString GetDefaultSQL();       // Default SQL for Recordset
    virtual void DoFieldExchange(CFieldExchange* pFX);  // RFX support
    DECLARE_DYNAMIC(CStateSet)
};
```

Using a *CRecordSet*-Derived Class

As soon as you've created your **CRecordSet**-derived class, you should be ready to use it. To show how the class is used, I will first create a new application that has the following attributes:

- A single document interface
- Toolbar and status bar support
- No database support of any kind will be included with the initial program.

I will create this program using ClassWizard and call it ADDB.

Because AppWizard won't directly create a **CFormView**-based application, you must modify the default program to include a **CFormView** object. To create a formview program, follow these steps:

1. Use AppWizard to create a standard program (either SDI or MDI).

2. Create a dialog box that will become the application's main window form. ADDB's dialog box is shown in Figure 18.2. In the Form dialog box, make sure that no controls have the identifiers **IDOK** or **IDCANCEL**, because ClassWizard generates incorrect handlers for controls with these two identifiers.

Figure 18.2. ADDB's dialog box.

3. Using ClassWizard, create a new class based on **CFormView**. In ADDB we'll call the new view class **CMainView**. When creating this class, use the identifier for the dialog box created in step 2.

4. In ADDB.CPP, change the original view class to **CMainView**. Also, delete the include of the original view class's header file (**#include "addbview.h"**) and add an include for your new view class (**#include "mainview.h"**). These changes are shown in Listing 18.6.

5. You no longer need the original view class source files (ADDBVIEW.CPP and ADDBVIEW.H), so you should delete them. Using the Visual Workbench's project edit feature, remove the reference to ADDBVIEW.CPP in your project. Tell Visual Workbench to scan all dependencies.

6. Optionally, you can force Windows to size your formview application's main window to match the size of the form dialog. This is done in two steps, as shown in Listings 18.7 and 18.8.

7. Next, we include the necessary **CRecordSet** derived class. I've chosen to include the class **CStateSet**, which we created earlier in this chapter. Typically, the **CRecordSet** class object would be connected to the application's document class. Some programs have their database support as part of a dialog box, so perhaps the database support will be at the level of the applicable dialog box.

8. The final step is to connect the column variables in **CStateSet** to the output controls in the **IDD_DISPLAY** dialog.

MORE ON USING *CFormView* CLASSES

Microsoft has published a document (available on the MSDN library disk or from Microsoft directly) titled *INF: Using CFormView in SDI and MDI Applications*. The document's ID number is PSS ID Number: Q98598.

Let's start by taking a look at the original program that AppWizard created and the changes needed to add the **CFormView** support. I will follow the steps shown in the preceding list, showing the final listings.

Listing 18.6 shows ADDB.CPP, the main file for the ADDB program. The changes I made appear in bold.

LISTING 18.6. ADDB's MAIN FILE (ADDB.CPP).

```
// ADDB.CPP: Defines the class behaviors for the application
//

#include "stdafx.h"
#include "addb.h"

#include "mainfrm.h"
#include "addbdoc.h"
// #include "addbview.h"
#include "mainview.h"

#ifdef _DEBUG
#undef THIS_FILE
static char BASED_CODE THIS_FILE[] = __FILE__;
#endif
```

```
/////////////////////////////////////////////////////////////////////////
// CAddbApp

BEGIN_MESSAGE_MAP(CAddbApp, CWinApp)
    //{{AFX_MSG_MAP(CAddbApp)
    ON_COMMAND(ID_APP_ABOUT, OnAppAbout)
        // NOTE: ClassWizard will add and remove mapping macros here
        // DC NOT EDIT what you see in these blocks of generated code!
    //}}AFX_MSG_MAP
    // Standard file-based document commands
    ON_COMMAND(ID_FILE_NEW, CWinApp::OnFileNew)
    ON_COMMAND(ID_FILE_OPEN, CWinApp::OnFileOpen)
    // Standard print setup command
    ON_COMMAND(ID_FILE_PRINT_SETUP, CWinApp::OnFilePrintSetup)
END_MESSAGE_MAP()

/////////////////////////////////////////////////////////////////////////
// CAddbApp construction

CAddbApp::CAddbApp()
{
    // TODO: Add construction code here
    // Place all significant initialization in InitInstance
}

/////////////////////////////////////////////////////////////////////////
// The one and only CAddbApp object

CAddbApp NEAR theApp;

/////////////////////////////////////////////////////////////////////////
// CAddbApp initialization

BOOL CAddbApp::InitInstance()
{
    // Standard initialization
    // If you are not using these features and wish to reduce the size
    // of your final executable, you should remove from the following
    // the specific initialization routines you do not need

    SetDialogBkColor();         // Set dialog background color to gray
    LoadStdProfileSettings();   // Load standard .INI file options
                                // (including MRU)

    // Register the application's document templates. Document templates
    // serve as the connection between documents, frame windows, and views.

    CSingleDocTemplate* pDocTemplate;
    pDocTemplate = new CSingleDocTemplate(
        IDR_MAINFRAME,
        RUNTIME_CLASS(CAddbDoc),
        RUNTIME_CLASS(CMainFrame),   // Main SDI frame window
//      RUNTIME_CLASS(CAddView)); (Deleted, added 'CMainView':
        RUNTIME_CLASS(CMainView));
    AddDocTemplate(pDocTemplate);

    // Create a new (empty) document
```

continues

LISTING 18.6. CONTINUED

```
    OnFileNew();

    if (m_lpCmdLine[0] != '\0')
    {
        // TODO: Add command-line processing here
    }


    return TRUE;
}

/////////////////////////////////////////////////////////////////////////////
// CAboutDlg dialog used for App About

class CAboutDlg : public CDialog
{
public:
    CAboutDlg();

// Dialog data
    //{{AFX_DATA(CAboutDlg)
    enum { IDD = IDD_ABOUTBOX };
    //}}AFX_DATA

// Implementation
protected:
    virtual void DoDataExchange(CDataExchange* pDX);   // DDX/DDV support
    //{{AFX_MSG(CAboutDlg)
        // No message handlers
    //}}AFX_MSG
    DECLARE_MESSAGE_MAP()
};

CAboutDlg::CAboutDlg() : CDialog(CAboutDlg::IDD)
{
    //{{AFX_DATA_INIT(CAboutDlg)
    //}}AFX_DATA_INIT
}

void CAboutDlg::DoDataExchange(CDataExchange* pDX)
{
    CDialog::DoDataExchange(pDX);
    //{{AFX_DATA_MAP(CAboutDlg)
    //}}AFX_DATA_MAP
}

BEGIN_MESSAGE_MAP(CAboutDlg, CDialog)
    //{{AFX_MSG_MAP(CAboutDlg)
        // No message handlers
    //}}AFX_MSG_MAP
END_MESSAGE_MAP()

// App command to run the dialog
void CAddbApp::OnAppAbout()
```

```
{
    CAboutDlg aboutDlg;
    aboutDlg.DoModal();
}

/////////////////////////////////////////////////////////////////////////////
// CAddbApp commands
```

Only two changes occurred in CADDB.CPP: The view class changed from **CAddView**, which is the default nonformview class, to **CMainView**, the **CFormView** class that we created. Also, the view class's included header file changed to MAINVIEW.H.

Listing 18.7 shows MAINFRM.CPP. This file has been changed to make it impossible for the user to resize the window. The window displayed will always be sized to fit the **IDD_DISPLAY** dialog.

LISTING 18.7. CHANGES TO LIMIT THE USER'S RESIZING OF ADDB'S MAIN WINDOW (MAINFRM.CPP).

```
// MAINFRM.CPP: Implementation of the CMainFrame class
//

#include "stdafx.h"
#include "addb.h"

#include "mainfrm.h"

#ifdef _DEBUG
#undef THIS_FILE
static char BASED_CODE THIS_FILE[] = __FILE__;
#endif

/////////////////////////////////////////////////////////////////////////////
// CMainFrame

IMPLEMENT_DYNCREATE(CMainFrame, CFrameWnd)

BEGIN_MESSAGE_MAP(CMainFrame, CFrameWnd)
    //{{AFX_MSG_MAP(CMainFrame)
        // NOTE: ClassWizard will add and remove mapping macros here
        // DO NOT EDIT what you see in these blocks of generated code!
    ON_WM_CREATE()
    //}}AFX_MSG_MAP
END_MESSAGE_MAP()

/////////////////////////////////////////////////////////////////////////////
// Arrays of IDs used to initialize control bars

// Toolbar buttons. IDs are command buttons
static UINT BASED_CODE buttons[] =
{
```

continues

LISTING 18.7. CONTINUED

```
    // Same order as in the bitmap toolbar.bmp
    ID_FILE_NEW,
    ID_FILE_OPEN,
    ID_FILE_SAVE,
        ID_SEPARATOR,
    ID_EDIT_CUT,
    ID_EDIT_COPY,
    ID_EDIT_PASTE,
        ID_SEPARATOR,
    ID_FILE_PRINT,
    ID_APP_ABOUT,
};

static UINT BASED_CODE indicators[] =
{
    ID_SEPARATOR,              // Status line indicator
    ID_INDICATOR_CAPS,
    ID_INDICATOR_NUM,
    ID_INDICATOR_SCRL,
};


/////////////////////////////////////////////////////////////////////////////
// CMainFrame construction/destruction

CMainFrame::CMainFrame()
{
    // TODO: Add member initialization code here
}

CMainFrame::~CMainFrame()
{
}

int CMainFrame::OnCreate(LPCREATESTRUCT lpCreateStruct)
{
    if (CFrameWnd::OnCreate(lpCreateStruct) == -1)
        return -1;

    if (!m_wndToolBar.Create(this) ||
        !m_wndToolBar.LoadBitmap(IDR_MAINFRAME) ||
        !m_wndToolBar.SetButtons(buttons,
          sizeof(buttons)/sizeof(UINT)))
    {
        TRACE("Failed to create toolbar\n");
        return -1;        // Fail to create
    }

    if (!m_wndStatusBar.Create(this) ||
        !m_wndStatusBar.SetIndicators(indicators,
          sizeof(indicators)/sizeof(UINT)))
    {
        TRACE("Failed to create status bar\n");
        return -1;        // Fail to create
    }
```

```
    return 0;
}

//////////////////////////////////////////////////////////////////////////
// CMainFrame diagnostics

#ifdef _DEBUG
void CMainFrame::AssertValid() const
{
    CFrameWnd::AssertValid();
}

void CMainFrame::Dump(CDumpContext& dc) const
{
    CFrameWnd::Dump(dc);
}

#endif //_DEBUG

//////////////////////////////////////////////////////////////////////////
// CMainFrame override handlers

BOOL CMainFrame::PreCreateWindow(CREATESTRUCT &cs)
{
    cs.style &= ~WS_THICKFRAME;
    return(CFrameWnd::PreCreateWindow(cs));
}

//////////////////////////////////////////////////////////////////////////
// CMainFrame message handlers
```

The overriding of the **PreCreateWindow()** function allows us to change the window attribute from the standard sizing frame to a thin (nonsizing) frame. In the new **CFormView** class, we add code that will resize the application's main window to the size of the dialog box. This change is shown in Listing 18.8.

LISTING 18.8. CHANGES TO FORCE THE MAIN WINDOW TO THE DIALOG'S SIZE (MAINVIEW.CPP).

```
// MAINVIEW.CPP: Implementation file
//

#include "stdafx.h"
#include "addb.h"
#include "mainview.h"

#ifdef _DEBUG
#undef THIS_FILE
static char BASED_CODE THIS_FILE[] = __FILE__;
#endif

//////////////////////////////////////////////////////////////////////////
// CMainView
```

continues

LISTING 18.8. CONTINUED

```
IMPLEMENT_DYNCREATE(CMainView, CFormView)

CMainView::CMainView()
    : CFormView(CMainView::IDD)
{
    //{{AFX_DATA_INIT(CMainView)
        // NOTE: ClassWizard will add member initialization here
    //}}AFX_DATA_INIT
}

CMainView::~CMainView()
{
}

void CMainView::DoDataExchange(CDataExchange* pDX)
{
    CFormView::DoDataExchange(pDX);
    //{{AFX_DATA_MAP(CMainView)
        // NOTE: ClassWizard will add DDX and DDV calls here
    //}}AFX_DATA_MAP
}


BEGIN_MESSAGE_MAP(CMainView, CFormView)
    //{{AFX_MSG_MAP(CMainView)
        // NOTE: ClassWizard will add and remove mapping macros here
    //}}AFX_MSG_MAP
END_MESSAGE_MAP()


/////////////////////////////////////////////////////////////////////
// CMainView override functions

void CMainView::OnInitialUpdate()
{
    CFormView::OnInitialUpdate();
    GetParentFrame()->RecalcLayout();
    ResizeParentToFit(FALSE);
}

/////////////////////////////////////////////////////////////////////
// CMainView message handlers
```

When these changes are complete, you have a standard formview application. This application could be used in virtually any manner consistent with a formview-type application. It isn't limited to being a program that interfaces with an ODBC database.

Adding ODBC support to ADDB is a simple process. First, in your document class, you need to add an object based on **CStateSet**.

The **CStateSet** object will be part of our document class. Even though, in this program, we don't have a true document (meaning that nothing in the document is either saved or retrieved), you can consider the DataSource to be part of the document. In ADDB, the DataSource is a read-only text file. If the DataSource were an Access database, it could also be updated and therefore would be an excellent example of a document, because the user could work with it and changes would be saved to the original document.

Let's take a look at the changes that we'll make to the program. First, in Listing 18.9, is ADDBDOC.H, which contains the header definitions for the document class.

LISTING 18.9. ADDB's DOCUMENT CLASS HEADER FILE **(ADDBDOC.H).**

```
// ADDBDOC.H: Interface of the CAddbDoc class
//
/////////////////////////////////////////////////////////////////////////////

#include "stateset.h"

class CAddbDoc : public CDocument
{
protected: // Create from serialization only
    CAddbDoc();
    DECLARE_DYNCREATE(CAddbDoc)

// Attributes
public:

    CStateSet    CState;

// Operations
public:

    void CAddbDoc::GetNext();
    void CAddbDoc::GetPrevious();

// Implementation
public:
    virtual ~CAddbDoc();
    virtual void Serialize(CArchive& ar);   // Overridden for document I/O
#ifdef _DEBUG
    virtual void AssertValid() const;
    virtual void Dump(CDumpContext& dc) const;
#endif

protected:
    virtual BOOL OnNewDocument();

// Generated message map functions
protected:
```

continues

LISTING 18.9. CONTINUED

```
//{{AFX_MSG(CAddbDoc)
    // NOTE: ClassWizard will add and remove member functions here
    // DO NOT EDIT what you see in these blocks of generated code!
//}}AFX_MSG
DECLARE_MESSAGE_MAP()
};


/////////////////////////////////////////////////////////////////////////////
```

Notice that I have an **#include** to include **CStateSet**'s header file:

```
#include "stateset.h"
```

Including the header for **CStateSet** inside the header for the document class is necessary because we define a **CStateSet** object in this header. This header may be included in other files, so we must ensure that the **CStateSet** object's definition is available.

Next, we define a **CStateSet** member object. I've called this member **CState**:

```
// Attributes
public:

    CStateSet     CState;
```

Finally, we add prototypes for two functions used to navigate through the records in the dataset. We could have included more than these two functions, such as functions to select the first record, the last record, or a specific record:

```
// Operations
public:

    void CAddbDoc::GetNext();      // Select the next record
    void CAddbDoc::GetPrevious();  // Select the previous record
```

In the source file we added additional code to support our **CState** object. Shown in Listing 18.10 is ADDBDOC.CPP. Our changes appear in bold.

LISTING 18.10. ADDB's DOCUMENT CLASS SOURCE CODE (ADDBDOC.CPP).

```
// ADDBDOC.CPP: Implementation of the CAddbDoc class
//

#include "stdafx.h"
#include "addb.h"

#include "addbdoc.h"
```

```
#ifdef _DEBUG
#undef THIS_FILE
static char BASED_CODE THIS_FILE[] = __FILE__;
#endif

/////////////////////////////////////////////////////////////////////////
// CAddbDoc

IMPLEMENT_DYNCREATE(CAddbDoc, CDocument)

BEGIN_MESSAGE_MAP(CAddbDoc, CDocument)
    //{{AFX_MSG_MAP(CAddbDoc)
        // NOTE: ClassWizard will add and remove mapping macros here
        // DO NOT EDIT what you see in these blocks of generated code!
    //}}AFX_MSG_MAP
END_MESSAGE_MAP()

/////////////////////////////////////////////////////////////////////////
// CAddbDoc construction/destruction

CAddbDoc::CAddbDoc()
{
    // TODO: Add one-time construction code here
}

CAddbDoc::~CAddbDoc()
{
//    Close the DataSource if it is open
    if (CState.IsOpen())
        CState.Close();
}

BOOL CAddbDoc::OnNewDocument()
{
    if (!CDocument::OnNewDocument())
        return FALSE;

//    Open the DataSource if it is not already open
    if (!CState.IsOpen())
        CState.Open();

    // TODO: Add reinitialization code here
    // (SDI documents will reuse this document)

    return TRUE;
}

/////////////////////////////////////////////////////////////////////////
// CAddbDoc serialization

void CAddbDoc::Serialize(CArchive& ar)
{
    if (ar.IsStoring())
    {
        // TODO: Add storing code here
    }
```

continues

LISTING 18.10. CONTINUED

```
    else
    {
        // TODO: Add loading code here
    }
}

////////////////////////////////////////////////////////////////////////////
// CAddbDoc diagnostics

#ifdef _DEBUG
void CAddbDoc::AssertValid() const
{
    CDocument::AssertValid();
}

void CAddbDoc::Dump(CDumpContext& dc) const
{
    CDocument::Dump(dc);
}
#endif //_DEBUG

////////////////////////////////////////////////////////////////////////////
// CAddbDoc commands

void CAddbDoc::GetNext()
{
    if (!CState.IsEOF())
        CState.MoveNext();
}

void CAddbDoc::GetPrevious()
{
    if (!CState.IsBOF())
        CState.MovePrev();
}
```

Now, let's take a closer look at each of the changes that have been made to our document class. First, in the document class's destructor, we need to close our DataSource. This is simply a check to make sure that the DataSource is actually open (if it isn't open, the program probably failed). If the DataSource is open, a call to **CRecordSet**'s **Close()** member function is made to close the connection to the DataSource:

```
CAddbDoc::~CAddbDoc()
{
//    Close the DataSource if it is open
    if (CState.IsOpen())
        CState.Close();
}
```

In the document class's **OnNewDocument()** function, we need to add code to open the DataSource. Again, there is a check to see whether the DataSource is open. If it isn't yet open, we call the **CRecordSet** member function **Open()**:

```
BOOL CAddbDoc::OnNewDocument()
{
    if (!CDocument::OnNewDocument())
        return FALSE;

//    Open the DataSource if it is not already open
    if (!CState.IsOpen())
        CState.Open();

    // TODO: Add reinitialization code here
    // (SDI documents will reuse this document)

    return TRUE;
}
```

The final change we make is to create our two functions to allow ADDB's user to navigate through the DataSource's records. We have a function called **GetNext()** that accesses the next record if the current record isn't the last record in the DataSource.

Like **GetNext()**, the **GetPrevious()** function checks the current record and, if it isn't the first record in the DataSource, accesses the previous record:

```
void CAddbDoc::GetNext()
{
    if (!CState.IsEOF())
        CState.MoveNext();
}

void CAddbDoc::GetPrevious()
{
    if (!CState.IsBOF())
        CState.MovePrev();
}
```

The next part of the source that needs to be updated is the view class. Listing 18.8 showed the view prior to our adding the support for displaying and navigating through records in the DataSource. Listing 18.11 shows the view class's source file with the necessary additions to access the information in the current record in the DataSource.

LISTING 18.11. THE VIEW CLASS WITH SUPPORT FOR A CRecordSet OBJECT (MAINVIEW.CPP).

```
// MAINVIEW.CPP: Implementation file
//

#include "stdafx.h"
```

continues

LISTING 18.11. CONTINUED

```
#include "addb.h"
#include "mainview.h"
#include "addbdoc.h"

#ifdef _DEBUG
#undef THIS_FILE
static char BASED_CODE THIS_FILE[] = __FILE__;
#endif


///////////////////////////////////////////////////////////////////////////
// CMainView

IMPLEMENT_DYNCREATE(CMainView, CFormView)

CMainView::CMainView()
    : CFormView(CMainView::IDD)
{
    //{{AFX_DATA_INIT(CMainView)
        // NOTE: ClassWizard will add member initialization here
    //}}AFX_DATA_INIT
}

CMainView::~CMainView()
{
}

void CMainView::DoDataExchange(CDataExchange* pDX)
{
    CFormView::DoDataExchange(pDX);
    //{{AFX_DATA_MAP(CMainView)
        // NOTE: ClassWizard will add DDX and DDV calls here
    //}}AFX_DATA_MAP
    // We manually add the DDX_Text() calls since we're
    // using GetDocument() to locate the variables

    DDX_Text(pDX, IDC_FIPS, ((CAddbDoc *)GetDocument())->CState.m_FIPS);
    DDX_Text(pDX, IDC_STATE, ((CAddbDoc *)GetDocument())->CState.m_Name);
    DDX_Text(pDX, IDC_DATA1, ((CAddbDoc *)GetDocument())->CState.m_D1);
    DDX_Text(pDX, IDC_DATA2, ((CAddbDoc *)GetDocument())->CState.m_D2);
    DDX_Text(pDX, IDC_DATA3, ((CAddbDoc *)GetDocument())->CState.m_D3);
    DDX_Text(pDX, IDC_DATA4, ((CAddbDoc *)GetDocument())->CState.m_D4);
    DDX_Text(pDX, IDC_DATA5, ((CAddbDoc *)GetDocument())->CState.m_D5);
    DDX_Text(pDX, IDC_DATA6, ((CAddbDoc *)GetDocument())->CState.m_D6);
    DDX_Text(pDX, IDC_DATA7, ((CAddbDoc *)GetDocument())->CState.m_D7);
}


BEGIN_MESSAGE_MAP(CMainView, CFormView)
    //{{AFX_MSG_MAP(CMainView)
    ON_BN_CLICKED(IDC_NEXT, OnNext)
    ON_BN_CLICKED(IDC_PREVIOUS, OnPrevious)
    //}}AFX_MSG_MAP
END_MESSAGE_MAP()
```

```
/////////////////////////////////////////////////////////////////////
// CMainView Override functions

void CMainView::OnInitialUpdate()
{
    CFormView::OnInitialUpdate();
    GetParentFrame()->RecalcLayout();
    ResizeParentToFit(FALSE);
}

/////////////////////////////////////////////////////////////////////
// CMainView message handlers


void CMainView::OnNext()
{
//    Tell the document to get the next record:
    ((CAddbDoc *)GetDocument())->GetNext();
    UpdateData(FALSE);
}

void CMainView::OnPrevious()
{
//    Tell the document to get the previous record:
    ((CAddbDoc *)GetDocument())->GetPrevious();
    UpdateData(FALSE);
}
```

The first change is to include the header file for the document class, which is necessary because we must access member functions and variables found in both the document class and the **CState** class object within the document class:

```
#include "addbdoc.h"
```

It's necessary to link with the form's output controls the variables in which **CStateSet** stores the current record's data columns. This is done in the **DoDataExchange()** function. Because we'll be accessing data objects that are outside the view class, we can't use ClassWizard to create the linkage. Instead, we must create the **DDX_Text()** function calls ourselves. The **DDX_Text()** function is overloaded to transfer the data types shown in the following list:

- **BYTE**: A pointer to an unsigned 8-bit value.
- **int**: A pointer to a signed 16-bit value.
- **UINT**: A pointer to an unsigned 16-bit value.
- **long**: A pointer to a signed 32-bit value.
- **DWORD**: A pointer to an unsigned 32-bit value.
- **CString**: A pointer to a **CString** type object.

- **float**: A pointer to a 32-bit floating-point value.
- **double**: A pointer to a 64-bit floating-point value.

There are other **DDX_...()** functions to interface with dialog controls other than text type. See the AFXDD_.H include file for a list of these **DDX_...()** functions.

In ADDB, all of our variables are of standard types (character, integer, or floating-point). We can use calls to **DDX_Text()** for each:

```
void CMainView::DoDataExchange(CDataExchange* pDX)
{
    CFormView::DoDataExchange(pDX);
    //{{AFX_DATA_MAP(CMainView)
        // NOTE: ClassWizard will add DDX and DDV calls here
    //}}AFX_DATA_MAP
    // We manually add the DDX_Text() calls since we're
    // using GetDocument() to locate the variables

    DDX_Text(pDX, IDC_FIPS, ((CAddbDoc *)GetDocument())->CState.m_FIPS);
    DDX_Text(pDX, IDC_STATE, ((CAddbDoc *)GetDocument())->CState.m_Name);
    DDX_Text(pDX, IDC_DATA1, ((CAddbDoc *)GetDocument())->CState.m_D1);
    DDX_Text(pDX, IDC_DATA2, ((CAddbDoc *)GetDocument())->CState.m_D2);
    DDX_Text(pDX, IDC_DATA3, ((CAddbDoc *)GetDocument())->CState.m_D3);
    DDX_Text(pDX, IDC_DATA4, ((CAddbDoc *)GetDocument())->CState.m_D4);
    DDX_Text(pDX, IDC_DATA5, ((CAddbDoc *)GetDocument())->CState.m_D5);
    DDX_Text(pDX, IDC_DATA6, ((CAddbDoc *)GetDocument())->CState.m_D6);
    DDX_Text(pDX, IDC_DATA7, ((CAddbDoc *)GetDocument())->CState.m_D7);
}
```

Notice how we specify the variable by using the **GetDocument()** function, which returns a pointer to the current document class, and cast this pointer to be a pointer to a **CAddbDoc** type object. Once this pointer is cast, we can access the **CState** member object. Each of the column variables in **CState** is public, which allows the **DDX_Text()** functions to modify them.

```
void CMainView::OnNext()
{
//    Tell the document to get the next record:
    ((CAddbDoc *)GetDocument())->GetNext();
    UpdateData(FALSE);
}

void CMainView::OnPrevious()
{
//    Tell the document to get the previous record:
    ((CAddbDoc *)GetDocument())->GetPrevious();
    UpdateData(FALSE);
}
```

The final addition to the view class is the addition of two member functions to navigate through the DataSource's records. To add these functions, we use

ClassWizard to create functions for both the Next and Previous buttons. When ClassWizard has created the shell functions, we can add the code to call the document class's record navigation functions.

The changes just outlined show one way to use **CRecordSet** class objects. There are other ways in which the **CRecordSet** class objects can be used.

Reviewing CRecordSet

In review, follow these steps to create and use a **CRecordSet** class object:

1. Use ClassWizard to create a class based on **CRecordSet**. For example, the class created might be called **COurRecordSet**.

2. Add to the appropriate source files the header file created for the **COurRecordSet** class.

3. Open a connection to **COurRecordSet**'s DataSource, and use **CRecordSet**'s functions to work with data in the DataSource.

4. When you're done with the DataSource, close the connection.

The complete ADDB program can be found on the sample source code disk.

THE SQL...() FUNCTIONS

For programs that aren't written in C++, and in which you don't want to include C++ code, you can use the ODBC interface **SQL...()** functions. The **SQL...()** functions also offer functionality that is simply not available in **CRecordSet**-derived objects.

The **SQL...()** functions are listed in Table 18.2. It's beyond the scope of this book to provide a comprehensive reference for each of the **SQL...()** functions, but Table 18.2 provides information about what each function does.

TABLE 18.2. SQL...() FUNCTION DESCRIPTIONS.	
Function	Description
SQLAllocConnect()	Allocates memory for the connection handle in the identified environment.
SQLAllocEnv()	Allocates the environment handle memory. Also initializes the ODBC interface for this

continues

TABLE 18.2. CONTINUED

Function	Description
	application. This function must be called before any other **SQL...()** function is called.
SQLAllocStmt()	Allocates the statement's memory. The statement will be associated with the connection specified.
SQLBindCol()	Assigns storage and the data type for a given column in a result set.
SQLBrowseConnect()	Determines, at runtime, the attributes and their associated values needed to connect to a given DataSource.
SQLCancel()	Cancels a synchronously executing SQL command.
SQLColAttributes()	Returns the attributes (length, name, precision, and so on) for a given column.
SQLColumnPrivileges()	Returns a recordset listing columns and their privileges.
SQLColumns()	Returns a recordset listing the column names for the specified table.
SQLConnect()	Loads the DataSource driver and establishes a connection between the DataSource and the application.
SQLDataSources()	Enumerates available DataSource names.
SQLDescribeCol()	Returns the name, type, and length of the specified column.
SQLDescribeParam()	Returns a description of the specified parameter in a prepared SQL statement.
SQLDisconnect()	Breaks the connection established using **SQLConnect()** or **SQLDriverConnect()**.
SQLDriverConnect()	An extended version of **SQLConnect()** for ODBC drivers that require more information than **SQLConnect()** can provide.

Function	Description
SQLError()	Returns information about any errors that have occurred.
SQLExecDirect()	Executes an SQL statement that is stored in a character string.
SQLExecute()	Executes a prepared SQL statement.
SQLExtendedFetch()	Returns, in arrays, each bound column. The number of rows to be fetched and the first row to be fetched may be specified.
SQLFetch()	Accesses the recordset's data, row by row.
SQLForeignKeys()	Returns a list of column names that are foreign keys.
SQLFreeConnect()	Releases the connection handle and its memory that was allocated using **SQLAllocConnect()**.
SQLFreeEnv()	Releases the environment handle and its memory that was allocated using **SQLAllocEnv()**.
SQLFreeStmt()	Releases the statement handle and its memory that was allocated using **SQLAllocStatement()**.
SQLGetConnectOption()	Retrieves the specified connect option.
SQLGetCursorName()	Returns the cursor name for the specified statement.
SQLGetData()	Gets data from a single column in the current row.
SQLGetFunctions()	Determines whether a given function is available in the specified ODBC driver.
SQLGetInfo()	Returns information about the specified driver and DataSource specified.
SQLGetStmtOption()	Retrieves the current statement option.
SQLGetTypeInfo()	Provides information about which data types are supported by the specified DataSource.
SQLMoreResults()	Determines if more results are available from the statement.

continues

TABLE 18.2. CONTINUED	
Function	*Description*
SQLNativeSql()	Returns the SQL string as translated by the driver.
SQLNumParams()	Returns the number of parameters in an SQL statement.
SQLNumResultCols()	Returns the number of columns in a result set.
SQLParamData()	Provides parameter data for SQL statements at the time of execution.
SQLParamOptions()	Permits an application to provide multiple parameter values.
SQLPrepare()	Prepares an SQL statement for execution.
SQLPrimaryKeys()	Returns the column names for columns that comprise the primary key.
SQLProcedureColumns()	Returns the list of input and output parameters and columns that make up a result set.
SQLProcedures()	Returns the procedure names that are stored in a given DataSource.
SQLPutData()	Sends parameter data to a driver at the time of statement execution.
SQLRowCount()	Returns the count of rows affected by an **UPDATE**, **DELETE**, or **INSERT** operation.
SQLSetConnectOption()	Sets the options for a given connection.
SQLSetCursorName()	Sets a statement's cursor name.
SQLSetParam()	Allows the specification of data type, storage, and length of a parameter marker found in an SQL statement.
SQLSetPos()	Positions a cursor in the block of data that has been fetched.
SQLSetScrollOptions()	Defines the behavior of cursors.
SQLSetStmtOption()	Sets a statement's options.
SQLSpecialColumns()	Returns information about columns that uniquely identify a row and columns that are

Function	Description
	automatically updated when a row's data changes.
SQLStatistics()	Returns information about a table and its indexes.
SQLTablePrivileges()	Returns a list of tables and their associated privileges.
SQLTables()	Returns the tables found in a specified DataSource.
SQLTransact()	Commits or rolls back all pending operations for DataSources that support transactions.

As Table 18.2 shows, there are many **SQL...()** type functions, which can be used to create applications that access different types of DataSources.

Using the SQL...() Functions

The final part of this chapter looks at routines that use the **SQL...()** functions. These routines should serve only as an example of how the **SQL...()** functions are used.

Listing 18.12 shows the **WM_INITDIALOG** handler for a dialog box that displays data from a user-selected DataSource. This dialog box is intended to allow the user to select a column to use in the main program.

LISTING 18.12. THE **WM_INITDIALOG** HANDLER CALLING **SQL...()** FUNCTIONS IN A C PROGRAM.

```c
#define STRICT

#include "STAR.H"

#include <COMMDLG.H>

#include <string.h>
#include <stdlib.h>
#include <io.h>
#include <stdio.h>
#include <float.h>

#include "sql.h"
#include "sqlext.h"
```

continues

LISTING 18.12. CONTINUED

```
/***************************************************************************
**
**        STAR: The Sales Territory Alignment Resource
**
**       TITLE: NEWDATA -
**
**    FUNCTION: The various routines that enable STAR to OPEN its files,
**              as when it's loading an initial problem
**
**
**      INPUTS: Various
**
**     OUTPUTS: Various
**
**     RETURNS: Errors
**
**     WRITTEN: 07-Dec-1993 18:58:42
**
**       CALLS: System, etc.
**
**   CALLED BY: STAR
**
**      AUTHOR: Peter D. Hipson
**
**       NOTES: for WINDOWS 3.1 16-bit
**
**    COPYRIGHT 1989-1994 BY PETER D. HIPSON. All rights reserved.
**
***************************************************************************/

extern LPOFSTRUCT        lpofTempXrefFiles;
extern LPCARTOGRAPHY     lpTempCartography;
extern DATAVARIABLE   huge * lpTempDataVariable;

extern HANDLE hGlobalMemoryXRF;
extern HANDLE hGlobalMemoryCRT;
extern HANDLE hGlobalMemoryDAT;

extern int     nCurrentSelection;
extern char    *szDataFileFilter[];

// Found in ODBC1.C
void    SQLPrintError(HENV henv, HDBC hdbc, HSTMT hstmt);

BOOL FAR PASCAL AccountProc(
    HWND      hDlg,
    unsigned  iMessage,
    WORD      wParam,
    LONG      lParam)
{
BOOL    bCanEnd;
BOOL    bAllColumns = FALSE;
BOOL    bHaveNumbers = FALSE;
```

```
int      i = 0;
int      j = 0;
int      k = 0;
int      l = 0;
static   int      nMax;
WORD     wCtrlID = 0;
WORD     wResult = 0;
HFONT    hFont;
HWND     hCtrl = 0;
DWORD    dwReturn;
PDATAVARODBC      TempDatavarODBC;
//-ODBC variables:
char     szDSN[256];
char     szUID[32];
char     szAuthStr[32];
char     szConStrOut[512];
char     szName[128];
char     szTemp[132];
HENV     henv;
HDBC     hdbc;
HSTMT    hstmt = SQL_NULL_HSTMT;
RETCODE    RC;
char     *     pSQL;
int        nTotalLength;
int        nColumnLength;
int        nNumberColumns;
int        nConStrOut;
int        nType;
long     lReturnLength;
SDWORD     sdReturn;
SWORD     swReturn;

    switch(iMessage)
    {
        case WM_INITDIALOG:
//          Allocate a buffer 4096 bytes long for SQL string
            pSQL = ALLOCP(4096);

            LocateDialog(hDlg);
            hFont = GetStockObject(OEM_FIXED_FONT);
            (VOID)SendDlgItemMessage(hDlg, ID_LISTBOX, WM_SETFONT, (WORD)hFont,
                                (LONG)TRUE);

            CheckDlgButton(hDlg, ID_DESCRIPTION, TRUE);

            bAllColumns = GetPrivateProfileInt(szAppName, "AllDataColumns",
                                    FALSE, szIniFile);

            LoadString(hInst, IDS_UNDEFINED, Info.szBuffer,
                        sizeof(Info.szBuffer));
            SendDlgItemMessage(hDlg, ID_GEOCODE,  CB_ADDSTRING, 0,
                            (LONG)(LPSTR)Info.szBuffer);
            SendDlgItemMessage(hDlg, ID_DATAVALUE, CB_ADDSTRING, 0,
                            (LONG)(LPSTR)Info.szBuffer);
            SendDlgItemMessage(hDlg, ID_ACCOUNTS, CB_ADDSTRING, 0,
                            (LONG)(LPSTR)Info.szBuffer);
```

continues

LISTING 18.12. CONTINUED

```
//          Get the columns in the user's table:

            SQLAllocEnv(&henv);
            SQLAllocConnect(henv, &hdbc);

//          We must include support for userID and passwords:
            sprintf(Info.szBuffer, "DSN=%s",
               lpTempDataVariable[nCurrentSelection].DatavarODBC.szDataSource);
            strcpy(szDSN, Info.szBuffer);
            strcpy(szUID, "UserName");
            strcpy(szAuthStr, "PassWord");

            RC = SQLDriverConnect(hdbc, hWnd,
               (unsigned char far *)szDSN, SQL_NTS,
               (unsigned char far *)szConStrOut, sizeof(szConStrOut),
               (short far *)&nConStrOut, SQL_DRIVER_COMPLETE);

            if (RC != SQL_SUCCESS && RC != SQL_SUCCESS_WITH_INFO)
            {
                CommMessage("SQLDriverConnect   Failed!:");
                 SQLPrintError(henv, hdbc, hstmt);
            }
            else
            {
                CommMessage("SQLDriverConnect() returned szConStrOut[]:");
                CommMessage(szConStrOut);
            }

            RC = SQLAllocStmt(hdbc, &hstmt);
            if (RC != SQL_SUCCESS && RC != SQL_SUCCESS_WITH_INFO)
            {
                CommMessage("SQLAllocStmt   Failed!:");
                SQLPrintError(henv, hdbc, hstmt);
            }

//          Get the columns in the specified table:
            RC = SQLColumns(hstmt,
               (lpTempDataVariable[nCurrentSelection].DatavarODBC.szDataDir[0]
                   == '\0') ? NULL :
               lpTempDataVariable[nCurrentSelection].DatavarODBC.szDataDir,
                   SQL_NTS,    // Qualifiers
               NULL, 0,        // Owners
               lpTempDataVariable[nCurrentSelection].DatavarODBC.szDataTable,
                   SQL_NTS,    // Table name
               NULL, 0);       // All columns

            if (RC != SQL_SUCCESS && RC != SQL_SUCCESS_WITH_INFO)
            {
                CommMessage("SQLColumns   Failed!:");
                CommMessage(lpTempDataVariable[nCurrentSelection].
                            DatavarODBC.szDataTable);
                SQLPrintError(henv, hdbc, hstmt);
            }
```

```
            SQLGetInfo(hdbc, SQL_DBMS_VER, szConStrOut, sizeof(szConStrOut),
                    &swReturn);
            CommMessage(szConStrOut);

//          Now bind variables to columns! Get the name, length,
//          and type of column:
            RC = SQLBindCol(hstmt, 4,  SQL_C_CHAR, szName, sizeof(szName),
                        &lReturnLength);
            RC = SQLBindCol(hstmt, 8,  SQL_C_SHORT, &nColumnLength,
                        sizeof(nColumnLength), &lReturnLength);
            RC = SQLBindCol(hstmt, 5,  SQL_C_SHORT, &nType, sizeof(nType),
                        &lReturnLength);

//          Then fetch the column information:
            Info.szBuffer[0] = '\0';
            nTotalLength = 0;
            while(TRUE)
            {
                RC = SQLFetch(hstmt);
                if (RC == SQL_ERROR ¦¦ RC == SQL_SUCCESS_WITH_INFO)
                {
                    CommMessage("SQLFetch   Failed!:");
                    SQLPrintError(henv, hdbc, hstmt);
                }
                if (RC == SQL_SUCCESS ¦¦ RC == SQL_SUCCESS_WITH_INFO)
                {
                    SendDlgItemMessage(hDlg, ID_GEOCODE       , CB_ADDSTRING,
                                    0, (LONG)(LPSTR)szName);
                    SendDlgItemMessage(hDlg, ID_ACCOUNTS       , CB_ADDSTRING,
                                    0, (LONG)(LPSTR)szName);
//          For ID_DATAVALUE, put in only the columns that are numeric
//          (unless forced):
                    if (bAllColumns ¦¦
                        nType == SQL_DECIMAL ¦¦
                        nType == SQL_NUMERIC ¦¦
                        nType == SQL_SMALLINT ¦¦
                        nType == SQL_TINYINT ¦¦
                        nType == SQL_BIGINT ¦¦
                        nType == SQL_REAL ¦¦
                        nType == SQL_FLOAT ¦¦
                        nType == SQL_DOUBLE)
                    {// We should count the number of columns.
                     // If less than 1, give error message!
                        SendDlgItemMessage(hDlg, ID_DATAVALUE       ,
                        CB_ADDSTRING, 0, (LONG)(LPSTR)szName);
                    }

                    sprintf(szTemp, "%-12.12s_", szName);

                    if (nTotalLength + strlen(szTemp) < sizeof(Info.szBuffer))
                    {
                        nTotalLength += strlen(szTemp);
                        lstrcat(Info.szBuffer, szTemp);
                    }
                    sprintf(szTemp, "%s_ ", szName);
                    strcat(pSQL, szTemp);
                }
```

continues

LISTING 18.12. CONTINUED

```
        else
        {// That's all, folks...
            break;
        }
    }

    SQLFreeStmt(hstmt, SQL_CLOSE);
    SQLFreeStmt(hstmt, SQL_UNBIND);
```

```
//      Add the data window's title line
```

```
    WAddExtentEntry(GetDlgItem(hDlg, ID_LISTBOX), Info.szBuffer);
    SendDlgItemMessage(hDlg, ID_LISTBOX,  LB_ADDSTRING, 0,
                        (LONG)(LPSTR)Info.szBuffer);
    for (i = 0; Info.szBuffer[i]; i++)
    {
        if (Info.szBuffer[i] != '_')
        {
            Info.szBuffer[i] = 'Ä';
        }
    }
    SendDlgItemMessage(hDlg, ID_LISTBOX,  LB_ADDSTRING, 0,
                        (LONG)(LPSTR)Info.szBuffer);
```

```
//      END: Get the columns in the specified table:
```

```
    SendDlgItemMessage(hDlg, ID_LISTBOX,  LB_GETTEXT, 0,
                        (LONG)(LPSTR)Info.szBuffer);
    nNumberColumns = 0;

    for (i = 0; *(pSQL + i); i++)
    {
        if (*(pSQL + i) == '_')
        {
            *(pSQL + i) = ',';
            ++nNumberColumns;
        }
    }
    *(pSQL + (strlen(pSQL) - 1)) = '\0';
    *(pSQL + (strlen(pSQL) - 1)) = '\0';
```

```
//      Get sample of the user's DataSource:
```

```
    strcpy(szConStrOut, "SELECT ");
    strcat(szConStrOut, pSQL);

    szDSN[0] = '\0';

    if (strlen(lpTempDataVariable[nCurrentSelection].
        DatavarODBC.szDataDir) > 0)
    {
        strcat(szDSN,
                lpTempDataVariable[nCurrentSelection].
```

```
                    DatavarODBC.szDataDir);
        strcat(szDSN, "\\");
}

strcpy(Info.szBuffer,
        lpTempDataVariable[nCurrentSelection].
        DatavarODBC.szDataTable);
QuoteName(Info.szBuffer, sizeof(Info.szBuffer));
strcat(szDSN, Info.szBuffer);



strcat(szConStrOut, " FROM ");
strcat(szConStrOut, szDSN);

RC = SQLExecDirect(hstmt, (unsigned char far *)szConStrOut,
                    SQL_NTS);

if (RC != SQL_SUCCESS && RC != SQL_SUCCESS_WITH_INFO)
{
    CommMessage("SQLExecDirect   Failed!:");
    SQLPrintError(henv, hdbc, hstmt);
}
else
{
    for (i = 0; i < nNumberColumns; i++)
    {
        SQLBindCol(hstmt, i + 1, SQL_C_CHAR,
            (unsigned char far *)&szConStrOut[i * 13], 12,
            &sdReturn);
    }

    j = 0;
    while(++j < 100)
    {
        RC = SQLFetch(hstmt);
        if (RC == SQL_ERROR)
        {
            CommMessage("SQLFetch() FAILED!!!!");
            SQLPrintError(henv, hdbc, hstmt);
        }
        if (RC == SQL_SUCCESS || RC == SQL_SUCCESS_WITH_INFO)
        {
            Info.szBuffer[0] = '\0';
            for (i = 0; i < nNumberColumns; i++)
            {
                sprintf(szTemp, "%-12.12s_", &szConStrOut[i * 13]);
                strcat(Info.szBuffer, szTemp);
            }
            WAddExtentEntry(GetDlgItem(hDlg, ID_LISTBOX),
                            Info.szBuffer);

            SendDlgItemMessage(hDlg, ID_LISTBOX, LB_ADDSTRING,
                0, (LONG)(LPSTR)Info.szBuffer);
        }
         else
        {// That's all, folks...
```

continues

LISTING 18.12. CONTINUED

```
            break;
        }
    }
}

SQLFreeStmt(hstmt, SQL_DROP);
SQLDisconnect(hdbc);
SQLFreeConnect(hdbc);
SQLFreeEnv(henv);

FREEP(pSQL);
return(TRUE);
```

Let's take a closer look at how the ODBC DataSource is used in this example. First, it's necessary to initialize the ODBC driver and establish a connection to the DataSource that the user specified. The following code fragment shows the allocation of the environment and the connection. After the environment and connection have been allocated, it's possible to connect to the DataSource. To connect this program, use the **SQLDriverConnect()** function. For DataSources that don't require the flexibility of **SQLDriverConnect()**, the **SQLConnect()** function could be used:

```
        SQLAllocEnv(&henv);
        SQLAllocConnect(henv, &hdbc);

//      We must include support for userID and passwords:
        sprintf(Info.szBuffer, "DSN=%s",
            lpTempDataVariable[nCurrentSelection].DatavarODBC.szDataSource);
        strcpy(szDSN, Info.szBuffer);
        strcpy(szUID, "UserName");
        strcpy(szAuthStr, "PassWord");

        RC = SQLDriverConnect(hdbc, hWnd,
            (unsigned char far *)szDSN, SQL_NTS,
            (unsigned char far *)szConStrOut, sizeof(szConStrOut),
            (short far *)&nConStrOut, SQL_DRIVER_COMPLETE);
```

After the connection to the DataSource is made, if the DataSource's columns are unknown, it's necessary to get information about the columns in the DataSource. To be able to work with a DataSource, you need to allocate a statement whose handle will be passed to other ODBC functions. The **SQLColumns()** function creates a recordset that contains information about each of the columns in the table.

When ODBC has created the recordset containing information about the columns in the table, the application can select which attributes are needed. Each attribute is a column in the result set. The columns of the **SQLColumns()** result set are described in Table 18.3. Notice that because the names shown in the Name column in Table 18.3 aren't `typedefed`, you must use the column number (such as 4, 8, or 5), as the following example shows:

```
RC = SQLBindCol(hstmt, 4,  SQL_C_CHAR, szName, sizeof(szName),
                       &lReturnLength);
        RC = SQLBindCol(hstmt, 8,  SQL_C_SHORT, &nColumnLength,
                       sizeof(nColumnLength), &lReturnLength);
        RC = SQLBindCol(hstmt, 5,  SQL_C_SHORT, &nType, sizeof(nType),
                       &lReturnLength);
```

TABLE 18.3. RESULT SET COLUMNS FOR THE SQLColumns() FUNCTION.

Column Number	Name	SQL Data Type	Description
1	**TABLE_QUALIFIER**	Varchar(128)	Table qualifier identifier. This field is **NULL** if it isn't applicable to the DataSource.
2	**TABLE_OWNER**	Varchar(128)	Table owner identifier. This field is **NULL** if it isn't applicable to the DataSource.
3	**TABLE_NAME**	Varchar(128), not **NULL**	Table name.
4	**COLUMN_NAME**	Varchar(128), not **NULL**	Column name.
5	**DATA_TYPE**	Smallint, not **NULL**	The column's SQL data type.
6	**TYPE_NAME**	Varchar(128), not **NULL**	The column's native data type.
7	**PRECISION**	Integer	The column's precision.

continues

TABLE 18.3. RESULT SET COLUMNS FOR THE `SQLColumns()` FUNCTION.

Column Number	Name	SQL Data Type	Description
8	**LENGTH**	Integer	The column's data length, in bytes. If the column represents numeric data, the returned size may be different than the size as stored in the DataSource.
9	**SCALE**	Smallint	The column's scale.
10	**RADIX**	Smallint	The data's radix, which is either 10 or 2.
11	**NULLABLE**	Smallint, not **NULL**	Is **SQL_NO_NULLS** if the column won't allow **NULL** values or **SQL_NULLABLE** if the column accepts **NULL** values. If it isn't known if the column accepts **NULL** values, **NULLABLE** is **SQL_NULLABLE_UNKNOWN**.
12	**REMARKS**	Varchar(254)	The column's description.

In the code fragment that follows, you see that I've used column numbers 4 (**COLUMN_NAME**), 5 (**DATA_TYPE**), and 8 (**LENGTH**). Are you confused? Here we're using columns in a result set to return information about columns in a table. It's rather confusing that ODBC returns column information for a table in a result set that is itself made up of columns.

```
        RC = SQLAllocStmt(hdbc, &hstmt);
//      Get the columns in the specified table:
```

```
RC = SQLColumns(hstmt,
    (lpTempDataVariable[nCurrentSelection].DatavarODBC.szDataDir[0]
        == '\0') ? NULL :
    lpTempDataVariable[nCurrentSelection].DatavarODBC.szDataDir,
        SQL_NTS,     // Qualifiers
    NULL, 0,         // Owners
    lpTempDataVariable[nCurrentSelection].DatavarODBC.szDataTable,
        SQL_NTS,     // Table name
    NULL, 0);        // All columns

SQLGetInfo(hdbc, SQL_DBMS_VER, szConStrOut, sizeof(szConStrOut),
        &swReturn);

//        Now bind variables to columns! Get the name, length,
//        and type of column:
RC = SQLBindCol(hstmt, 4,  SQL_C_CHAR, szName, sizeof(szName),
                &lReturnLength);
RC = SQLBindCol(hstmt, 8,  SQL_C_SHORT, &nColumnLength,
                sizeof(nColumnLength), &lReturnLength);
RC = SQLBindCol(hstmt, 5,  SQL_C_SHORT, &nType, sizeof(nType),
                &lReturnLength);
```

When the desired columns in the result set have had variables bound to them, the application can then retrieve each row in the result set. Generally, retrieving rows in a result set is done using a **while()** or **do...while()** loop.

The following code fragment shows how to retrieve each of the names of the columns in the result set:

```
while(TRUE)
{
    RC = SQLFetch(hstmt);
    if (RC == SQL_ERROR ¦¦ RC == SQL_SUCCESS_WITH_INFO)
    {
        CommMessage("SQLFetch   Failed!:");
        SQLPrintError(henv, hdbc, hstmt);
    }
    if (RC == SQL_SUCCESS ¦¦ RC == SQL_SUCCESS_WITH_INFO)
    {
//          Work with the information provided
    }
     else
    {// That's all, folks. There is no more information...
        break;
    }
}
```

Your application can use the information that is fetched for a column in the result set by adding code to the if statement at the comment line that reads Work with the information provided.

The last two chapters cover each of the different aspects of interfacing with an ODBC DataSource.

SUMMARY

This chapter presented methods of accessing ODBC DataSources. The following methods were discussed:

- The use of MFC's **CDatabase**, **CRecordView**, and **CRecordSet** classes
- The use of the SQL library's **SQL...()** functions

CONNECTING TO DIFFERENT DATASOURCES

Using ODBC to access a DataSource is an excellent resource for the programmer. However, it's also necessary for the programmer to know about the different DataSources that can be used with the application, and how to work with each different DataSource.

If you're writing an application that will access only a single ODBC DataSource, you probably can skip this chapter. Programs that access a single DataSource are best created using AppWizard. This chapter is intended to assist programmers whose applications will access a variety of different ODBC DataSources. An example of such an application is the MSQuery program provided by Microsoft.

DataSources come in many flavors. This chapter discusses those that are provided with the stock set of ODBC drivers. Drivers are available for a vast number of other DataSources (with new drivers being introduced constantly), in case you have an application that must access a DataSource that isn't supported by the stock Microsoft ODBC driver set.

DataSources range from complex SQL servers, in which the data may be accessed by many users at the same time, to simple text files. Here are some of the more common formats for DataSources:

- Remote DataSources, which are provided by a server. Typically, SQL servers and Oracle servers are remote DataSources. Other common servers include DataSources provided using IBM's AS/400 systems. The application, the user, and often the programmer never see the actual DataSource; instead, they see it as an abstract set of records and rules.

- Local DataSources, which are either found on the user's machine or shared over a network. Access to the DataSource isn't routed through a database server; it's provided by the operating system. Local Data-Sources can be divided into two broad categories:

  Single-file DataSources, in which the table or tables, the information about the DataSource, and usually the DataSource's indexes are found in a single file. An example of a single-file DataSource is a Microsoft Access database.

  Multifile DataSources, in which each table is a separate file. Each index also often occupies a file. Examples of multifile DataSources include dBASE and text format files.

ODBC can gather a certain amount of information about each DataSource. For DataSources that were produced using database programs (for example, dBASE or Access), the ODBC drivers can determine information such as table names, column names, and column data types.

For a text-based DataSource that hasn't been previously installed, ODBC can guess at the column names and column data types. If the text-based DataSource has been installed, ODBC can determine information about the columns. For many of the multifile-based DataSources, the table name usually is the same as the filename.

The ODBC driver manager provides a method for listing DataSources, using the **SQLDriverConnect()** function and passing an empty string for the **DSN** parameter. **SQLDriverConnect()** then displays the SQL Data Sources dialog box (see Figure 19.1). This dialog box enables the user to select any DataSource that has been installed on his or her system.

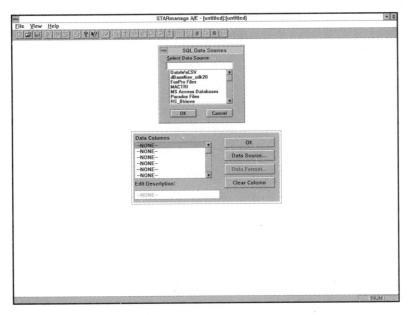

Figure 19.1. The SQL Data Sources dialog box.

After selecting a DataSource, the user must select a table. Usually, a table is a database table or, for text files, a specific text format data file.

To select a table from a DataSource, the user must be presented with a list of available tables. While ODBC provides table names for all DataSources, including text format sources, many applications extend the text table selection (using either **GetOpenFileName()** or a **CFileDialog** class object) to allow selection of text tables located outside the default directory. You should decide whether to support changing directories when the user is selecting tables in a text DataSource.

GETTING THE DATASOURCE NAME

To get a DataSource name, the user must be presented with a list of DataSources to select from. The easiest way to present this list is to allow the **SQLDriverConnect()** function to display it in a dialog box.

An example of the code that performs this by creating a simple DataSource open function is shown in Listing 19.1.

LISTING 19.1. THE GetODBC() FUNCTION (ODBC2.CPP).

```
//   ODBC2.CPP

#include "stdafx.h"
#include <afxdb.h>

#include "sql.h"
#include "sqlext.h"
#include <stdio.h>
#include <stdlib.h>
#include <string.h>
#include <commdlg.h>
#include "odbctabl.h"
#include "odbcinfo.h"

/******************************************************************************
**
**          STAR: The Sales Territory Alignment Resource.
**
**         TITLE: ODBC2.cpp
**
**      FUNCTION: Open DataBase Connectivity interface code
**
**
**        INPUTS: VARIOUS
**
**       OUTPUTS: VARIOUS
**
**       RETURNS: YES
**
**       WRITTEN: 17 March 1994
**
**         CALLS: ODBC routines: SQL...()
**
**     CALLED BY: Things that need data from databases
**
**        AUTHOR: Peter D. Hipson
**
**         NOTES: Win 3.11 and later.
**
**     COPYRIGHT 1994 BY PETER D. HIPSON. All rights reserved.
**
*******************************************************************************/
```

```
// Static, for this module only:


// Functions (may be shared):


// Shared data objects, not otherwise allocated:


// Routines:

BOOL GetODBC(
    char * szDataSource,
    int    nDataSourceSize,
    char * szDataTable,
    int    nDataTableSize,
    char * szDataDir,
    int    nDataDirSize)
{
BOOL        bReturnCode = TRUE;

    CODBCInfo    COdbcInfo;

    COdbcInfo.GetInfo();

    TRACE("At the *very* end: Datasource '%s' ", COdbcInfo.m_DataSourceName);
    TRACE(" table '%s'\n",    COdbcInfo.m_DataTableName);

    if (szDataSource != NULL)
    {// User wants the datasource name
        if (COdbcInfo.m_DataSourceName.GetLength() < nDataSourceSize)
        {
            strcpy(szDataSource, COdbcInfo.m_DataSourceName);
        }
        else
        {
            szDataSource[0] = '\0';
            bReturnCode = FALSE;
        }
    }

    if (szDataTable != NULL)
    {// User wants the DataTable name
        if (COdbcInfo.m_DataTableName.GetLength() < nDataTableSize)
        {
            strcpy(szDataTable, COdbcInfo.m_DataTableName);
        }
        else
        {
            szDataTable[0] = '\0';
            bReturnCode = FALSE;
        }
    }

    if (szDataDir != NULL)
```

continues

LISTING 19.1. CONTINUED

```
    {// User wants the DataTable directory name
        if (COdbcInfo.m_DataTableDir.GetLength() < nDataTableSize)
        {
            strcpy(szDataDir, COdbcInfo.m_DataTableDir);
        }
        else
        {
            szDataDir[0] = '\0';
            bReturnCode = FALSE;
        }
    }

// And return either success or failure
    return(bReturnCode);
}
```

The GetODBC() function is quite simple. It creates a **CODBCInfo** class object
(**COdbcInfo**) and then calls the **GetInfo()** member function. When **GetInfo()**
returns, the szDataSource, szDataTable, and szDataDir passed buffers are filled
in. Checks are made to ensure that these passed buffers aren't too short for the
information that will be stored in them. If the passed buffers are too small, the
buffer isn't saved and the function returns false.

Listing 19.2 shows the code for the **GetInfo()** function that does the real work.
This function is called from the GetODBC() function that was shown in Listing
19.1.

LISTING 19.2. THE CODBCInfo::GetInfo() FUNCTION (ODBCINFO.CPP).

```
//   ODBCINFO.CPP

#include "stdafx.h"
#include <afxdb.h>
#include "STAR.H"

#include "sql.h"
#include "sqlext.h"
#include "odbcinfo.h"
#include <stdio.h>
#include <stdlib.h>
#include <string.h>
#include <commdlg.h>
#include "odbctabl.h"

/*****************************************************************************
**
**      STAR: The Sales Territory Alignment Resource.
**
```

```
**       TITLE: CODBCInfo
**
**    FUNCTION: Open DataBase Connectivity interface code
**
**
**      INPUTS: VARIOUS
**
**     OUTPUTS: VARIOUS
**
**     RETURNS: YES
**
**     WRITTEN: 17 March 1994
**
**       CALLS: ODBC routines: SQL...()
**
**   CALLED BY: Things that need data from databases
**
**      AUTHOR: Peter D. Hipson
**
**       NOTES: Win 3.11 and later.
**
**   COPYRIGHT 1994 BY PETER D. HIPSON. All rights reserved.
**
****************************************************************************/

// Static, for this module only:


// Shared data objects, not otherwise allocated:


// Routines:

// Construction

CODBCInfo::CODBCInfo()
{// Initialize variables, etc.

    m_Synonyms = TRUE;
    m_SystemTables = TRUE;
    m_Tables = TRUE;
    m_Views = TRUE;
}

void CODBCInfo::GetInfo()
{
HSTMT        hstmt = SQL_NULL_HSTMT;
char         szConStrOut[256];
SWORD        swReturn;
CString       CDBType;
RETCODE       RC;

    TRACE("CODBCInfo::GetInfo(), gets ODBC datasource and table name!\n");

    if (!m_CDodbc.Open(m_TableInfo))
    {//User selected cancel; go home; no more playing for 'im.
      return;
```

continues

LISTING 19.2. CONTINUED

```
    }

    m_DatabaseName = m_CDodbc.GetDatabaseName();
    TRACE("Our database is %s \n", m_DatabaseName);
    m_Connect = m_CDodbc.GetConnect();
    TRACE("Our Connect is %s \n", m_Connect);

    m_CanUpdate = m_CDodbc.CanUpdate();
    m_CanTransact = m_CDodbc.CanTransact();

// C++'s MFC CRecordSet() class is a bit too inflexible to
// really work well with an undefined database. Therefore,
// we simply break into the older API (SQL...()) calls.

    RC = SQLGetInfo(m_CDodbc.m_hdbc, SQL_DATA_SOURCE_NAME, szConStrOut,
        sizeof(szConStrOut), &swReturn);

    m_DataSourceName = szConStrOut;

    TRACE("STATUS: After SQL_DATA_SOURCE_NAME\n");

// Lines below are simply for debugging and the programmer's information:
//
//      TRACE("Datasoure: '%s'\n", m_DataSourceName);
//      SQLGetInfo(m_CDodbc.m_hdbc, SQL_DRIVER_NAME, szConStrOut,
//          sizeof(szConStrOut), &swReturn);
//      TRACE("1 %s\n", szConStrOut);
//      SQLGetInfo(m_CDodbc.m_hdbc, SQL_DRIVER_VER, szConStrOut,
//          sizeof(szConStrOut), &swReturn);
//      TRACE("2 %s\n", szConStrOut);
//      SQLGetInfo(m_CDodbc.m_hdbc, SQL_ODBC_VER, szConStrOut,
//          sizeof(szConStrOut), &swReturn);
//      TRACE("3 %s\n", szConStrOut);
//      SQLGetInfo(m_CDodbc.m_hdbc, SQL_SERVER_NAME, szConStrOut,
//          sizeof(szConStrOut), &swReturn);
//      TRACE("4 %s\n", szConStrOut);
//      SQLGetInfo(m_CDodbc.m_hdbc, SQL_DATABASE_NAME, szConStrOut,
//          sizeof(szConStrOut), &swReturn);
//      TRACE("5 %s\n", szConStrOut);
//      SQLGetInfo(m_CDodbc.m_hdbc, SQL_DBMS_VER, szConStrOut,
//          sizeof(szConStrOut), &swReturn);
//      TRACE("6 %s\n", szConStrOut);
//
// Once a DataSource is provided, we need to get the TABLE that
// the user will want. If the DataSource is a text file, we use
// a CFileDialog object (with modifications...).

    SQLGetInfo(m_CDodbc.m_hdbc, SQL_DBMS_NAME,
        szConStrOut, sizeof(szConStrOut), &swReturn);

    TRACE("After SQL_DBMS_NAME\n");
    CDBType = szConStrOut;

//      TRACE("%s\n", CDBType);
```

```
//      SQL_SUCCESS, SQL_SUCCESS_WITH_INFO , SQL_ERROR or
//   SQL_INVALID_HANDLE.

    if (CDBType == "TEXT")
    {// Data type is text
        CFileDialog dlg(TRUE, "txt", NULL,
            OFN_FILEMUSTEXIST ¦ OFN_HIDEREADONLY,
            "CSV Files (*.csv)¦*.csv¦"
            "Text Files (*.txt)¦*.txt¦"
            "Data Files (*.dat)¦*.dat¦"
            "¦");

// Patch to use our dialog box template:
        dlg.m_ofn.hInstance = AfxGetInstanceHandle();
        dlg.m_ofn.lpTemplateName = MAKEINTRESOURCE(TABLESELECT);
        dlg.m_ofn.Flags ¦= OFN_ENABLETEMPLATE;

        if (dlg.DoModal() == IDOK)
        {
            m_DataTableName = dlg.GetPathName();
            int nPosition = m_DataTableName.ReverseFind('\\');
            if (nPosition > 0)
            {
// Get directory
                m_DataTableDir = m_DataTableName.Left(nPosition);
// Get filename
                m_DataTableName = m_DataTableName.Mid(nPosition + 1);
            }

            TRACE("IN IDOK ODBCINFO.CPP, table is '%s' ", m_DataTableName);
            TRACE("Dir is '%s' \n", m_DataTableDir);
        }
    }
    else
    {// Data type is not text; possibly Access, dBASE, or FoxPRO
     // (but could be others)
        CODBCTable OTDlg;

        OTDlg.m_Synonyms = m_Synonyms;
        OTDlg.m_SystemTables = m_SystemTables;
        OTDlg.m_Tables = m_Tables;
        OTDlg.m_Views = m_Views;
        OTDlg.m_CDB = &m_CDodbc;

        if (OTDlg.DoModal() == IDOK)
        {
            m_DataTableName = OTDlg.m_TableName;

            TRACE("IN IDOK ODBCINFO.CPP, table is '%s' ", m_DataTableName);
            TRACE(" and '%s'\n", OTDlg.m_TableName);
        }
    }
}

void    CODBCInfo::PrintError(HENV henv, HDBC hdbc, HSTMT hstmt)
{
```

continues

LISTING 19.2. CONTINUED

```
RETCODE RC;
char    szSqlState[256];
char    szErrorMsg[256];
SDWORD    pfNativeError;
SWORD    pcbErrorMsg;

    RC = SQLError(
        henv,
        hdbc,
        hstmt,
        (UCHAR FAR*)szSqlState,
        &pfNativeError,
        (UCHAR FAR*)szErrorMsg,
        sizeof(szErrorMsg),
        &pcbErrorMsg);

    TRACE("SQL ERROR:\n");
    if (RC == SQL_SUCCESS || RC == SQL_SUCCESS_WITH_INFO)
    {
        TRACE("%s\n", szSqlState);
        TRACE("%s\n", szErrorMsg);
    }
    else
    {
        TRACE("%s\n", "SQLError() returned an error!!!");
    }
}

#ifdef DONOTCOMPILE

// A typical SQL-type query (from Microsoft's Student Registration example):

SELECT
DYNABIND_SECTION.CourseID,
DYNABIND_SECTION.InstructorID,
DYNABIND_SECTION.LabSchedule,
DYNABIND_SECTION.LabRoomNo,
DYNABIND_SECTION.SectionNo,
DYNABIND_SECTION.Schedule
FROM DYNABIND_SECTION DYNABIND_SECTION
ORDER BY DYNABIND_SECTION.LabRoomNo

#endif
```

Notice that in `GetInfo()` we check to see what the ODBC database type is. If it's **TEXT**, we create a **CFileDialog** object and use it to get the name of the desired table. If, however, the database type isn't **TEXT**, we create an object of the CODBCTable class. This object lists for the user the tables in the DataSource.

As you should know, C++ classes rely greatly on the header file. The header for ODBCINFO.CPP is shown in Listing 19.3. This listing shows the member variables and the function prototypes.

LISTING 19.3. ODBCINFO.CPP'S HEADER FILE (ODBCINFO.H).

```
// odbctabl.h: header file
//

///////////////////////////////////////////////////////////////////////////////
// CODBCTable dialog

class CODBCInfo
{
// Construction
public:
                CODBCInfo();      // Standard constructor
    void        GetInfo();

// Next n objects are for initializing (generally by caller):
    BOOL        m_Synonyms;       // List synonym tables
    BOOL        m_SystemTables;   // List system tables
    BOOL        m_Tables;         // List normal tables
    BOOL        m_Views;          // List view tables
    CDatabase   m_CDodbc;         // The CDatabase object used
    CString     m_TableInfo;      // Database name to pass to m_CDodbc.Open()

//    Next n objects are for returning information to the caller:
    CString     m_DataSourceName; // User's returned DataSource name.
                                  // If null, no go.
    CString     m_DataTableName;  // User's returned table name.
                                  // If null, no go.
    CString     m_DataTableDir;   // User's returned table directory
                                  // for TEXT files
    BOOL        m_CanUpdate;      // If TRUE, the database can be updated
    BOOL        m_CanTransact;    // If TRUE, the database
                                  // supports transactions
    CString     m_DatabaseName;   // User's database name
                                  // (usually != m_DataSourceName)
    CString     m_Connect;        // Connect string (DSN, DBQ, FIL, etc.)
// End of public stuff...

private:
// Data used internally. Keep private.

// Functions called by us, not externally:

    void        PrintError(HENV henv, HDBC hdbc, HSTMT hstmt);

};
```

GETTING A TABLE NAME

In our sample program, we use two methods to prompt the user for table names. If the DataSource is text format, we use a slightly modified **CFileDialog** object. If the DataSource is not text format, we use an object based on our CODBCTable class.

Table Names for a Text Format DataSource

For DataSources that are text-based, we use a **CFileDialog** object with a custom dialog box template. Figure 19.2 shows our custom template, which simply has minor changes to the titles of the dialog box and the tables list box.

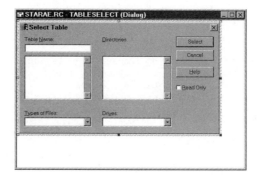

Figure 19.2. The custom template for ***CFileDialog*** *to select tables.*

To use this customized dialog box with a **CFileDialog** object, we must tell the **CFileDialog** object which dialog box template to use. The **CFileDialog** object has an **OFN** structure as a member variable. The **OFN** structure enables you to specify the dialog template and other options (check out the Visual C++ help topic for **CFileDialog**). **CFileDialog** must know the program's instance handle, which is returned by the **AfxGetInstanceHandle()** function, as well as the dialog box's identifier. In addition, the **OFN** structure's flags must include the flag to enable a custom dialog box (**OFN_ENABLETEMPLATE**). This process is shown in the following code fragment:

```
CFileDialog dlg(TRUE, "txt", NULL,
    OFN_FILEMUSTEXIST | OFN_HIDEREADONLY,
    "CSV Files (*.csv)|*.csv|"
    "Text Files (*.txt)|*.txt|"
    "Data Files (*.dat)|*.dat|"
    "|");
```

```
// Patch to use our dialog box template:
    dlg.m_ofn.hInstance = AfxGetInstanceHandle();
    dlg.m_ofn.lpTemplateName = MAKEINTRESOURCE(TABLESELECT);
    dlg.m_ofn.Flags |= OFN_ENABLETEMPLATE;

    if (dlg.DoModal() == IDOK)
    { //...
```

Table Names for a Nontext Format DataSource

For DataSources that aren't text-based, we call our own dialog function to list the tables in a given DataSource. This allows us to format the display in whatever manner we choose. I initially used the table selection dialog in the Microsoft application MSQUERY as an example. I found MSQUERY's two-tiered dialog (with a dialog for selecting the table to be used and a second nested dialog for setting options) too cumbersome, so I combined the two dialog boxes into one. Figure 19.3 shows the table selection dialog box that `CODBCTable` uses.

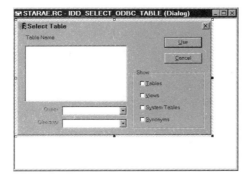

Figure 19.3. `CODBCTable`'s table selection dialog.

The table selection dialog is managed by a `CODBCTable` class object. The process of creating, initializing, and displaying this dialog is shown in the code fragment that follows. In our example, we retain the initial values of the four check boxes (synonyms, system tables, views, and tables) and pass the retained values to the dialog box. We also pass a pointer to our **CDatabase** object that has been opened for the user-specified DataSource:

```
    CODBCTable OTDlg;
 // Initialize the check boxes
    OTDlg.m_Synonyms = m_Synonyms;
    OTDlg.m_SystemTables = m_SystemTables;
    OTDlg.m_Tables = m_Tables;
    OTDlg.m_Views = m_Views;
 // Pass a pointer to the CDatabase object
```

```
OTDlg.m_CDB = &m_CDodbc;

if (OTDlg.DoModal() == IDOK)
{
    m_DataTableName = OTDlg.m_TableName;

    m_Synonyms = OTDlg.m_Synonyms;
    m_SystemTables = OTDlg.m_SystemTables;
    m_Tables = OTDlg.m_Tables;
    m_Views = OTDlg.m_Views;
  // Debugging output for the programmer:

    TRACE("IN IDOK ODBCINFO.CPP, table is '%s' ", m_DataTableName);
    TRACE(" and '%s'\n", OTDlg.m_TableName);
}
```

The dialog box displayed by CODBCTable poses an interesting problem. Whenever the user changes the state of any of the four check boxes (Synonyms,
System Tables, Views, and Tables), the dialog box must change the contents
of the Tables list box. This process consists of handlers for the four check boxes
and a single function that queries the DataSource for table names. When the
DataSource is queried for table names (using SQLTables()), there is a parameter
to specify which table types are to be returned. Listing 19.4 shows the listing for
ODBCTABL.CPP.

LISTING 19.4. LISTING TABLES IN A DATASOURCE (ODBCTABL.CPP).

```
// odbctabl.cpp: implementation file
//

#include "stdafx.h"
#include <afxdb.h>
#include "starae.h"
#include "sql.h"
#include "sqlext.h"
#include "odbctabl.h"

#ifdef _DEBUG
#undef THIS_FILE
static char BASED_CODE THIS_FILE[] = __FILE__;
#endif


/////////////////////////////////////////////////////////////////////////////
// CODBCTable dialog


CODBCTable::CODBCTable(CWnd* pParent /*=NULL*/)
    : CDialog(CODBCTable::IDD, pParent)
{
    //{{AFX_DATA_INIT(CODBCTable)
```

```
    m_Synonyms = FALSE;
    m_SystemTables = FALSE;
    m_Tables = FALSE;
    m_Views = FALSE;
    //}}AFX_DATA_INIT
}

void CODBCTable::DoDataExchange(CDataExchange* pDX)
{
    CDialog::DoDataExchange(pDX);
    //{{AFX_DATA_MAP(CODBCTable)
    DDX_Control(pDX, IDC_SYNONYMS, m_CSynonyms);
    DDX_Control(pDX, IDC_VIEWS, m_CViews);
    DDX_Control(pDX, IDC_TABLES, m_CTables);
    DDX_Control(pDX, IDC_SYSTEM_TABLES, m_CSystemTables);
    DDX_Control(pDX, IDC_LIST1, m_TableList);
    DDX_Check(pDX, IDC_SYNONYMS, m_Synonyms);
    DDX_Check(pDX, IDC_SYSTEM_TABLES, m_SystemTables);
    DDX_Check(pDX, IDC_TABLES, m_Tables);
    DDX_Check(pDX, IDC_VIEWS, m_Views);
    //}}AFX_DATA_MAP
}

BEGIN_MESSAGE_MAP(CODBCTable, CDialog)
    //{{AFX_MSG_MAP(CODBCTable)
    ON_BN_CLICKED(IDC_SYNONYMS, OnSynonyms)
    ON_BN_CLICKED(IDC_SYSTEM_TABLES, OnSystemTables)
    ON_BN_CLICKED(IDC_TABLES, OnTables)
    ON_BN_CLICKED(IDC_VIEWS, OnViews)
    //}}AFX_MSG_MAP
END_MESSAGE_MAP()


/////////////////////////////////////////////////////////////////////////////
// CODBCTable message handlers

BOOL CODBCTable::OnInitDialog()
{
    CDialog::OnInitDialog();

// LocateDialog() centers dialog in parent's window
    LocateDialog(m_hWnd);

    m_TableList.SetTabStops(75);
    LoadTableList();
    return TRUE;  // Return TRUE unless you set the focus to a control
}

void CODBCTable::LoadTableList()
{
HSTMT    hstmt = SQL_NULL_HSTMT;
long     lReturnLength;
int      i;
SWORD    swReturn;
RETCODE  RC;
char     szQualifier[128];
```

continues

LISTING 19.4. CONTINUED

```
char     szOwner[128];
char     szName[128];
char     szType[128];
char     szConStrOut[256];
char     szRemarks[254];

    RC = SQLAllocStmt(m_CDB->m_hdbc, &hstmt);

    if (RC != SQL_SUCCESS && RC != SQL_SUCCESS_WITH_INFO)
    {
        TRACE("SQLAllocStmt() FAILED!!!!\n");
        PrintError(SQL_NULL_HENV, m_CDB->m_hdbc, hstmt);
    }

    RC = SQLTables (hstmt,
        (unsigned char far *)"%", SQL_NTS, (unsigned char far *)"", 0,
        (unsigned char far *)"", 0, (unsigned char far *)"", 0);

    SQLFreeStmt(hstmt, SQL_CLOSE);
    SQLFreeStmt(hstmt, SQL_UNBIND);

    SQLGetInfo(m_CDB->m_hdbc, SQL_MAX_OWNER_NAME_LEN, &i,
        sizeof(int), &swReturn);
    TRACE("maxownernamelen = %d\n", i);

    szRemarks[0] = '\0';
    if (m_CTables.GetCheck() == 1)
    {
        strcat(szRemarks, "'TABLE'");
    }
    if (m_CSystemTables.GetCheck() == 1)
    {
        if (strlen(szRemarks) > 0)
            strcat(szRemarks, ", ");

        strcat(szRemarks, "'SYSTEM TABLE'");
    }
    if (m_CViews.GetCheck() == 1)
    {
        if (strlen(szRemarks) > 0)
            strcat(szRemarks, ", ");

        strcat(szRemarks, "'VIEW'");
    }
    if (m_CSynonyms.GetCheck() == 1)
    {
        if (strlen(szRemarks) > 0)
            strcat(szRemarks, ", ");

        strcat(szRemarks, "'SYNONYM'");
    }
    TRACE("Listing tables: '%s' \n", szRemarks);

    RC = SQLTables(hstmt,
        NULL, SQL_NTS,    // Table qualifier
```

```
        NULL, SQL_NTS,    // Table owner
        NULL, SQL_NTS,    // Table name
        (unsigned char far *)szRemarks, strlen(szRemarks));


    if (RC != SQL_SUCCESS && RC != SQL_SUCCESS_WITH_INFO)
    {
        CommMessage("SQLTables() FAILED!!!!\n");
        PrintError(SQL_NULL_HENV, m_CDB->m_hdbc, hstmt);
    }

    SQLGetInfo(m_CDB->m_hdbc, SQL_DBMS_VER, szConStrOut,
        sizeof(szConStrOut), &swReturn);

    TRACE("%s\n", szConStrOut);

// Now bind variables to columns!

    RC = SQLBindCol(hstmt, 1, SQL_C_CHAR, szQualifier,
        sizeof(szQualifier), &lReturnLength);
    RC = SQLBindCol(hstmt, 2, SQL_C_CHAR, szOwner,
        sizeof(szOwner), &lReturnLength);
    RC = SQLBindCol(hstmt, 3, SQL_C_CHAR, szName,
        sizeof(szName), &lReturnLength);
    RC = SQLBindCol(hstmt, 4, SQL_C_CHAR, szType,
        sizeof(szType), &lReturnLength);
    RC = SQLBindCol(hstmt, 5, SQL_C_CHAR, szRemarks,
        sizeof(szRemarks), &lReturnLength);

// Then get the table names:
    m_TableList.ResetContent();

    while(TRUE)
    {
        RC = SQLFetch(hstmt);
        if (RC == SQL_ERROR ¦¦ RC == SQL_SUCCESS_WITH_INFO)
        {
            TRACE("SQLFetch() FAILED!!!!\n");
            PrintError(SQL_NULL_HENV, m_CDB->m_hdbc, hstmt);
        }
        if (RC == SQL_SUCCESS ¦¦ RC == SQL_SUCCESS_WITH_INFO)
        {
            sprintf(szRemarks, "%s\t%s", szType, szName);
            TRACE("'%s'\n", szRemarks);
            m_TableList.AddString(szRemarks);
        }
        else
        {// That's all, folks...
            break;
        }
    }

    m_TableList.SetCurSel(0);

    SQLFreeStmt(hstmt, SQL_CLOSE);
    SQLFreeStmt(hstmt, SQL_UNBIND);
```

continues

LISTING 19.4. CONTINUED

```
    SQLFreeStmt(hstmt, SQL_DROP);
}

void CODBCTable::OnSynonyms()
{
    // TODO: Add your control notification handler code here
     LoadTableList();
}

void CODBCTable::OnSystemTables()
{
    // TODO: Add your control notification handler code here
     LoadTableList();
}

void CODBCTable::OnTables()
{
    // TODO: Add your control notification handler code here
     LoadTableList();
}

void CODBCTable::OnViews()
{
    // TODO: Add your control notification handler code here
     LoadTableList();
}

void CODBCTable::OnOK()
{
CString        TempString;
    // TODO: Add extra validation here
    m_TableList.GetText(m_TableList.GetCurSel(), TempString);

// Get everything after the tab...
    m_TableName    = TempString.Mid(TempString.Find('\t') + 1);

    TRACE("OK in ODBCTABL.CPP '%s'\n", m_TableName);

    CDialog::OnOK();
}

void    CODBCTable::PrintError(HENV henv, HDBC hdbc, HSTMT hstmt)
{
RETCODE RC;
char    szSqlState[256];
char    szErrorMsg[256];
SDWORD    pfNativeError;
SWORD    pcbErrorMsg;

    RC = SQLError(henv, hdbc, hstmt,
        (UCHAR FAR*)szSqlState,
        &pfNativeError,
        (UCHAR FAR*)szErrorMsg,
        sizeof(szErrorMsg),
        &pcbErrorMsg);
```

```
    TRACE("SQL ERROR:\n");
    if (RC == SQL_SUCCESS || RC == SQL_SUCCESS_WITH_INFO)
    {
        TRACE("%s\n", szSqlState);
        TRACE("%s\n", szErrorMsg);
    }
    else
    {
        TRACE("%s\n", "SQLError() returned an error!!!");
    }
}
```

Notice that the CODBCTable class creates a dialog box that has a list box to display the table names for the user to select from.

You might wonder why we didn't just use a CODBCTable class object for DataSources that are of the TEXT format. Actually, we could have quite easily. However, by using a CFileDialog class object, we allow the user to change directories and save ourselves from writing a great deal of code to support directory management. Because the CFileDialog class has this directory support built in, we can use it. If the users can change directories, they don't have to define multiple text-based DataSources that would be identical except for the directory in which the tables were located.

SUMMARY

This chapter presented a method to access both a DataSource and tables within the DataSource. The following topics were discussed:

- Getting the DataSource's name using a call to **SQLDriverConnect()**.
- Getting the names of tables in a text-based DataSource using a **CFileDialog**-based object.
- Getting the names of tables in a non-text–based DataSource. We access table names using an object based on our CODBCTable class.

OBTAINING INFORMATION ABOUT DRIVERS

Four ODBC `SQL...()` functions are used to return information about drivers and DataSources:

- `SQLDataSources()`: Provides a list of available DataSources.
- `SQLGetInfo()`: Returns information about a specific DataSource and driver.
- `SQLGetFunctions()`: Returns information about which `SQL...()` functions a given driver supports.
- `SQLGetTypeInfo()`: Allows the application to determine which data types a given DataSource supports.

This chapter documents each of these four functions and describes their uses.

SQLDataSources( )

The **SQLDataSources()** function is an extension level 2 function that is implemented by the driver manager and that returns the information found in the ODBC.INI file (or the Windows registry, depending on which version of Windows you're using).

As an example, if your ODBC.INI file is like mine (see Listing 20.1), **SQLDataSources()** returns the output shown in Table 20.1.

LISTING 20.1. A TYPICAL ODBC.INI FILE.

```
; -----------------------------------------------------------------------
; WARNING:  Do not make changes to this file without using the ODBC Control
;           panel device or other utilities provided for maintaining data
;           sources.
;
;           Incorrect changes to this file could prevent ODBC from
;           operating or operating correctly.
; -----------------------------------------------------------------------

[ODBC Data Sources]
Student Registration=Access Data (*.mdb)
MS Access Databases=Access Data (*.mdb)
FoxPro Files=FoxPro Files (*.dbf)
Paradox Files=Paradox Files (*.db )
MACTRI=Access Data (*.mdb)
StarDatabase files=Access Data (*.mdb)
STARmanager dBase Output=dBase Files (*.dbf)
RS_dBase=dBase Files (*.dbf)
RS_FoxPro=FoxPro Files (*.dbf)
RS_Excel=Excel Files (*.xls)
RS_Paradox=Paradox Files (*.db )
RS_MS_Access=Access Data (*.mdb)
RS_Text=Text Files (*.txt; *.csv)
RS_Btrieve=Btrieve Data (file.ddf)
dBaseNav_sdk20=dBase Nav Enabled Test Driver
Sample_sdk20=Template Sample Driver
DataWaCSV=Text Files (*.txt; *.csv)
States=Text Files (*.txt; *.csv)

[Student Registration]
Driver=C:\WINDOWS\SYSTEM\simba.dll
FileType=RedISAM
DataDirectory=D:\MSVC15\MFC\SAMPLES\ENROLL\STDREG.MDB
SingleUser=False
UseSystemDB=False

[MS Access Databases]
Driver=C:\WINDOWS\SYSTEM\SIMBA.DLL
FileType=RedISAM
SingleUser=False
UseSystemDB=False
```

```
[FoxPro Files]
Driver=C:\WINDOWS\SYSTEM\SIMBA.DLL
FileType=FoxPro 2.5
SingleUser=False

[Paradox Files]
Driver=C:\WINDOWS\SYSTEM\SIMBA.DLL
FileType=Paradox
SingleUser=False

[ODBC]
TraceAutoStop=0
Trace=1
TraceFile=E:\NEWSTAR\ODBC.LOG

[MACTRI]
Driver=C:\WINDOWS\SYSTEM\simba.dll
Description=Our Access test db.
FileType=RedISAM
DataDirectory=e:\odbc\access.mdb
SingleUser=True
UseSystemDB=False

[StarDatabase files]
Driver=C:\WINDOWS\SYSTEM\simba.dll
Description=A test of creating a database with C++
FileType=RedISAM
DataDirectory=e:\odbc\star01.mdb
SingleUser=False
UseSystemDB=False

[STARmanager dBase Output]
Driver=C:\WINDOWS\SYSTEM\SIMBA.DLL
Description=Used as ODBC server
FileType=dBase3
DataDirectory=e:\newstar
SingleUser=False

[RS_dBase]
Driver=C:\WINDOWS\SYSTEM\simba.dll
FileType=dBase4
SingleUser=False
DataDirectory=D:\RPTSMITH\video

[RS_FoxPro]
Driver=C:\WINDOWS\SYSTEM\simba.dll
FileType=FoxPro 2.5
SingleUser=False
DataDirectory=D:\RPTSMITH\video

[RS_Excel]
Driver=C:\WINDOWS\SYSTEM\simba.dll
FileType=Excel
MaxScanRows=200
DataDirectory=D:\RPTSMITH\video
```

continues

LISTING 20.1. A TYPICAL **ODBC.INI** FILE.

```
[RS_Paradox]
Driver=C:\WINDOWS\SYSTEM\simba.dll
FileType=Paradox
SingleUser=False
DataDirectory=D:\RPTSMITH\video

[RS_MS_Access]
Driver=C:\WINDOWS\SYSTEM\simba.dll
FileType=RedISAM
SingleUser=False
UseSystemDB=False

[RS_Text]
Driver=C:\WINDOWS\SYSTEM\simba.dll
FileType=Text
ColNameHeader=False
Format=CSVDelimited
MaxScanRows=25
CharacterSet=OEM

[RS_Btrieve]
Driver=C:\WINDOWS\SYSTEM\simba.dll
FileType=Btrieve
SingleUser=False

[dBaseNav_sdk20]
Driver=C:\WINDOWS\SYSTEM\simbanav.dll
Description=Sample dBase Data
FileType=dBase4
DataDirectory=G:\ODBCSDK2\SMPLDATA\DBASE
SingleUser=False

[Sample_sdk20]
Driver=C:\WINDOWS\SYSTEM\sample.dll
Description=Sample Driver (null functionality)
Option1=Yes
Option2=Yes

[ODBCSPY]
TargetDSN=
TargetDriver=

[DataWaCSV]
Driver=C:\WINDOWS\SYSTEM\simba.dll
Description=Starmanager Alpha test files
FileType=Text
DataDirectory=e:\newstar\alpha
ColNameHeader=False
Format=CSVDelimited
MaxScanRows=25
CharacterSet=OEM

[States]
Driver=C:\WINDOWS\SYSTEM\simba.dll
Description=State information for WEVCPSK
```

```
FileType=Text
DataDirectory=e:\odbc
Extensions=None,ASC,CSV,TAB,TXT
ColNameHeader=True
Format=CSVDelimited
MaxScanRows=25
CharacterSet=OEM

[ODBC 32 bit Data Sources]
SQL Server=SQL Server (32 bit)

[SQL Server]
Driver32=C:\WINDOWS\SYSTEM\sqlsrv32.dll
```

Notice in Table 20.1 that the *szDescription* returned is the driver's description and not the DataSource's description. The *szDescription* field is obtained from the [ODBC Data Sources] section of the ODBC.INI file. As an example, looking at the [ODBC Data Sources] entry for the Student Registration DataSource, you see that the file associated with this DataSource is an Access data file with an extension of .MDB.

TABLE 20.1. AN EXAMPLE OF OUTPUT FROM **SQLDataSources()**.

szDSN Value	*szDescription* Value
Student Registration	Access data (*.MDB)
MS Access databases	Access data (*.MDB)
FoxPro files	FoxPro files (*.DBF)
Paradox files	Paradox files (*.DB)
MACTRI	Access data (*.MDB)
StarDatabase files	Access data (*.MDB)
STARmanager dBase output	dBASE files (*.DBF)
RS_dBase	dBASE files (*.DBF)
RS_FoxPro	FoxPro files (*.DBF)
RS_Excel	Excel files (*.XLS)
RS_Paradox	Paradox files (*.DB)
RS_MS_Access	Access data (*.MDB)
RS_Text	Text files (*.TXT, *.CSV)
RS_Btrieve	Btrieve data (FILE.DDF)

continues

TABLE 20.1. CONTINUED	
szDSN Value	*szDescription* Value
dBaseNav_sdk20	dBASE nav enabled test driver
Sample_sdk20	Template sample driver
DataWaCSV	Text files (*.TXT, *.CSV)
States	Text files (*.TXT, *.CSV)

This information is useful if you're going to use a **CFileDialog** class object to allow the user to select a DataSource table (when dealing with text-based files and **ISAM** files, such as dBASE files).

Parameters and Return Codes

The **SQLDataSources()** function takes a total of eight parameters. The function prototype is as follows:

```
RETCODE SQLDataSources(
    HENV          henv,
    UWORD         fDirection,
    UCHAR FAR *   szDSN,
    SWORD         cbDSNMax,
    SWORD FAR *   pcbDSN,
    UCHAR FAR *   szDescription,
    SWORD         cbDescriptionMax,
    SWORD FAR *   pcbDescription);
```

The **SQLDataSources()** parameters are shown in Table 20.2.

TABLE 20.2. **SQLDataSources()** PARAMETERS.		
Parameter	*Data Type*	*Description*
henv	**HENV**	The ODBC environment handle.
fDirection	**UWORD**	Use **SQL_FETCH_FIRST** to get the first DataSource in the list and use **SQL_FETCH_NEXT** to get the next DataSource in the list.

Parameter	Data Type	Description
szDSN	UCHAR FAR *	A far pointer to a character string buffer. This buffer should be long enough to hold the results, but it need not be longer than **SQL_MAX_DSN_LENGTH** + 1 (for the terminating null character).
cbDSNMax	SWORD	The length of szDSN. You can use the C/C++ **sizeof()** operator to obtain this parameter's value, or code an absolute value.
pcbDSN	SWORD FAR *	A pointer to an **SWORD** (short unsigned int) variable that receives the count of the number of bytes used in szDSN. If szDSN isn't large enough to hold the returned string, the string is truncated to cbDSNMax − 1 bytes in length.
szDescription	UCHAR FAR *	A far pointer to a character string buffer. This buffer should be at least 255 bytes in length.
cbDescriptionMax	SWORD	The length of szDSN. You can use the C/C++ **sizeof()** operator to obtain this parameter's value, or code an absolute value.
pcbDescription	SWORD FAR *	A pointer to an **SWORD** (short unsigned int) variable that receives the count of the number of bytes used in szDescription. If szDescription isn't large enough to hold the returned string, the string is truncated to cbDescriptionMax − 1 bytes in length.

The **SQLDataSources()** function returns a **RETCODE** (int) value. Table 20.3 shows the valid return codes for **SQLDataSources()**.

TABLE 20.3. `SQLDataSources()` RETURN CODES.	
RETCODE	*Description*
`SQL_SUCCESS`	The call to `SQLDataSources()` was successful. There is no further information.
`SQL_SUCCESS_WITH_INFO`	The call to `SQLDataSources()` was successful, but an error might have occurred. Further information can be obtained by calling `SQLError()`.
`SQL_NO_DATA_FOUND`	No more DataSource names remain.
`SQL_ERROR`	The call to `SQLDataSources()` failed. Call `SQLError()` to obtain specific information about the error(s).
`SQL_INVALID_HANDLE`	The environment handle passed to `SQLDataSources()` was invalid. There is no further information, so calling `SQLError()` won't be useful for this error condition.

Error Details

When the `SQLDataSources()` function returns either `SQL_ERROR` or `SQL_SUCCESS_WITH_INFO`, calling `SQL_ERROR()` returns one of the error messages listed in Table 20.4. Remember that because the error codes aren't unique, you should rely on the text of the error message rather than the error code.

TABLE 20.4. `SQLDataSources()` ERROR CONDITIONS WHEN `SQLError()` IS CALLED.		
Error Code	*Error Message*	*Description*
`01000`	General warning	A driver-specific error occurred. This error code is returned when `SQLDataSources()` returns `SQL_SUCCESS_WITH_INFO`.

Error Code	Error Message	Description
01004	Data truncated	Your buffer, *szDSN*, was too small for the current DataSource name. Only the amount of the DataSource name that would fit was returned. **SQLDataSources()** returns **SQL_SUCCESS_WITH_INFO**, and the *pcbDescription* parameter contains the actual (not truncated) length of the DataSource name.
S1000	General error	An undefined error occurred. No other error code is defined for this error. The text returned in **SQLError()**'s *szErrorMsg* parameter describes the error.
S1001	Memory allocation failure	ODBC's driver manager couldn't allocate the memory to execute this function.
S1090	Invalid string or buffer length	Either *cbDSNMax* or *cbDescriptionMax* or both contained a value less than 0.
S1103	Direction option out of range	The parameter *fDirection* wasn't equal to **SQL_FETCH_FIRST** or **SQL_FETCH_NEXT**.

SQLGetInfo( )

The **SQLGetInfo()** function enables you to obtain a vast array of information about a given DataSource. You can query a total of 139 different types of information. Not all parameters return valid information for all DataSources.

Using the Student Registration DataSource provided by Microsoft, I executed **SQLGetInfo()** for each available *fInfoType* parameter. Table 20.5 lists the results. Notice that many of the calls to **SQLGetInfo()** returned `SQL_ERROR`, indicating that this particular DataSource wasn't able to return any information for the specified *fInfoType* parameter value.

TABLE 20.5. TYPICAL **SQLGetInfo()** RETURN RESULTS.

fInfoType	ID	pcbInfoValue (*rgbInfoValue* Length)	*rgbInfoValue*/ Identifier
SQL_ACTIVE_CONNECTIONS	0	2	0
SQL_ACTIVE_STATEMENTS	1	2	0
SQL_DATA_SOURCE_NAME	2	20	"Student Registration"
SQL_DRIVER_HDBC	3	4	0x4387:0x0000
SQL_DRIVER_HENV	4	4	0x0ACF:0x0000
SQL_DRIVER_HSTMT	5	4	0x501F:0x0000
SQL_DRIVER_NAME	6	9	"SIMBA.DLL"
SQL_DRIVER_VER	7	10	"1.01.2115"
SQL_FETCH_DIRECTION	8	4	**SQL_FD_FETCH_NEXT**
SQL_ODBC_API_CONFORMANCE	9	2	**SQL_OAC_LEVEL1**
SQL_ODBC_VER	10	10	"02.00.0000"
SQL_ROW_UPDATES	11	1	"Y"
SQL_ODBC_SAG_CLI_CONFORMANCE	12	2	**SQL_OSCC_COMPLIANT**
SQL_SERVER_NAME	13	6	"ACCESS"
SQL_SEARCH_PATTERN_ESCAPE	14	1	"\"
SQL_ODBC_SQL_CONFORMANCE	15	2	**SQL_OSC_MINIMUM**

fInfoType	ID	pcbInfoValue (rgbInfoValue Length)	rgbInfoValue/ Identifier
SQL_DATABASE_NAME	16	39	"D:\MSVC15\ MFC\SAMPLES\ ENROLL\STDREG. MDB"
SQL_DBMS_NAME	17	6	"ACCESS"
SQL_DBMS_VER	18	3	"1.1"
SQL_ACCESSIBLE_TABLES	19	1	"N"
SQL_ACCESSIBLE_PROCEDURES	20	1	"N"
SQL_PROCEDURES	21	1	"N"
SQL_CONCAT_NULL_BEHAVIOR	22	2	SQL_CB_NON_NULL
SQL_CURSOR_COMMIT_BEHAVIOR	23	2	SQL_CC_PRESERVE
SQL_CURSOR_ROLLBACK_BEHAVIOR	24	2	SQL_CR_DELETE
SQL_DATA_SOURCE_READ_ONLY	25	1	"N"
SQL_DEFAULT_TXN_ISOLATION	26	4	0
SQL_EXPRESSIONS_IN_ORDERBY	27	1	"Y"
SQL_IDENTIFIER_CASE	28	2	SQL_IC_MIXED
SQL_IDENTIFIER_QUOTE_CHAR	29	1	"'"
SQL_MAX_COLUMN_NAME_LEN	30	2	64
SQL_MAX_CURSOR_NAME_LEN	31	2	18
SQL_MAX_OWNER_NAME_LEN	32	2	0
SQL_MAX_PROCEDURE_NAME_LEN	33	2	0
SQL_MAX_QUALIFIER_NAME_LEN	34	2	66
SQL_MAX_TABLE_NAME_LEN	35	2	64
SQL_MULT_RESULT_SETS	36	1	"N"
SQL_MULTIPLE_ACTIVE_TXN	37	1	"N"
SQL_OUTER_JOINS	38	1	"Y"
SQL_OWNER_TERM	39	0	""
SQL_PROCEDURE_TERM	40	0	""
SQL_QUALIFIER_NAME_SEPARATOR	41	1	"\"

continues

TABLE 20.5. CONTINUED

fInfoType	ID	pcbInfoValue (rgbInfoValue Length)	rgbInfoValue/ Identifier
SQL_QUALIFIER_TERM	42	9	"DIRECTORY"
SQL_SCROLL_CONCURRENCY	43	4	SQL_SCCO_READ_ONLY
SQL_SCROLL_OPTIONS	44	4	SQL_SO_FORWARD_ONLY
SQL_TABLE_TERM	45	5	"TABLE"
SQL_TXN_CAPABLE	46	2	SQL_TC_NONE
SQL_USER_NAME	47	5	"Admin"
SQL_CONVERT_FUNCTIONS	48	4	SQL_FN_CVT_CONVERT
SQL_NUMERIC_FUNCTIONS	49	4	SQL_FN_NUM_MOD
SQL_STRING_FUNCTIONS	50	4	SQL_FN_STR_CONCAT
SQL_FN_STR_LEFT			
SQL_FN_STR_LTRIM			
SQL_FN_STR_LENGTH			
SQL_FN_STR_LOCATE			
SQL_FN_STR_LCASE			
SQL_FN_STR_RIGHT			
SQL_FN_STR_RTRIM			
SQL_FN_STR_SUBSTRING			
SQL_FN_STR_UCASE			
SQL_SYSTEM_FUNCTIONS	51	4	SQL_FN_SYS_USERNAME
SQL_FN_SYS_DBNAME			
SQL_TIMEDATE_FUNCTIONS	52	4	SQL_FN_TD_CURDATE
SQL_FN_TD_DAYOFMONTH			
SQL_FN_TD_DAYOFWEEK			
SQL_FN_TD_MONTH			
SQL_FN_TD_YEAR			
SQL_FN_TD_CURTIME			
SQL_CONVERT_BIGINT	53	4	0

fInfoType	ID	pcbInfoValue (rgbInfoValue Length)	rgbInfoValue/ Identifier
SQL_CONVERT_BINARY	54	4	0
SQL_CONVERT_BIT	55	4	SQL_CVT_CHAR
SQL_CVT_NUMERIC			
SQL_CVT_INTEGER			
SQL_CVT_SMALLINT			
SQL_CVT_REAL			
SQL_CVT_DOUBLE			
SQL_CVT_LONGVARCHAR			
SQL_CVT_BIT			
SQL_CVT_TINYINT			
SQL_CONVERT_CHAR	56	4	SQL_CVT_CHAR
SQL_CVT_INTEGER			
SQL_CVT_SMALLINT			
SQL_CVT_REAL			
SQL_CVT_DOUBLE			
SQL_CVT_LONGVARCHAR			
SQL_CVT_BIT			
SQL_CVT_TINYINT			
SQL_CVT_TIMESTAMP			
SQL_CONVERT_DATE	57	4	SQL_CVT_CHAR
SQL_CVT_TIMESTAMP			
SQL_CONVERT_DECIMAL	58	4	0
SQL_CONVERT_DOUBLE	59	4	SQL_CVT_CHAR
SQL_CVT_NUMERIC			
SQL_CVT_INTEGER			
SQL_CVT_SMALLINT			
SQL_CVT_REAL			
SQL_CVT_DOUBLE			
SQL_CVT_LONGVARCHAR			

continues

TABLE 20.5. CONTINUED			

fInfoType	*ID*	*pcbInfoValue (rgbInfoValue Length)*	*rgbInfoValue/ Identifier*
SQL_CVT_BIT			
SQL_CVT_TINYINT			
SQL_CONVERT_FLOAT	60	4	**SQL_CVT_CHAR**
SQL_CVT_NUMERIC			
SQL_CVT_INTEGER			
SQL_CVT_SMALLINT			
SQL_CVT_REAL			
SQL_CVT_DOUBLE			
SQL_CVT_LONGVARCHAR			
SQL_CVT_BIT			
SQL_CVT_TINYINT			
SQL_CONVERT_INTEGER	61	4	**SQL_CVT_CHAR**
SQL_CVT_NUMERIC			
SQL_CVT_INTEGER			
SQL_CVT_SMALLINT			
SQL_CVT_REAL			
SQL_CVT_DOUBLE			
SQL_CVT_LONGVARCHAR			
SQL_CVT_BIT			
SQL_CVT_TINYINT			
SQL_CONVERT_LONGVARCHAR	62	4	**SQL_CVT_CHAR**
SQL_CVT_LONGVARCHAR			
SQL_CONVERT_NUMERIC	63	4	**SQL_CVT_CHAR**
SQL_CVT_NUMERIC			
SQL_CVT_INTEGER			
SQL_CVT_SMALLINT			
SQL_CVT_REAL			

fInfoType	ID	pcbInfoValue (rgbInfoValue Length)	rgbInfoValue/ Identifier
SQL_CVT_DOUBLE			
SQL_CVT_LONGVARCHAR			
SQL_CVT_BIT			
SQL_CVT_TINYINT			
SQL_CONVERT_REAL	64	4	SQL_CVT_CHAR
SQL_CVT_NUMERIC			
SQL_CVT_INTEGER			
SQL_CVT_SMALLINT			
SQL_CVT_REAL			
SQL_CVT_DOUBLE			
SQL_CVT_LONGVARCHAR			
SQL_CVT_BIT			
SQL_CVT_TINYINT			
SQL_CONVERT_SMALLINT	65	4	SQL_CVT_CHAR
SQL_CVT_NUMERIC			
SQL_CVT_INTEGER			
SQL_CVT_SMALLINT			
SQL_CVT_REAL			
SQL_CVT_DOUBLE			
SQL_CVT_LONGVARCHAR			
SQL_CVT_BIT			
SQL_CVT_TINYINT			
SQL_CONVERT_TIME	66	4	SQL_CVT_CHAR
SQL_CVT_TIMESTAMP			
SQL_CONVERT_TIMESTAMP	67	4	SQL_CVT_CHAR
SQL_CVT_TIMESTAMP			
SQL_CONVERT_TINYINT	68	4	SQL_CVT_CHAR
SQL_CVT_NUMERIC			

continues

TABLE 20.5. CONTINUED			

fInfoType	ID	pcbInfoValue (rgbInfoValue Length)	rgbInfoValue/ Identifier
SQL_CVT_INTEGER			
SQL_CVT_SMALLINT			
SQL_CVT_REAL			
SQL_CVT_DOUBLE			
SQL_CVT_LONGVARCHAR			
SQL_CVT_BIT			
SQL_CVT_TINYINT			
SQL_CONVERT_VARBINARY	69	4	0
SQL_CONVERT_VARCHAR	70	4	SQL_CVT_CHAR
SQL_CVT_INTEGER			
SQL_CVT_SMALLINT			
SQL_CVT_REAL			
SQL_CVT_DOUBLE			
SQL_CVT_LONGVARCHAR			
SQL_CVT_BIT			
SQL_CVT_TINYINT			
SQL_CVT_TIMESTAMP			
SQL_CONVERT_LONGVARBINARY	71	4	0
SQL_TXN_ISOLATION_OPTION	72	4	0
SQL_ODBC_SQL_OPT_IEF	73	1	"N"
SQL_CORRELATION_NAME	74	2	SQL_CN_ANY
SQL_NON_NULLABLE_COLUMNS	75	2	SQL_NNC_NON_NULL
SQL_DRIVER_HLIB	76	4	0x0000:0x431E
SQL_DRIVER_ODBC_VER	77	5	"01.00"
SQL_FILE_USAGE	78		SQL_ERROR
SQL_GETDATA_EXTENSIONS	79		SQL_ERROR
SQL_NULL_COLLATION	80		SQL_ERROR

fInfoType	ID	pcbInfoValue (rgbInfoValue Length)	rgbInfoValue/ Identifier
SQL_ALTER_TABLE	81		SQL_ERROR
SQL_COLUMN_ALIAS	82		SQL_ERROR
SQL_GROUP_BY	83		SQL_ERROR
SQL_KEYWORDS	84		SQL_ERROR
SQL_ORDER_BY_COLUMNS_IN_SELECT	85		SQL_ERROR
SQL_OWNER_USAGE	86		SQL_ERROR
SQL_POSITIONED_STATEMENTS	87		SQL_ERROR
SQL_QUALIFIER_USAGE	88		SQL_ERROR
SQL_QUOTED_IDENTIFIER_CASE	89		SQL_ERROR
SQL_SPECIAL_CHARACTERS	90		SQL_ERROR
SQL_SUBQUERIES	91		SQL_ERROR
SQL_UNION	92		SQL_ERROR
SQL_MAX_COLUMNS_IN_GROUP_BY	93		SQL_ERROR
SQL_MAX_COLUMNS_IN_INDEX	94		SQL_ERROR
SQL_MAX_COLUMNS_IN_ORDER_BY	95		SQL_ERROR
SQL_MAX_COLUMNS_IN_SELECT	96		SQL_ERROR
SQL_MAX_COLUMNS_IN_TABLE	97		SQL_ERROR
SQL_MAX_INDEX_SIZE	98		SQL_ERROR
SQL_MAX_ROW_SIZE_INCLUDES_LONG	99		SQL_ERROR
SQL_MAX_ROW_SIZE	100		SQL_ERROR
SQL_MAX_STATEMENT_LEN	101		SQL_ERROR
SQL_MAX_TABLES_IN_SELECT	102		SQL_ERROR
SQL_MAX_USER_NAME_LEN	103		SQL_ERROR
SQL_TIMEDATE_ADD_INTERVALS	104		SQL_ERROR
SQL_TIMEDATE_DIFF_INTERVALS	105		SQL_ERROR
SQL_CONVERT_C_BINARY	106		SQL_ERROR
SQL_CONVERT_C_BIT	107		SQL_ERROR
SQL_CONVERT_C_CHAR	108		SQL_ERROR

continues

TABLE 20.5. CONTINUED			
fInfoType	ID	pcbInfoValue (rgbInfoValue Length)	rgbInfoValue/ Identifier
SQL_CONVERT_C_DATE	109		SQL_ERROR
SQL_CONVERT_C_DOUBLE	110		SQL_ERROR
SQL_CONVERT_C_FLOAT	111		SQL_ERROR
SQL_CONVERT_C_SLONG	112		SQL_ERROR
SQL_CONVERT_C_SSHORT	113		SQL_ERROR
SQL_CONVERT_C_STINYINT	114		SQL_ERROR
SQL_CONVERT_C_TIME	115		SQL_ERROR
SQL_CONVERT_C_TIMESTAMP	116		SQL_ERROR
SQL_CONVERT_C_ULONG	117		SQL_ERROR
SQL_CONVERT_C_USHORT	118		SQL_ERROR
SQL_CONVERT_C_UTINYINT	119		SQL_ERROR
SQL_CONVERT_SQL_BIGINT	120		SQL_ERROR
SQL_CONVERT_SQL_BINARY	121		SQL_ERROR
SQL_CONVERT_SQL_BIT	122		SQL_ERROR
SQL_CONVERT_SQL_CHAR	123		SQL_ERROR
SQL_CONVERT_SQL_DATE	124		SQL_ERROR
SQL_CONVERT_SQL_DECIMAL	125		SQL_ERROR
SQL_CONVERT_SQL_DOUBLE	126		SQL_ERROR
SQL_CONVERT_SQL_FLOAT	127		SQL_ERROR
SQL_CONVERT_SQL_INTEGER	128		SQL_ERROR
SQL_CONVERT_SQL_LONGVARBINARY	129		SQL_ERROR
SQL_CONVERT_SQL_LONGVARCHAR	130		SQL_ERROR
SQL_CONVERT_SQL_NUMERIC	131		SQL_ERROR
SQL_CONVERT_SQL_REAL	132		SQL_ERROR
SQL_CONVERT_SQL_SMALLINT	133		SQL_ERROR
SQL_CONVERT_SQL_TIME	134		SQL_ERROR
SQL_CONVERT_SQL_TIMESTAMP	135		SQL_ERROR

fInfoType	ID	pcbInfoValue (rgbInfoValue Length)	rgbInfoValue/ Identifier
SQL_CONVERT_SQL_TINYINT	136		SQL_ERROR
SQL_CONVERT_SQL_VARBINARY	137		SQL_ERROR
SQL_CONVERT_SQL_VARCHAR	138		SQL_ERROR

As you can see from Table 20.5, **SQLGetInfo()** returns a vast amount of information. In the great majority of ODBC programs, **SQLGetInfo()** is called with only a few of the available *fInfoType* codes.

Parameters and Return Codes

The **SQLGetInfo()** function takes a total of eight parameters. The function prototype is as follows:

```
RETCODE SQLGetInfo(
    HDBC        hdbc,
    UWORD       fInfoType,
    PTR         rgbInfoValue,
    SWORD       cbInfoValueMax,
    SWORD FAR * pcbInfoValue)
```

The **SQLGetInfo()** parameters are shown in Table 20.6.

TABLE 20.6. **SQLGetInfo()** PARAMETERS.		
Parameter	*Data Type*	*Description*
hdbc	**HDBC**	The ODBC connection handle.
fInfoType	**UWORD**	Uses one of the values from Table 20.7.
rgbInfoValue	**PTR**	A far pointer to a character string buffer. This buffer should be long enough to hold the results (see Table 20.7). For *fInfoType*s that return character strings, this buffer should be long enough to hold the string returned.

continues

	TABLE 20.6. CONTINUED	
Parameter	Data Type	Description
cbInofValueMax	SWORD	The length of *rgbInfoValue*. See Table 20.7 for information about buffer sizes.
pcbInfoValue	SWORD FAR *	This is a pointer to an **SWORD** (short unsigned int) variable that receives the count of the number of bytes used in *rgbInfoValue*. If *rgbInfoValue* isn't large enough to hold the returned string, the string is truncated to *cbInfoValueMax* − 1 bytes in length.

Table 20.7 shows values that can be used with *fInfoType*.

	TABLE 20.7. **SQLGetInfo()**'S *fInfoType* VALUES.	
fInfoType	Bytes Returned	Returns
SQL_ACTIVE_CONNECTIONS	2	*rgbInfoValue* contains a short integer that specifies the maximum number of **HDBC**s that this driver/ DataSource can support. The limiting factor can be either the driver or the DataSource. When the maximum number can't be determined, a zero value is returned.

fInfoType	*Bytes Returned*	*Returns*
SQL_ACTIVE_STATEMENTS	2	*rgbInfoValue* contains a short integer that specifies the maximum number of **HSTMT**s that this driver/ DataSource can support. The limiting factor can be either the driver or the DataSource. When the maximum number can't be determined, a zero value is returned.
SQL_DATA_SOURCE_NAME	Varies	The *rgbInfoValue* buffer contains a character string that is the DataSource name used with the call to **SQLConnect()**, **SQLDriverConnect()**, or **SQLBrowseConnect()**.
SQL_DRIVER_HENV	4	The **HENV** for this DataSource.
SQL_DRIVER_HDBC	4	The **HDBC** for this DataSource.
SQL_DRIVER_HSTMT	4	The driver's **HSTMT**. In *rgbInfoValue*, you pass a valid, open **HSTMT**.
SQL_DRIVER_NAME	Varies	*rgbInfoValue* contains a character string that holds the filename of the ODBC driver.

continues

	Bytes	
fInfoType	*Returned*	*Returns*
SQL_DRIVER_VER	Varies	*rgbInfoValue* contains a string that holds the version code for the driver in the format of *nn.nn.nnnn*. The first two digits are the major version, the second two are the minor version, and the last four are the release version. The return string can, optionally, include a description of the driver.
SQL_FETCH_DIRECTION	4	*rgbInfoValue* contains a **DWORD** bitmask. Support for the following options can be determined with a Boolean **AND** operation: **SQL_FD_FETCH_NEXT** **SQL_FD_FETCH_FIRST** **SQL_FD_FETCH_LAST** **SQL_FD_FETCH_PREV** **SQL_FD_FETCH_ABSOLUTE** **SQL_FD_FETCH_RELATIVE** **SQL_FD_FETCH_RESUME**
SQL_ODBC_API_CONFORMANCE	2	*rgbInfoValue* contains a short integer that indicates the level of ODBC conformance for this driver/ DataSource. Return values are the following: 0: None 1: Level 1 supported 2: Level 2 supported

TABLE 20.7. CONTINUED

fInfoType	Bytes Returned	Returns
SQL_ODBC_SAG_CLI_CONFORMANCE	2	*rgbInfoValue* contains a short integer that indicates compliance to the **SAG** specifications: 0: Not all functions are **SAG**-compliant 1: **SAG**-compliant
SQL_ODBC_SQL_CONFORMANCE	2	*rgbInfoValue* contains a short integer indicating the SQL grammar supported by this driver/DataSource combination: 0: Minimum grammar supported 1: Core grammar supported 2: Extended grammar supported
SQL_ODBC_SQL_OPT_IEF	1	*rgbInfoValue* contains a Y if the optional integrity enhancement facility is supported, or an N if it's not.
SQL_ODBC_VER	Varies	*rgbInfoValue* contains a string that holds the version code for the driver manager in the format of *nn.nn.nnnn*. The first two digits are the major version, the second two are the minor version, and the last four are the release version.

continues

	TABLE 20.7. CONTINUED	

fInfoType	Bytes Returned	Returns
SQL_PROCEDURES	1	*rgbInfoValue* contains a Y if the driver and the Data-Source support procedures, or an N if they don't.
SQL_ROW_UPDATES	1	*rgbInfoValue* contains a Y if the driver can detect changes in rows between multiple fetches of the same rows, or an N if it can't.
SQL_SEARCH_PATTERN_ESCAPE	Varies	*rgbInfoValue* contains the character string specifying the escape character to be used when trying to match the metacharacters underscore (_) and percent (%) in building search patterns. The escape search character is used only in catalog functions.
SQL_SERVER_NAME	Varies	*rgbInfoValue* contains a character string that holds the data-source–specific server name. You can use this string when calling the **SQLConnect()**, **SQLDriverConnect()**, and **SQLBrowseConnect()** functions.

fInfoType	Bytes Returned	Returns
SQL_DATABASE_NAME	Varies	*rgbInfoValue* points to a character string containing the name of the current database in use, if the DataSource is defined as a database.
SQL_DBMS_NAME	Varies	*rgbInfoValue* contains a character string that holds the name of the DBMS (database management system) being accessed by the driver.
SQL_DBMS_VER	Varies	*rgbInfoValue* contains a string that holds the version code for the DBMS manager in the format of *nn.nn.nnnn*. The first two digits are the major version, the second two are the minor version, and the last four are the release version. The *nn.nn.nnnn* format is documented as being required, but it's possible for the driver to append a version string in another format as well.
SQL_ACCESSIBLE_TABLES	1	*rgbInfoValue* contains a character string that holds a Y if the user has SELECT privileges for all the tables returned by **SQLTables()**. It contains an N if not.

continues

	Bytes	
fInfoType	*Returned*	*Returns*
SQL_ACCESSIBLE_PROCEDURES	1	*rgbInfoValue* points to a character string containing a Y when the user can execute all procedures returned by **SQLProcedures()**.
SQL_CONCAT_NULL_BEHAVIOR	2	*rgbInfoValue* contains a short integer defining how the DataSource handles concatenation of DataColumns containing a mixture of null and non-null values. Return values are the following: 0: The result will be null. 1: The result will be a concatenation of columns that are not null.
SQL_CURSOR_COMMIT_BEHAVIOR	2	*rgbInfoValue* contains a short integer that indicates how COMMIT operations affect the cursor. Return values are the following: 0: The cursors will be closed and deleted. 1: The cursors will be closed. 2: The cursors will be saved and retain the same positions they had prior to the call to COMMIT.

TABLE 20.7. CONTINUED

fInfoType	Bytes Returned	Returns
SQL_CURSOR_ROLLBACK_BEHAVIOR	2	*rgbInfoValue* contains a short integer that indicates how a ROLLBACK operation will affect the cursors. Return values are the following: 0: The cursors will be closed and deleted. 1: The cursors will be closed. 2: The cursors will be saved and retain the same positions they had prior to the call to COMMIT.
SQL_DATA_SOURCE_READ_ONLY	1	*rgbInfoValue* contains a Y if the DataSource is read-only, and an N if it isn't.
SQL_DEFAULT_TXN_ISOLATION	4	*rgbInfoValue* contains a long integer used to show the default truncation isolation level. Return values are the following: 0: The driver or Data-Source doesn't support transactions. **SQL_TXN_READ_UNCOMMITTED**: Any changes will be seen by all transactions. **SQL_TXN_READ_COMMITTED**: A row read by a transaction can be altered and committed by the transaction.

continues

	Bytes	
fInfoType	Returned	Returns
		SQL_TXN_REPEATABLE_READ: A transaction can add or delete rows matching the search condition or a pending transaction. **SQL_TXN_SERIALIZABLE**: Any data that will be affected by pending transactions isn't made available to other transactions. **SQL_TXN_VERSIONING**: Any data that will be affected by other pending transactions won't be available.
SQL_EXPRESSIONS_IN_ORDERBY	1	rgbInfoValue contains a Y if the DataSource supports expressions in the ORDER BY list; otherwise, it contains an N.
SQL_IDENTIFIER_CASE	2	rgbInfoValue contains a short integer that will be one of the following values: 1: All names will be in uppercase. 2: All names will be in lowercase. 3: All names will be in mixed case. The names will be case-sensitive. 4: All names will be in mixed case. The names will not be case-sensitive.

TABLE 20.7. CONTINUED

fInfoType	Bytes Returned	Returns
SQL_IDENTIFIER_QUOTE_CHAR	Varies	*rgbInfoValue* contains the character that will be used to surround (delimit) a delimited identifier. For DataSources that don't support delimited identifiers, this value will be an empty string.
SQL_MAX_COLUMN_NAME_LEN	2	*rgbInfoValue* contains a short integer that specifies the maximum length of the column name.
SQL_MAX_CURSOR_NAME_LEN	2	*rgbInfoValue* contains a short integer that specifies the maximum length of the cursor name.
SQL_MAX_OWNER_NAME_LEN	2	*rgbInfoValue* contains a short integer that specifies the maximum length of the DataSource's owner name. For DataSources that don't support owner names, this value is zero.
SQL_MAX_PROCEDURE_NAME_LEN	2	*rgbInfoValue* contains a short integer that specifies the maximum length of the procedure name. For Data-Sources that don't support procedure names, this value is zero.

continues

	TABLE 20.7. CONTINUED	
fInfoType	*Bytes Returned*	*Returns*
SQL_MAX_QUALIFIER_NAME_LEN	2	*rgbInfoValue* contains a short integer that specifies the maximum length of the qualifier name. For DataSources that don't support qualifier names, this value is zero.
SQL_MAX_TABLE_NAME_LEN	2	*rgbInfoValue* contains a short integer that specifies the maximum length of the table name.
SQL_MULT_RESULT_SETS	1	*rgbInfoValue* contains a Y for DataSources that support multiple result sets, and an N for those that don't.
SQL_MULTIPLE_ACTIVE_TXN	1	*rgbInfoValue* contains a Y for DataSources that support active transactions on multiple connections, and an N for those that don't.
SQL_OUTER_JOINS	1	*rgbInfoValue* contains a Y if the DataSource and driver support outer joins, and an N if they don't.
SQL_OWNER_TERM	Varies	*rgbInfoValue* contains a string that holds the name of the DataSource's vendor.

fInfoType	Bytes Returned	Returns
SQL_PROCEDURE_TERM	Varies	rgbInfoValue contains a pointer to a string that holds the name of the DataSource's vendor for a procedure.
SQL_QUALIFIER_NAME_SEPARATOR	1	rgbInfoValue contains a string that holds the separator used between the qualifier name and the qualified name that follows. Typical values include \ and a period.
SQL_QUALIFIER_TERM	Varies	rgbInfoValue contains a string that holds the source vendor's qualifier name. Typical values include "database" and "directory."
SQL_SCROLL_CONCURRENCY	4	rgbInfoValue contains a DWORD bitmask. Support for the following options can be determined with a Boolean AND operation: SQL_SCCO_READ_ONLY SQL_SCCO_LOCK SQL_SCCO_OPT_TIMESTAMP SQL_SCCO_OPT_VALUES
SQL_SCROLL_OPTIONS	4	rgbInfoValue contains a DWORD bitmask. Support for the following options can be determined with a Boolean AND operation: SQL_SO_FORWARD_ONLY SQL_SO_KEYSET_DRIVEN SQL_SO_DYNAMIC SQL_SO_MIXED

continues

	Bytes	
fInfoType	*Returned*	*Returns*
SQL_TABLE_TERM	Varies	*rgbInfoValue* contains a string that holds the vendor's name for a table. Typical values could be "table" or "file."
SQL_TXN_CAPABLE	2	*rgbInfoValue* contains a short integer showing the level of transaction support. This value contains one of the following values: 0: No transactions are supported. 1: Transactions may contain only the DML statements SELECT, INSERT, UPDATE, and DELETE. 2: Transactions may also contain the DDL statements CREATE TABLE, DROP INDEX, and so on.
SQL_TXN_ISOLATION_OPTION	4	*rgbInfoValue* contains a **DWORD** bitmask. Support for the following options can be determined with a Boolean **AND** operation: **SQL_TXN_READ_UNCOMMITTED** **SQL_TXN_READ_COMMITTED** **SQL_TXN_REPEATABLE_READ** **SQL_TXN_SERIALIZABLE** **SQL_TXN_VERSIONING**

TABLE 20.7. CONTINUED

fInfoType	Bytes Returned	Returns
SQL_USER_NAME	Varies	*rgbInfoValue* contains a string that holds the name used for a given database. This name may differ from the name used to log in to the DataSource.
SQL_CONVERT_FUNCTIONS	4	*rgbInfoValue* contains a **DWORD** bitmask. Support for the following option can be determined with a Boolean **AND** operation: **SQL_FN_CVT_CONVERT**
SQL_NUMERIC_FUNCTIONS	4	*rgbInfoValue* contains a **DWORD** bitmask. Support for the following options can be determined with a Boolean **AND** operation: **SQL_FN_NUM_ABS** **SQL_FN_NUM_ACOS** **SQL_FN_NUM_ASIN** **SQL_FN_NUM_ATAN** **SQL_FN_NUM_ATAN2** **SQL_FN_NUM_CEILING** **SQL_FN_NUM_COS** **SQL_FN_NUM_COT** **SQL_FN_NUM_EXP** **SQL_FN_NUM_FLOOR** **SQL_FN_NUM_LOG** **SQL_FN_NUM_MOD** **SQL_FN_NUM_PI** **SQL_FN_NUM_RAND** **SQL_FN_NUM_SIGN** **SQL_FN_NUM_SIN** **SQL_FN_NUM_SQRT** **SQL_FN_NUM_TAN**

continues

	TABLE 20.7. CONTINUED	
fInfoType	Bytes Returned	Returns
SQL_STRING_FUNCTIONS	4	rgbInfoValue contains a **DWORD** bitmask. Support for the following options can be determined with a Boolean **AND** operation: **SQL_FN_STR_ASCII** **SQL_FN_STR_CHAR** **SQL_FN_STR_CONCAT** **SQL_FN_STR_INSERT** **SQL_FN_STR_LCASE** **SQL_FN_STR_LEFT** **SQL_FN_STR_LENGTH** **SQL_FN_STR_LOCATE** **SQL_FN_STR_LTRIM** **SQL_FN_STR_REPEAT** **SQL_FN_STR_REPLACE** **SQL_FN_STR_RIGHT** **SQL_FN_STR_RTRIM** **SQL_FN_STR_SUBSTRING** **SQL_FN_STR_UCASE**
SQL_SYSTEM_FUNCTIONS	4	rgbInfoValue contains a **DWORD** bitmask. Support for the following options can be determined with a Boolean **AND** operation: **SQL_FN_SYS_DBNAME** **SQL_FN_SYS_IFNULL** **SQL_FN_SYS_USERNAME**

fInfoType	Bytes Returned	Returns
SQL_TIMEDATE_FUNCTIONS	4	*rgbInfoValue* contains a **DWORD** bitmask. Support for the following options can be determined with a Boolean **AND** operation: SQL_FN_TD_NOW SQL_FN_TD_CURDATE SQL_FN_TD_DAYOFMONTH SQL_FN_TD_DAYOFWEEK SQL_FN_TD_DAYOFYEAR SQL_FN_TD_MONTH SQL_FN_TD_QUARTER SQL_FN_TD_WEEK SQL_FN_TD_YEAR SQL_FN_TD_CURTIME SQL_FN_TD_HOUR SQL_FN_TD_MINUTE SQL_FN_TD_SECOND SQL_CONVERT_BIGINT SQL_CONVERT_BINARY SQL_CONVERT_BIT SQL_CONVERT_CHAR SQL_CONVERT_DATE SQL_CONVERT_DECIMAL SQL_CONVERT_DOUBLE SQL_CONVERT_FLOAT SQL_CONVERT_INTEGER SQL_CONVERT_LONGVARBINARY SQL_CONVERT_LONGVARCHAR SQL_CONVERT_NUMERIC SQL_CONVERT_REAL SQL_CONVERT_SMALLINT SQL_CONVERT_TIME SQL_CONVERT_TIMESTAMP SQL_CONVERT_TINYINT SQL_CONVERT_VARBINARY

continues

TABLE 20.7. CONTINUED		
fInfoType	*Bytes Returned*	*Returns*
SQL_CONVERT_VARCHAR	4	*rgbInfoValue* contains a **DWORD** bitmask. The bitmask indicates which conversions are supported. If the bitmask is zero, there are no supported conversions. Support for the following options can be determined with a Boolean **AND** operation: **SQL_CVT_BIGINT** **SQL_CVT_BINARY** **SQL_CVT_BIT** **SQL_CVT_CHAR** **SQL_CVT_DATE** **SQL_CVT_DECIMAL** **SQL_CVT_DOUBLE** **SQL_CVT_FLOAT** **SQL_CVT_INTEGER** **SQL_CVT_LONGVARBINARY** **SQL_CVT_LONGVARCHAR** **SQL_CVT_NUMERIC** **SQL_CVT_REAL** **SQL_CVT_SMALLINT** **SQL_CVT_TIME** **SQL_CVT_TIMESTAMP** **SQL_CVT_TINYINT** **SQL_CVT_VARBINARY** **SQL_CVT_VARCHAR**

As the preceding table shows, the **SQLGetInfo()** function is capable of providing a substantial amount of information about a DataSource and the driver.

The **SQLGetInfo()** function returns a **RETCODE** (int) value. Table 20.8 shows the valid return codes for **SQLGetInfo()**.

TABLE 20.8. **SQLGetInfo()** RETURN CODES.

RETCODE	Description
SQL_SUCCESS	The call to **SQLGetInfo()** was successful. There is no further information.
SQL_SUCCESS_WITH_INFO	The call to **SQLGetInfo()** was successful, but an error might have occurred. Further information can be obtained by calling **SQLError()**.
SQL_ERROR	The call to **SQLGetInfo()** failed. Call **SQLError()** to obtain specific information about the error(s).
SQL_INVALID_HANDLE	The environment handle passed to **SQLGetInfo()** was invalid. There is no further information, so calling **SQLError()** won't be useful for this error condition.

Error Details

When the **SQLGetInfo()** function returns either **SQL_ERROR** or **SQL_SUCCESS_WITH_INFO**, calling **SQL_ERROR()** returns one of the error messages listed in Table 20.9. Remember that the error codes are not unique and that you should rely on the text of the error message rather than the error code.

TABLE 20.9. `SQLGetInfo()` ERROR CONDITIONS WHEN `SQLError()` IS CALLED.

Error Code	Error Message	Description
01000	General warning	A driver-specific error occurred. This error code is returned when `SQLDataSources()` returns `SQL_SUCCESS_WITH_INFO`.
01004	Data truncated	Your buffer, *rgbInfoValue*, was too small for the current Data-Source name. The amount of the DataSource name that would fit was returned. `SQLGetInfo()` returns `SQL_SUCCESS_WITH_INFO`, and the *pcbInfoValue* parameter contains the actual (not truncated) length of the DataSource name.
08003	Connection not open	The *fInfoType* value specified requires an open connection. (Only `SQL_ODBC_VER` can be requested without an open connection.)
22003	Numeric value out of range	A numeric result was too large for the buffer provided, and there would be a loss of significance.
IM001	Driver doesn't support this function	The *fInfoType* isn't supported by this driver.
S1000	General error	An undefined error occurred. No other error code is defined for this error. The text returned in `SQLError()`'s *szErrorMsg* parameter describes the error.
S1001	Memory allocation failure	ODBC's driver manager couldn't allocate the memory to execute this function.

Error Code	Error Message	Description
S1009	Invalid argument value	You specified **SQL_DRIVER_HSTMT**, and the value pointed to by *rgbInfoValue* wasn't a valid handle.
S1010	Function sequence error	A synchronously executing function was still executing when **SQLGetInfo()** was called.
S1090	Invalid string or buffer length	The *cbInfoValue* contained a value less than 0.
S1096	Information type out of range	The *fInfoType* was invalid.
S1C00	Driver not capable	The *fInfoType* value was valid but not supported by the driver applied to the DataSource.
S1T00	Timeout expired	The DataSource didn't return the requested information before the timeout period expired.

SQLGetFunctions()

The **SQLGetFunctions()** function returns information as to whether the driver supports a specific ODBC function. Not all drivers support all functions.

The information is returned in a **UWORD** variable, a pointer to which is passed as a parameter to **SQLGetFunctions()**.

Parameters and Return Codes

The **SQLGetFunctions()** function takes a total of three parameters. The function prototype is as follows:

```
RETCODE SQLGetFunctions(
    HDBC          hdbc,
    UWORD         fFunction,
    UWORD FAR * pfExists);
```

The **SQLGetFunctions()** parameters are shown in Table 20.10.

	TABLE 20.10. `SQLGetFunctions()` PARAMETERS.	
Parameter	Data Type	Description
hdbc	**HDBC**	The ODBC connection handle.
fFunction	**UWORD**	The function for which support must be determined.
pfExists	**UWORD FAR ***	A pointer to a **UWORD** (short unsigned int) variable that is zero (**FALSE**) if the function isn't supported and nonzero (**!FALSE**) if the function is supported.

The **SQLGetFunctions()** function returns a **RETCODE** (int) value. Table 20.11 shows the valid return codes for **SQLGetFunctions()**.

	TABLE 20.11. `SQLGetFunctions()` RETURN CODES.
RETCODE	Description
SQL_SUCCESS	The call to **SQLGetFunctions()** was successful. There is no further information.
SQL_SUCCESS_WITH_INFO	The call to **SQLGetFunctions()** was successful, but an error might have occurred. Further information can be obtained by calling **SQLError()**.
SQL_ERROR	The call to **SQLGetFunctions()** failed. Call **SQLError()** to obtain specific information about the error(s).
SQL_INVALID_HANDLE	The environment handle passed to **SQLGetFunctions()** was invalid. There is no further information, so calling **SQLError()** won't be useful for this error condition.

Table 20.12 lists the functions for which **SQLGetFunctions()** checks.

TABLE 20.12. FUNCTIONS THAT `SQLGetFunctions()` CHECKS FOR.	
Function	*Function Class*
`SQL_API_SQLALLOCCONNECT`	Core
`SQL_API_SQLFETCH`	Core
`SQL_API_SQLALLOCENV`	Core
`SQL_API_SQLFREECONNECT`	Core
`SQL_API_SQLALLOCSTMT`	Core
`SQL_API_SQLFREEENV`	Core
`SQL_API_SQLBINDCOL`	Core
`SQL_API_SQLFREESTMT`	Core
`SQL_API_SQLCANCEL`	Core
`SQL_API_SQLGETCURSORNAME`	Core
`SQL_API_SQLCOLATTRIBUTES`	Core
`SQL_API_SQLNUMRESULTCOLS`	Core
`SQL_API_SQLCONNECT`	Core
`SQL_API_SQLPREPARE`	Core
`SQL_API_SQLDESCRIBECOL`	Core
`SQL_API_SQLROWCOUNT`	Core
`SQL_API_SQLDISCONNECT`	Core
`SQL_API_SQLSETCURSORNAME`	Core
`SQL_API_SQLERROR`	Core
`SQL_API_SQLSETPARAM`	Core
`SQL_API_SQLEXECDIRECT`	Core
`SQL_API_SQLTRANSACT`	Core
`SQL_API_SQLEXECUTE`	Core
`SQL_API_SQLCOLUMNS`	Extension Level 1
`SQL_API_SQLPARAMDATA`	Extension Level 1
`SQL_API_SQLDRIVERCONNECT`	Extension Level 1
`SQL_API_SQLPUTDATA`	Extension Level 1
`SQL_API_SQLGETCONNECTOPTION`	Extension Level 1

continues

TABLE 20.12. CONTINUED	
Function	*Function Class*
SQL_API_SQLSETCONNECTOPTION	Extension Level 1
SQL_API_SQLGETDATA	Extension Level 1
SQL_API_SQLSETSTMTOPTION	Extension Level 1
SQL_API_SQLGETFUNCTIONS	Extension Level 1
SQL_API_SQLSPECIALCOLUMNS	Extension Level 1
SQL_API_SQLGETINFO	Extension Level 1
SQL_API_SQLSTATISTICS	Extension Level 1
SQL_API_SQLGETSTMTOPTION	Extension Level 1
SQL_API_SQLTABLES	Extension Level 1
SQL_API_SQLGETTYPEINFO	Extension Level 1
SQL_API_SQLBROWSECONNECT	Extension Level 2
SQL_API_SQLNUMPARAMS	Extension Level 2
SQL_API_SQLCOLUMNPRIVILEGES	Extension Level 2
SQL_API_SQLPARAMOPTIONS	Extension Level 2
SQL_API_SQLGETFUNCTIONS	Extension Level 2
SQL_API_SQLPRIMARYKEYS	Extension Level 2
SQL_API_SQLDESCRIBEPARAM	Extension Level 2
SQL_API_SQLPROCEDURECOLUMNS	Extension Level 2
SQL_API_SQLEXTENDEDFETCH	Extension Level 2
SQL_API_SQLPROCEDURES	Extension Level 2
SQL_API_SQLFOREIGNKEYS	Extension Level 2
SQL_API_SQLSETPOS	Extension Level 2
SQL_API_SQLMORERESULTS	Extension Level 2
SQL_API_SQLSETSCROLLOPTIONS	Extension Level 2
SQL_API_SQLNATIVESQL	Extension Level 2
SQL_API_SQLTABLEPRIVILEGES	Extension Level 2

Error Details

When the **SQLGetFunctions()** function returns either **SQL_ERROR** or **SQL_SUCCESS_WITH_INFO**, calling **SQL_ERROR()** returns one of the error messages listed in Table 20.13. Remember that because the error codes are not unique, you should rely on the text of the error message rather than the error code.

TABLE 20.13. SQLGetFunctions() ERROR CONDITIONS WHEN SQLError() IS CALLED.

Error Code	Error Message	Description
01000	General warning	A driver-specific error occurred. This error code is returned when **SQLGetFunctions()** returns **SQL_SUCCESS_WITH_INFO**.
S1000	General error	An undefined error occurred. No other error code is defined for this error. The text returned in **SQLError()**'s *szErrorMsg* parameter describes the error.
S1001	Memory allocation failure	ODBC's driver manager couldn't allocate the memory to execute this function.
S1010	Function sequence error	The **SQLGetFunctions()** function can be called only after a successful call to **SQLConnect()**, **SQLBrowseConnect()**, or **SQLDriverConnect()**.
S1095	Function index option out of range	The parameter *fFunction* wasn't one of the values specified in Table 20.12.

SQLGetTypeInfo( )

The **SQLGetTypeInfo()** function is used to obtain information about which data types are supported by the DataSource specified. This function returns the results as a recordset.

Parameters and Return Codes

The **SQLGetTypeInfo()** function takes a total of eight parameters. The function prototype is as follows:

```
RETCODE SQLGetTypeInfo(
    HSTMT        hstmt,
    SWORD        fSqlType,
```

The **SQLGetTypeInfo()** parameters are shown in Table 20.14.

Parameter	Data Type	Description
TABLE 20.14. **SQLGetTypeInfo()** PARAMETERS.		
hstmt	**HSTMT**	An ODBC statement handle.
fSqlType	**SWORD**	The ODBC SQL data type (or **SQL_ALL_TYPES**) about which information is being requested. See Table 20.15 for valid data-type identifiers.

Table 20.15 shows the valid identifiers for the *fSqlType* parameter.

Parameter	Description
TABLE 20.15. VALID *fSqlType* PARAMETERS.	
SQL_ALL_TYPES	Specifies that information about all data types should be returned.
SQL_DECIMAL	A signed, exact number with a specified precision and scale.
SQL_NUMERIC	A signed, exact number with a specified precision and scale.

Parameter	Description
SQL_TINYINT	An exact number with a precision of 3 and a scale of 0.
SQL_SMALLINT	An exact number with a precision of 5 and a scale of 0.
SQL_INTEGER	An exact number with a precision of 10 and a scale of 0.
SQL_BIGINT	An exact number with a precision of 19 if signed or 20 if unsigned and a scale of 0.
SQL_BIT	Binary data 1 bit long.
SQL_BINARY	Fixed-length binary data 1 to 254 bytes long.
SQL_VARBINARY	Variable-length binary data 1 to 254 bytes long.
SQL_LONGVARBINARY	Variable-length binary data whose maximum length is dependent on the source.
SQL_CHAR	Character string 1 to 254 bytes long.
SQL_VARCHAR	Variable-length character string 1 to 254 bytes long.
SQL_LONGVARCHAR	Variable-length character data whose maximum length is dependent on the source.
SQL_REAL	A signed, inexact number with a mantissa precision of 7.
SQL_DOUBLE	A signed, inexact number with a mantissa precision of 15.
SQL_FLOAT	A signed, inexact number with a mantissa precision of 15.
SQL_DATE	Data in a date format.
SQL_TIME	Data in a time format.
SQL_TIMESTAMP	Combination date and time data.

The **SQLGetTypeInfo()** function returns a **RETCODE** (int) value. Table 20.16 shows the valid return codes for **SQLGetTypeInfo()**. The **SQLGetTypeInfo()** function returns its results as a standard result set. This result set is ordered by **DATA_TYPE** and **TYPE_NAME**. Table 20.16 lists, in order, the columns in the result set. For columns with a data type of **VARCHAR**, the length listed is the maximum that will be returned.

	TABLE 20.16. `SQLGetTypeInfo()` RESULT SET COLUMNS.	
Column Name	Column Data Type	Description
TYPE_NAME	Varchar(128), not **NULL**	A data type name, DataSource-dependent, such as CHAR, VARCHAR, or MONEY.
DATA_TYPE	Smallint, not **NULL**	The ODBC SQL data-type identifier.
PRECISION	Integer	Returns the precision of the data type. Returns **NULL** for data types that don't have precision.
LITERAL_PREFIX	Varchar(128)	The literal prefix character, such as 0x for hexadecimal data types or a single quote (') for character data objects.
LITERAL_SUFFIX	Varchar(128)	The literal postfix character, such as a single quote (') for character data objects.
CREATE_PARAMS	Varchar(128)	Describes the column's data definition, such as the maximum length of a VARCHAR column.

Column Name	Column Data Type	Description
NULLABLE	Smallint, not **NULL**	One of the following: **SQL_NO_NULLS**: The data type can't have null values. **SQL_NULLABLE**: The data type may have nulls. **SQL_NULLABLE_UNKNOWN**: It's unknown whether the data type can have nulls.
CASE_SENSITIVE	Smallint, not **NULL**	Indicates whether the data is case-sensitive when collating. If **FALSE**, the data can't be case-sensitive.
SEARCHABLE	Smallint, not **NULL**	Indicates how the **WHERE** clause is defined: **SQL_UNSEARCHABLE**: Data type can't be used in a **WHERE** clause. **SQL_LIKE_ONLY**: Data type can be used only in a **LIKE** predicate. **SQL_ALL_EXCEPT_LIKE**: Data type can be used in a **WHERE** clause, except where the **LIKE** predicate is used.

continues

	TABLE 20.16. CONTINUED	
Column Name	*Column Data Type*	*Description*
UNSIGNED_ATTRIBUTE	Smallint	Indicates whether the data is to be treated as signed. If **FALSE**, the data is signed; if **NULL**, the data type isn't numeric.
MONEY	Smallint, not **NULL**	Indicates whether the data is the MONEY type. If **FALSE**, the data type isn't MONEY.
AUTO_INCREMENT	Smallint	Indicates whether the data type is an auto-incrementing field.
LOCAL_TYPE_NAME	Varchar(128)	Returns the localized name for the data type, or **NULL** if local names aren't supported.

Table 20.17 shows the **SQLGetTypeInfo()** return codes.

	TABLE 20.17. **SQLGetTypeInfo()** RETURN CODES.
RETCODE	*Description*
SQL_SUCCESS	The call to **SQLGetTypeInfo()** was successful. There is no further information.
SQL_SUCCESS_WITH_INFO	The call to **SQLGetTypeInfo()** was successful, but an error might have occurred. Further information can be obtained by calling **SQLError()**.

RETCODE	Description
SQL_STILL_EXECUTING	An unfulfilled asynchronous operation is pending.
SQL_ERROR	The call to SQLGetTypeInfo() failed. Call SQLError() to obtain specific information about the error(s).
SQL_INVALID_HANDLE	The environment handle passed to SQLGetTypeInfo() was invalid. There is no further information, so calling SQLError() won't be useful for this error condition.

Error Details

When the SQLGetTypeInfo() function returns either SQL_ERROR or SQL_SUCCESS_WITH_INFO, calling SQL_ERROR() returns one of the error messages listed in Table 20.18. Remember that because the error codes aren't unique, you should rely on the text of the error message rather than the error code.

TABLE 20.18. SQLGetTypeInfo() ERROR CONDITIONS WHEN SQLError() IS CALLED.

Error Code	Error Message	Description
01000	General warning	A driver-specific error occurred. This error code is returned when SQLGetTypeInfo() returns SQL_SUCCESS_WITH_INFO.
S1000	General error	An undefined error occurred. No other error code is defined for this error. The text returned in SQLError()'s szErrorMsg parameter describes the error.

continues

	TABLE 20.18. CONTINUED	
Error Code	*Error Message*	*Description*
08S01	Communication link failure	Communications with the DataSource, which is located on a remote server, were lost prior to completion of the function.
24000	Invalid cursor state	There were pending results with this **hstmt** from a previous SELECT, or a cursor associated with the **hstmt** hasn't been closed.
IM001	Driver doesn't support this function	This function isn't supported by this driver.
S1004	SQL data type out of range	A parameter was passed in *fSqlType*.
S1008	Operation canceled	The asynchronous request was canceled using **SQLCancel()**.
S1010	Function sequence error	A pending asynchronous function is still executing for the **hstmt**.
S1T00	Timeout expired	The function didn't complete prior to the completion of the timeout interval.
S1001	Memory allocation failure	ODBC's driver manager couldn't allocate the memory to execute this function.

SUMMARY

This chapter provided a reference to the functions that supply information about drivers and DataSources. The following functions were described:

- **SQLDataSources()**: Provides a list of available DataSources.
- **SQLGetInfo()**: Returns information about a specific DataSource and driver.
- **SQLGetFunctions()**: Returns information about which **SQL...()** functions a given driver supports.
- **SQLGetTypeInfo()**: Allows the application to determine which data types a given DataSource supports.

GLOSSARY

AboutBox   A dialog box that displays information about an application.

accelerator key   A key that can be used (usually in combination with Alt, Ctrl, or Shift) to make a selection without using the mouse.

aftermarket   A product that supports a prior product and is supplied by a different company.

AFX   Application Frameworks, part of the MFC system.

afxdb.h   The standard include file for the database classes.

AFXTraceOptions   Options that control what the programmer sees when debugging.

afxwin.h   The standard include file for a C++ program that supports MFC.

ANSI   American National Standards Institute. Under Windows, ANSI refers to the character set.

API   Applications Program Interface. Any function not part of the application could be called an API. API functions are often grouped by type.

applet   A small, simple program that is used to support Windows or another application.

AppStudio   A program that was used with prior versions of Visual C++ to edit resources.

AppWizard   An applet used to create new Windows applications.

argument   1. Data that is passed to a function. 2. Something that happens between you and your spouse when you spend too much time working with the computer.

Arial   A standard True Type font supplied with Windows.

AssertValid   A macro that checks to see if the expression is valid.

automation servers   An OLE automation server is an application that exposes a programmable object (the server's functionality) to an OLE container application.

Bézier   A type of curve that is defined as two endpoints and two control points.

bitmap   An image formed by creating a record of the bits in the original image.

bitmask   A mask specifying a certain pattern of bits.

bitwise   An operation that is performed in a bit-by-bit manner.

Boolean   Having a value of either 1 or 0.

BorderStyle   The style of a border of a window, such as thin, sizing, or dialog.

CAboutDlg   The standard About dialog box class created by AppWizard.

CArray   An MFC class that consists of arrays.

CBrush   An MFC object that defines a brush.

CByteArray   An MFC object that consists of an array of bytes.

CDatabase   The MFC class object for database work.

CDBException   The exception condition that is raised when an error occurs in the MFC database class objects.

CDialog   The MFC class object for dialog boxes.

CDK   Control Developer's Kit, used to develop OLE Custom Controls.

CDocument   The MFC class object for documents.

CFont   The MFC class object for fonts.

CFrameWnd   The MFC class object for frame windows.

check box   A Windows dialog box control that can be checked, unchecked, or indeterminate.

Class Wizard   The Visual C++ applet that enables the programmer to smanipulate classes in an AppWizard-created program.

CLSID   A unique OLE identification tag (a UUID/GUID) that is associated with a class object.

CodeView   The debugger often used with Visual C++ 1.5 and earlier. Visual C++ 2.0 doesn't use CodeView.

combo box   A Windows dialog control consisting of both an edit box and a list box together.

compound document   A document that contains OLE embedded or linked objects.

container   An application that may contain OLE embedded or linked objects.

ControlWizard   The applet used to create OLE Controls.

CWnd   The MFC class object for a window.

database   A system used to store data in a fixed format.

dataset   A set of records retrieved from a database.

DataSource   A source of data, such as a file or a database.

data type   The data's type, such as integer, character, or floating point.

dBASE   A database program marketed by Borland International.

DDE   Dynamic Data Exchange. A method for passing information between two Windows applications. DDE is a base system used by OLE.

destructor   A function found in all C++ objects that is called when the object is being destroyed.

DLL   Dynamic Link Library, a set of functions that are linked at runtime rather than when the program is created.

dockable   A window that can be attached to the top, bottom, or side of its parent window. Visual C++ 2.0's standard windows (such as Output) are dockable.

dropdown   A form of combo box in which the list box portion is hidden until the user needs it.

DrWatson   An applet used to gather information about an application when there has been a fault such as a GPF.

DrWatson.LOG   The file containing information about a system failure.

DumpBin   A utility to dump executable files. Replaces EXEHDR.

dynaset   A set of records retrieved from a query.

EditBin   A utility used to modify an executable file.

embeddable   An OLE object that may be placed in a container document. An embedded object has both the object and its data in the container.

embedded   An OLE object that is contained within a compound document.

event   An action such as a mouse click or a keyboard press.

FoxPro   A database system sold by Microsoft.

goto   A C programming statement that transfers execution to a specified location.

group box   A labeled box around a group of controls in a dialog box.

GUID   Globally Unique Identifier. This is the same as a UUID (Universally Unique Identifier).

HDBC   Handle to a database connection.

HeapWalk   A utility that enables the programmer to examine memory under Windows 3.x.

hot key   A key that, when pressed, causes a special action to take place.

hot spot   A point on a graphic image that, when clicked on, causes an action to take place.

HSTMT   Handle to an ODBC statement.

HWND   Handle to a window.

hypergraphic   A file format that is used in a Windows help file.

iconized   An application that is displayed using only a symbol called an *icon*.

initializer   A statement or value that sets a variable to a known value.

int   An integer variable type.

Internet A collection of computers formed into a network. Perhaps on its way to becoming the "information superhighway."

Katakana A phonetic form of Japanese writing.

linked object An OLE object whose data is contained externally to the container object.

list box A Windows dialog box control that contains a list of items.

makefile The input file to the NMake program. All Visual C++ projects are valid makefiles.

MessageBox A dialog box that displays a message for the user.

metafile A file that contains a collection of graphics commands.

modeless A dialog box that has no parent and its own thread of execution.

mono One, as in *monochrome* (one-colored).

multi One or more, as in *multiselection* (allowing one or more selections).

OCX The short name for an OLE Custom Control.

ODBC Open Database Connectivity. A method for a Windows application to access data from a number of different DataSources, such as Access or dBASE files.

OLE Object Linking and Embedding. A method for allowing Windows applications to create and edit documents that will contain data created by other, different applications. A single document may contain text, graphics, spreadsheets, sound, video, and other types of data.

OLE Container An OLE application that may contain embedded or linked OLE objects.

OLE Control An OLE application that serves as an automation server.

OLE Server An OLE application that provides either embedded or linked objects to an OLE Container.

overridable A C++ class function that can be replaced with a child class's function.

params One or more items passed to a function.

Pentium Intel's successor to the I486 processor.

PortTool   A program that is used to help convert 16-bit Windows applications to 32-bit versions. Flags questionable usage of variables and functions that might have changed.

postfix   A symbol or character appended to the end of an object.

printf()   A C standard library function to print to the stdout stream.

QuickC for Windows   Microsoft's first C language compiler with an integrated Windows development environment.

QuickWatch   A method to check the contents of a variable and to optionally place the variable in the watch window.

QuickWin   An easy method to convert DOS character-based applications to Windows.

radio button   A Windows dialog control consisting of descriptive text and a small circle that is filled in if the radio button is on. Radio buttons are used in groups. Only one button of the group can be on at a time.

rand()   The C runtime library function for generating random numbers.

RecalcLayout()   A function that tells Afx to resize the windows. Often called after adding or removing a toolbar or status bar.

recordset   A collection of records returned by a query.

RedISAM   The driver used to access ISAM files.

RegEdit   The program used to modify the Windows registry file.

RegisterClass   A function used to add a new object to the registry file.

shareware   A software distribution method in which the user receives the application without paying for it, and pays to register the application if he or she decides to keep it.

sizeof()   The standard C operator that returns the size of the specified object.

sprintf()   The standard library function that prints a formatted string to a character buffer.

Spy++   The replacement for Window 3.x's Spy program. Provides enhanced features and an improved user interface.

srand()   The standard C function to seed the random-number generator.

statusbar   A small window at the bottom of the application's main window, indicating the application's status.

stdafx.h   The standard Afx include file.

stdout   The standard output stream filename.

strcpy()   The standard library function used to copy two strings.

strftime()   The standard library function used to obtain a time formatted in a specified manner.

strlen()   The standard library function that returns the length of a null-terminated character string.

struct   A collection of objects of basic types, structures, and unions.

subdirectory   Any directory that is found inside another directory. The root directory is the only directory on a drive that isn't a subdirectory.

time.h   The include file for time functions.

tm   The structure that is used to hold a time value.

traceback   Following back a set of function calls to determine the flow of program execution.

typedef   A standard C keyword used to create a new basic data type.

typelib   A library of OLE Control properties that are used when the control is registered.

underflow   A condition in which a number's value is too small to be represented by the variable type selected.

Unicode   A 16-bit character set definition in which all characters in nearly all languages are available at any time. Windows NT 3.5 supports Unicode.

userid   The identification code for a certain user. Typically used by networks and database programs to verify that the user has the authority to use the system.

UUID   Universally Unique Identifier. This is the same as a GUID (Globally Unique Identifier).

VBX   Visual Basic Control. The predecessor to an OLE Control.

void*   A pointer to an object whose type is either unknown or not specified.

WinDiff   A program to determine the difference between two files under Windows.

WinHelp   The Windows help system.

COMPILER OPTIONS

This appendix lists the compiler command-line options, which are described in Chapter 6. Most programmers won't set these options directly, but will use the Visual Workbench as their tool to manage projects and to set the compiler options for projects.

TABLE B.1. THE COMPILER'S COMMAND-LINE OPTIONS.

Option	Description
	Optimization Category
/O1	Optimizes to create the smallest output.
/O2	Optimizes to create the fastest code.
/Oa	Turns off aliasing.
/Ob<n>	Enables (= 1 or = 2) or disables (= 0) inline expansion.
/Od	Disables all optimizations.
/Og	Enables optimization at the global level.
/Oi	Turns on intrinsic (inline rather than calls to library) functions.
/Op[-]	Optimizes to create floating-point consistency.
/Os	Optimizes to minimize code size.
/Ot	Optimizes to improve code speed.
/Ow	Establishes that aliasing may occur between functions.
/Ox	Maximum optimization. Equivalent to /Ogityb1/Gs.
/Oy[-]	Tells the compiler not to create stack frames on the call stack.
	Code Generation Category
/G3	Optimizes for the 80386 CPU.
/G4	Optimizes for the 80486 CPU.
/G5	Optimizes for the Pentium CPU.
/GB	Optimizes to favor the Pentium, but not to seriously affect performance when run on 80386/80486 systems.
/Gd	Uses the __cdecl calling convention.
/Ge	Turns on stack calls when functions are entered.
/Gf	Turns on string pooling. String constants are reused if possible.

Option	Description
/Gh	Generates a call to **__penter** for each function or method called.
/Gr	Uses the **__fastcall** calling convention.
/Gs[num]	Customizes the stack probes. Setting a nondefault value for **[num]** can cause problems.
/GX	Enables the calling of destructors when the stack is unwound during exception handling.
/GX-	Disables the calling of destructors when the stack is unwound during exception handling.
/Gy	Creates separate functions for the linker.
/Gz	Uses the **__stdcall** calling convention.
Output Files Category	
/Fa[file]	Creates and optionally names the assembly listing file.
/FA[sc]	Customizes the **/Fa** assembly listing. **s** = assembly with source, **c** = assembly with machine code, and **sc** = assembly with machine code and source.
/Fd[file]	Creates and optionally names the .PDB file.
/Fe<file>	Specifies the name of the executable file.
/Fm[file]	Creates and optionally names the map file.
/Fo<file>	Specifies the name for the object file.
/Fp<file>	Specifies the name for the precompiled header file.
/Fr[file]	Creates and optionally names the source Browser file.
/FR[file]	Creates and optionally names the extended .SBR file.
/C	Leaves comments in the preprocessor output.
/D<name>{=¦#}<text>	Creates a macro.
/E	Writes the preprocessor output to stdout.

continues

TABLE B.1. CONTINUED	
Option	Description
	Output Files Category
`/EP`	Writes the preprocessor output to stdout, suppressing the line numbers.
`/FI<file>`	Forces the named file to be included.
`/I<dir>`	Adds an additional path to the include search path.
`/P`	Writes the preprocessor output to a file.
`/u`	Removes all existing macros.
`/U<name>`	Removes an existing macro.
`/X`	Ignores the standard search order.
	Language Category
`/vd{0¦1}`	Enables or disables the addition of the hidden **vtordisp** constructor displacement member. Useful only if virtual bases are used.
`/vm<x>`	Member pointer type. **s** = single inheritance, **m** = multiple inheritance, and **v** = any class.
`/Z7`	Creates CodeView debugging information in C7 style.
`/Za`	Disables Microsoft extensions to the C/C++ language (implies `/Op`).
`/Zd`	Writes line number information to the object file.
`/Ze`	Enables Microsoft extensions to the C/C++ language (implies `/Op`).
`/Zg`	Generates function prototypes.
`/Zi`	Creates CodeView-compatible output.
`/Zl`	Doesn't write library names in the object files.
`/Zp[n]`	Packs (aligns) structures to be on n byte boundaries.
`/Zs`	Performs a syntax check only; doesn't write an object file.

Option	Description
	Miscellaneous Category
/? or /help	Displays a quick list of options.
/c	Performs a compile only; doesn't link.
/H<num>	Sets the maximum external name length. Used for some aftermarket linkers.
/J	Makes the default **char** type be unsigned.
/nologo	Doesn't display the sign-on banner and copyright message.
/Tc<source file>	Compiles as if the input file had an extension of .C.
/Tp<source file>	Compiles as if the input file had an extension of .CPP.
/V<string>	Adds a string to the object file. Useful for copyright branding.
/w	Turns off all warnings.
/W<n>	Sets the warning level. The default is **n** = 1.
/WX	Treats all warnings as errors.
/Yc[file]	Creates a .PCH (precompiled header) file.
/Yd	Adds debugging information to each object file created.
/Yu[file]	Uses the user-specified .PCH file.
/YX[file]	Uses a precompiled header file and creates the .PCH if it doesn't exist.
/Zn	Disables source Browser packing for .SBR files.
	Linker Category
/F<num>	Defines the stack size.
/LD	Creates a DLL (Dynamic Link Library) rather than an executable program.
/link	Allows the passing of options and libraries to the linker.
/MD	Creates a multithreaded application using MSVCRT.LIB.

continues

TABLE B.1. CONTINUED	
Option	Description
	Linker Category
/ML	Creates a single-threaded application using LIBC.LIB.
/MT	Creates a multithreaded application using LIBCMT.LIB.

LINKER OPTIONS

This appendix lists the linker's command-line options, which are described in Chapter 6. Most programmers won't set these options directly, but will use the Visual Workbench as their tool to manage projects and set the linker options for projects.

Linker options can be specified on the CL commmand line when the linker is being invoked directly by the compiler.

TABLE C.1. THE LINKER'S COMMAND-LINE OPTIONS.	
Option	*Description*
`/ALIGN:n`	A command-line option used to specify the alignment of each section within the linear address space. The default for *n* is 4096, and it must be a power of 2.
`/BASE:{address ¦ @filename, key}`	An output type option used to set the base address of the program. For Windows NT programs, the default address is 0x400000. When loading the program, Windows can alter the base if necessary. However, altering the program's base significantly affects the program's loading performance. Remember that Windows NT and Windows 95 have different program-loading addresses. If you're targeting a specific version of Windows, be sure that the correct base address is specified.
`/COMMENT:comment`	A command-line option used to insert a comment string into the header of the output file. The comment can be used for copyright information or version identification.
`/DEBUG`	A debugging option that tells the linker to include debugging information in the output file.
`/DEBUGTYPE:{CV ¦ COFF ¦ BOTH}`	A debugging option used to specify which type of debugging information is included with the output file. You can choose to have the debugging information stored in CodeView, COFF, or both formats.

Option	Description
/DEF:filename	A command-line option used to specify the module definition file. A module definition file isn't required with this version of the linker.
/DEFAULTLIB:library[, library]	A command-line option used to add libraries in addition to the ones already defined.
/DLL	A command-line option used to tell the linker to build a dynamic link library instead of an executable file.
/ENTRY:symbol	An output option that sets the entry point for an executable program or a dynamic link library.
/EXETYPE:{DEV386 ¦ DYNAMIC}	A command-line option used when creating a virtual device driver (a VXD). You specify **DEV386** to create a VXD that is loaded when the calling program is loaded. If **DYNAMIC** is specified, the VXD is dynamically loaded.
/EXPORT:symbol	A command-line option that allows you to specify which functions are exported and accessible to other programs.
/FIXED	A command-line option that tells Windows that the program may be loaded only at its specified base address (see /**BASE**).
/FORCE[:{MULTIPLE ¦ UNRESOLVED}]	An option that tells the linker to create a valid executable file, even if there are unresolved or multiply-defined symbols.

continues

TABLE C.1. CONTINUED	
Option	*Description*
`/HEAP:reserve[,commit]`	A command-line option that sets the heap size. The default size is 1,048,576 (1 MB).
`/IMPLIB:filename`	A command-line option that is used to override the default name for the import library created by Link. An import library is created whenever an output file contains exported functions.
`/INCLUDE:symbol`	An input option that tells the linker to include a symbol in the symbol table.
`/INCREMENTAL:{YES¦NO}`	An option used to change the default behavior of the incremental linker.
`/MAC:creator:name`	Specifies the name of the creator of the Macintosh application.
`/MAC:type:`	Specifies the type of Macintosh application. The default is **APPL**.
`/MAC:{BUNDLE ¦ NOBUNDLE}`	Specifies whether the application has a bundled resource. The bundled resource has information about the application's icons for both the application and the application's documents.
`/MACDATA:path`	Specifies the path of the Macintosh Data Fork File Name box.
`/MACHINE:{IX86 ¦ M68K}`	A command-line option used to specify the target machine as either Intel 80x86/Pentium (IBM PC-compatible) or Motorola 68xxx (Macintosh-compatible).
`/MACRES:filename`	Specifies the name of the Macintosh resources file.

Option	Description
/MAP[:filename]	An option used to specify the creation of a map file (which lists the symbols and their locations in a program) and optionally the name of the map file.
/NODEFAULTLIB[:library [, library...]]	An option that tells the linker to ignore all the default libraries that may be specified in an object module.
/NOENTRY	A command-line option used to create a dynamic link library that has only resources and no callable functions.
/NOLOGO	An option that tells the linker not to display a startup logo or copyright notice.
/OPT:{REF ¦ NOREF}	A command-line option used to tell the linker how to optimize the output file.
/ORDER:@filename	An option that allows you to specify the order of certain packaged functions in the final output file.
/OUT:filename	An option used to specify an output filename that is different from the default.
/PDB:{filename ¦ NONE}	An option that tells the linker whether or not to create a program database, a file used for debugging.
/PROFILE	An option that enables the inclusion, in the output file, of information that the profiler requires.

continues

Option	Description
/RELEASE	An option used to set the output file's checksum. Device drivers are required to have a valid checksum, and it's recommended that all files include checksum information.
/SECTION:section,[E][R][W][S] [D][K][L][P][X]	An option used to change the attributes of the specified section.Options include E (execute),R (read), W (write), S (shared), P (paged virtual memory), D (discardable), and K (cached virtual memory).
/STACK:reserve[, commit]	An option that allows the stack size to be specified. The default size is 1,048,576 (1 MB).
/STUB:filename	An option that enables you to specify the name of the stub program. The stub program is run when a Windows program is executed under DOS without Windows running.
/SUBSYSTEM:{NATIVE ¦ WINDOWS ¦ CONSOLE ¦ POSIX}[,#[.##]]	A command-line option that enables you to specify the type of application you will generate. A NATIVE subsystem is a Windows NT device driver. A WINDOWS subsystem is an application that creates its own windows. A CONSOLE application runs in Windows NT and Windows 95 console mode (Windows 95's DOS windows mode). A POSIX application runs under POSIX in Windows NT.

TABLE C.1. CONTINUED

Option	Description
/VERBOSE	An option that tells the linker to provide a detailed report of the progress of the link.
/VERSION:#[.#]	An option that allows you to specify the version information (a major version and optionally a minor version) to the output file's header.
/VXD	A command-line option that tells the linker to create a VXD (virtual device driver) file.
/WARN[:*warninglevel*]	A command-line option that specifies what level of warnings you want to see. Setting *warninglevel* to 0 suppresses all warnings. Setting *warninglevel* to 1 displays most warnings. Setting *warninglevel* to 2 displays all warnings.

RESOURCE COMPILER OPTIONS

This appendix lists the resource compiler's command-line options, which are also described in Chapter 6. Most programmers won't set these options directly, but will use the Visual Workbench as their tool to manage projects and to set the compiler options for projects.

	TABLE D.1. THE RESOURCE COMPILER'S COMMAND-LINE OPTIONS.

Option	Description
-r	Tells RC to create a .RES compiled resource file.
-v	Tells RC to display progress messages.
-d	Defines a symbol for the resource file being compiled.
-fo	Renames an existing .RES file. (Don't use the DOS RENAME command.)
-l	Sets the default language ID. Specify the value in hex.
-i	Sets an additional path for include file searches.
-x	Tells RC to ignore the INCLUDE environment variable.
-c	Sets the CodePage used by NLS (national language support) conversion.

PRODUCTS TO MAKE VISUAL C++ PROGRAMMING EASY

When Visual C++ 2.0 was released, there were a number of products to help Visual C++ programmers build and debug applications. Most of the products listed in this appendix should have become available either when Visual C++ 2.0 was released or shortly thereafter. Sometimes, however, a product is delayed in getting to market. If you can't find a product from your traditional sources, you should contact the product's manufacturer to see if it's available.

This appendix lists some of these products, but it doesn't review or recommend them. You must decide whether a product meets your needs and whether the product's reputation makes it worthy of purchase.

I've listed these products by name rather than function. At the beginning of each section describing a product, I've listed the type, or category, of product. A blank field signifies that the information wasn't available. The prices shown were current when this book was written. However, software prices fluctuate, so you should check pricing for any product that you're seriously considering purchasing.

Affinity Publishing, Inc., 100 West Harrison, North Tower, Suite 225, Seattle, WA 98119 produces a number of valuable catalogs that list suppliers of Microsoft products. For example, two catalogs offered by Affinity are *Microsoft ODBC Drivers Catalog* and *Microsoft Visual C++ Resource Guide*. All of Affinity's catalogs are available from Microsoft, or you can get on Affinity's mailing list. These catalogs are produced on a periodic basis as needed.

Product	**3d Graphic Tools**
Type	Graphics developer tool set
Price	$150
Description	Tools to assist the 3D graphics programmer
Produced by	Micro System Options
Address	P.O. Box 95167
	Seattle, WA 98145
Telephone	1-800-868-5418
Other Information	CIS 71530,2232
Product	**Accusoft Image Format Library 4.0**
Type	Graphics file utilities, including a format converter
Price	
Description	This program lets you work with images that have the following image formats: JPEG, CALS, GIF, TGA, TIFF, PCX, DCX, BMP, DIB, EPS, WMF, WPG, and PICT.
Produced by	AccuSoft
Address	112 Turnpike Road
	Westborough, MA 01581
Telephone	1-800-525-3577
Other Information	Available by electronic distribution
Product	**Bounds-Checker for Windows**
Type	Debugging tool
Price	$250

Description	Performs a number of very valuable application integrity checks, including parameter checking, API parameter checking, and memory overwriting.
Produced by	Nu-Mega Technologies, Inc.
Address	P.O. Box 7780
	Nashua, NH 03060
Telephone	1-603-889-2386
Other Information	An excellent tool to help create bug-free applications
Product	**Bounds-Checker32 for Windows NT**
Type	Debugging tool
Price	$250
Description	Performs a number of very valuable application integrity checks, including parameter checking, API parameter checking, and memory overwriting. This version is compatible with Windows NT and should work well with future versions of Windows.
Produced by	Nu-Mega Technologies, Inc.
Address	P.O. Box 7780
	Nashua, NH 03060
Telephone	1-603-889-2386
Other Information	An excellent tool to help create bug-free applications
Product	**BugBase**
Type	Product bug management tool
Price	
Description	This tool enables developers to track and manage reports of product problems.
Produced by	Archimedes Software
Address	2159 Union St.
	San Francisco, CA 94123
Telephone	1-415-567-4010
Other Information	Try GO BUGBASE on CompuServe.

Product	**Crystal Reports Pro**
Type	Report generator package
Price	$395
Description	An add-in report generator for Visual C++ programmers. Uses either VBX or DLL interfaces.
Produced by	Crystal Services
Address	Suite 2200
	1050 W. Pender St.
	Vancouver, BC, Canada
Telephone	1-800-663-1244
Other Information	Royalty-free distribution

Product	**DataTable SpreadSheet Control**
Type	Spreadsheet add-in control
Price	$495
Description	A VBX (and DLL) type add-in control that can be used with Visual C++ applications
Produced by	ProtoView Development Corporation
Address	353 Georges Road
	Dayton, NJ 08810
Telephone	1-800-231-8588
Other Information	

Product	**DELTA**
Type	File comparison utility
Price	$60
Description	Does comparisons to determine the differences between two different files.
Produced by	OPENetwork
Address	215 Berkeley Place
	Brooklyn, NY 11217
Telephone	1-800-542-0938
Other Information	Site licensing is available.

Product	**FarPoint VBX controls**
Type	VBX controls for Visual C++ programmers
Price	$49 to $249
Description	A series of three libraries that offer spreadsheet, tab, and miscellaneous VBX controls
Produced by	FarPoint Technologies

Address	569 Southlake Blvd.
	Richmond, VA 23236
Telephone	1-804-378-0432
Other Information	

Product	**Graphics Server SDK**
Type	Graphics builder library
Price	$299
Description	Creates plots and other images from your data.
Produced by	Pinnacle Publishing Inc.
Address	P.O. Box 888
	Kent, WA 98035
Telephone	1-800-321-1293
Other Information	

Product	**ImageMan**
Type	Graphics Image Manager
Price	$495
Description	A program to manage and manipulate graphics images in JPEG, PCX, DCX, IMG, WPG, GIF, BMP, DIB, WMF, and Targa formats
Produced by	Data Technologies Inc.
Address	340 Bowditch Street
	Suite 6
	Burnsville, NC 28714
Telephone	1-800-955-8015
Other Information	Royalty-free distribution

Product	**InstallSHIELD**
Type	Product installation tool kit
Price	
Description	A system that allows automated installation of your Windows application. Features include a wide variety of options, templates, and hardware/system determination.
Produced by	Stirling
Address	1100 Woodfield Road
	Suite 108
	Schaumburg, IL 60173-9946
Telephone	1-708-307-9197
Other Information	CIS 76702,1607

Product	**Integra Visual Database Builder**
Type	Database applications builder
Price	
Description	This application helps the Visual C++ programmer build complex database applications.
Produced by	Coromandel Industries, Inc.
Address	70-15 Austin Street
	Third Floor
	Forest Hills, NY 11375
Telephone	1-800-535-3267
Other Information	Royalty-free distribution
Product	**Magna-Comm C**
Type	Communications library
Price	$299
Description	A library of functions to aid the applications developer who is creating programs that must interface with communications ports and other communications products
Produced by	SofDesign
Address	1303 Columbia Drive
	Suite 209
	Richardson, TX 75081
Telephone	1-800-755-7344
Other Information	Royalty-free distribution
Product	**OML Learning Series**
Type	Computer-aided training
Price	$69 per series, per user
Description	The OML Learning Series helps with learning Visual C++, MFC, and other aspects of Windows programming.
Produced by	Object Management Laboratory
Address	2666 Country Lane
	Westlake Village, CA 91361
Telephone	1-800-678-9665
Other Information	Available in English, French, Spanish, and German.

Product	**POET**
Type	Object Database System
Price	$499
Description	Allows easy interfacing with objects without using flat files or an RDBMS to store the objects.
Produced by	Poet Software
Address	4633 Old Ironsides Dr.
	Suite 110
	Santa Clara, CA 95054
Telephone	1-800-950-8845
Other Information	Supports Windows 3.x, Windows NT, Win32s, Windows for Workgroups, Novell, SUN, AIX, HP, SCO, Macintosh, OS/2, NeXTStep, and most major C/C++ compilers.

Product	**ProtoView Interface Component Set**
Type	Add-in controls
Price	$495
Description	VBX (and DLL) type add-in controls that can be used with Visual C++ applications
Produced by	ProtoView Development Corporation
Address	353 Georges Road
	Dayton, NJ 08810
Telephone	1-800-231-8588
Other Information	

Product	**QuickApp**
Type	Client/Server application builder
Price	
Description	Used to create client/server applications.
Produced by	DCA
Address	1000 Alderman Drive
	Alpharetta, GA 30202
Telephone	1-800-348-3221
Other Information	

Product	**RavenWrite**
Type	Multimedia interface
Price	$495

Description	A set of utilities to assist the multimedia programmer
Produced by	Looking Glass Software, Inc.
Address	11222 La Cienega Blvd.
	Inglewood, CA 90304
Telephone	1-310-348-8240
Other Information	Other products include RavenText, RavenDraw, Raven3D, RavenBase, and RavenSpeak.
Product	**ReportEase Plus**
Type	Report generator
Price	
Description	A report generator package that can be included with Visual C++ applications. Includes source code.
Produced by	Sub Systems Inc.
Address	159 Main Street
	Stoneham, MA 02180
Telephone	1-800-447-6819
Other Information	
Product	**ReportSmith**
Type	Report generator package
Price	$99 to $299
Description	Reporting facility for Visual C++ programs. This powerful package offers excellent facilities for programmers who want their applications to have full reporting capabilities.
Produced by	ReportSmith, Inc.
Address	2755 Campus Drive
	Suite 205
	San Mateo, CA 94403
Telephone	1-415-312-0147 or 1-800-336-8428
Other Information	ReportSmith was acquired by Borland International Inc.
Product	**TNT-Extender**
Type	32-bit DOS extension tools
Price	$495

Description	A system to allow the building of 32-bit applications that will run under DOS and Windows NT
Produced by	Phar Lap Software, Inc.
Address	60 Aberdeen Avenue Cambridge, MA 02138
Telephone	1-617-876-2972
Other Information	

Product	**VBtrv\C++**
Type	Btrieve application builder
Price	$249
Description	An application builder for Btrieve applications. Includes a number of useful tools.
Produced by	Classic Software Inc.
Address	3542 Pheasant Run Circle Suite Eight Ann Arbor, MI 48108
Telephone	1-800-677-2952
Other Information	Source is available.

Product	**VtoolsD for Windows**
Type	VxD development system
Price	$495
Description	A library to assist in developing Windows VXD drivers
Produced by	Vireo Software, Inc.
Address	385 Long Hill Road Bolton, MA 01740
Telephone	1-508-779-8352
Other Information	Vireo has announced that it will have versions for Windows 95 when it's released.

Product	**Win/U 2.0**
Type	Applications converter
Price	
Description	Allows a Microsoft Windows application to run under UNIX/Motif.
Produced by	Bristol Technology, Inc.
Address	241 Ethan Allen Highway Ridgefield, CT 06877

Telephone	1-203-438-6969
Other Information	Internet: info@bristol.com

Product	**WindowsMAKER**
Type	Windows development tool
Price	
Description	This program helps the Windows developer create more-complex Windows applications with ease. Creates applications templates and supports Visual Basic-like code editing and the addition of code directly to objects.
Produced by	Blue Sky Software
Address	7486 La Jolla Blvd.
	Suite 3
	La Jolla, CA 92037
Telephone	1-800-677-4946
Other Information	

Product	**WinWidgets 3.0**
Type	Custom controls package
Price	$350 to $700
Description	A set of custom controls available in both 16-bit and 32-bit versions.
Produced by	Simple Software
Address	543 Third Street
	Brooklyn, NY 11215
Telephone	1-800-653-3234
Other Information	Source code is available. Royalty-free distribution.

Product	**zApp Developer's Suite for Windows**
Type	Application development package
Price	$695
Description	An application developer available in versions for Windows, Windows NT, OS/2, and many other platforms
Produced by	ZINMARK Development Corporation
Address	2065 Landings Drive
	Mountain View, CA 94043
Telephone	1-800-346-6275
Other Information	

Many programmers have difficulty obtaining ODBC drivers. Microsoft and Affinity Publishing periodically produce the *Microsoft ODBC Driver Catalog*, which lists most of the producers of ODBC drivers. You can order a copy by contacting Affinity Publishing.

Table E.1 is a list of many ODBC driver producers. You should contact the driver producer for more information about its products. Many of these driver producers also produce drivers other than the ones I've listed.

TABLE E.1. ODBC DRIVER SUPPLIERS.

Producer	Telephone	Drivers
Apple Computer Inc.	1-408-862-3385	ODBC/DAL for Macintosh, ODBC/DAL for Windows
Born Software Development Group	1-800-624-5102	AS/400
Bull	1-602-862-6062	Oracle, Informix, DB2
Cincom	1-800-543-3010	RDBMS
Computer Associates	1-800-342-5224	CA-IDMS, CA-DATACOM, CA-DB
Computer Corporation of America	1-617-492-8860	Select
Coromandel	1-800-535-3267	Integra
Cross Access Corporation	1-708-684-2345	IMS, DB2, VSAM, IDMS, and others
Digital	1-800-344-4825	DEC Rdb
EDA/SQL	1-800-969-4636	EDA/SQL Servers
Hewlett Packard	1-800-637-7740	Allbase/SQL, RDBMS
Informix	1-800-876-3101	Informix Servers
Ingres	1-800-446-4737	INGRES Servers
Micro Decisionware	1-800-221-3634	ODS
Microsoft	1-800-227-4679	Various, including Access and FoxPro

continues

	TABLE E.1. CONTINUED	
Producer	*Telephone*	*Drivers*
MUST Software International	1-800-441-6878	DB2
Oracle Corporation	1-800-345-3267	ORACLE-7
PAL Consulting	011-44-81-659-8826	Various, including SQL Server, INGRES, and others
Progress Software	1-800-477-6473	RDBMS
Q+E Software	1-800-876-3101	Various
RAIMA	1-800-327-2462	Access, Excel, FoxPro, Visual Basic
ShowCase	1-800-829-3555	AS/400
Software AG	1-800-843-9543	SQL Server
Sybase	1-800-879-2273	SQL Server and others
Tandem	1-800-482-6336	Contact company for information
TechGnosis, Inc.	1-407-997-6687	Oracle, Ingress, Sybase, and others
VisionWare Headquarters	1-800-949-8474	Contact company for information
Watcom	1-800-265-4555	SQL Server
White Cross Systems	011-44-344-300770	Contact company for information
XDB	1-301-317-6800	DB2

INDEX

Add to Your Sams Library Today with the Best Books for Programming, Operating Systems, and New Technologies

The easiest way to order is to pick up the phone and call

1-800-428-5331

between 9:00 a.m. and 5:00 p.m. EST.
For faster service, please have your credit card available.

ISBN	Quantity	Description of Item	Unit Cost	Total Cost
0-672-30409-0		What Every Borland C++ 4 Programmer Should Know	$29.95	
0-672-30533-X		What Every Paradox 5 for Windows Programmer Should Know, Second Edition (Book/2 Disks)	$45.00	
0-672-30370-1		Visual C++ Developer's Guide (Book/Disk)	$49.95	
0-672-30512-7		DB2 Developer's Guide, Second Edition	$59.99	
0-672-30440-6		Database Developer's Guide with Visual Basic 3	$44.95	
0-672-30485-6		Navigating the Internet, Deluxe Edition (Book/Disk)	$29.95	
0-672-30520-8		Your Internet Consultant	$25.00	
0-672-30473-2		Client/Server Computing, Second Edition	$40.00	
0-672-30486-4		Rightsizing Information Systems, Second Edition	$40.00	
0-672-30173-3		Enterprise-Wide Networking	$39.95	
0-672-30445-7		OS/2 2.11 Unleashed (Book/CD-ROM)	$39.95	
0-672-30338-8		Inside Windows File Formats (Book/Disk)	$29.95	
0-672-30306-X		Memory Management for All of Us, Deluxe Edition (Book/Disk)	$39.95	
0-672-30249-7		Multimedia Madness! (Book/Disk/CD-ROM)	$44.95	
❏ 3 ½" Disk		Shipping and Handling: See information below.		
❏ 5 ¼" Disk		TOTAL		

Shipping and Handling: $4.00 for the first book, and $1.75 for each additional book. Floppy disk: add $1.75 for shipping and handling. If you need to have it NOW, we can ship product to you in 24 hours for an additional charge of approximately $18.00, and you will receive your item overnight or in two days. Overseas shipping and handling adds $2.00 per book and $8.00 for up to three disks. Prices subject to change. Call for availability and pricing information on latest editions.

201 W. 103rd Street, Indianapolis, Indiana 46290

1-800-428-5331 — Orders   1-800-835-3202 — FAX   1-800-858-7674 — Customer Service

Book ISBN 0-672-30493-7